16 $\frac{25}{01}$ EC

MUSIC IN PHILADELPHIA

A DISSERTATION

IN MUSIC

PRESENTED TO THE FACULTY OF THE GRADUATE SCHOOL OF THE
UNIVERSITY OF PENNSYLVANIA IN PARTIAL FULFILLMENT
OF THE REQUIREMENTS FOR THE DEGREE OF
DOCTOR OF PHILOSOPHY

ROBERT A. GERSON

GREENWOOD PRESS, PUBLISHERS
WESTPORT, CONNECTICUT

Copyright 1940 by Theodore Presser Co.

Reprinted by permission
of the University of Pennsylvania Press

First Greenwood Reprinting 1970

Library of Congress Catalogue Card Number 76-95121

SBN 8371-3930-9

Printed in the United States of America

PREFACE

When a book on Music in Philadelphia was first considered, the idea was fondly entertained that by attaching a dictionary and index to include the less important names, the text could be kept readable and interesting. The style of Ernest Walker, for example, is a model of pleasant and easy narrative—a goal to be striven for in a work that must include thousands of facts. As material was collected, however, even in the preliminary stages of scratching the surface of Philadelphia music history, it became obvious that no first book with this inclusive scope could contain even the more important facts and still be as readable as might be desired. The following pages are admittedly reference material for the most part. This is a necessary characteristic since there has been no work that has claimed to be a study of the entire musical history of Philadelphia, up to the time that this account was written. Some of the material here assembled might serve as nuclei and be utilized in the preparation of more specialized works dealing with many phases of Philadelphia's musical history. Music publishing in Philadelphia, the life and works of William H. Fry, Leopold Stokowski in Philadelphia, and the Philadelphia Academy of Music are among many topics about which a more detailed account might well be written in book form. A monograph could also be written on music by Haydn, Mozart, Beethoven, and other European composers commissioned by American publishers and musical organizations.

The early music of Philadelphia and Pennsylvania has been the subject of many volumes, which are mentioned in the bibliography. Nineteenth century music and that of the present day has not been previously summed up even for reference purposes, much less treated in an exhaustive manner. One book cannot pretend to follow the latter method, but if it does the former, summing up with any degree of completeness, its usefulness for reference purposes will constitute its main value.

Students of the present day, who are in the midst of a period of musical specialization, will be impressed by the varied activities

v

and surprising versatility of each musician in early days of Music in Philadelphia. Everyone, with the exception of the very few musicologists who have troubled to look at the progress and state of music in the local region, is inclined to think of Philadelphia music in terms of its superlatives, that is to say, the specialized products of super-trained individuals and groups. We consider with justifiable pride the Curtis Institute of Music, where artistic training is of the highest order, or the Philadelphia Orchestra, where musical interpretation has reached the loftiest levels; but do we remember the 1,000 members of the Philadelphia Music Teachers' Association, the 20,000 students of music in organized conservatories, or the 7,500 trained instrumental musicians earning an average salary of $1,500 a year?[1] It will be found by any student who investigates Music in Philadelphia, whether past or present, that the sheer number of those engaged in that art in a sufficiently professional manner to be readily counted, is an inescapable and ever-present impression.

As the historical panorama is unfolded we shall see how, from modest beginnings amid unfavorable conditions, a steady progress in local music has characterized each period since the founding of the city. This has been shown in the increased regard for music and the growing esteem in which the musical expert is held.

Recent developments in Philadelphia, as elsewhere, tend to produce great specialization and resulting proficiency in every musical field. The growth in the actual amount of music is largely responsible for this division and subdivision of its fields. And yet if any trend can be stated as outstanding during the last few years of Philadelphia music, it is the great tendency to join musical organizations on the part of thousands of people. Twenty years of increased popularity of music as a school subject accounts for some of this mass participation, but more is probably due to the constant gain of our art over a period of two hundred years.

---

[1] Figures from the Chamber of Commerce Report for 1917, brought up to date by information from Dr. Hipsher and others.

CONTENTS

PART I

viii CONTENTS

PART III

THOMAS à BECKET, JR.

PART I

CHAPTER ONE

COLONIAL MUSIC

I

Music is a delicate plant that needs long and patient cultivation. It will not thrive—as does the church—on persecution. The blood of the martyrs is the seed of the church, for man's indomitable religious instinct is a sturdy plant, but the aphorism does not apply to persecution of the fine arts.

The Society of Friends, dominant in early Philadelphia, was openly hostile to public musical gatherings. The class that could write, or took the trouble to do so in a permanent form, seems to have opposed music on all occasions. Beyond doubt this intense disapproval of music was only the official side of the leading citizens' attitude: the presence of song could not have been totally banned in every private scene. Their formal pronouncements were so unequivocal in condemning music that it is not surprising that persons who wished to be successful did not make their own possible tolerance of vocal or instrumental music a matter of written record. Nearly all of the early references to Music in Philadelphia evidence this general lack of interest, or even open hostility.

Evidence of musical activity is mainly to be found in the frequent warnings or exhortations to stay away from it. We may assume that the forbidden evils existed somewhere in the city, or else why did the yearly meeting of the Friends in 1716 advise against "going to or being in any way concerned in plays, games, lotteries, music, and dancing"?[1] Other condemnations are numerous, betraying the fact that the tolerant Quakers were admitting colonists whom they could not approve in certain respects.

---

[1] Louis C. Madeira, *Annals of Music in Philadelphia and the Musical Fund Society* (Lippincott 1896), p. 17.

The Friends, with their predilection for plain religious meetings, must have been repeatedly shocked by the music at Christ Church. In 1728 this Episcopal congregation spent two hundred pounds for a "new organ." This was a large amount of money for colonial Philadelphians to spend on a musical instrument. The term *new organ* connotes that there had been an old organ some of the time, in the preceding thirty-five years of the parish. In the story of this very early musical transaction in Philadelphia, it may be noted that the "new" organ purchased in 1728 was probably not new at all, but was rebuilt from an instrument used by the Hermits of the Wissahickon for many years. These Hermits were German mystics, and had been noted organ builders since about 1700.

Many historians in treating Philadelphia music begin with the quarrels of theatres and authorities, or of high churchmen with Quakers. The beginning of music in and near Philadelphia is far earlier than these controversies. The difficulty in attempting to discuss the early Swedish and German music lies in the lack of first hand information about the remote men who made the music of the Pennsylvania Germans an important part of religious music in Philadelphia. Again, the need for discussion of the music in Bethlehem or Ephrata, their two important early musical centers, makes any treatment of the music of the German sects seem to call for chapters not concerned with Philadelphia music history. Yet the early religious music of many of the German groups was composed, sung and played in and near Philadelphia. Such material as concerned the Swedes at Wicaco or the Germans in Germantown belongs to the story of Music in Philadelphia, and constitutes its earliest chapter.

The Swedes who preceded William Penn in this region antedated Philadelphia also. Their music continued during the early years of Penn's settlement, however, and as a rival religious force, the Swedes and their music make an interesting beginning to Philadelphia music. The settlement at Wicaco was one of the few Swedish communities north of Fort Christina.[1] The music at the Old Swedes' Church is the oldest of which we have any record in

---

[1] Wicaco is now in the southeast section of Philadelphia; Fort Christina was located approximately on the site of Willingston—now Wilmington.

Philadelphia. We know that there was an organ in this building in the year 1703, for Jonas [1] played it during the ordination of Justus Falckner on November twenty-sixth of that year. This same Falckner is remembered as a musician, clergyman, and hymnologist. His evangelical enthusiasm bears an interesting relation to music in the earliest days of this city. It was Justus Falckner who wrote in 1700 to Schleswig, Germany, begging the authorities of his church to send an organ to Philadelphia. The lack of music in Friends' Meetings constituted a great weakness in popular appeal; and, said Falckner, if they could have an organ at the church at Wicaco, many people would flock to worship there. Falckner joined the Hermits of the Wissahickon in 1700. Three years later he was ordained at Old Swedes' Church—to the music of an organ, believed by some to have been sent from Germany. The instrument may have been sent in response to his own entreaties, while the organist, as has been mentioned above, was a Swede who had been in Philadelphia for about seven years.

Not many years after the famous musical ordination of Justus Falckner we read of an interesting expedient designed to improve congregational singing in the Swedish churches. Samuel Hesselius was pastor of the Wicaco church (Old Swedes') at the same time that his brother Andreas Hesselius was Provost of the Swedish churches in and near Christina. Drummond in his account of *Early German Music in Pennsylvania* (p. 14), relates how Provost Hesselius urged those who could sing easily and well to do so, while "those who were unfitted for this should not with their harsh voices hinder others and make confusion. By softly singing after the others they should train themselves to correct singing. During the singing he went around the church and aided where they failed." How many musically sensitive ministers since Hesselius have longed to do just that, and how few would dare to do it today!

The Hermits of the Wissahickon constitute the second early musical influence in Philadelphia. This pietist group came from Germany in 1694, about twelve years after the founding of Philadelphia. They settled on a large tract of land in the Wissahickon

---

[1] Probably Jonas Auren, a musician, a Swedish mystic; also a Lutheran pastor. He came to Philadelphia in 1697.

Valley, about six miles northwest of the original city.[1] Strong mystical leanings of the Hermits' religious persuasion seem to have been conducive to the use of a varied musical program in their church life. Not content with the numerous fine chorales and other vocal forms which flourished everywhere among German Protestants, the Hermits of the Wissahickon brought with them an organ, a viol, hautboy, trumpets, and kettledrums when they came to Philadelphia. The location of their settlement is well within the present city limits, in the Wissahickon Valley between Germantown and Roxborough.[2] The sincere piety and thorough musicianship of the leader of the Hermits, Johannes Kelpius, were in all probability responsible for their carrying such a cargo of musical instruments into the wilderness north of Philadelphia, and for their cultivation of vocal and instrumental music to such a high degree. Between the years 1698 and 1708 Kelpius composed a book of hymns, with German words. The nineteen works in that collection constitute the first musical composition in Pennsylvania of the eighteenth century. The original Kelpius Hymn Book consisted of seventy pages. The twelve hymns that exist in the remains of his original copy are reproduced in the interesting collection "Church Music in Pennsylvania in the Eighteenth Century."[3]

Among the original band of Wissahickon Hermits, the names of Henry Bernhard Köster and Johann Gottfried Seelig should be

[1] The settlement of the adjacent country for over ten years by Germans under Franz Daniel Pastorius doubtless encouraged the Hermits to pick a site near Germantown for their community life. Pastorius was born in Germany in 1651. He is said to have been a very learned man, a leader of the German settlers in 1683, schoolmaster for some years, Bürgermeister for many. His writings include one secular song of lyric beauty, *Come Corinna*, and many hymns of standard excellence for his period. He died in 1719 at Germantown, thus outliving Johannes Kelpius, the leader of the Hermits of the Wissahickon, by about ten years, just as he had arrived in Germantown ten years earlier than Kelpius. His musical importance is slight, however, while that of the Hermits and Kelpius is considerable.

[2] The writer has the dubious distinction of residing directly above the reputed burial ground of the Hermits of the Wissahickon.

[3] *Church Music and Musical Life in Pennsylvania in the Eighteenth Century,* by Mrs. A. A. Parker, is the fourth publication of the Pennsylvania Society of Colonial Dames of America. Published in Philadelphia, 1926. The Kelpius hymns are photographically reproduced in pages 21-165 of the first volume.

A PAGE FROM THE KELPIUS HYMNAL

mentioned as writers and composers of hymns. Köster is said [1] to have composed thirteen hymns, Seelig at least four.

Any attempt at judging the musical worth of these hymns— or of any of the compositions recorded as forming a part of the history of Philadelphia music—would be merely the setting up of a single opinion on a decidedly shifting question of musical taste. When we hear writers of 1880 criticize music in the period of Palestrina as harsh or sadly wanting in tonal stability, we realize that 1940 considers 1500 quite differently. It is very possible that tomorrow's critic will smile at today's verdict on the Kelpius Hymnal. Beyond doubt most present day hymnologists would declare his words severe and his music angular. Readers who are interested in forming a first-hand opinion concerning Philadelphia's earliest known original music are referred to the reproductions of these hymns previously mentioned. Their importance in Philadelphia music is slight. The Hermits of the Wissahickon either migrated to Ephrata under the leadership of Conrad Beissel, or stayed in Philadelphia and Germantown and forgot about being hermits.

J. Conrad Beissel is a name of great importance in early Pennsylvania music. He was the founder of the Sabbatarians in Pennsylvania. Beissel came from Germany in 1720, settling in the Wissahickon colony at Germantown. The move to Ephrata was made in 1735 under his leadership. Since most of his composition and writing on musical subjects was done at Ephrata, where he remained for thirty-three years, little concerning him should be said in this book. He was the second important musical leader in the colony of the Hermits of the Wissahickon, and far surpassed the earlier Kelpius in volume and diversity of musical works. A Treatise on the Voice, a Dissertation on Harmony, and a collection of Choral Songs (1754) are important works by Beissel. He composed over 400 hymns, which were printed in Germantown and Ephrata.[2]

The Mennonite schoolmaster, Christopher Dock, came to Pennsylvania in 1714. Most of the years between that date and his death

---

[1] By Robert Rutherford Drummond on p. 8 of *Early German Music in Pennsylvania*; publ. by Appleton, New York, 1910.

[2] Some of his poems made up the first German book issued in America. They were printed by Franklin in 1730.

in 1771 were spent in Germantown. Like all of the German pietist leaders—and unlike the leading Quakers—he made music an important part in his life. His book on "Schul-Ordnung" (it would be called "Pedagogy" today) contains an account of his methods in teaching music. He used a special narrow blackboard which had three staves cut into each side. Another work, the "Rules of Conduct," contains the words and music of several hymns.[1]

From the year 1739, the print shop of Christopher Saur in Germantown was responsible for the publication of many early German books of music. An important collection of nine hundred and seventeen hymns was printed by Saur in 1762. This large hymnal was used by several of the German sects in Pennsylvania and elsewhere. Noted hymnologists of the day in and near Philadelphia who contributed to this book were Dr. Abraham Wagner (thirty-five hymns), Balzer Hoffman (thirty-eight hymns), and George Weiss (twenty-five hymns).[2]

In Germantown at the same period as Dock and Saur, was the versatile Christopher Witt. Dr. Witt joined the Hermits of the Wissahickon in 1704. While in that colony he painted the first known portrait in Pennsylvania. Since his subject was John Kelpius, the first musician in Philadelphia, this painting is doubly significant to students of music. At the death of Kelpius in 1708, Witt moved to Germantown, where he lived until his death in 1765, at the age of ninety. His home was torn down in 1914, amid many historical protests. This house, situated at Germantown Avenue and High Street, was the first colonial home to house a large pipe organ. Dr. Witt had built the organ while at the Hermit colony, and moved it to Germantown shortly after 1708. We know little about the organ, except that it was built and played by Christopher Witt, and that it brought the large sum of forty pounds at the time

---

[1] Some of these hymns are reproduced in *Church Music and Musical Life in Pennsylvania,* volume 2, pages 20-25.

[2] Robert R. Drummond mentions no less than twenty-two printed editions of German hymn books issued in Philadelphia (including Germantown) during the eighteenth century. In addition to these printings, there was a tremendous interest and effort among some of the German pietists in the copying of both words and music of hymn collections. Dr. Drummond lists and describes these collections in his book on *Early German Music in Pennsylvania,* p. 10.

of his death. Varied interests of this extraordinary nonagenarian included the cultivation of Philadelphia's first botanical garden, and playing upon the virginals.[1]

Before taking leave of these remarkable and mysterious German[2] musicians, a group that had particular fondness for hymn composing and copying should be mentioned. The Schwenkfelders settled in the northern section of what is now Philadelphia, and in Bucks county, in 1734. Forty families strong, they occupied a considerable section of Pennsylvania's most valuable farming country. Judging from their musical industry, the farming duties left the Schwenkfelders considerable leisure time for musical pursuits. A single hymn book brought from Silesia was copied by hand on paper from the David Rittenhouse paper mill of Germantown. They added tunes and words of their own in many hand-written volumes. Their painstaking and ambitious works were often of more than a thousand pages in length.[3]

In most ways the Swedish and German music and musicians must be regarded as very old and interesting preludes to a generally unrelated course of later musical development. We know little concerning the actual musicianship of Dr. Witt, or the tonal qualities of the Hermits' orchestra. There are few points of contact between the later stream of English influence, which dominated Philadelphia's musical life from 1780 to about 1840, and the mystic music of the Germans who led in musical matters for almost one hundred years before this British ascendency. The Moravians were recognized as accomplished musicians both in Philadelphia and in Bethlehem by later musicians from England like Andrew Adgate and Benjamin Carr. An ex-hermit of the Wissahickon, Ludovic Sprogel, sold Christ Church its first adequate organ in 1728.[4] David Tanneberger, or Tannenberg, was probably a Moravian from

---

[1] The virginals owned by Christopher Witt were purchased from the celebrated Mary Margaret Zimmerman, who founded the community of the Woman in the Wilderness. Miss Zimmerman's lady hermits settled near Kelpius' colony in 1694. The virginals which she sold to Dr. Witt in 1725 had been the first instrument of its kind in Pennsylvania.

[2] Except of course Dr. Witt, who was born in England in 1675.

[3] Cf. Allen A. Seipt, *Schwenkfelder Hymnology,* Germania-Americana Press, Philadelphia, 1909.

[4] This instrument may have been brought from Germany by the Hermits, although they are said to have built an organ in 1700, and in (about) 1705.

Bethlehem, and certainly the builder of the largest organ in America, in 1790, for Zion Lutheran Church in Philadelphia. While this instrument belongs to a later period than that under discussion, its Moravian-American origin suggests it as one of many points of contact of the early German influence and later Philadelphia. The organ possessed about ten stops. Its dedication was attended by President and Mrs. Washington, many members of Congress and of the Pennsylvania Assembly. This famous organ was destroyed by fire in 1794.

The Sabbatarians in Ephrata and the Moravians in Bethlehem were long famous for their musical talent, but the Philadelphia history of music seems to have started on a new course with the arrival of a group of men from Great Britain. The music for the theatre would have to make a fresh start—for the Germans were hardly more interested in theatrical music than the Friends themselves. The more versatile English musicians were frequently members of the Episcopal church, a religious body sympathetic to good music, and tolerant of most dramatic productions. This does not mean that the earlier German tradition was completely lost. The Lutheran church and several smaller denominations continued beside the original Quaker and the growing Catholic, Episcopal and Presbyterian congregations throughout the eighteenth century. But when we consider music of the stage—the only form of music of which there is plentiful record in the early press—the lighter style encouraged by English colonists is seen to be the accepted one. And when concert music is discussed, the wealthy and worldly will be seen to have monopolized that field, so far as finished (or at least ambitious) musical performance is concerned.[1] Let us then return to the account of the earliest musical records in the city itself, leaving the still older influences of the surrounding Germanic settlements to seep in in the inconspicuous manner which must have been their actual method as Philadelphia became more English in musical styles.

---

[1] A fondness for German works characterized even these most ardent admirers of the English ballad opera. Handel was always popular, of course, as were Gluck, Haydn, Mozart, and Beethoven. These European German influences which dominated so much of American musical life in the eighteenth and nineteenth centuries should be considered as quite different from the interesting, but perhaps crude, writings by Pennsylvania German Pietists.

II

The early colonial period, 1682-1740, seems to have witnessed a slowly growing toleration of the music of the religious type and the most restrained secular forms. The Friends were tolerant, if hard to change; hence the Episcopal and Catholic colonists were welcomed in Philadelphia with their varying religious doctrines and their definitely set church music.

One of the earliest musical records in the colonial period [1] concerned the first mention of dancing lessons in Philadelphia schools (1728). The first music printed in Philadelphia was issued the following year, 1729, when the Franklin Press issued a reprint of Watts' *Psalms of David.* In 1730, Miss Ball, "lately arrived from London," taught "singing, playing on the spinet, dancing, and all sorts of needle work." [2] Though Miss Ball has been regarded as Philadelphia's first music teacher, there is some question concerning the fact, for the *Pennsylvania Gazette* in July of the same year advertised Daniel Warner's *The Singing Master's Guide to His Scholars* as a publication of the Franklin Press. Daniel Warner could not advertise "lately arrived from London," the great probability being that he was one of many humbler Philadelphia musicians who flourished long before their more publicized colleagues crossed from Europe. Two printers besides Franklin are known to have published music as early as 1739. Andrew Bradford and Christopher Saur published music in that year and Isaiah Warner in 1742. These early musical collections consisted almost entirely of sacred music.

Three men became active in music teaching in Philadelphia near the year 1750. John Beals, a music master from London, advertised that he would teach "Violin, Hautboy, German Flute, Common Flute, and Dulcimer by note," at his house in Fourth Street.[3] Robert Coe declared in the same periodical, in January, 1753, that he "conceiving himself capable of teaching the German Flute, thought proper to inform the Publick that he would attend

---

[1] Most of these early happenings are quoted from O. Sonneck's introductory chapter to *Francis Hopkinson and James Lyon:* H. L. McQueen, Washington, 1905.

[2] *Pennsylvania Gazette,* March 5, 1730.

[3] *Pennsylvania Gazette,* March 21, 1749.

to that purpose four nights in the week at his house." Still in the
Pennsylvania Gazette, December 27, 1753, Josiah Davenport advertised that he would give lessons in psalmody. The chronicle
grows crowded with names after about 1760, teachers of music and
of dancing, and musical concerts and ballad operas becoming very
numerous in the rapidly growing city. In the periods that follow
the Revolution, we could not name all that happened in Philadelphia
music, but must rather single out the best, or the most historically
significant events.

The Kean-Murray company is known to have given musical
plays, possibly ballad operas, in Plumstead's warehouse, King
Street, Philadelphia, as early as 1749. A much better cast visited
Philadelphia in 1754, performing twenty-four times at the same
warehouse. This company came from London, backed by William
Hallam and managed by Lewis Hallam the elder. There was scant
publicity for their productions; indeed their plays were given only
after vigorous opposition by both the governor and the Society of
Friends. Sonneck supposes [1] that their repertory resembled that
of the Kean-Murray company, basing this theory upon New York
programs of the Hallam troupe. Lewis Hallam died in Jamaica
shortly after the Philadelphia performances of 1754. However,
Mrs. Hallam's second husband, David Douglass, soon reorganized
the troupe, which returned to colonial cities as the Old American
Opera Company in 1758. In 1759, many operas were given on
"Society Hill," Philadelphia, by Douglass' Company. In 1766 this
troupe opened the Southwark Theatre, reputed to have been the first
American building to be given the title *Opera House.*

Music had been largely an adjunct of the church, or the theatre,
prior to 1757, but after that time there are records of music programs, *i.e.,* concerts. The first public concert took place at the
Assembly Room in Lodge Alley on January 25, 1757, "under the
direction of Mr. John Palma, to begin exactly at six o'clock."
Tickets were required for admittance; they were procurable at the
London Coffee House, and cost one dollar. George Washington
attended the second Philadelphia concert, his ledger for 1757 showing the following entry, "Mar. 17th, By Mr. Palmas Tickets 52

---

[1] *Francis Hopkinson and James Lyon,* pages 20-21.

s. 6. . . ." Sonneck, in quoting this entry,[1] adds, "This was presumably the first, though by no means the last, concert attended by George Washington." Possibly these two early concerts were not well supported by the public. In any case, there was no further advertisement of a musical performance in concert form open to the public for seven years following Mr. Palma's two early efforts. In 1764, musicians seemed to venture once again from under the protective mantle of private soirées—where we must assume they had led a continuous musical life—and an increasing number of public concerts are to be noted from that year. The advent of two British musicians, the Scottish James Bremner and the English Andrew Adgate, may be said to have stirred up a large part of the growing interest in fine music.

James Bremner was the earlier of these two concert organizers to reach America. He settled in Philadelphia in 1763, opening a music school in December of the year. St. Peter's Church secured his services as organist, also in 1763. In the same concert season, on February 21, 1764, Bremner directed a public musicale for the benefit of the St. Peter's organ fund. This early concert was held in the Assembly Room in Lodge Alley. A few years later we find James Bremner as organist at Christ Church, in addition to St. Peter's. These two organ positions and public concerts by groups trained by him seem to have constituted the occupation of Philadelphia's first professional musician of distinction, until his death in 1780.[2] Bremner was a composer as well as an inspiring conductor and expert performer. Unlike most of the professional musicians of the generation which followed him, James Bremner seems to have kept his own works off programs he conducted. Through his better known pupil, Francis Hopkinson, we learn of many original works and arrangements by Bremner. In the Hopkinson collection are preserved copies of the *Variations on a Minuet, March,* and other pieces noncommittally entitled *Lessons,* which Bremner had written for his pupil. A piano arrangement which

---

[1] *Early Concert Life*, p. 65.
[2] Bremner's concert in College Hall in 1765 included a Stamitz Overture, Geminiani Concerto, Martini Overture, and the *Artaxerxes Overture* by Arne. A later concert at the same hall (April 10, 1775), included a different assortment by similar composers.

he made of the popular *Overture* by the Earl of Kelly was printed
by G. Willig and Company in about the year 1800.

III

Christ Church and St. Peter's led a closely connected life, both
in music and in church organization. St. Peter's and St. James'
churches were started as missions of the older Christ Church.
Bremner, Hopkinson and William Young were among the musicians connected with music in these churches. Bishop White, early
in the following century (1808), championed the musical form of
Anglican worship, mentioning in his report to the general convention ". . . . as it is by the gospel that life and immortality are
brought to light, . . . its high design . . . may reasonably be rendered the more impressive by their being carried to the heart on
the wings of poetry and music." [1] An early attempt to define
sacred music as such may be found in White's pamphlet "Thoughts
on the Singing of the Psalms and Anthems in Churches" (1808),
in the "distinction . . . between the making of devotion pleasing
by the aid of music and the applying of music to convey a pleasure
not intended to be instrumental to devotion. . . . Nothing in inter-
ludes and voluntaries contrary either to good taste or decency should
be tolerated for the gratification of private whim." Light airs
which tended to send the people "dancing out of the church" were
heartily condemned.

St. Joseph's, Willing's Alley, is called [2] the first Catholic
church in the United States, although, the first building not having
been erected until 1733, it is difficult to imagine how the Catholics
in Maryland got along in the previous one hundred years! An
organ is mentioned as having been in use from about 1748. Another organ used by St. Joseph's in 1780 is still in existence. The
choir was a noted organization, even in pre-Revolution days. Benjamin Carr was organist at St. Joseph's at one time. Lafayette,
de Rochambeau, and de Grasse were among notable visitors to
St. Joseph's.

---

[1] Madeira, *op. cit.*, page 20.
[2] Madeira, *op. cit.*, p. 21.

In the Presbyterian church, located in the Barbados Warehouse from 1698 to 1704, and at Market above Second Street, from 1704 to 1788, a precentor, or singing leader, was an important officer. He stood beneath the pulpit with a tuning fork in his hand, at a table or desk placed on a slight elevation from the church floor, and lined out the hymns.[1] Unaccompanied unison singing must have proven a bit barren musically, for early in the colonial period a somewhat amusing controversy was occasioned by the proposal to introduse a bass viol to provide some instrumental support. "Its introduction into the church met with vigorous opposition, especially on the part of the ministers. To one of these musical Tories a singer wishing to improve on the lines of Dr. Watts' Ninety Second Psalm

> 'O let my heart in tune be found
> Like David's harp of solemn sound'

gravely proposed this change:

> 'O may my heart be tuned within
> Like David's sacred violin,'

to which the reverend wag suggested as amendment:

> 'Oh, may my heart go diddle-diddle
> Like Uncle David's sacred fiddle.' "

This ministerial disapproval has been quoted in full[2] since it shows not only a typical obstacle in the path of early Presbyterian music in Philadelphia, but, especially in the last quotation, a decidedly low appreciation for instrumental music as a whole by a cultivated group. Surely the music for fiddle being composed by Bach for the accompaniment of his immortal Passions and Cantatas at the very time of the reverend's slighting characterization is considerably more than diddle-diddle. It is very possible that in the English colonies settled by a majority of dissenting colonists, a reaction to the gaiety of the English life of 1600-1700 is felt in the

---

[1] Scharf and Westcott's *History of Philadelphia*, p. 1075.
[2] Madeira, *op. cit.*, p. 23.

extreme disapproval of all instrumental music. The organ was not primarily an ecclesiastical instrument in the early eighteenth century. Organs in amusement gardens and hotels of early Philadelphia were more widely advertised than the few instruments used in the churches. An organist named Bowen played the following recital in Boston on July 30, 1799:

> Battle of Prague
> Within a mile of Edinburgh
> Dead of Night
> Fal la la
> The Topsail Shivers in the Wind
> Heaving the Lead
> Sailor's Journal
> Tom Bowling
> You Gentlemen of England and Little Sally
> On Board the Arethusa
> Dutch Fishmonger
> British Grenadiers
> Freemasons' Song
> Meg of Wapping
> Delights of the Chase
> [and fifteen more like them].[1]

The use of the organ for such programs as played by Mr. Bowen of Boston may shed some light upon why it was not regarded as a religious instrument. Quakers, Presbyterians, even the Catholics, and Martin Luther, did not favor instrumental music in church and included the organ in their disapproval. Typical of this opposition is the remark of a preacher who, asked to lead in prayer after the organ had been heard with the singers, cried out, "Call on the machine! If it can sing and play to the glory of God, it can pray to the glory of God also. Call on the machine!" [2]

The Reverend James Lyon is notable as a Presbyterian clergyman who was also a talented musician. He favored vocal and instrumental music in the service of his church. Although James Lyon spent only a few years in Philadelphia, the period was an

---

[1] Sonneck, *Early Concert Life*, p. 308.
[2] Madeira, p. 25.

important one in his career, coming as it did immediately after his college days at Princeton. His musical works most important to a Philadelphia history are those composed in Princeton both as an undergraduate (1757-1759) and as a divinity student (1762-1764), and in Philadelphia during the intervening years of 1760 to 1762.

The significance of *Urania* and its connection with Philadelphia, both as to its publication and early use, make it seem proper to treat this chief work by James Lyon at some length, rather than to follow biographical details of his somewhat wandering later life.[1] *Urania* was a psalm tune collection, begun at Princeton, and completed and published at Philadelphia in 1761. James Lyon may well have declared [2] that "the whole collection is better fitted to the Use of Churches and private Families than any ever published in America." Some tunes are original with Lyon, as were many of "the plainest and most necessary rules of Psalmody" used as an introduction to *Urania*. There were one hundred and ninety-eight pages of music in the collection, comprising twelve anthems, fourteen hymns, and seventy psalm tunes. Parts of the work were printed as early as 1760, and the whole was advertised for public sale in June, 1762. It had been sold to subscribers in the intervening two years. There were new editions in 1767 and 1773—suggesting that the collection was used extensively.

The practicality of the rules of psalmody recommended them to the public. Lyon's first rules treat the notes and rests, the staves and "cliffs," and have caused this introduction to *Urania* to be considered as elementary. However, his sections on syncopation, transposition, and "of the graces in music" (*i.e.,* grace notes, ornaments) are sufficiently advanced for both teachers and pupils to have benefited by their study. Lyon's directions for singing and his

---

[1] The following data on James Lyon's life are condensed from Sonneck's book *Francis Hopkinson and James Lyon*. Lyon was born in Newark, New Jersey, in 1735. He attended Princeton College from 1757 to 1759, lived in Philadelphia from 1760 to 1762, and studied at Princeton as a graduate student from 1762 to 1764. Obtaining a license as a Presbyterian minister in 1764, he served in several districts of Nova Scotia. In about 1772, he accepted a call to Machias, Maine, where he preached until 1794, the year of his death. Lyon was an ardent patriot during the American Revolution, and made valuable suggestions to the Congress and to George Washington, pertaining to the best conduct of that war.

[2] In the *Pennsylvania Journal* and *Gazette*, May 22, 1760.

use of the treble clef for tenor parts are noteworthy contributions to the art of psalmody, and to all subsequent vocal music.[1]

The music of *Urania* is arranged mainly for four voices, with a small number of two- and three-part harmonizations. The choral style prevails—a fortunate condition since the "fuguing" work of the collection is not of the highest order. Solos occur in many of the anthems and even in a few hymns.

This collection is an important link in the chain of such sacred music from the Massachusetts *Bay Psalm Book* of 1640 to hymnals of the present day. Unfortunately for the historian, no mention is made of the composer of any music in *Urania*. The advertisements mention Dr. Watts and Addison as authors of metrical texts. Lyon also notes in the index that "All Tunes marked with an Asterism are new." The six so marked, two anthems and four psalm tunes, are presumed to have been composed by James Lyon.[2]

Of Lyon's many later works, few are known and still fewer concern us here. The Uranian concert in Philadelphia, 1786, included his anthem *The Lord Descended from Above,* while that of 1787 included his *Friendship.* These and other known works by James Lyon mark him to have been a composer of talent, though his lack of training and musical opportunities prevented his ever becoming a great musical figure. We shall see how men with more complete musical backgrounds were able to develop their own opportunities for first class musical organizations in post-Revolutionary Philadelphia. It is worthy of notice that directors like Andrew Law [3] and Andrew Adgate [4] saw fit to produce compositions by the pioneer composer James Lyon.

The Baptists and the German Reformed body sang hymns in their services. The music of the Swedes and Lutherans then, as now, resembled that of the Anglican church in their sacred music. The music of the Methodists and Catholics impressed John Adams in a visit to Philadelphia. His diary, 1774, states that he found the

---

[1] Oscar Sonneck's book on *Francis Hopkinson and James Lyon* contains a full reproduction of Lyon's *Most Necessary Rules of Psalmody* on pages 154-160.

[2] They are: *The Lord descended from above, Let the shrill trumpets,* and the 8th, 23rd, 95th and 104th psalm tunes.

[3] Influential psalmodist, editor, teacher and composer in various parts of the United States; b. 1748, d. 1821.

[4] Cf. *infra.,* p. 26.

chanting in the Catholic Church in Philadelphia (St. Joseph's) "exquisitely soft and sweet." The emotional quality of the singing in the Methodist church of St. George impressed him deeply. He describes it as "the finest music I have heard in any society except the Moravians, and once in a church with an organ."

The Moravians, so singled out by Adams, certainly deserve special mention in the colonial period. While the episcopal seat of the Moravians was at Bethlehem, the Moravian congregation at Bread and Race Streets in Philadelphia had remarkably fine music. They favored the use not only of the organ, but of other brass and string instruments. There were two organs in use as early as 1743. The great organ became too old in 1796 and a new one was installed by David Tannenberg. There is record of the Second Moravian Church purchasing an organ in 1805 from E. N. Scherr.

The most ancient of religions to be represented in colonial Philadelphia is that of the Jews. Hebrew traders were in Philadelphia before 1682, although their first synagogue was not officially founded until 1745. This earliest Jewish congregation, known as Mickve Israel, is noted for the activities of the Gratz family throughout most of its long history. The two reformed Jewish congregations that became so influential in the nineteenth century are more recent in their organization, Rodeph Shalom having been founded in 1802 and Keneseth Israel in 1847. The music at Mickve Israel was limited to chants and hymns in its first years. Later developments have enriched Jewish music by the addition of several fine organs and well trained chorus choirs.[1]

IV

Public musical performances of dramatic and concert nature seem to have been tolerated, although not always well supported, from about 1750 throughout the late colonial period. In addition to productions by the Kean-Murray and Hallam companies mentioned above, many less important, or at least, less professional

---

[1] Russell King Miller, Walter Sinclair Knodle, N. Lindsay Norden, and Isadore Freed are a few Philadelphia organists who have played at leading synagogues. Among their regular vocal soloists have been such noted artists as Max Heinrich, Nicholas Douty, and Abbie Keely.

events might be mentioned at this time. Some of the theatrical performances were spoken of somewhat vaguely as operas, which usually means that several musical numbers were introduced. In the performance of Arne's *Masque of Alfred* (1757) by the students of the College of Philadelphia, it is reported that "several young ladies condescended to sing the songs." Another public performance of amateur musicians took place in December, 1759, when "an interlude of concert music was performed by some gentlemen of the city for the purpose of purchasing an organ for the College Hall in this city, and instructing the college children in psalmody." This organ was installed in 1760, and Francis Hopkinson frequently played it. Hopkinson was largely responsible for the University of Pennsylvania's having so much good music in the eighteenth century, according to an article by Otto E. Albrecht, *Francis Hopkinson, Musician, Poet and Patriot.*[1]

A series of concerts was thus announced in the *Pennsylvania Journal* in the autumn of 1764: "Subscription Concert at the Assembly Room, Lodge Alley, begins on Thursday the 8th of Nov. next, to continue every other Thursday till the 14th of March following. Each subscriber paying 3£ to be entitled to two Ladies' tickets for the season. Tickets to be had at the bar of the London Coffee House." Evidently the musical devotees were becoming bolder and more ambitious at this period.

One work of particular importance stands out in the colonial period of music in Philadelphia. *The Disappointment, or The Force of Credulity,* by Andrew Barton, was advertised in various journals of 1767[2] as a new comic opera of two acts. This ballad opera was printed in 1767, and though the music is named rather than printed, *The Disappointment* is claimed by many to be the oldest American opera. The libretto calls for eighteen songs, among them *Yankee Doodle.* This printed and dated document, of which several copies are preserved,[3] should establish, once and for all, the pre-Revolutionary origin of *Yankee Doodle.*

---

[1] Library Chronicle of the University of Pennsylvania, March, 1938. Cf. *infra*, pp. 30-36 for an account of Hopkinson.

[2] Among them the *Pennsylvania Chronicle* of April 26 and 27, 1767.

[3] A copy may be seen at the Boston Public Library, New York Public Library, The Library Company of Philadelphia, and the Pennsylvania Historical Society.

A mystery concerning any traces of Andrew Barton beyond the authorship of *The Disappointment,* has caused some historians to ascribe the play to Colonel Forrest of Germantown, who may possibly have used Andrew Barton, Esquire, as a pseudonym. There is very little evidence that Forrest wrote the play, however,[1] and since the tunes are largely chosen from English, rather than American ballad airs, the entire question belongs to the study of literature rather than the history of Philadelphia music.

Even earlier than *The Disappointment* is *The Fashionable Lady,* written by a Philadelphian, James Ralph, while he was in London, and first produced in that city in 1730. The lack of connection between the play and Ralph's earlier years in Philadelphia (1698-1724), renders it remote in its importance for discussion in this book. Again, the words only were written by Ralph, making the entire work more in the literary field than the musical. *The Fashionable Lady,* and not *The Disappointment,* was quite definitely the first opera by an American; and as such must be at least mentioned as the work of an ex-Philadelphian.[2] This play was produced in New York in 1750, but there is no record of its being given in Philadelphia, the city of Ralph's birth.

This questionable celebrity, James Ralph, was noted for his friendship with Benjamin Franklin as well as his censure by Alexander Pope. Franklin's connections with music were scientific rather than artistic. He did write the words for vocal ballads in his early years, but soon abandoned the lighter vein for his philosophical and acoustical study of music. His scientific improvement of the musical glasses, or Armonica, is not only practical as we should expect of him, but based on sound acoustics. This instrument will be mentioned in connection with its first appearance in Philadelphia (1764), Franklin having been in London in the years of his interest in its improved construction. The great popularity of the Armonica for forty years (1760-1800) was largely the result of Franklin's improvements in its facility and tone.

Benjamin Franklin expressed an interesting theory on the question of the composition of beautiful melodies. He declared

---

[1] Says Sonneck, in his *Bibliography of Early Secular American Music.*
[2] Mrs. Ralph and the children, incidentally, were still Philadelphians at the time of their absent parent's notoriety as a character in Pope's *Dunciad,* and the nine London performances of his *Fashionable Lady.*

that a melody with inherent harmonic basis, or even with arpeggio passages in it, is more agreeable than one which needs too much harmonic support from other voices or instruments.[1] He laments that so much melody of his day is quite unsingable when compared to the old songs. Franklin's idea of melodic construction is strikingly true when applied to great tunes that have lasted for long periods of time.

If *Watson's Annals* are correct in the supposition that the song in the Trades Procession of 1787 was written by Dr. Franklin, we may say that Benjamin Franklin returned in his eighties to the writing of light ballad verses in which he had delighted as a youth. The song was sung in a Philadelphia parade in honor of the state's ratification of the Constitution. Each trade had its stanza in a lively rhythm [2] well suited to a marching crowd.

Two concert announcements showing the nature of the programs in the colonial period are quoted: Signor Gualdo announces in 1770: "a concert of vocal and instrumental music, solos and concertos in various instruments, the favorite mandolin not excepted." An announcement of the time of Gualdo's concert sheds an interesting light on the rise of music in popular estimation since it was classed with gambling and dancing in 1716: "Admission ten shillings, and if any lady or gentleman chooses to go away after the concert [*i.e.,* omitting the ball] the porter will return half a crown." An earlier concert (1764) was thus advertised: "For the benefit of Mr. Forrage and others, assistant performers at the Subscription Concerts in this city, on Monday, [December] 31st instant, at the Assembly Room on Lodge Alley will be performed A Concert of Music, consisting of a variety of the most celebrated pieces now in taste, in which will be introduced the famous Armonica or Musical Glasses so much admired for the great Sweetness and Delicacy of its tone.[3] Tickets at 7/6 each, to be had at the bar of the London Coffee House. . . . The concert to begin at six o'clock precisely."

---

[1] *The Writings of Benjamin Franklin,* ed. Albert H. Smyth, N. Y., 1905-1907 (Volume 4, pp. 373-381).

[2] "Ye merry mechanics, come join in my song . . . . Ye tailors . . . . Ye joiners . . . . Ye masons, etc." The verses are given on p. 345 of Vol. 2, Watson's *Annals of Philadelphia.*

[3] Mr. Forrage himself appeared as soloist on the Armonica.

The colonial chapter should close, as it began, with the mention of an accomplishment by one of the German-Swedish element in Philadelphia. John Behrent achieved distinction by the manufacture of the first American piano, in Philadelphia, 1775. His accomplishment reminds us of the reputed skill of the Germans at instrument making as well as instrumental performance in the earliest days of Philadelphia. Although the city was rapidly becoming imbued with the English musical forms—the ballad opera, the lighter styles of composition—Behrent, and the earlier Hesselius,[1] exemplify a continuing craftsmanship in instrument making.[2]

In closing the account of colonial music in Philadelphia, it should also be noted that most of the legal restrictions proposed by Pennsylvania's proprietary government were vetoed by the British colonial authorities. Gradually even such laws against entertainment as were in effect began to be interpreted as excepting music. At least, it seems that we are justified in so assuming from the many concerts announced from 1765 to 1774. Such names as *Interlude, Subscription concert,* or *Benefit Program* seem to suggest a popular approval of musical entertainments, since many performances so announced contained plays hiding under a musical aegis. However, legal compulsion was seldom invoked to prevent out-and-out dramatic entertainment. Individual fanaticism was long present, but it must be said for the Pennsylvania Friends that as a group, they tolerated nearly anything for the entertainment of non-Quaker audiences, while most of the relatively few attempts at legal restriction that they did propose were not approved by English authorities. It is reasonable and natural to suppose that the Church of England group who favored nearly all of the theatri-

---

[1] Gustavus Hesselius, Swedish organ builder in Philadelphia, who built the first American spinets and virginals as early as 1742.

[2] Other names of less importance to Philadelphia itself, but noted in the history of early American instruments, are those of Johann Gottlob Klemm and Matthias Zimmerman. Klemm came to Philadelphia in 1726, but soon moved to New York. He was famous as the builder of the Trinity Church organ in 1740. Zimmerman bequeathed an organ that he had made, in a will of 1737. These early instruments, and the earlier ones made by the Hermits of the Wissahickon, make it difficult to establish the date of the first American organ. Similarly, a "first American opera" depends on many factors—chief of which is the question as to just which of the first attempts was an opera worthy of the name. So, the earliest organs built in Germantown or Philadelphia were undoubtedly very limited instruments.

cal ventures should have the support of authorities in the court of the early Georges of England. Hence, the main difficulty in public performances of a musical and dramatic nature must have been to get an appreciative audience large enough to make the professional organization of theatres a profitable undertaking. In this connection it should be noted that the Friends were far from being the only religious sect to disapprove of musical entertainments. The Presbyterians, Baptists, and Methodists were decidedly opposed to the assembling of audiences for the hearing of light music or dramatic entertainment; while Mennonites, Dunkards, and the many sects that settled early Pennsylvania, even the musical Moravians, were not in favor of the use of music for "profane gratifications." From 1750 on there was not so much a change in the Quaker viewpoint as there was a tremendous increase in population, from 4,500 in 1700 to 42,500 in 1770. These many thousands of newer colonists were not as a rule so religiously minded as the company of Johannes Kelpius, or the original colonists of William Penn.

CHAPTER TWO

THE REVOLUTION AND AFTER

I

During the Revolution a wave of seriousness swept over Philadelphia authorities. Possibly the party that had never succumbed to concerts managed by Palma or Signor Gualdo, or to plays produced by Hallam or Douglass (1750-1770), found the struggle against England an opportunity to impose a sterner environment on their more musically or theatrically minded neighbors. Even in 1773, when the seriousness of desperate patriotism was a possibility of the future, the newspapers contained such cards as that by Philadelphus in the *Pennsylvania Gazette* of November tenth, 1773: ". . . and it is much to the disreputation of this city that more encouragement [to theatrical musicians] is given here than in any other place on the continent."

Philadelphus, the die-hard, overstates the truth concerning his city's welcome to music and drama. It may be claimed that in no city was there such a great increase in the number of concerts and musical plays during the twenty years prior to his card to the Gazette, that is, 1753-1773. Per thousand population, there is little doubt that Philadelphia encouraged music and the theatre less heartily than other colonial towns. As to the character of late colonial music, both New York and Philadelphia are said to have balanced sacred and secular forms rather evenly.[1] Boston and New England in general were dominated by religious elements in music, while in Charleston and the South secular music predominated.[1]

While the Continental Congresses were dictating stern policies, theatrical and musical ventures were almost non-existent. Laws passed in 1775 prohibited "theatrical performances and other vain

---

[1] O. Sonneck, *Francis Hopkinson and James Lyon*, pp. 10-11.

23

diversions."[1] The Southwark Theatre, opened in 1766, had to be renamed "Temple of Apollo" for concerts of vocal and instrumental music. Its advertisements were models of ingenious subterfuge. Operettas, mainly "ballad operas," were announced as "Lectures, being a mixed entertainment of Representation and Harmony." Under the comprehensive title "Lecture" were presented *Hamlet* and *The Gamester* among other plays. *Hamlet* was called a "moral and instructive tale, introduced between the parts of the concert, called Filial Piety exemplified in the History of the Prince of Denmark." When *The Gamester* was produced, an announcement reassured the public that "between the acts of the Concert will be presented a serious and moral lecture in five parts, on the sin of gambling at the request of several ladies and gentlemen." We are led to wonder whether the sin of gambling is greater or less if the ladies and gentlemen have neglected to request it. Our press agent was even more ambiguous than he intended.

Little further need be noted concerning the various evasive attempts at public musical functions from 1774 to 1777. However, the gayety of the Tories in entertaining the British during the winter of 1777-1778 is well known. The story is told[2] that Major André painted a drop scene for amateur British actors in Philadelphia which was used twenty years later as the scene of his own capture in a play written on the subject.

The outstanding entertainment of the British in Philadelphia was the Meschianza[3] given on May 18, 1778. Beginning at four in the afternoon a regatta rowed down the Delaware River and landed in the southern part of the city. A tournament was staged, with officers in knightly costumes. This was followed by a ball which lasted until ten in the evening, then there were fireworks, a great dinner with much drinking of toasts, and finally dancing until four in the morning. The entire program was given by the officers in the army of General Howe, on the occasion of his quitting the command of the British army in America to return to England. Music was featured throughout the Meschianza. The regatta was

---

[1] Jane Campbell, *Old Philadelphia Music*, p. 182.
[2] Madeira, *op. cit.*, p. 33.
[3] From *mischiare* (Ital.) to mix, hence a medley of various forms of entertainment.

in three divisions, each headed by a flat boat containing a "band
of music."[1]   The boats were rowed in time to this music from
Green Street wharf to below Old Swedes' Church.   The tournament
and the later toasts were made colorful by many trumpet fanfares,
while the two sessions of dancing and the dinner were accompanied
by the usual music incidental to such functions.

A further bit of "negative evidence" that music was still present in public performances is the recommendation by Congress on
October 2, 1778, that "States should pass laws to prevent theatrical
and musical diversions as are productive of idleness."   Recommendations and public opinion did render any musical undertaking haz-
ardous during the war, if its standards were not definitely amateur.

II

The rise of music after the Revolutionary War was much more
uniform than its progress in the colonial period.   During the years
which closed the eighteenth century, Philadelphia music achieved
an eminent position in America which it has never since regained.
Let us compare the orchestra which Oscar Sonneck, the foremost
authority on early national music in this country, has imagined to
have played at colonial performances [2] with one similarly made up
of men who were known to have played in Philadelphia groups between 1780 and 1800.   The group of the 1764 Subscription Concerts probably included Francis Hopkinson at the harpsichord;
James Bremner, Stephen Forrage, John Schneider, and Governor
John Penn on stringed instruments, George d'Eissenburg and
Ernst Barnard, German flutes.   John Schneider also played the
horn.   John Deals is a likely selection among several oboists in the
vicinity of Philadelphia.   Within a decade after the Revolution,
however, an imposing list of professional musicians could be made
from contemporary accounts and press notices.   These musical personages were almost all from Europe.   The more important ones
in the following list constitute the center of Music in Philadelphia
throughout the brilliant period which closed the eighteenth century.

---

[1] Watson's *Annals* contain two accounts of this affair, and several additional references to it.
[2] Cf. *Francis Hopkinson and James Lyon* by Sonneck, p. 48.

Andrew Adgate was the foremost choral conductor from 1784 to 1793. Alexander Reinagle, the famous manager and conductor, was active in Philadelphia from 1786 to about 1800. Benjamin Carr, the latest to arrive of these three English musicians, exerted the greatest influence of them all on Philadelphia music. Reinagle's former teacher, Raynor Taylor, came to Philadelphia in the same year as did Benjamin Carr, 1793. His important influence in Philadelphia music lasted but a few years less than that of Carr himself, Carr remaining active in the city until 1831, Taylor until 1825. Other noted instrumentalists were Jean Gehot, George Gillingham, Alexander Juhan and Philip Phile, violin; George Schetky and Henry Capron, 'cello; William Young and William Brown, flute; A. Wolff and Mr. Dubois, clarinet; William Priest, bassoon and trumpet; Robert Shaw, oboe and bassoon. Both William Roth and John Bentley were harpsichord soloists—which Francis Hopkinson did not claim to be. It should be borne in mind that this rapid increase in both musicians and musicianship so close to the year 1790 was an *addition* to existing musical forces. The new and the old musicians alike benefited by the removal of the official ban on theatrical performances, which took place in the year 1789.

We must retrace our steps into the period of the theatrical prohibition to consider the musical work of Andrew Adgate. His arrival in Philadelphia in 1784 followed the death of James Bremner by only a few years. Doubtless both the current ban on secular music and his own special ability led Adgate to concentrate on sacred musical productions, particularly in the choral field.

Andrew Adgate was a celebrated organizer of choral musical events and singing schools from 1784 to 1793. The Institute for the Encouragement of Church Music, founded 1784, later the Free School for Spreading the Knowledge of Vocal Music, 1785; and its final development, the Uranian Academy of 1787, are important organizations in the history of Philadelphia choral singing. The Uranian Academy was possibly named in honor of the collection *Urania* by James Lyon. Adgate's chorus surely sang the type of music contained in Lyon's collection of 1761.[1] The Uranian Acad-

---

[1] The unusual name *Uranian* suggests Urania the muse of astronomy, and thus heavenly music; although Uranus, the father of the furies, might at times seem the patron of choral groups!

emy interested many leading Philadelphians in the late eighteenth
century. Dr. Benjamin Rush and Judge Francis Hopkinson were
among the trustees and patrons.[1] Although the number of students
was set at three hundred, with three teaching positions, the Uranian
Academy did not long survive the plague of 1793, which took Andrew Adgate to the real heavenly music, the eternal Urania.

Adgate's selections and plans for a great number of excellent
vocal programs are fully and appreciatively treated in Oscar Sonneck's *Early Concert Life in America*. The loyalty to American
composers' efforts in many of Andrew Adgate's programs seems
to have limited the artistic significance of the events under his management. On the other hand he transplanted the current British
admiration for Handel's Hallelujah Chorus with such success and
insistence that Philadelphia audiences have admired and demanded
its frequent performance ever since! Some of the most important
musical events in the period of theatrical prohibition, 1775-1789,
were managed by this early professional musician. Particularly
noteworthy was a *"Grand Concert of Sacred Song* given on May 4,
1786, at the Reformed German Church on Race Street, for the benefit of the Pennsylvania Hospital, Philadelphia Dispensary and the
Poor." Among the numbers are an overture by Martini, a concerto
for flute by W. Brown and one for violin by Mr. Juhan, five anthems, and the Hallelujah Chorus from Handel's *Messiah*. One
of the anthems was composed by a Mr. W. Billings of Boston, who
is often called the first American composer. Another anthem was
by James Lyon, who probably composed it while a resident of
Philadelphia. The chorus numbered over two hundred, the band
fifty.

Adgate furnishes us with an early example of choric recita-
tion. At a concert in the Hall of the University twenty boys in
white robes recited *The Messiah* in unison. The boys were from
Mr. Ely's school, an institution at which psalmody was thoroughly
taught. Mr. Adgate directed some more advanced musical numbers in the gallery in order to render the occasion more agreeable

---

[1] The *Pennsylvania Mercury* of March 30, 1787, gives the officers of the
Uranian Academy as Reverend Dr. Andrews, President; Reverend Dr. Henry
Helmuth, Vice-President; Mr. John Swanick, Secretary; and Mr. Azariah
Horton, Treasurer.

to the ladies and gentlemen who would "be so kind as to favor this infant exhibition with their notice."[1] Adgate's choir figured on nearly all of the important concert programs which included music for vocal chorus.

Andrew Adgate died in the 1793 epidemic of yellow fever as has been said. A Uranian Society, or Academy, seems to have lived up until about 1800, however, and is known to have given concerts at the hall of the University of Pennsylvania until at least that year. Also, the interest in psalmody, and vocal music in general, that he awakened did not die,[2] but continued in a relatively unbroken tradition down to the present time, as will be discussed later.

John Bentley was the first to organize post-Revolutionary City Concerts. In the two winter seasons following the war, 1783-1784, and 1784-1785, his fortnightly orchestral evenings at the Lodge Room drew capacity houses. The quick success of these concerts which followed the actual cessation of the war seems to have been of brief duration. The leading musical spirits had difficulties within their ranks, and it was not until 1786 with the arrival of Alexander Reinagle that any important series of city concerts was resumed. Reinagle's management was evidently of a high order of efficiency, while his programs were both interesting and musically worthy. It is true that his own compositions and those of members of his orchestra (William Brown, A. Juhan, and H. Capron), were performed quite frequently at his concerts, but this was quite a universal method of securing recognition—to say nothing of securing music to play. And it is decidedly to Reinagle's credit that the European composers who shared his attention with such local geniuses included men like Corelli, Mozart, Haydn, Stamitz, Grétry, and Bach—probably C. P. E. Bach. The ever popular Overture by the Earl of Kelly, or, as Reinagle's programs name him, *Lord Kelly,* was given repeatedly during Brown and Reinagle's two winters of program building for the Philadelphia City Concerts.

Washington's diary mentions attending several theatrical performances during his stay in Philadelphia as president of the Constitutional Convention. At a benefit concert, May 29, 1787, at the

---

[1] Quoted from the Pennsylvania Journal, April 4, 1788, by O. Sonneck in *Early Concert Life in America,* p. 118.
[2] Though in the decade following Adgate's death, 1793-1803, the great popularity of English opera caused it to languish considerably.

City Tavern, he heard a grand overture by Martini, a sonata by Haydn, and many musical numbers by local composers.

The beginning of theatrical music in quantity seems to have followed closely the repeal of the laws against theatres in 1789. In about 1790 a new series of musical entertainments was given at Harrowgate Garden, near Frankford. Operas and "Musical Pieces" were given in quite regular series at the Southwark Theatre. Seventeen ninety-one saw the opening of the Northern Liberties Theatre, and two years later the famous Chestnut Street Theatre was opened at Sixth Street and Chestnut.[1]

George Gillingham was an English violinist who was imported to become the concert master of the Chestnut Street, or New Theatre. The twenty accomplished musicians led by him, and by Reinagle, were said to possess a skill "deemed equal with the stage artists." However absolute such a criticism of the Chestnut Street Theatre orchestra may or may not be, it was surely intended to be complimentary, and it showed a sincere appreciation of the talents of the musical accompanists to some of Philadelphia's earliest drama. A performance of *Robin Hood* in 1794, probably in the Ballad Opera form which appealed strongly to English audiences, stands out as one of many theatrical performances. *Tammany, or The Indian Chief* by James Hewitt was produced twice in Philadelphia in that same year. *Tammany* is the earliest opera on an American Indian theme, and one of the first to be composed by an American. It had been previously produced three times in New York, and was given once in Boston after its Philadelphia performances in 1794.

III

The musical productions on a professional scale, from 1790 on, are so numerous that they eclipse, in the records of the time, the many amateur entertainments. Doubtless the tradition of amateur musical organizations was a continuous one; for we noted its beginnings in the colonial period when the province was too small and too narrow to permit of much music of the professional type;

---

[1] Cf. *Infra*, p. 39, in the account of Reinagle, for this New Theatre's early events.

its second period of prominence when theatrical companies were largely excluded, 1775-1785; and we shall find constant presence of amateur musicianship in the increasingly affluent days of the early nineteenth century. In the Post-Revolutionary period the advertising and the actual increase in professional music hide what was undoubtedly a time of expanding study of music and participation in its performance by amateurs.

The amateur concerts are decidedly more difficult to trace than the more widely advertised professional and benefit concerts. Some few are noted in Sonneck's *Early Concert Life in America*—as a New Concert, December 2, 1783, a series of about twelve concerts in the season 1786-1787, and similar series up to 1791. Most of these were given by a Music Club—so named in current press announcements—but unfortunately programs were not advertised or preserved. Their existence was most probably a continuous one, the more frequent mention of them merely coinciding with the seasons when City Concerts failed to materialize.

A permanently successful combination of professional and amateur musicians occurred in 1794. The appearance of many new names, both Philadelphia musicians and local and foreign composers, marks the long and impressive list of programs from 1794 quite continuously to 1860. The severe yellow fever epidemic of 1793 had occasioned a musical hiatus of about two years. From the close of the Revolution to 1792 the musical life of Philadelphia was active and important in both amateur and professional fields. After the resuming of concert and dramatic music in 1794, the development of Philadelphia music is a consistent process, not seriously interrupted until the American Civil War of 1861. The great popularity of summer concerts in the open air, and winter operas in the New Theatre, mark the closing years of the century. The Pennsylvania Coffee House had inaugurated series of summer concerts under Vincent Pelosi in 1786. Harrowgate Gardens and Bush Hill began summer concerts before 1800.

The name of Francis Hopkinson, 1737-1791, inevitably comes to mind whenever one considers the gentleman-musician of Revolutionary and Post-Revolutionary days. The sanity and sincerity with which Philadelphians appreciated the scholarly yet simple works by Hopkinson reflect credit on the musical taste of the times. His importance was recognized in his own time, and though slighted from 1800 to 1900, he is becoming increasingly known and appreciated today. The recent celebration in 1937 of the bicentennial of his birth has done much to make his life and work known to the musical public. Those who have studied the earliest music produced in the United States have recognized Hopkinson's importance for many years. To such musical antiquarians, the details of his life were familiar long before the data assembled at his bicentennial anniversary spread information about him. His political importance coupled with that of his musical contributions make it well-nigh unbelievable that most nineteenth century specialists on Philadelphia history either barely mention his music, or ignore it completely.

Francis Hopkinson was born in Philadelphia, 1737, educated in the College of Philadelphia,[1] and admitted to the bar in 1761. He was a delegate to the Continental Congress of 1776, and a signer of the Declaration of Independence; assisted in drafting the Articles of the Confederation, and was a member of the Constitutional Convention. His Federal and local appointments included Judge of Admiralty for Pennsylvania, 1779-1789, Pennsylvania District Judge 1790-1791, and first Secretary of the Navy.

Hopkinson was a man of exceptionally varied accomplishments. He composed music for his facile songs, painted, was a dilettante in popular science, a humorist and political pamphleteer.

As to his musical interests, his library contained several manuscript copies taken from such contemporary masters as Handel, Corelli, Geminiani, Vivaldi, Alberti, and Guglielmi. An interesting collection of the period, probably used by his son Joseph, is also in the Hopkinson library, *The Essex Harmony, a Collection of Songs, Catches, Canzonets, Canons and Glees,* published in 1796. *The Musical Miscellany Songs and Lyric Poems, with the Basses to Each Tune, and Transposed for the Flute,* was a printed collection. An antiquarian treasure, even in 1780, was Hopkinson's copy of Giles Farnaby's, "The Psalmes of David to Fower Parts for viols and voyce, the First Book Doric Mottoes, the Second Divine Canzonets, composed by Giles Farnaby Bachilor of Musicke with a

---

[1] Later called the University of Pennsylvania. Francis Hopkinson was the first graduate of the University of Pennsylvania.

prelude before the psalmes cromaticke." Only the soprano part book seems to have been in the Hopkinsons' possession.[1]

There is some possibility that Hopkinson assisted in the composition as well as the performance of the *Masque of Alfred* given by the College of Philadelphia in 1757. In 1759, the celebrated song *My Days have been so Wondrous Free* was composed. It has been widely recognized as the first secular song by a native American composer. In the same year the song *With Pleasure have I spent my Days* was composed by Hopkinson. A two hundred page manuscript notebook, containing the two songs mentioned above and at least three others by Francis Hopkinson, is preserved in the Library of Congress. The remaining songs in the book are taken from the works of Handel, Purcell, Pergolesi, Boyce, Arne, and Pepusch. Many of Hopkinson's compositions are thus sandwiched in between copied works in the large manuscript notebooks in his library. Another notebook contains his piano and organ lessons studied with James Bremner. The lessons are copied from works of Handel, Scarlatti, Corelli, Geminiani, Vivaldi, Galuppi, and Stamitz. Fragments of a manuscript book copied before 1755 contain Handel's Aria from *Atalanta* (p. 78), with the harpsichord part for the right hand in treble clef and left hand in the alto clef. This book was given to his sister when both Francis and Elizabeth were very young.

Hopkinson's brilliance in other fields besides music may be briefly mentioned. A declamation written and delivered at the age of fifteen (1753) in honor of the granting of a charter to the Academy by the Proprietaries of Pennsylvania is still treasured by his descendants.

An interesting sample of his literary awareness is provided by the pamphlet "Errata, or the Art of Printing Incorrectly by a Variety of Examples taken from a Latin Grammar lately printed by Andrew Stewart for the Use of the College and Academy of this City"—to which already lengthy title he appends a couplet by Pope:

---

[1] Otto E. Albrecht mentions this Farnaby book as "an otherwise unknown work" in his article *Francis Hopkinson Musician, Poet and Patriot,* p. 8. (Library Chronicle of the University of Pennsylvania, March 1938.)

"Still her old Empire to restore she tries,
For born a Goddess, Dulness never dies." [1]

An early literary work is "Science," a poem, written 1762. From the same period we have "Exercise containing a Dialogue and Ode, Sacred to the memory of his Late Majesty George II," words and music by Francis Hopkinson, 1761. Another similar literary-musical composition was produced in honor of George III's accession.

In 1763 he compiled a collection of "Psalm Tunes, with a few Anthems and Hymns, some of them Entirely New, for the United Churches of Christ Church, and St. Peter's in Philadelphia." From about the same period there comes a letter of strikingly mature wisdom written by Hopkinson to Reverend Dr. White, rector of the two churches, on the "conduct of a church organ," and religious music in general. This letter was reproduced in the *Columbian Magazine* for September, 1792. Hopkinson's remarks on the rhythm of words in chanting are' still a pertinent guide for this type of religious music. His plea for dignity in church music, and for unity of thought in religious services will still repay consideration by our church musical authorities. For example, Hopkinson suggests that the postlude following a sermon should be related to the thought contained in the address. He even suggested that various psalm verses dealing with contrasting subjects should receive contrasting organ accompaniments. [2]

Hopkinson composed both words and music of a "Psalm of Thanksgiving," performed at Christ Church, March 30, 1766. From 1765 we hear less of musical contributions by Hopkinson due possibly to his appointment as an "attourney of the Supream Court for the Province of Pennsylvania." During the Revolution Francis Hopkinson was a wholehearted supporter of the colonial cause. On hearing of Jacob Duché's proposal to Washington in 1777 that "the Congress should recall the hasty and Ill-advised Declaration of Independency," Hopkinson's encouragement to the Valley Forge

---

[1] Stewart's prompt answer is as bitter as Hopkinson's attack, and with considerably less restraint!
[2] For the letter itself, the reader is referred to Oscar Sonneck's *Francis Hopkinson and James Lyon*, pp. 59-62.

headquarters was prompt and positive. This was during the British occupation of the city, when Hopkinson was living in New Jersey and his classmate, friend, and brother-in-law, Duché, had remained in Philadelphia. His letter expressed surprise and sorrow at the suggestion of his friend and kinsman, and renewed his own expressions of interest and encouragement to his friend George Washington. Hopkinson was made Treasurer of Loans for Congress, holding this office from 1778 to 1782. The lengthy ballad *The Battle of the Kegs* was a timely patriotic song with words and music by Francis Hopkinson. Its nineteen stanzas relate how the British fleet wasted a large quantity of ammunition on a number of empty kegs floated down the Delaware River from Philadelphia. British sailors had been told that these kegs were infernal machines sent out to destroy their ships. The Battle of the Kegs, as a historical event and as a song by Hopkinson, dates from the year 1778.

In 1781 Hopkinson wrote one of his most important works. *The Temple of Minerva* was called an *Oratorial Entertainment* in two acts; but in reality it was a short opera in two scenes. In effect it resembled a masque in that it contained solos, a duet, a trio and choruses, although it did not include dancing. *The Temple of Minerva* closely parallels what was later termed grand opera, in that nothing was spoken in its performance. Its fragmentary size forbids its being classed as the first American opera, yet it certainly bears a more musical right to that distinction than *The Fashionable Lady,* or *The Disappointment,* in both of which the authors are known to have written only the words to familiar music. Hopkinson's *Oratorial Entertainment* contains some if not all original music, and boasted an overture for its initial performance; which took place before the French Minister, the Washingtons, and other notables in Philadelphia, December, 1781. We shall not be misled by the classification *oratorial entertainment,* if we remember that 1781 falls in the period in which operas were forbidden in public, and probably frowned upon for private performance. It was surely not an oratorio in any way. The use of the words *Hail Columbia* in the concluding chorus of this work has been said [1] to have sug-

---

[1] By Sonneck. *Francis Hopkinson and James Lyon,* p. 110.

gested that phrase to his son Joseph. Joseph Hopkinson's particular importance in music lies in his authorship of the patriotic song
Hail Columbia.

Doubtless Hopkinson's admiration for Washington was responsible for the dedication of an important musical collection, *Seven
Songs for Harpsichord or Forte-Piano,* to the President. This
collection contained eight songs, with words and music by Hopkinson, and was published in Philadelphia in 1788. It was the first
publication of its kind by a native composer. That the above mentioned admiration was mutual, a quotation from Washington's reply
to Hopkinson will make clear. Hopkinson had sent the copy of the
songs and the customary apologetic statement concerning their
value, together with his hopes that Washington would not object
to having "so bad a thing" dedicated to him, to the president at
Mt. Vernon. Mr. Washington replied in a long and appreciative
letter within a week after receiving the songs (February 5, 1789)
"If they [the ancients] could even charm the powers of Hell by
their Musick, I am sure that your productions would have had at
least enough virtue in them (without the aid of voice or instrument) to soften the ice of the Delaware and Potomack—and in
that case you should have had an earlier acknowledgment of your
favor of the first of December which came to hand but last Saturday," two months later. Referring to a deprecatory phrase in
Hopkinson's dedication of the songs, Washington states "I do not
believe that you would do a 'very bad thing indeed,' and would defend your performance if necessary to the last effort of my musical
abilities." Later in the same letter the writer says, "What alas!
can I do to support it [the quality of Hopkinson's songs]? I can
neither sing one of the songs, nor raise a single note on any instrument to convince the unbelieving.—But I have, however, one argument which will prevail with persons of true taste (at least in
America)—I can tell them that it is the production of Mr. Hopkinson."

Hopkinson's interest in scientific matters caused Franklin to
bequeath to him most of his philosophical paraphernalia. Thomas
Jefferson was deeply interested in Francis Hopkinson's improvements in quilling and tuning the harpsichord, and in his invention

of a keyboard for the harmonica (musical glasses) which resulting instrument he called the Bellarmonic. Jefferson and Hopkinson's correspondence, which extended over a period of several years, is described in *Francis Hopkinson, Musician, Poet and Patriot,* an article by Otto E. Albrecht in the Library Chronicle of the University of Pennsylvania, March, 1938. Their letters discussed the new "ballons" and their potential influence on fortifications, the proposed introduction of decimals into arithmetic, as well as the harpsichord and the harmonica.[1] Of the plentiful tributes to Hopkinson in his many fields, the most musical is probably that of William Brown who composed *Three Rondos for Pianoforte or Harpsichord,* and "humbly dedicated" them to the Honourable Francis Hopkinson, Esquire.[2]

Francis Hopkinson's life and works have been discussed at considerable length because, first, his was the most lasting importance among Philadelphia musicians of the eighteenth century, and second, a picture of his career helps the general as well as the musical student to form an idea of the Revolutionary times in and around Philadelphia. He is therefore the first composer whose musical influence is treated in Music in Philadelphia with any attempt at completeness. With his death in 1791, the outstanding amateur development of the eighteenth century seems to have drawn to a close—at least so far as contemporary records reveal.

IV

The final years of the century saw a great increase in the concerts known as benefits. Sometimes these were advertised as charitable affairs, as to help a man impoverished by the San Domingo uprising. At other times the public servant-musician counted on the gratitude of his former audiences to put across a concert for his own benefit; and finally, purely spectacular events claimed the interest of the concert goers, such as an infant prodigy or a pro-

---

1 Albrecht, *op. cit.*, p. 13.
2 William Brown was active in Philadelphia between 1783-1787 as flutist, concert manager, and composer. He took part also in musical activities in New York, Baltimore and Charleston.

digious instrument. The musicians seem to have taken part in each others' benefit concerts, or at least not been rude enough to be absent on these occasions. There were, of course, some exceptions in this rule of courteous attendance, which were apt to cause quarrelsome notice by the friends of the main organizer of the concert. Two concerts for the benefit of women vocalists—Miss Broadhurst, April 3, 1800, and Mrs. M'Donald, August 11, 1800—marked the close of the eighteenth century with elaborate but not excellent programs. It is to be regretted that the increase of professional music in the closing years of the eighteenth century was accompanied by a less sincere effort to perform the best works. Regrettable, but not amazing, for a professional in a newly developing community must please first, and edify when possible. Certainly at benefit concerts we have the emphasis on pleasing, on virtuosity, and showmanship. The many earlier subscription concerts were less abject in their promises to have everything agreeable, while the amateur programs probably never considered such a phase at all. Such men as Gillingham, Taylor, Reinagle, and Carr would never descend to the standards of some of the earliest musical pioneers (Tuckey, Billings), and yet in the rapidly multiplying concerts of benefit-professional nature about the year 1800 there is a decided falling off from the artistic level achieved in the preceding twenty years.

V

In these early days there was little mention of the first performance in America of musical works. Later in our historical chapters, the American premières in Philadelphia are less frequent, and occasioned more mention on contemporary programs than they did in the eighteenth century. This is to be expected since the early musicians were constantly introducing works to America at Philadelphia performances. At present, when Philadelphia does produce an important piece of music for the first time in this country, it is considered to be news, and as such should be mentioned in the twentieth century sections of Music in Philadelphia.

Among the eightenth century first performances in America, the *Battle of Prague* is one of the most interesting to record. A Bohemian composer, Franz Kotzwara, wrote this piano sonata in 1792. Shortly after that year it was introduced to this country at a concert at Oellers' Hotel at Chestnut Street, between Sixth and Seventh, Philadelphia. George Gillingham and Benjamin Carr directed this concert. George Schetky, also a Philadelphian, orchestrated *The Battle of Prague,* but its piano version remained particularly popular well into the nineteenth century.[1]

Benjamin Carr and Raynor Taylor will be more fully discussed in the chapter on music of the early ninetenth century. Alexander Reinagle, however, seems to have left Philadelphia shortly after 1800; thus the enormous influence he exerted on its music springs from a period of only about fifteen years. The following biographical data are condensed from the account in John Tasker Howard's *Our American Music,* pp. 75-81.

Alexander Reinagle was born in Portsmouth, England, in 1756, and died in 1809 at Baltimore, Maryland. He studied with Raynor Taylor in Scotland. Carl Philip E. Bach and other noted European musicians were known to Reinagle, some of them intimately. In 1786 Alexander Reinagle came to America, spending a few months in New York. By September of that year he had settled permanently in Philadelphia.

A song and sonata of Reinagle's were given on Henri Capron's benefit program of September 21, 1786. In October, Reinagle gave a benefit performance, opening and closing with works by Haydn. Reinagle, Capron, William Brown, and Alexander Juhan managed subscription concerts in the 1786-1787 season. Reinagle and Brown managed them in the following year. At about this time, 1787, Reinagle introduced four-hand piano music to America, playing with Juhan one of the *Sonates a quatre mains* (arranged

---

[1] This popular patriotic effort of Kotzwara was imitated by many composers, notably the American, James Hewitt, in his *Battle of Trenton.* The 'sonata,' *The Battle of Trenton,* was published by Hewitt in New York and by Benjamin Carr in Philadelphia in 1797. Mr. Olin Downes, editor, lecturer, and music critic for the New York *Times,* has revived interest in *The Battle of Trenton* by selecting it as the final and climactic example in his delightful lecture on Humor and Characterization in Music.

AN EARLY PHILADELPHIA MARCH

from a symphony), by Haydn, at a benefit concert for Juhan. Washington attended this program, and many concerts managed by Reinagle. He is said to have engaged Reinagle to teach the harpsichord to his step-grand-daughter, Nelly Custis. Reinagle returned to New York in 1788, but in 1789 the repeal of the Anti-Theatre laws brought him back to Philadelphia. He managed the city concerts of 1791-1792 with J. C. Moller, and with Moller and Capron in 1792-1793. The fact that he was always one of the managing figures in the various seasons may account for the definite improvement in the calibre of the music played. Haydn, Grétry, Bach, and Mozart appeared frequently on these concert programs. Most noted among this great director's many managerial combinations is that of Reinagle and Thomas Wignell in the building and management of the New Theatre on Chestnut Street. Planned and begun in 1791, the New Theatre was ready just as the plague of the winter of 1792-1793 began. Its opening was therefore delayed until April 2, 1793. A grand concert of vocal and instrumental music was given for that occasion. This New Theatre, or Chestnut Street Theatre, as it was later called, was widely advertised as one of the seven wonders of America. It was as large as Covent Garden, and an exact copy of the Theatre Royal at Bath. The building was located on Chestnut Street near Sixth, where it remained as the home of the finest music in Philadelphia until 1855. Not until February, 1794, did a true theatrical opening take place with the production of *The Castle of Andalusia*. George Gillingham was brought from England to act as principal violin at the New Theatre. The Old American Opera Company decided against competition with the flourishing Wignell-Reinagle company at the New Theatre; thus from 1794 to 1803, their productions were supreme in the Philadelphia theatrical field. Wignell having died in 1803, Reinagle continued to conduct the music at the New Theatre for a short time with Mrs. Wignell as dramatic director. He soon moved to Baltimore, and managed a theatre there until his death, September 21, 1809.

Many of Reinagle's compositions are listed in the index of this book. He wrote piano sonatas, and preludes, some miscellaneous quartets, numerous songs, music for the play *Slaves in Algiers*

(1794) ; for the musical farce *The Savoyard* (1797) ; and he collaborated with Raynor Taylor in the *Monody* on the death of Washington, and the plays *Pizarro* and *The Castle Spectre*. A piano concerto, many overtures and song collections are among works by Reinagle.[1]   He was beyond question Philadelphia's most important musician and prolific composer in the closing decade of the eighteenth century.

---

[1] A complete list, by date of production, of Alexander Reinagle's works is contained in pp. 85-88 of Drummond's *Early German Music in Pennsylvania*.

CHAPTER THREE

MUSIC FROM 1800 TO 1860

I

Raynor Taylor and Benjamin Carr are the two most important musicians whose careers extend from the closing years of the eighteenth century until well into the nineteenth. The withdrawal of Alexander Reinagle to Baltimore soon after 1800 seems to have left the musical leadership quite definitely in the able hands of Carr and Taylor. Taylor had been Reinagle's teacher in Scotland, although the pupil preceded the teacher in America by about seven years. Raynor Taylor by his agreeable personality must have seemed younger than his years, possibly younger than his efficient and established pupil Alexander Reinagle. He has been aptly styled the Nestor of the fine circle to which Reinagle, Carr, and Schetky belonged.[1] As the sage counsellor, Raynor Taylor's biography should be given at the beginning of any discussion of nineteenth century music in Philadelphia. Most of the following facts are taken from John Tasker Howard's book on *Our American Music*, pages 92-97.

Raynor Taylor was born in England in 1747, and received his first schooling as a choir boy at the Chapel Royal. In this capacity he is said[2] to have assisted at Handel's funeral in 1759, and to have lost his hat in the great man's grave. He became an organist and theatrical conductor as a young man. In 1792 Taylor came to America. After short residences in Baltimore and Annapolis, he settled in Philadelphia in May, 1793. In that year, St. Peter's Church engaged him as organist, which position he filled until almost the year of his death, 1825. His *Ode to the New Year*, given January eighteenth and twenty-eighth, 1794, was an early Philadelphia production. In 1796 Taylor staged a benefit concert at

---

[1] *Grove's Dictionary*, American Supplement.
[2] In *Grove's Dictionary*.

41

Oellers' hotel on April twenty-first.   The small band, or concertino, consisted of :

1st violin and leader	Mr. Gillingham
Violoncello	Mr. Menel
Double Bass	Mr. Demarque
Oboe	Mr. Shaw
Tenor [*i.e.*, viola]	Mr. Berenger
Bassoon and Trumpet	Mr. Priest
Horns	Messrs. Gray and Homman
Violins	Messrs Daugel, Bouchony, Stewart, Schetky.

Three numbers by Taylor were on the program, his violin concerto being played by Gillingham.   When Vauxhall Garden opened for the season of 1814, Taylor was the organist, playing an organ concerto of his own composition.   At Vauxhall on May 23, 1815, a group of amateurs gave his *May Day, or The Peasant's Invitation,* a musical play.   Taylor also wrote the music for *The Rose of Arragon* (1822), a melodrama.   Several anthems and songs are by Raynor Taylor.   *The Wounded Sailor, The Nightingale, The Philadelphia Hymn, The Merry Piping Lad, The Wandering Village Maid,* and a four hand arrangement of the *President's March,* are among his works.   His *La Petite Piedmontese,* a serious ballet, was produced in Philadelphia in 1795.   In 1797 Taylor's *The Iron Chest* was given in Baltimore.   His *La Bonne Petite Fille, or The Shipwrecked Marriner,* was produced in Philadelphia, Baltimore, and Boston.   Taylor collaborated with Reinagle in music for *Pizarro,* which was given in Philadelphia, 1800; and in the *Monody* on the death of Washington, 1799.   Carr published his piano method in 1797.   His cantata, *Morning Hymn,* was introduced and repeatedly given by the Handelian Society in 1815.   Taylor's musical play, *Buxom Joan,* was produced at the New Theatre on January 30, 1801.

Like his great contemporary, Benjamin Carr, Raynor Taylor was a singer and actor as well as a composer of vocal and instrumental music of all kinds.   Unfortunately very little is preserved of the many works credited to him on the programs of 1794-1825.

Two somewhat less notable men in Philadelphia music share Carr and Taylor's distinction of being very active in both eighteenth and nineteenth centuries. George Schetky and Charles Taws [1] were both influential in musical affairs for as long a period as were Carr and Taylor themselves. Schetky was a fine 'cellist, who came to Philadelphia in 1787, a year later than the arrival of his noted uncle Reinagle. He took part in many programs for a longer period of years than any previous musician. Schetky was one of the founders of the Musical Fund Society in 1820, remaining interested in its orchestra for about ten years after that date. His partnership with Carr as a publisher and music dealer belongs only to the first year or two of the nineteenth century, but his association with Benjamin Carr in the years 1800-1830 is one of the finest examples of a musical friendship. The names Carr and Schetky were linked in many ways beyond their official partnership of 1800. The two men died during the same year, 1831.

George Schetky was a singer, composer and arranger as well as an able 'cellist. He is mentioned as a violinist on the program of Raynor Taylor's benefit concert of April 21, 1796. His arrangement for a "full band" of Kotzwara's *Battle of Prague* has also been previously mentioned.[2] An interesting reference to Schetky's compositions appeared in *Les noms inconnus bons a connoitre*, or Unknown Names Worth Knowing, published by Venier in Paris in 1764. Haydn's name is linked with Schetky's in a criticism of early works by both men.

II

As we advance toward the present years it becomes constantly more difficult to give a picture of the general musical situation in Philadelphia. The accounts must become more topical as we progress through the nineteenth century, while the following century will be considered only by the topical method.

The early nineteenth century constituted Philadelphia's most important period in the manufacture of pianos. Since piano making has been this country's main musical industry—at least until

---

[1] For account of Charles Taws cf. *infra* pp. 45.6.
[2] Cf. *supra*. p. 38.

1930—some of the important men in Philadelphia's years of piano leadership should be discussed. The years of this musical-manufacturing dominance are 1780-1835, without any question.[1] With considerable debate the leadership of Philadelphia piano makers might be extended to 1860. Rather than indulge in any such comparative estimates, let us consider some of the firms in the history of Philadelphia piano manufacture. This commercial excursion from our trip through the clouds of concert artists and opera stars will not be the last such in our discussion of music in Philadelphia, for that city has always been an important center in the commercial phases of music life. We shall abandon the chronological limits of this chapter and mention the most important names in our history of piano making, with particular stress on the early nineteenth century, since it was the main period of Philadelphia's influence in that field.

Gustavus Hesselius has been mentioned, albeit rather parenthetically,[2] as a maker of virginals and spinets from as early as 1742. Little is known concerning his instruments, but his workmanship is supposed to have been of a fine character as should be expected of a member of the distinguished Swedish family to which he belonged. He is called an organ maker also. His spinets and virginals are very probably the first to have been made in this country.

James Julian is another early figure among Philadelphia piano makers. He announced in 1785 that he would sell "piano-fortes" of his own invention. His advertisements appear frequently in the newspapers of that year, and 1786.

When we discuss the piano manufacturing interests of Charles Albrecht we are on more certain and surely more permanent ground. He made pianos in Philadelphia from 1789 or earlier. The Albrecht piano on display at the Pennsylvania Historical Society bears that date. Charles Albrecht remained as a successful piano maker until 1824. C. F. L. Albrecht, doubtless a son of Charles, remained active in piano manufacture until 1842, when his concern was pur-

---

[1] According to Daniel Spillane's *History of the American Pianoforte*, p. 72.

[2] Cf. *supra*, p. 21.

chased by the Blasius Piano Company. This C. F. L. Albrecht won a medal for piano construction at the Franklin Institute Exhibition of 1833.

One of Schetky's early friends in Philadelphia was Joseph Charles Taws, a Scottish piano maker. Schetky and Taws were both Scots, coming to America within a year of each other. Taws spent somewhat more than a year in New York, where he had arrived in 1786, moving to Philadelphia in 1788. Within a few years Charles Taws was engaged in piano manufacture in Philadelphia. He and his sons were regarded as makers of fine instruments for many years. We read in the history of St. Luke's church that after Mr. Armat had lent the church an organ in 1817, a Mr. Taws came to play it, on July sixth of that year.[1] This "Mr. Taws" was described as a professional organist and organ builder, but unfortunately his full name is not given. One of C. Taws' many advertisements, that in the *American Daily Advertiser,* November 12, 1810, shows him to have been an importer as well as builder of pianos. We read "Charles Taws has opened a quantity of superb Piano Fortes from best London manufactories" at his new store, 61 S. 3rd St. Charles Taws was a close friend of the Austrian-English Reinagle as well as of his own compatriot George Schetky. He displayed the versatility so common to the musicians of the day. Probably this very versatility was necessary for financial success in the early days of professional music in the United States. Taws was a piano maker, an importer of pianos and other instruments, an authority on acoustics, a teacher of piano and theory, a music publisher—and was in addition said to have constructed the first barrel organ in America. Two sons of Charles Taws, James B. Taws and Lewis Taws, were instrument makers. James began his business in 1829, and Lewis in 1837, both having doubtless been associated with their father's firm in previous years. J. Charles Taws died in Philadelphia about 1833.

The invention and development of the upright piano dates from the year 1800. Spillane divides the credit for the "entirely new shape of the pianoforte which was sent to London and Paris"

---

[1] *History of St. Luke's Church, Germantown,* by Royden K. Yerkes, p. 17. Phila. 1912, private printing.

between Charles Taws and John I. Hawkins.[1] The latter's father, Isaac Hawkins of London, patented this upright piano from designs communicated to him in confidence by his son. The Philadelphia inventor John I. Hawkins is discussed later in this chapter.

While the Blakes' importance seems to lie in the publishing and selling of music, they were early importers of instruments, and later manufacturers of them in Philadelphia. E. Blake declared in 1790 that "native made pianos were braced with screws, not glue as in English pianos, to withstand our dryer climate."[2] George E. Blake, a son of the earlier Blake, came to Philadelphia in 1793. He was deeply interested in musical instrument construction. His pianos were on display at the Franklin Institute from 1824, the first year of that organization's important series of annual exhibitions. George Blake was a member of the committee on instruments at the Franklin Institute in 1824. Although the Blake firm will be discussed in a later chapter for its more important publishing work, a few facts concerning George Blake are included here.

George E. Blake was born in 1775, and died in Philadelphia in 1871. His music publishing dates from 1802. Blake's musical interests were varied: he was a charter member of the Musical Fund Society, a frequent exhibitor at the Franklin Institute; he edited and published *Vocal Harmony*, a sacred collection, in 1810; and for almost seventy years was actively engaged in professional music in Philadelphia.

While George E. Blake was midway in his career and the Taws instrument making concern was in its later years, the fame of both firms as manufacturers was somewhat eclipsed by that of Thomas Loud, later Loud Brothers, who were active in the field from about 1820.

This Thomas Loud was the son of Thomas Loud, Sr., an English piano maker who came to New York in 1816. The son had settled in Philadelphia in 1812, becoming a well-known pianist and piano maker. There were four Loud Brothers in an enterprising piano concern from 1824 to 1837. Thomas C. Loud, the son of the Philadelphia Thomas Loud, continued as a piano manufacturer

---

[1] *History of the American Pianoforte*, p. 81.
[2] Quoted by Spillane, p. 111, from the *General Advertiser*.

in that city until 1854. The Louds all had inventive ability, and contributed many improvements to piano construction.[1]

The English-New York Thomas Loud patented an upright piano in 1802. In 1800 another Englishman, John Isaac Hawkins, had patented an upright piano, styled a cottage piano, which seems to have been the first of its kind.[2] This is of particular interest to Philadelphians, since Hawkins was a resident of Philadelphia at the time he developed, patented, and marketed this instrument. He is styled a Philadelphia inventor in those years, his family residing in this city and Bordentown, New Jersey. A public demonstration of Hawkins' cottage piano took place at the Franklin Institute in 1802. Hawkins used coiled strings for bass tones; this was also a new feature, and protected by the 1800 patent. Thomas Jefferson, who had been deeply interested in Hopkinson's harpsichord improvements ten years earlier, was enthusiastic about Hawkins' cottage piano, and wanted to buy one for his Virginia home, Monticello. Claypoole's *American Daily Advertiser*[3] printed the fol-

---

[1] More detailed facts concerning the Louds in Philadelphia are herewith condensed from Spillane's account (*History of the American Pianoforte*, pp. 112-118).

Thomas Loud settled in Philadelphia in 1812, or earlier. His piano business, begun in 1816, was located at 5th and Prune Streets in 1817. In 1818 John Loud became a partner, the firm having moved to 361 High Street. A third brother, Philologus Loud, joined the firm in 1822, the concern being officially named Loud Brothers. Joseph Loud was the fourth brother. Loud Brothers was the most important piano making firm in this country in 1824. Six hundred and eighty pianos were made in that year by the Louds. In the second annual exhibition, 1825, the Franklin Institute awarded the Loud Brothers first place among the exhibitors of upright pianos.

A piano made in 1826 for the nouveau riche Louisiana planter, Gordon, attracted much attention. Ornately cased and built on an enlarged scale, this instrument had the phenomenal range of seven and a half octaves. While this ninety-toned piano possessed almost the identical range of our present day instruments, it was declared worthless by contemporary musicians of 1826.

The patents by Loud Brothers from 1827 to 1837 were related to improvements in the action and in the construction of the plate. In 1837 the firm moved to 306 Chestnut Street, and suspended manufacturing during the same year. There is record of a short lived firm, Loud and Co., at 170 Chestnut Street from about 1838 to 1840. Thomas C. Loud, the son of the first Loud brother, had a longer career as piano maker at 305 S. 10th Street, from 1838 to 1854.

[2] See Spillane (*History of American Pianoforte*, pp. 80-83).

[3] Claypoole's newspaper became *Poulson's American Daily Advertiser* on March 20, 1800. This paper and the *Daily Aurora* contain a great amount of information concerning important musical happenings, throughout the early nineteenth century.

lowing notice concerning Hawkins' early upright piano on February 19, 1800:

> Because of the unwieldy size of Grand Pianofortes, Mr. Hawkins has patented an instrument in which all sweetness of tone is preserved. It occupies one-quarter of the room required by a grand; is an elegant piece of furniture, and will keep in tune five to six times as long. There are four pedals which by combination produce twenty-four different changes or imitations of different instruments, and a gradual swell much admired in wind instruments and harmonica [musical glasses]. The cost is one half the price of a common grand pianoforte. To be seen at Mr. Willig's Musical Magazine, ♯ 185 Market Street.

Important improvements in strengthening the frame of the grand piano were made by this same inventor in 1800. Hawkins left Philadelphia in 1802, and gave up piano making.

Among nineteenth century piano makers, there are other early Philadelphia names which should be added to those of the pioneer firms of Taws and Loud. The period between 1800 and 1850 was an important one in the improvements of piano construction throughout the eastern United States. Knabe of Baltimore and Chickering of Boston, founded leading firms of piano manufacture in those years. Steinway and Mason and Hamlin companies began a few years after 1850. A Philadelphia piano maker, Conrad Meyer, was one of the first to construct a piano with a full metal plate. His piano of 1832, exhibited 1833, antedated Jonas Chickering's patent on a metal plate by several years. Meyer was active in Baltimore from 1819 to 1829, and in Philadelphia for almost fifty years after the latter date. The credit for the first use of a single cast metal frame of piano plate belongs probably to neither Conrad Meyer nor Jonas Chickering. Alpheus Babcock of Boston patented this metal plate in 1825. A Babcock square piano won the first place in the Franklin Institute exposition of 1825—the same year that Loud Brothers' upright won first prize in its class. In 1829 Alpheus Babcock moved to Philadelphia, where he was associated with the Klemm firm of instrument makers. An early use of the overstrung scale was developed by Babcock in Philadelphia at about 1830, and perfected by the Steinways in 1855. The probability is that Meyer knew of Babcock's improved piano construction, since both were interested in the Franklin Institute exhibitions. Conrad Meyer exhibited pianos in the Centennial Exposition, Philadelphia, 1876, and the Paris Universal Exposition, 1878, spreading his fame as a builder of fine pianos and his claim as inventor of the solid metal plate.

An even longer career than Meyer's was begun by Johann Heinrich Schomacker in Philadelphia, 1837. Schomacker was born in Schleswig-Holstein, in 1800, trained in Vienna, and worked as a piano maker in Bavaria. This varied background served him well in the construction of the long famous Schomacker pianos. Johann Schomacker died in 1875, but the firm continued to be active until about 1935 under the management of H. W. Gray, and the founder's son Henry C. Schomacker. Of the many patents registered by the Schomacker piano company since 1842, the one covering Colonel Gray's invention of 1876 is the most important. In that year Gray perfected a new method of electro-plating piano strings with gold. It was the first practically valuable method of coating piano strings with metals or metallic alloys.

The early nineteenth century was an important period in the growth of music publishing in Philadelphia and in the beginning of definite standards of music in the public schools. Since both of these fields are discussed later in this book [1] mere mention of their importance will suffice in this historical survey.

III

An important but little known figure in Philadelphia music of the early nineteenth century was Charles F. Hupfeld.

There were two musicians named Hupfeld or Hupfeldt, and certain references are made to a third. Scharf and Westcott mentions a Charles Hupfeld who gave concerts in the years between 1810 and 1818, and died in January, 1819. Since both or all of the Hupfelds combined forces in early nineteenth century programs, the records are not clear as to which of them took part in each event.

---

[1] Cf., *infra*, pp. 332-335, for music publishers of the period, and pp. 269-70 for an account of the earliest music in Philadelphia public schools.

Sonneck mentions Mr. Hupfeld, Hupfield, and Hopefield, in Philadelphia concerts prior to 1800—as at the Bush Hill concerts of 1797. This could not have been the celebrated Charles Frederick Hupfeld, for he was born in Germany in 1788, came to Philadelphia in 1801, and died there in 1864.[1]

The son of this best known Hupfeld, Charles F. Hupfeld, Jr., was also a musician and music dealer. Charles and John Hupfeld were both violinists of note in the early nineteenth century. They were both interested and influential members of the large and small instrumental groups which joined in forming the Musical Fund Society in 1820. Obviously their contribution was supplementary to that of many older Philadephia musicians such as Carr, Schetky, Taylor, and Gillingham.

The two Hupfeld brothers were members of a string quartet that practiced and performed in the winter months of the years 1816 to 1820. A larger group was also rehearsing at Earle and Sully's gallery of paintings during the same seasons.[2] Charles Hupfeld was the more active of the two brother violinists, becoming one of the conductors in the first concerts of the Musical Fund Society and their principal conductor between 1828 and 1845. Other activities of Charles F. Hupfeld included participation in the Quartet Party ensemble in 1810, making quintets possible. He gave annual concerts between 1812 and 1818.[3] A Concerto Militaire by Charles F. Hupfeld was played by the noted flutist Francis Blondau in concerts between 1810 and 1820. At Hupfeld's annual concert for 1815, a violin concerto, a double concerto, and a flute concerto were "played by the principal professors and amateurs of the city." This C. F. Hupfeld concert was given at the Masonic Hall on December 14. 1815, "to begin at 7 P. M."[4]

The coming of Benjamin Carr to Philadelphia at the age of twenty-three has been mentioned in a previous chapter. His extended period of active participation in all phases of music (1793-

[1] These vital statistics, and much other information about the Hupfelds, were contributed by a Philadelphia descendant of the Hupfelds, and the Hommanns, Mrs. Walter Hupfeld De Metz of Germantown.

[2] Mrs. W. H. De Metz still treasures two excellent portraits by Thomas Sully, one of Charles F. Hupfeld, the other of his son Charles, Jr.

[3] Scharf and Westcott's History of Philadelphia, p. 1078.

[4] Notice in Philadelphia Aurora of that date.

1831) has led him to be called the Father of Philadelphia Music. During the early years of his life in the city he devoted much time to his Musical Repository at Fifth and High Streets. This establishment was the most noted American music publishing headquarters of the eighteenth century. In it Carr composed, printed, and sold music and dealt in general musical merchandise for nearly ten years after his coming to Philadelphia. George Schetky was a partner in the firm about 1800. Benjamin Carr's, or Carr and Schetky, as the Repository was variously known, was not the oldest firm of its kind in Philadelphia, as has sometimes been claimed for it. M. Hillegas, Moller and Capron, and others had published and sold music long before Benjamin Carr left England in 1793. Carr and his greatest publishing rival George Willig are more fully discussed in a later chapter on Philadelphia Music Publishers.[1]

Benjamin Carr could give up his extensive publishing and music dealing—which he seems to have done at about 1800—and still remain a busy and important figure in Philadelphia music. He was organist in both Episcopal and Catholic churches in the city, a famous ballad and opera singer, an expert pianist, and a noted conductor. At the time of his retirement from music publishing, he edited a *Musical Journal,* 1800. His sacred collections, *The Chorister,* and others, date from 1805, 1811 and 1820. The music for these books was selected, arranged, and in many cases composed by Carr. The music is more scholarly than that of most early sacred collections since Benjamin Carr had received a thorough musical education at the hands of two of England's leading church musicians, Dr. Samuel Arnold and Samuel Wesley. Carr was steeped in dignified Anglican and Catholic tradition, doubtless superior to the somewhat arid sacred music of most Congregational and Presbyterian Psalmodists. It is interesting to observe that Samuel Sebastian Wesley taught both Kendrick Pyne and Minton Pyne, Philadelphia's most influential church musicians of the Anglican type of service in the later nineteenth century.

One of Benjamin Carr's best known sacred concerts was given at St. Augustine's Church on June 20, 1810. Selections from *The*

---

[1] Cf. *infra,* pp. 332-3.

Messiah and *The Creation* made up the entire program—a daring step in that period of Philadelphia music. An unusually large number of instrumentalists took part in this event. The conducting was divided among Carr, Taylor, and Schetky.[1] The organ and orchestra must have required expert management, since a chorus of but 34 voices was accompanied by a 53 piece orchestra: 21 violins, 6 violas, 5 'cellos, 3 string basses, 6 flutes, 4 clarinets, 3 bassoons, 4 trumpets and horns, and (strangest of all) 1 kettle drum.[2] *Poulson's Daily Advertiser* contains a "card" with full directions for drivers concerning how to face the horses when taking persons to St. Augustine's.[3] It is interesting that this very early suggestion for one way traffic was necessitated by Carr's conducting of Handel and Haydn.[4] He is known to have conducted many concerts at which leading soloists appeared, and may be said to have guided musical taste in Philadelphia at least from Reinagle's departure (c. 1803) until 1831.

Among the many compositions by Benjamin Carr, William Treat Upton selects his *Hymn to the Virgin*, or *Ave Maria*, as the finest.[5] This song is the third in Carr's Opus 7, which consisted of six ballads from Scott's *Lady of the Lake*. The songs were published by Carr and Schetky in 1810.

Carr's opera *The Archers* is probably his most ambitious work. Virtually nothing remains of the music to *The Archers,* two fragments—a Rondo from its overture, and the song, "Why, Huntress, Why?"—being noted by Sonneck [6] as coming from this opera. New York audiences heard *The Archers* in April, 1796, and a Boston production was staged the following year. No record has been traced of a performance of the opera in Philadelphia, but it is thought that in 1797 or shortly thereafter Carr's opera was given in that city. The libretto, written by William Dunlap, was based on the story of William Tell.

---

[1] According to Scharf and Westcott's *History of Philadelphia,* p. 1077.
[2] Further material on this program is included in a later section of this chapter, devoted to concerts. Cf. *infra,* p. 96.
[3] *Poulson's American Daily Advertiser,* June 20, 1810.
[4] The programs for the Academy of Music, 1857 *et seq.,* give quite regular directions to traffic incidental to functions at that celebrated theatre.
[5] William Treat Upton, *The Art Song in America,* 1930.
[6] In his *Early Opera in America,* pp. 98-100.

An early Philadelphia publication by Carr was a piano method, *The New Assistant for the Pianoforte*, 1796, containing arrangements and works by the publisher. His arrangement for Mrs. French, one of his pupils, of *Down the Burn, Davy Love*,[1] was popular in Philadelphia, as was his *Ellen, Arise*, and many other ballads. *The Federal Overture*, published 1794, is called a composition by B. Carr, although it included the "Marseilles hymn," *Ca Ira, O dear, what can the matter be?, Rose Tree, Carmagnole, The President's March*, and *Yankee Doodle*. Opus 11 was a piano sonata, *"The History of England*, from the close of the Saxon Heptarchy to the Declaration of American Independence, in familiar verse adapted to music by B. Carr, . . . combining Education and Music for young people."[2] Several songs were composed by Carr near the year 1800; among them are *How Sweet is the Morning, The Linnet, Little Sailor Boy, Spirits of the Blest*, and *The Widow*.

The leadership of Benjamin Carr in musical matters is seen in the early events of the Musical Fund Society. He was one of the early conductors of its orchestra. The portrait of Carr by his colleague in the Musical Fund Society, J. C. Darley, is the first of the invaluable series of paintings still treasured by that society. The monument erected by the Musical Fund Society in St. Peter's church yard still proclaims the members' indebtedness to Carr's musicianship during the first ten years of their organization.

Benjamin Carr may be considered the second figure in Philadelphia music to rise above the level of most experts of his time, and to have dominated the musical activities in that city. Just as Hopkinson typified the early national culture in Philadelphia with its constant atmosphere of history in the making, Carr personifies the civic growth of the early nineteenth century. Hopkinson was the most important amateur musician of early Philadelphia, Carr the leading professional of the following period. The dates of their influence mark them as true chronological successors, since Hopkinson died in 1791, and Carr arrived in Philadelphia only two

---

[1] Carr's printing of this song seems to be an early example of the great nineteenth century vogue for Scotch airs. The problem of representing the Scotch snap was solved by Carr in this fashion:

[2] This ambitious historical effort is (anomalously) undated, but was written after 1810, since that year saw the publication of his *Six Ballads*, Opus 7.

years after that date. The plague of 1792-3 having intervened, Carr
and Hopkinson were quite continuous in their influence on Philadelphia music. Andrew Adgate, Carr's most important professional
predecessor, died of the plague—just before Benjamin Carr's
arrival.

Soon after settling in Philadelphia, Carr composed the opera
The Archers (1796), one of many works called the First American
Opera.

The Disappointment was much older, of course, having been
composed about 1766, by Andrew Barton, also a Philadelphian.
The words only were written by Barton in *The Disappointment*,
hence the entirely valid claim for Carr's *Archers* as the first American opera. *The Archers* was written one year before Hewitt's
Tammany, and was produced in New York, Philadelphia and Boston in 1796 and 1797. The cry of admirers of exclusively European opera as to when a great American opera will really be composed is an old one. The fact that so many "first American operas"
are noted simply connotes that, despite numerous American productions, the public was never quite sure that any given one was
truly American, or if so, truly an opera. Sigmund Spaeth, a Philadelphian by birth and training, has a humorous but profound essay
on "The Great American Opera" in his small book *Words and
Music*.[1] The frequency with which American composers' dramatic
works have been hailed as the first American opera reflects nothing
so much as the unsettled state of opera itself in the early days of
our musical history. Just as operas were called lectures in the
days of banned opera performance, many works with spoken lines
were called operas in other periods of early Philadelphia. *The
Cossack and the Volunteer*, by an actor named Braun, is still another "first American Opera" by a Philadelphian. It was produced
in 1830. The title, *The Cossack and the Volunteer*, seems to suggest
a ballad opera of the type of *The Poor Soldier*—a decidedly sketchy
musical play which Washington is said to have heard in Philadelphia as an antidote to the strain and stress of the Constitutional
Convention in 1787 (July 10th). *Leonora*, widely heralded as a

---

[1] Simon and Schuster, N. Y. 1926.

grand opera, was the first American composition to deserve that grand title. This process of proclaiming a final answer to the nation's demand for an American opera has not yet ceased. Victor Herbert's *Natoma* and Deems Taylor's *The King's Henchman* are recently acclaimed great American operas; but despite Herbert's deliberate choice of Indian scenic background, these, as all American operas, are steeped in European tradition—as indeed is our entire musical system.

Joseph Carr of Baltimore was the father of Philadelphia's Benjamin Carr and his brother, Thomas Carr. The latter was organist at Christ Church, Baltimore, from 1798 to 1811, and succeeded his father as a music publisher in Baltimore in 1819. G. Willig bought the publishing firm in 1822, and Thomas Carr moved to Philadelphia in the following year. City registers list him as "Professor and Vender of music" from 1823 to 1837, and as "Professor of music" from the latter year until his death in 1849.[1] The importance of this Uncle of Philadelphia Music seems to have been slight, yet he carried on the Carr name in that city for almost twenty years after the death of his famous older brother. Thomas Carr is known to have been the first conductor of the St. Cecelia Society in Philadelphia.

Benjamin Carr is the guiding musical figure that links the rather uneven eighteenth century period to music of the middle nineteenth century in Philadelphia. Before his death in 1831, the Musical Fund Society was firmly established, an organization that for forty years unified the best musical talent in the city. While the influence of this society never regained its unique musical prominence after the Civil War, it has continued to exist with varying degrees of activity down to the present day. Since the Musical Fund Society is so outstanding in its influence on Philadelphia music during the years 1820-1860, it surely merits a complete historical account for that period.[2]

---

[1] Thomas Carr is discussed as a Baltimore publisher and Philadelphia musician in Wm. Arms Fisher's *One Hundred and Fifty Years of Music Publishing in the United States*, pp. 93-94.

[2] Madeira's account of this society is the more authoritative section of his book, *Annals of Music in Philadelphia and the Musical Fund Society*. The facts of the above short history are drawn mainly from Madeira's book.

IV

The Musical Fund Society was the outgrowth of small meetings in the homes of Philadelphians during the winter months of the years 1816-1820. String quartets were the main item of musical entertainment, those of "Beethoven, Boccherini, and others" being mentioned. The quartet members were Charles F. Hupfeld, 1st violin; John Hupfeld, 2nd violin, and viola; P. Gilles and George Schetky, violoncelli. Some of these musicians were endeavoring to rehearse regularly in a larger instrumental group in Earle and Sully's gallery of paintings, near Fifth and Chestnut. Their difficulty in keeping this larger ensemble intact led to the idea of a fund to assist poor musicians. The orchestral group and the regular audience at the quartet performances met jointly on January 7, 1820, to "institute a society for the relief and support of decayed musicians and their families." [1] At this first meeting, a constitution committee was appointed consisting of Carr, Hupfeld, Cross, and Patterson. The society may be said to date from that evening. The constitutional committee's report was unanimously adopted at a meeting on February 3rd. This report included the suggested name for the organization, "The Musical Fund Society of Philadelphia." Later in February the following officers were elected:

> Dr. William P. DeWees, President
> Dr. Robert M. Patterson, Vice-President
> Daniel Lammot, Treasurer
> John K. Kane, Secretary

Twelve Managers of the Fund included Carr and Schetky. Twelve Musical Directors included Raynor Taylor, Benjamin Carr, Charles Hupfeld, P. Gilles, Benjamin Cross, and George Schetky. Eighty-five members included all of the above mentioned notables and many additional names of prominent Philadelphians, musicians and others. Thomas Sully, George Womrath, Rêné La Roche, Jr., J. C. Hommann, Thomas Loud, Joseph C. Taws, Francis Hopkinson, Charles Poulson, and John Hupfeld were among these charter members.

---

[1] The purpose of the Society is so phrased in the original by-laws.

The early procedure was an unpretentious one. Directors and committees met in private homes, while the weekly rehearsals were held in large rooms or halls, mainly Carpenters' Hall. Both musical and beneficent activities were inaugurated from the start. As early as 1820 the distribution committee provided that two physicians be elected annually, to visit and prescribe gratuitously for needy members and their families. As a first year's musical venture, a concert was presented to the public in April, 1821. When we read of the difficulties encountered in the society's attempts to secure parts for Haydn's *Creation,* and the Hallelujah Chorus from Beethoven's *Mount of Olives,* we are somewhat disappointed in the selections actually presented on the program which follows:

SECOND PERFORMANCE

of the

FIRST CONCERT

for the benefit of the

MUSICAL FUND SOCIETY

OF PHILADELPHIA

Tuesday, May 8, 1821,
At the Grand Saloon, Washington Hall,
with the addition of some
Vocal Solos.

Conductors—Messrs. B. Carr, B. Cross, P. Gilles, C. F. Hupfeld,
T. Loud, G. Schetky.

PLAN OF THE CONCERT
PART FIRST

Grand Sinfonia in E. ....Romberg

Vocal Duett, "The Butterfly' ....Sale

Gay being, born to flutter thro' the day,
Sport in the sunshine of the present hour,
On the sweet rose thy painted wings display,
And cull the fragrance of the op'ning flower!

Time hastens on; the summer ends too soon;
    Take then the rosy minutes as they fly;
For soon, alas, your little life is gone,
    To-day you sparkle, and to-morrow die.

Concerto Violoncello—Mr. Gilles, from B. Romberg's Concerto in D, followed by an air with variations, composed by ......Mr. Gilles

Air, vocal, "Donald" ....Original Scottish Melody

When first you courted me, I own,
    I fondly favoured you;
Apparent worth and high renown
    Made me believe you true, Donald.

Each virtue then seem'd to adorn
    The man esteem'd by me;
But now the mask's thrown off, I scorn
    To waste one thought on thee, Donald.

O then for ever haste away,
    Away from love and me!
Go seek a heart that's like your own,
    And come no more to me, Donald.

For I'll reserve myself alone
    For one that's more like me;
If such a one I cannot find,
    I'll fly from love and thee, Donald.

Overture—Dell Opera Tancredi ....Rossini

Glee and Chorus—Awake, Aeolian Lyre, with orchestra......Danby
                          Accompaniments by B. Carr.

Glee and Chorus.

Awake, Æolian Lyre, awake!
And give to rapture all thy trembling strings:
From Helicon's harmonious springs,
A thousand rills their mazy progress take.

The laughing flow'rs that round them blow,
Drink life and fragrance as they flow.
Now the rich stream of music winds along,
Deep, majestic, smooth, and strong,

Thro' verdant vales and Ceres' golden reign;
Now rolling down the steep amain,
Headlong, impetuous, see it pour,
The rocks and nodding groves rebellow to the roar.

PART SECOND

Concerto Violin, Mr. Hupfeld ....Rode

Polacca, "Trifler, Forbear" ....Bishop

RECIT.

     Trifler, forbear; deceit in flattery lies;
     We may endure it, but we must despise.

AIR.

     Go, trifler, go; your flattery leave,
       That lure which leads our sex astray!
     Still smiling only to deceive,
       And more securely to betray!

     On Etna's side thus verdure bright
       Deludes the swain, and hope inspires;
     While, with an overwhelming might
       The dread Volcano pours its fires!

                       Trifler, forbear!

     Go, trifler, go, etc.

Grand Sinfonia in D ....Beethoven

New Glee and Chorus—Sequel to the "Red Cross Knight,"
    with orchestra accompaniments by B. Carr ....Dr. Clarke

SEQUEL TO THE RED CROSS KNIGHT

SOLO, BASS VOICE.

I cannot stay, cried the Red Cross Knight,
Nor can I feast with thee:
But I must haste to a pleasant bow'r,
Where a lady's waiting for me.

TRIO.

Oh, say not so, dear Red Cross Knight,
Nor heed that fond lady,
For she can't compare with my daughter so fair,
And she shall attend on thee.

SOLO, BASS VOICE.

Now must I go, cried the Red Cross Knight,
For that lady I'm to wed,
And the feast guests and bridesmaids all are met,
And prepared the bridal bed.

TRIO.

Now nay, now nay, thou Red Cross Knight,
My daughter shall wed with thee,
And the mass shall be sung,
And the bells shall be rung,
And we'll feast right merrily.

CHORUS.

And the mass shall be sung,
And the bells shall be rung,
And we'll feast right merrily.

TRIO.

And as the lady prest the Knight,
With her ladies clad in pall,
Oh then bespake a pilgrim boy,
As he stood in the hall.

SOLO, TREBLE VOICE.

Now Heav'n thee save, Sir Red Cross Knight,
I'm come from the North country,
Where a lady is laid all on her death bed,
And evermore calls for thee.

SOLO, BASS VOICE.
Alas! alas! thou pilgrim boy,
Sad news thou tellest me,
Now must I ride full hastily,
To comfort that dear lady.

TREBLE VOICES.
Oh heed him not, the ladies cried,
But send a page to see.

TRIO AND CHORUS.
While the mass is sung,
And the bells are rung,
And we feast merrily.

SOLO, TREBLE VOICE.
Again bespake the pilgrim boy:
Ye need not send to see,
For, know, Sir Knight, that lady's dead,
And died for love of thee.

TRIO.
Oh! then the Red Cross Knight was pale,
And not a word could say;
But his heart did swell, and his tears down fell,
And he almost swoon'd away.
And where is her grave, said the Red Cross Knight,
The grave where she doth lay?
Oh, I know well, cried the pilgrim boy,
And I'll shew thee the way.
The Knight was sad, the pilgrim sigh'd,

SOLO, TREBLE VOICE.
While the Warder loud did cry,
Let the mass be sung,
And the bells be rung,
And the feast eat merrily.

TRIO AND CHORUS.
Let the mass be sung,
And the bells be rung,
And the feast eat merrily.

Overture—De L'Opera Les Deux Aveugles De Toledo,
  full orchestra ....Méhul

LEADER—MR. C. F. HUPFELD.

Principal violins—Messrs. DeLuce, Heinrich, Kahn, Getze, etc., etc.
Principal violoncello—Mr. P. Gilles.
Violoncellos—Messrs. Hommann, senr., etc.
Tenors—Messrs. Cantor, C. Hommann, etc.
Principal double bass—Mr. Schetky.
Double basses—Messrs. J. Hommann and Klemm.
Principal flute—Mr. Dannenberg.
Principal bassoon—Mr. J. D. Weisse from Bethlehem.

The CONDUCTORS of the VOCAL Music will alternately
preside at the ORGAN.

The Orchestra will consist of one hundred Vocal and Instrumental performers.

TO COMMENCE AT 7 O'CLOCK.

Two concerts in 1822 exemplify an interesting transition in
musical taste and ambition. The concert of March 19th consisted
of eleven very miscellaneous compositions, written mainly by the
performers and their friends. That of June 10th was devoted to
a pretentious performance of Haydn's *Creation*. A sizable pamphlet, containing words and notes on the oratorio, was printed for
the occasion. Over one hundred musicians took part; many were
non-members of the society, recruited for this concert, and a few
were borrowed from the Moravian community at Bethlehem. The
popular Mrs. French sang the soprano solos with great success.[1]

---

[1] The same lady, a pupil of Benjamin Carr, caused most rhapsodic praise
from all critics whenever she sang. Lapsing into poetry one critic declares:

" 'Tis said that Orpheus played so well
He raised Euridice from Hell;
And St. Cecelia sang so clear
That angels leaned from heaven to hear.

But our Cecelia far excels
These fabled feats. Her trills and swells
Enchant the vaulted roof and walls
Until the azure ceiling falls.   Quoted by Madeira, p. 84.

The reference is to the actual collapse of part of the ceiling of Washington
Hall during one of Mrs. French's concerts.

Poulson's Daily Advertiser, June 11, 1822, states: ". . . A repetition of the performance would equally contribute to the improvement and benefit of the institution, to the diffusion of scientific and sublime music, and to the gratification of the public at large." A less lavish commendation is provided by another contemporary journalist who reports: "[*The Creation*] was attended by a numerous and respectable company, who appeared to be more pleased than it was expected they would be." This 'respectable company' numbered between 1800 and 2000. Six conductors were named on the program—the reason for this variety of leadership not being divulged.

Following concerts contained several miscellaneous programs, a repetition of *The Creation, The Seasons, The Messiah,* and Handel's *Dettingen Te Deum* (1823 and 1824). Washington Hall, The New Theatre in Chestnut Street, and St. Stephen's Church were used for the productions of the Musical Fund Society prior to the opening of their Musical Fund Hall.

In 1824 the site of the Fifth Presbyterian Church, Locust above 8th, was purchased for the erection of the still famous Musical Fund Hall. One of the original members of the society, William Strickland, designed the concert hall, which many declare to be still unsurpassed for acoustical excellence. The first concert in this new building was given December 20, 1824. The *Dettingen Te Deum* and three other Handel numbers were included in this historic program; Mozart's name appears twice on it. A full and strikingly up-to-date book of program notes was printed for the concert.

Musical Fund Hall cost $23,500 to build—including the lot and all furnishings—which will seem an amazingly low figure to those who know its location and construction. Early in its long history, the rentals from the hall and many rooms covered the cost of its site and erection. Commencements, concerts, lectures, and meetings were held there in great numbers from 1825 to the Civil War period. Even down to the present day, the hall or any of its rooms may be rented for a variety of uses.

The original double purpose of the Musical Fund Society has been stated as the relief of needy musicians and the advancement of musical taste. The first purpose suggests the many professional members, who from earliest times have been unfortunately in need of financial assistance. The second suggests the many amateur members who have acknowledged a constant need of education in musical taste and ability. This society has in its regular concerts, usually two a year, promoted both of its objectives. Employment in planning, preparing and performing these concerts has come to many hundreds of Philadelphia musicians; while high musical standards, maintained as uniformly as possible, have contributed to the amateurs' music appreciation. Many amateur instrumentalists and vocalists have, of course, joined with the professionals in the actual work of performing the music of these concerts.

A few landmarks not included in the above account may prove of interest. An Academy of Music was formed in 1825 to provide more skilled members for the society's orchestra. A Vocal Class was added in 1826. This society engaged Adolph Schmitz to take charge of its third class in the Academy of Music in 1826. Both Schmitz and his son William Adolph Schmitz became leading musicians in Philadelphia in the middle nineteenth century. The school was abandoned in 1832, although the activities of the professors continued in their private teaching and concert work. The premature end of the society's Academy of Music follows with significant proximity the death of Schetky and Carr in 1831. This double loss was a great blow to the professional side of the group.

Among important events at the Musical Fund Hall were many individual recitals and lectures, in addition to the regular and special events of the Musical Fund Society itself. Madame Malibran was the most noted in their early years. At her first concert in Philadelphia, June 16, 1827, she is said to have been so delighted with the acoustics of Musical Fund Hall that she extemporized songs while walking up and down the aisles, while her accompanist, Da Coninck of the Paris Conservatoire, improvised at the piano. Excellent programs were given at both Malibran concerts in that year, the first including Mozart's *Batti, batti,* Gluck's *Che faro,* and Rossini's *De tanti palpiti.*[1]

---

[1] The autumn of 1831 saw the delegates of an important free trade convention holding a week's meetings at Musical Fund Hall. Albert Gallatin was the guiding spirit of the convention. His opposition to Henry Clay on the free trade question is well known. Chief Justice John Marshall was

The famous singers Mrs. Austin and Madame Feron (Mrs. Glossop) gave recitals at Musical Fund Hall in the 1830's. Mr. Tyrone Power managed to insert and sing two Irish songs on Mrs. Austin's program of November 1833. This Mr. Power was a singer and writer, publishing novels and an interesting series of impressions of America (1836). He was drowned while returning from a later American visit on the ill-fated steamship *President* in 1841.[1]

At about the same time Mr. and Mrs. Joseph Wood became famous in Philadelphia musical circles. The popularity of the Woods lasted down into the period when William and Joseph Fry became active in writing and directing operas in Philadelphia. The Woods' productions of *La Sonnambula* and *Norma* were the most popular in the history of Philadelphia opera up to that time.[2] Caradori-Allan and Arthur and Anne Seguin sang several programs at Musical Fund Hall, in addition to their many theatrical appearances in mid-nineteenth century Philadelphia.

The theatrical leanings of some of the leading concert artists of the society may be said to have brought about an operatic performance at Musical Fund Hall. On February 8, 1841, Mozart's *Magic Flute* was produced for the first time in America, as the first operatic production by the Musical Fund Society. Benjamin Cross directed this momentous performance, "presiding at the piano." The orchestra contained 64 performers. Visitors came from New

---

among those present. The name of Mr. Preserved Fish, a New York member, is always included in the list of the delegates at this convention. Many other political meetings, lectures, and commencements were held in this famous old hall, which do not concern us here. Still, as the hall has been used by such lecturers as Edward Everett, R. H. Dana, George Bancroft, Ralph Waldo Emerson, William H. Furness, and Horace Greeley, it is not surprising that the present Musical Fund members point with pride to so historic an edifice.

1 Tyrone Power, the actor of the present day, is a descendant of the actor-musician mentioned above.

2 Singers too numerous to appear in the above text were heard in this rapidly expanding musical period. Among them the names of Mrs. and Miss Watson, Miss Wheatly, Elizabeth Poole, Mr. and Mrs. Morely, Mrs. Gibbs, and James Howard are frequently found on Philadelphia programs. Mr. Henry Russell carried the local talent system to its logical conclusion by singing on May 15, 1841 thirteen of his own songs at a Musical Fund Hall concert. The *Old Sexton*, *The Gambler's Wife*, and *The Maniac*, are worthy of the attention of Sigmund Spaeth, that twentieth century collector of nineteenth century morbid songs. Some of Henry Russell's more cheerful songs, like *A Life on the Ocean Wave*, are still sung, however.

York and Boston to hear this "Grand Musical Festival." The success was complete, and a repeat benefit performance was staged. *The National Gazette* declared: ". . . The Public has now had such samples of operatic excellence that mediocrity will no longer answer. What is now done in that way must be done fully and well to command success." [1]

Whatever the actual popularity of Mozart's "German Opera" when compared to those of the Italian school so plentifully provided in the Chestnut and Walnut Street Theatres, we find that the Musical Fund Society did not continue with its operatic ventures. It refused to perform musically tawdry compositions, and it looks very much as though the Philadelphia audiences refused just as decidedly to support anything else. In any case no further operas were given, and the orchestra rehearsals and the concerts were resumed in 1843. Ole Bull headed the list of the distinguished soloists in the autumn of that year. This Norwegian violinist played a concerto, a fantasie, *Niagara,* and *Solitude of the Prairie,* all of his own composition, at his second concert in Philadelphia, January 18th, 1845. "Bethovan," Auber, Rossini, and Mozart were also represented in the orchestral numbers of the program. Bull gave five concerts in Philadelphia in the same fortnight as his Musical Fund appearance of 1845.

W. V. Wallace, famous as the composer of *Maritana,* and Vieuxtemps, violinist and composer, also were soloists during the 1843-1844 season. Many other noted artists assisted at the concerts. The orchestra achieved fame by playing the entire first symphony of Beethoven. The directors reported in May, 1845: " . . . The ability with which these complicated, yet expressive, harmonies were produced, and their approval by one of the largest audiences ever gathered in the hall, is gratifying evidence of advancing musical skill and taste in the community." The symphony was not given as one selection. Its first movement began the program. Followed four operatic *entermets,* then Beethoven's *Andante,* and *Minuet.* The intermission came next, and then the *Finale allegro,* from the

---

[1] Madeira concludes his account of this first Musical Fund Hall opera with the statement: "The whole enterprise was the work of a single citizen, an eminent builder of locomotives." He undoubtedly refers to Matthias Baldwin.

symphony. Leopold Meignen, the conductor of the orchestra since Hupfeld's resignation, introduced Beethoven's "second symphony entire" (but in similarly homeopathic doses) the following season, spring, 1846. The *Eroica Symphony* was divided into only *two* sections, the next season—a daring step on Meignen's part. This same concert, the first of the 1846-1847 season, contained Weber's *Oberon* and Mendelssohn's *Midsummer Night's Dream* overtures. The Mendelssohn overture, and of course the *Eroica*, were played for the first time in Philadelphia. Henri Herz, pianist, was a soloist at this concert.

These four successful seasons moved the directors to alter and enlarge the Musical Fund Hall. The plans were made by Napoleon Le Brun, and the work accomplished during the summer of 1847. To help pay for these repairs a ladies' bazaar was held. Its chief importance historically is the *Bazaar Album,* a paper printed about the articles for sale, the uncertainties of the weather, and, particularly, the musical gossip of Philadelphia in 1847.

In the enlarged hall, the series of concerts continued with added brilliance. The membership in the Musical Fund orchestra varied from 80 to 120 members.[1] The many first rate artists who performed in the years 1847 to 1851 seem to have been eclipsed by the enormous popularity of Lind and Sontag in 1850 and 1852. Jenny Lind gave two concerts at Musical Fund Hall in 1850. She did not sign any agreement to participate in the regular concerts of the society, her commercially astute manager, P. T. Barnum, preferring to advertise lavishly and auction all tickets for her concerts. Henriette Sontag, however, sang many numbers at Musical Fund concerts, in addition to her own benefit recitals and opera performances in Philadelphia. In 1852 and 1853 Madame Sontag was the leading soloist in this city. There is even record of her having given a free concert at the Philadelphia Normal School.[2]

The other soloists were, as has been said, first-rank performers. For example, in the 1855 season the regular Musical Fund Concerts included solos by Elise Hensler, Brignoli, Amodio, Mme. La Grange, and Gottschalk. Even Mario and Grisi, who sang in Philadelphia opera performances, were rated mainly by comparison

---

[1] Scharf and Westcott, *op. cit.*, p. 1089.
[2] Given in October 1853.

with Lind and Sontag who had so completely captured the fancy of our musical public. Brignoli, Amodio, and La Grange will be mentioned later as leading figures in opera in Philadelphia. Miss Hensler was later the Queen of Portugal. Louis M. Gottschalk was the first, and with the exception of MacDowell probably the greatest American composer-pianist of the nineteenth century.

Adelina Patti's concert on September 23rd, 1852, was a celebrated child prodigy program at Musical Fund Hall. She was "not yet eight years old," yet she sang, according to the program, "the Bravura pieces of Malibran, Pasta, Lind, Sontag, Alboni, etc., with perfection and purity of style."

In leaving the most active period of the Musical Fund Society (1820-1858), let us plainly state it is not *adieu*, but *au revoir* that is the appropriate salutation. Most of the chronicles concerning the society consider that its brilliant concerts of the 1850's marked the final activities of this group. We shall find, however, that in both the late nineteenth century and twentieth, the Musical Fund Society has continued with considerable vitality. Yet it has never regained its importance as the main unifying musical influence in this city.

V

To trace the course of Philadelphia opera during the period 1800-1860 we must first attempt to arrive at a satisfactory meaning of the term opera. Most sources refuse the classification of "opera" to the Philadelphia musical plays prior to about 1820. Considerable mention of works in the style known as ballad-opera has been included in the preceding chapter. As might be expected, the turn of the century did not materially affect the type of dramatic music heard in Philadelphia. Mrs. Oldmixon remained active as a ballad opera favorite for several years after 1800. She lived in Philadelphia and Germantown, and died in 1814. The ballad operas that were given between 1800 and about 1840 were so numerous that they can be merely listed here: [1]

---

[1] The above list is taken from W. Armstrong's *Record of the Opera in Philadelphia*, pp. 11-13; and from the *Claypoole* (later *Poulson*) *Daily Advertiser*, and other newspapers of the period under discussion.

Arne, *Love in a Village.*
Arnold, *Castle of Andalusia, Mountaineers, Inkle and Yarico, Surrender of Calais.*
Barnett, *Midas, Olympic Revels.*
Bishop, *Guy Mannering, The Slave, Clari Maid of Milan, Miller and His Men.*
Braham, *The Cabinet, Devil's Bridge.*
Davy, *Rob Roy.*
Dibdin, *The Quaker, The Waterman.*
Jackson, *Lord of the Manor,* with words by General Burgoynè.
Kelly, *Blue Beard.*
Linley, *Carnival of Venice, The Camp, The Duenna* (the words of the *Camp* and *The Duenna* were writen by R. B. Sheridan, Linley's son-in-law), *Selina and Azor, Spanish Maid.*
Mazzinghi (an Englishman of Italian descent), *Paul and Virginia.*
Shield, *Poor Soldier, The Woodman.*
Storace, *Haunted Tower, No Song No Supper, Siege of Belgrade.*

The production of *The Libertine* at the Chestnut Street Theatre in 1818 has been pronounced [1] to be the earliest performance of grand opera in Philadelphia. Another 'earliest grand opera' is Weber's *Freischütz,* produced at the same theatre on March 18. 1825. It was sung in English by English and American singers.[2] Possibly a better choice for Philadelphia's first grand opera might be Rossini's *Barber of Seville,* brought out by the English vocalist Henry Phillips at the Walnut Street Theatre in March 1822. Phillips' performance was the American première of the work.[3] It is profitless to spend much time and space in considering which was the first. especially since ballad operas had been composed by Philadelphians and produced in that city ever since colonial days.[4] Obviously, the controversy here is similar to that mentioned earlier,[5] "What is an opera?" If some lines are spoken the term Ballad Opera is often used. *English Opera* formerly referred to such works, and now *operetta* and *light opera* are indiscriminately applied

---

[1] By the late John Curtis, president of the Behrens Opera Club, and founder of the Philadelphia Operatic Society.
[2] *Der Freishütz* is Armstrong's choice for the first grand opera in Philadelphia. W. G. Armstrong, *Record of the Opera in Philadelphia,* p. 11.
[3] Scharf and Westcott, *op. cit.,* p. 1078.
[4] Barton's *The Disappointment* was printed in Philadelphia in 1767.
[5] *Supra,* p. 21.

to modern works of a similar nature. Throughout the first quarter of the nineteenth century this light opera was the exclusive opera of Philadelphia.[1] *Der Freischütz* in Philadelphia and the unsuccessful opera series by the Garcia troupe in New York, also in 1825, were of a new order to American audiences.

Lest we should become too amazed at a conservative city's sudden acceptance of the *opera seria,* I quote from Scharf and Westcott's [2] comment on its 1825 performance in Philadelphia. "The artists saved the production of *Der Freischütz* on March 18th, which was not a success as a whole. . . . Some actors spoke their parts, although there were excellent singers in the cast." This reflected sadly our unregenerate ballad opera habits, but may have helped many in the audience to an idea of what was happening on the stage. "The music was of too high and scientific a character to be understood by the ordinary public." The ordinary public was given a compromise, however, in which spoken and sung lines were mixed, the probability being that more lines were spoken than Weber had intended. The artists who saved the performance included John Darley, who was the son of an earlier Philadelphia opera singer and probably a relative of the noted F. T. Sully Darley. Even more celebrated were Joseph Jefferson and Mrs. Burke, who later became Mrs. Joe Jefferson. "Mr. Jefferson" was the third in a line of actors, of which the fourth was the famous Joseph Jefferson, son of this Jefferson and the former Mrs. Burke. The same *Der Freischütz* cast included James William Wallack, a member of a hardly less noted theatrical family than the Jeffersons.

Philadelphia's first extended series of "serious opera" was provided by a French opera company from New Orleans. A number of performances by that company were given in Philadelphia, beginning in 1827, and continuing with more or less annual regularity until 1842. During the same season, 1827-1828, Mrs. Austin's company gave several English operas, the American première of Rossini's *Cinderella,* and the world première of *The Cossack and the Volunteer.* The music to the last is credited to Mr. Braun, a mem-

---

[1] The memoirs of Lorenzo da Ponte bewail Philadelphia's lack of the type of dramatic music that he later attempted to provide for New York. Da Ponte lived in Philadelphia in 1818, 1832, and 1833, and in Sunbury, Pennsylvania, for many years (1811 to 1818).

[2] *History of Philadelphia,* p. 1079.

ber of the Austin company,[1] although the Philadelphian John Clemens has also been named as its composer. Clemens' opera *Justina* was produced in Philadelphia during the season of 1829-1830.

The company of Mme. Fearon gave one of the earliest Italian opera performances in Philadelphia on May 5th, 1829. *La Trionfa della Musica* was the opera. Mme. Fearon had come to Philadelphia from London in 1828, while the better known Madame Feron arrived in the autumn of 1830.

In 1832 several operas were given by English singers and a few Italians who had remained in America when Manuel Garcia returned to Europe. The Montressor troupe of Italian singers came to Philadelphia in 1833. *Il Pirata* was the most popular opera in their repertoire. Rossini's *Otello* was well given by this company—a considerable achievement for any group. The Montressor company also gave the oratorio *Moses in Egypt* in Musical Fund Hall. Mr. and Mrs. Wood's company followed the New Orleans group during the fall of 1833. They performed twenty works, some ballad operas, some grand operas. The same season saw yet another operatic troupe, the Rivafinoli Company.[2] Their extended repertoire contained Italian operas exclusively.

The purchase of the Walnut Street Theatre by Francis Courtney Wemyss in 1834 coincides with the rise of that hall to a position of real rivalry with the Chestnut Street Theatre as a home for dramatic music in Philadelphia. This building, still located at Ninth and Walnut Streets, is America's oldest theatre. Both its original construction, as *The Circus* in 1808, and the years of its greatest brilliance lie in the period of the early nineteenth century. A stage was added to the Circus in 1811, the altered edifice being called the Olympic Theatre in the following year. Its present name, The Walnut Street Theatre, was first applied to it in 1820.[3] Wemyss called it the American Theatre in 1834. The noted actress Charlotte Cushman became its manager in 1842. From the years of her management to the present day this historic building has been known

---

[1] In Scharf and Westcott's *History of Philadelphia*, p. 1097.
[2] Both Montressor and Rivafinoli troupes were managed by Lorenzo da Ponte, Mozart's famous librettist.
[3] Edwin Forrest made his theatrical debut in the Walnut Street Theatre in November, 1820.

as the Walnut Street Theatre. In the period of grand opera's first popularity the Chestnut Street and Walnut Street Theatres divided the main musical events between them. The building of the Academy of Music in 1857 served to eclipse the glories of both of these older theatres. However, the operettas and lighter theatricals that have been given in this theatre at Ninth and Walnut Streets between 1860 and 1940 are numerous, and among the most notable in the city for that long period. The building has had many renovations and alterations in addition to the few mentioned above as belonging to the period under discussion. It still preserves the early architectural features, particularly since its remodelling of 1920, which was mainly a restoration of early nineteenth century details.[1]

In 1834-1835 an English company singing Italian works was featured at the Chestnut Street Theatre. These were sung mainly *in English* as were the many ballad operas also produced by them during the same season.

Novelty and instability marked the gradual change from English ballad operas of 1800 to the triumph of Italian Opera in 1835. On February 15, 1835, Mr. and Mrs. Wood's company introduced *La Sonnambula* which sealed the fate of the ballad opera so far as fashionable opera audiences were concerned. There were more than forty performances of this opera in the four years following its introduction. A few evenings of such old favorite ballad operas as *Love in a Village* or *Castle of Andalusia* lingered on until 1840. In that year the American première of *Norma* produced by William and Joseph Fry at the Chestnut Street Theatre provided new triumphs for Italian opera artists and admirers. About the only audible dissent to Bellini's supremacy was voiced by the Musical Fund Society's selection of Mozart's *Magic Flute* for the opera of their "Grand Musical Festival" of 1841.

The appearance of the names of Arthur and Anne Seguin in 1839 among principal singers in opera troupes is noteworthy. This bass-soprano couple seem to have supplanted Mr. and Mrs. Wood

---

[1] The recent selection of the Walnut Street Theatre as a home for the Philadelphia Federal Symphony Orchestra's concerts marks a renewal of this historic edifice's importance in Music in Philadelphia. The first concert by this orchestra in the Walnut Street Theatre took place on February 26, 1939. For an account of previous concerts by this group cf. *infra*, pp. 211-12.

in popular esteem at about the year 1841. In 1842 the troupe is described as the Seguin Company. Both of the Seguins were first class musicians, although his voice may have been somewhat worn when they sang in Philadelphia. They were popular and active in New York and Philadelphia until about 1850, Mrs. Seguin for several years after that date.

The first performance of *Leonora* by William H. Fry took place June 4, 1845. It was sung by the Seguin opera troupe, conducted by Leopold Meignen. The libretto was written by Joseph R. Fry, a brother of the composer. Fry surely thought and wrote 'in the large.' If size and fulness constitute the necessary attributes to a grand opera, *Leonora* is certainly one. While it was not Fry's earliest opera, *Aurelia The Vestal* having been composed nearly ten years before it, *Leonora* was the first of his operas to be performed successfully.

Original scores of *Leonora* and other works by Fry are valued possessions of the Philadelphia Library Company. It is thus possible to see how the contemporary accounts were properly impressed by the ambition and Italian manner of *Leonora*. William Fry was a thorough musician, though the epithet "the American Berlioz," often given to him, is rather high praise. Both Berlioz and Fry were masters of orchestral and choral composition, but Berlioz's originality far exceeds that of Fry. The two names were linked partly because of the sincere friendship they were known to share while Fry was in Paris.

William Henry Fry (1813-1864) was the son of William Fry the publisher of the *National Gazette*. He received a literary education, music being always a beloved hobby. His autodidactic methods of music study were supplemented by a musical home life, and by later studies in the theory of music under Leopold Meignen. Overtures were composed by this ambitious youth from the time he was fourteen years old. His fourth overture was awarded a gold medal, and performed at a concert of the Philadelphia Philharmonic Society in 1833. *Aurelia the Vestal* was an early but lengthy opera by William Fry, set to a libretto by his brother Edward P. Fry in 1838. The Frys were consistent advocates of opera in English, the *Leonora* performances noted above all being sung in that tongue. In 1844 William Fry became editor of the *Philadelphia Ledger,* a post he held but a short time, for in 1846 we find him in both London and Paris as the European correspondent for the New York *Tribune.* Returning to America in 1852, he gave a remarkable series of lectures on the history and art of music. Fry's lectures were probably the first of their kind, since they were of general and popular interest, being delivered to large audiences in New York. The final lecture centered around one of the earliest and most extreme musical declarations of independence for American music.[1]

During the following year, 1853, Jullien's orchestra played four symphonies by Fry, *Childe Harold, A Day in the Country, The Breaking Heart,* and *Christmas* (or *Santa Claus*). An occasional ode, composed in honor of the opening of the New York Crystal Palace, was played at the inaugural concert in that hall on May 4, 1854. In the same year Fry's one movement symphony *Niagara* was produced at the Crystal Palace. This same prolific composer wrote several cantatas, about a dozen string quartets, and considerable music for the Catholic church. A *Stabat Mater* for soloists, chorus, and orchestra is his largest sacred work. His many overtures include *Macbeth* and *Evangeline.* The opera *Leonora* was given in Italian in New York in 1858.[2] William Fry's *Notre Dame de Paris,* or *Esmerelda,* was brought out in Philadelphia on May 9, 1864, only a few months before his death. This performance will be discussed at the conclusion of our account of Philadelphia opera of the early and middle nineteenth century.

The preceding facts concerning the life and music of William H. Fry are gathered from many sources. Contemporary programs

---

[1] The original notes and charts of this lecture series are preserved in the Ridgway branch of the Library Co. of Philadelphia.

[2] Recent revivals of *Leonora* in New York, staged as quaint American musical antiquities, brought forth the same mixture of cheers and jeers Fry's operas seem to have produced in his own day. The occasion for this latest *Leonora* performance was an attempt to compare early American music with ultra modern works, the whole program being given in concert form at a meeting of the Pro Musica Society in May 1929. New York critics declared that *Leonora* was more reasonably tuneful than the modern compositions, and as interesting as the Bellini operas on which it was modelled. These 1929 critics were much kinder to Fry's "inexperienced and unoriginal opus" than their forerunners of *Leonora's* own days. This modern revival, and many quotations from criticisms of it, are recorded in Howard's *Our American Music,* pp. 246-249.

mention several of the works, while writings of the time mention the man and his music at great length. The comments on this strange man by students of his life and works are filled with striking details. Robert Patterson, an intimate friend of William Fry, recognized that *Leonora* and *Notre Dame* "were ambitious attempts well produced, and skillfully written for voice and orchestra. Some say they lack originality. His musical genius was really great, but he spent too much time and energy in his editorial work." [1] Upton in *The Art Song in America*, pp. 41-43, characterizes Fry as "'aggressive, opinionated, egotistical, but possessed of very real musical gifts," also as "the most quarrelled with musician in the America of his time." John S. Dwight [2] declared in 1853: "I should like him, but disagree with him," while a year later Willis [3] called him "a splendid frigate at sea without a helm." Readers may wonder how a Philadelphian ever became so well known to American critics. As the musical editor of the New York *Tribune*, Fry was in a position to spread his views on American music to a large groups of readers. Since those views, as expressed in an article in the New York *Musical Times and Musical World*, January 21, 1854, were diametrically opposed to the current trend in music in Philadelphia and New York, a lively controversy ensued. The *Musical World* article stated with much conviction and bitterness that the admiration bestowed on imported music and musicians was leading us to artistic suicide as a musical nation, and bringing about actual starvation for native men stubborn enough to depend on music as a profession. The earlier lecture on recognition for native composers, with which William Fry concluded his noted series of 1852, had stressed the same ideas. In the period of this early pleading for artistic independence, the many German musicians constituted the European element so bitterly opposed. The superior training

---

[1] Patterson's estimate is quoted by W. G. Armstrong in *Record of the Opera in Philadelphia*, p. 49. Armstrong himself was an acquaintance of the Fry family.

[2] John Sullivan Dwight, one of America's earliest music critics of ability. Dwight's *Journal of Music* was the leading periodical in its field from 1852 to 1881.

[3] Richard S. Willis, composer and editor of the *Musical Times and the Musical World* in New York at the time of Fry's connection with the *New York Tribune*.

and gifts of the Germans made short work of Fry's obstacles, of course, but his agitation for appreciation of American subjects and native composers was highly influential.

The entire Fry family was musically gifted. William's brother Joseph R. Fry wrote librettos for both *Leonora* and *Notre Dame de Paris*, while his first opera, *Aurelia the Vestal* or *Christians and Pagans* was composed in 1838 to words by Edward Fry. A third brother, Charles, who died as a young man was said to have possessed a fine baritone voice. One of the marvels of early telephone communication concerns the experiences of a fourth brother, Edward Fry, who listened at a telephone in New York to Philadelphia opera performances, particularly those featuring Mme. Gerster. These operas were transmitted to Edward Fry in 1883.[1]

In 1847 the first visit of a new company was announced for the coming season. The Italian Opera Company from Havana rapidly became the favorite troupe in Philadelphia. Opening in July 1847, the five years to 1852 were characterized by their leadership in number and significance of the operas produced. This company was the first to introduce Verdi's music to Philadelphia audiences. Angiolina Bosio was their greatest singer. Salvi, Badiali, Marino, and Bettini were also noted singers in the Havana Italian Opera Company.

The musical public of the city had long ceased to be dependent on one theatre or one musical organization for its entertainment. The American première of *Luisa Miller*, October 27, 1852, was an independent operatic venture at the close of the Havana troupe's period of dominant influence. Miss Caroline Richings sang the leading part in this opera. Alboni, Sontag and Patti sang their first Philadelphia concerts at Musical Fund Hall during the same year. The Seguins gave what was probably their last important concert, at the Walnut Street Theatre—also in 1852.

In 1853 Mme. Alboni and later Mme. Sontag were the main attractions at the opera in Philadelphia. The Walnut Street and National Theatres seem to have become more prominent opera

---

[1] This opera-by-telephone is recounted as a remarkable achievement in W. G. Armstrong's *Record of the Opera in Philadelphia*. The book having been published in 1884, Mr. Fry's telephone sessions were considered, quite properly, as the most recent in scientific marvels.

houses than the older Chestnut Street Theatre. W. G. Armstrong, the chronicler of nineteenth century opera in Philadelphia, quotes from his diary: "April 11th 1853, Badiali says smoking improves his voice. Pozzolini also says that since he smokes, his voice is better. Madame Sontag has taken to it, and now will smoke a whole cigar at a time." He follows this startling diary picture with the sentence "*In Don Pasquale* they dressed in the costume of the present day, and Mme. Sontag was the very impersonation of feminine grace."[1] We may be sure that Mme. Sontag did not smoke a cigar on that occasion.

The season of 1854 witnessed the continued popularity of Italian opera, although *Guy Mannering* and the *Beggar's Opera* were both produced in that year. The baritone Graziani sang in several operas at the Chestnut Street Theatre. He was later to reach even greater fame as the Count di Luna in numerous London and Paris performances of *Il Trovatore*. This was one of the few early instances of young singers' leaving the United States to secure greater fame in Europe. Madame Malibran, Signorina Bosio, and Mme. Viardot were other singers who did this at about the same period. The reverse process—that of worn and old voices coming to America—had been so prevalent that this country had been repeatedly styled the "burying ground of European talent." W. G. Armstrong, whose *Record of the Opera in Philadelphia* provides much of our information concerning the early productions of grand opera, records his disappointment in many instances. Thus: "Severi [tenor] lost his voice in crossing the ocean."[2] "Braham, nearly seventy years old when he came to the Untied States, had the wreck of a great voice."[3] "Mr. Seguin had an excellent bass voice. In England he sang at the oratorio festivals always with great applause. In this country, having to sing every night, his voice of course became impaired; but his good acting carried him through with approbation."[4] Signora de Paez as Lucia was declared abominable,[5] and her manager, Maretzek, was warned that she

---

[1] Armstrong, *op. cit.*, p. 78.
[2] Armstrong, *op. cit.*, p. 57.
[3] *Ibid.*, p. 46.
[4] Pp. 45-46.
[5] The performance was at the Academy of Music on March 4, 1857. Armstrong, *Record of the Opera in Philadelphia*, p. 88.

would be hissed off the stage if she appeared again. "Ronconi's knowledge of the voice enables him to conceal in a great measure the ravages which time and labor had made upon it in 1860."[1] Mlle. Tostée, who headed the cast in the Philadelphia première of Offenbach's *Grand Duchess,* Feb. 11, 1867, is described as showing the effects of time and wear. 'But she was full of fun and had comic audacity that was very droll.' There are other examples of disapproval nearly as outspoken as the above, while the many aging European artists damned with faint praise are still more numerous.

The Maretzek Company's operas of September 1854 were the last to be given in the historic Chestnut Street Theatre, which was torn down in 1855.

Grisi and Mario opened the next year with three Italian operas (January, 1855; *Puritani, Lucrezia Borgia, Norma*) at the Walnut Street Theatre. Armstrong declares that "Mario is far the best tenor I have heard" and adds many other superlative statements. He feels that "Madame Grisi when she came to this country was a vocalist no longer young," and mentions general disappoint in her voice.[2]

January 14, 1856, marks the American première of *Il Trovatore* at the Walnut Street Theatre. It was also the first appearance of Mme. La Grange's opera company in Philadelphia. This troupe having remained for so long the favorite opera group in Philadelphia, the names of some of their leading soloists are given: Anna La Grange, soprano; Nantier Didiée, mezzo-soprano; Brignoli, tenor; Amodio and Morelli, baritones; Rovere, buffo. Elise Hensler was also a soprano in their productions, other leading parts being sung by Arnoldi, Gasparoni, and Salviani. Adelaide Phillips made her first Philadelphia appearance in the La Grange production of *Semiramide,* 1856.

Il Trovatore was chosen as the inaugural opera for the Philadelphia Academy of Music, February 25, 1857. Caroline Richings and Mme. Gazzaniga are among the new names that appear in the somewhat changed personnel of the opera cast at the new Academy.

---

[1] *Ibid.,* p. 107.
[2] Armstrong, *Record of Opera in Philadelphia,* pp. 83-84. It is interesting to compare Madeira's rating of the same two singers. He greatly prefers Grisi to Mario. (Madeira, *Musical Fund Society,* pp. 170-171.)

A long and varied series of Italian operas lasted from February to June of this year. *La Traviata* was introduced in this season (March 13th, with four repeat performances). There were five German Operas produced in June 1857 (*Freischütz, Fidelio, Le Maçon*—by Auber, but sung in German—*Martha*, and *The Czar and the Carpenter*).

The fall season witnessed a long series of Italian operas, *Rigoletto* being presented for the first time in Philadelphia, January 25, 1858. "Herr Carl Formes," basso, appeared in several operas in the Philadelphia Academy of Music in 1858. His voice, declared to have been magnificent as Sarastro in 1842, was found to be a bit worn when first heard in Philadelphia. Gustav Hinrichs declares in his *Memoirs* that Carl Formes was the greatest basso of the nineteenth century. Madame Colson came to this city from New Orleans in the same year (1858). In 1859 Mlle. Piccolomini made her Philadelphia debut as "The Daughter of the Regiment"—that favored role for first appearances. Conductors Muzio and Anschütz are mentioned on operatic programs of that year.[1]

In December 1859 Adelina Patti made her operatic debut as "Lucia." Throughout the following years Patti, her teacher Maurice Strakosch, Mesdames Strakosch and Colson, Miss Phillips, Sig. Brignoli, Amodio, Ferri, and Susini played most of the parts in the many operas at the Academy of Music. A German company occasionally appears for a few nights, but the large majority of productions were Italian operas. This German Company introduced *Faust to American* audiences in November 1863. They gave frequent performances of *Fidelio, Magic Flute, Stradella, Martha,* and the still popular *Freischütz*.

Let us close this long record of opera history with a brief account of the second performed opera of William Fry. *Notre Dame de Paris* was produced May 9th, 1864, for the benefit of the Sanitary Fair. Fry wrote this opera in nineteen days, and paid most of the expenses of staging it. Ninety musicians were in the orchestra, hundreds on the stage.[2] Theodore Thomas conducted the

---

[1] Programs of the Philadelphia Academy of Music from 1857 are preserved, some in bound volumes, at the Pennsylvania Historical Society, 13th and Locust Streets, Philadelphia.
[2] Armstrong's *Record of Opera in Philadelphia*, p. 126.

opera. The orchestra, as would be expected of Fry orchestration and Thomas conducting, was outstanding. There were seven performances of this work, doubtless to the vast gain of sanitation.

VI

Since Philadelphia is truly a city of homes, it is also a city of families. Father and son musicians are very frequently encountered among Philadelphia's well known names. Among so many family combinations it is remarkable that almost no third generation musicians of importance have appeared in any of them. The biography of one of Philadelphia's most noted musicians, so far omitted, suggests the outstanding father and son of Philadelphia musical history. Benjamin Cross was surely a personage in that city from at least as early as 1820 until his death in 1857. His son Michael Hurley Cross was a leading musical figure from 1860 to 1897. While chronological regulation suggests that Michael Cross belongs to a far different period than that of this chapter, one cannot consider Benjamin Cross without remembering the long years of important influence that father and son exerted on Music in Philadelphia.[1] Possibly the long period served by Benjamin and Michael Cross is rendered the more conspicuous in that when Benjamin was born, 1786, musicians were usually an imported species in this country; thus it seems the more remarkable when a native born Philadelphian achieves musical fame, and produces a son possibly still more famous. The earlier Francis Hopkinson's musical celebrity is in large part due to the fact that he was the first native born American to compose the sort of music that he did.

Benjamin Cross was identified very closely with Philadelphia from his earliest years. Born in that city in 1786, he attended the University of Pennsylvania and was one of its early graduates. His

---

[1] Other families possessing noted musicians for two successive generations include E. Blake and George E. Blake, Thomas Loud and Thomas C. Loud, J. C. Taws and his two sons, among those already discussed; and Charles Jarvis senior and junior, the two Thomas à Becket's, Henry Gordon Thunder and his two sons, Henry G. Thunder, Jr., and William Sylvano Thunder, among men who will be mentioned later in this book. If we were to consider the musically great whose parents were musically gifted we should have to include many more names in the above list. The list contains only families where both representatives have been outstanding among Philadelphia musicians.

teachers of music were the distinguished Benjamin Carr and Raynor Taylor. As a young man Benjamin Cross was organist at St. Mary's Roman Catholic Church. Cross became a noted vocal soloist from about 1810. His influence was important as teacher, singer and conductor. In 1820 he was one of the founders of the Musical Fund Society, and conducted many of its concerts. His solo work was included in so many programs between 1810 and 1830 that it is difficult to pick only a few of the most important performances. His appearances in *The Creation,* at Washington Hall, June 10, 1822; in the *Dettingen Te Deum* at the opening of Musical Fund Hall, December, 29, 1824; and in *The Messiah,* Musical Fund Hall, April 30, 1828, reveal not only his prominence as a vocal performer, but remind us of the ambitious music undertaken in that remote era in Philadelphia. Equally notable are many performances which Benjamin Cross directed in his later years as a member of the Musical Fund Society. The American première of Mozart's *Magic Flute,* already mentioned as the main musical event in 1841, was under Cross's direction. Benjamin Cross may well be considered to have been the guiding spirit of this Society after the year of Carr and Schetky's death, 1831, a position he shared with both Charles Hupfeld and Leopold Meignen at different periods. The sudden cessation of the society's concerts in 1857 was due to the death of Benjamin Cross as well as to the simultaneous completion of the new Academy of Music.

VII

If we should consider the three main developments of Music in Philadelphia during the years 1800-1860, they would undoubtedly be those already discussed in this chapter: the founding and great influence of the Musical Fund Society; the firm establishment of *opera seria,* culminating in the building and early successes at the Academy of Music; and the great growth of Philadelphia as a center for the manufacture of musical instruments, particularly the piano. It would not be so easy to pick three men who were similarly outstanding during this long period of the early nineteenth century. Many of the late eighteenth century musicians exerted their main influence in the period after 1800; among them Carr, Schetky,

Taylor, Taws, and Gillingham have been noted as important. In our exact period, 1800-1860, some main musical figures were Cross, Hupfeld, Meignen, and Fry. The names of men who were in Philadelphia prior to 1860, but whose influence was felt in the years after that date, are very numerous indeed; since they are connected with a later chapter a few of their names will be merely listed here. Important among them are Michael Cross, Henry Gordon Thunder (Sr.), Thomas à Becket, Charles Jarvis, David D. Wood, Simon and Mark Hassler, and Septimus Winner. To students familiar with recent developments in Philadelphia music, the preceding list may seem a heterogeneous assortment of names, but those very readers should be interested to discover how many present day musicians in the city are directly descended, by birth or training, from men who were active in Philadelphia prior to the end of the period arbitrarily chosen as Early Nineteenth Century. This musical inbreeding has both advantages and disadvantages too obvious to need stating here. The following biographical chart of Philadelphia musicians shows by its arrangement of names the connection of certain famous men to each other in family relationship; and, as often as possible, in the important relation of teacher and pupil. Chronological sequence and similarity of musical fields have been the main factors in the arrangement of the chart.

Before we leave this period we must discuss a few less exalted and ambitious phases of its Music in Philadelphia. The popular music of the early nineteenth century had already begun to show that morbid sentimentality so often ascribed to the ballads of the 1890's, or to music after the Civil War. Many Philadelphians composed doleful songs long before 1860 however. Jane Campbell[1] lists several such Philadelphia ballads coming from the early nineteenth century. Among them are J. Haynes Bayly's *She Wore a Wreath of Roses,* c.1835; Mrs. Norton's *Love Not Ye Hapless Sons of Clay,* 1831; Elam Ives' *Weep, Weep, for the Maid of Song is Dead,* c. 1845; Thomas Fitzgerald's, *Mary Bell, . . . tenderest blossom Fare Thee Well,* 1849; and E. L. Walker's *Agnes May . . . she sleeps beneath the Withered Grass,* 1850. Philadelphia's outstanding contribution to the literature of the nineteenth century popular

---

[1] Jane Campbell, *Old Philadelphia Music,* pp. 200-202.

music was composed before the Civil War. It was Septimus Winner's *Listen to the Mocking Bird*, written in 1854. This song will be treated more fully in a biography of Winner, which is included in the following chapter.[1] Its cheerful melody disguises, but should not conceal, the fact that the text of this song is as sad as that of most of the morbid songs listed above.[2]

Sigmund Spaeth has collected so many sentimental songs from nineteenth century America in his two entertaining volumes, *Read 'Em and Weep*, and *Weep Some More My Lady*,[3] that we need only say that many such songs were written in Philadelphia in the period under discussion. Nor does their musical or literary significance justify more than mention of a few titles that appear to be typical. If Mr. Spaeth investigated the voluminous bound collections of such early popular music preserved in the Ridgway Branch of the Library Company of Philadelphia, he was doubtless bewildered by the problem of selecting songs for his two books.[4] Many individual songs composed and published in Philadelphia are listed in the index of this book. Their general sentimental emphasis, while noted as prophesying the sorrowful ballads of the century, is to be preferred to the political nature of the popular songs that were waning as the sentimental ballads waxed. A rare volume in the Philadelphia Library Company collection entitled *The Philadelphia Songster*, or *Complete Vocal Pocket Companion*, "being a collection of The Most approved Anacreontic Political and Sentimental Modern Songs . . . selected from a variety of volumes," was printed by B. Graves in

---

[1] Cf. p. 110.

[2] Readers familiar with only the music of this song may be surprised to discover that its gay prattle is a setting for these words:

> I am dreaming now of Hallie
> Sweet Hallie, sweet Hallie
> She's sleeping in the valley
> And the mocking bird is singing where she lies.
> Listen to the mocking bird [bis.]
> The mocking bird is singing where she lies

[or *o'er her grave*, a variant ending that states more definitely what happened to Hallie].

[3] Published by Doubleday, Page and Co., New York, 1927.

[4] The James Rush, Richard Vaux and other collections contain many volumes of popular songs, composed mainly by Philadelphians, published almost exclusively in Philadelphia. The guitar seems to have superseded the mandolin in popularity as a general alternate to the piano as accompanying instrument during the 1820's. George E. Blake's numerous popular publications frequently feature the guitar.

1805. When the political bombast and crudity is compared with the early sentimental songs in the Philadelphia Songster, we must admit that the ousting of politics as the dominant theme for popular music was a mark of progress. In the two books by Spaeth on early American songs the same conclusion is reached, in spite of their author's conspicuous lack of sympathy with the adolescents who caused a prolonged vogue for morbidity to characterize our nineteenth century popular songs. Mr. Spaeth aptly classes the political and anacreontic songs of the period 1800 to 1820 as musically monstrous.[1]

Songs and dances constitute the two main realms of popular music in this or any period. Prior to 1800 a wide variety of themes engaged the writers of popular songs. Hunting songs, sea songs, patriotic and political songs, even songs based on classic mythology shared the field with the love songs of the day. From 1820 on, the love song has been seen to have crowded all others from the popular favor, taking on a sad, usually funereal, character as it did so. Dance music, however, increased in liveliness, even as the very texts of the songs played in dance form became their saddest. While all of the foregoing sounds frivolous and trivial in our discussion of Music in Philadelphia, especially following the account of the beginnings of the lofty Musical Fund Society and the equally serious first Grand Operas in Philadelphia, the tremendous quantity of popular songs and dances forbids that they be ignored entirely.

A figure of considerable interest in the years 1815-1840 was that of Francis Johnson. He was a colored musician, an unrivalled trumpeter and an expert bandmaster, a prolific and popular composer. Johnson organized a band of colored men (The Washington Guards, Company Three Band) in Philadelphia, in 1815, which soon outshone the other musical groups of the city.[2] Willig published a *Collection of Cotillions* by Francis Johnson, in 1818.[3] In

---

[1] *Weep Some More My Lady*, p. 5.

[2] Some of these other instrumental groups of the period were: The Republican Greens, a twenty-piece band, founded 1805; the Independent Blues, 1808, Columbian Light Infantry Band, 1820; Philadelphia Band 1833 (c.); managed by a family named Beck, a rival of Johnson's band in popular esteem; German Washington Guards Band, 25 instruments, 1837; and Hazzard's Band, a second noted negro organization, 1840. Later bands were Bayley's, Breiter's, and others, until the Civil War days and their numerous regimental musical units.

[3] A copy may be seen at the Philadelphia Library Company.

1821 we learn of his presenting to Mrs. Ann Rush piano arrangements for eighty-seven of his own compositions.[1] Johnson's' band
furnished the music for the grand ball given to Lafayette in 1825.
Stringed instruments were included in concert and dance appearances of this band. They played marches and cotillions of Frank
Johnson's composition on that occasion. This celebrated band made
a European tour in 1837, probably the first American musical organization so to do; and, of course, 'played before royalty' abroad.
The Philadelphia Grays' *Quick Step* was a noted march by Johnson.
It was composed for the State Fencibles,[2] for whom Johnson's band
played regularly, providing music for their drills and exhibitions.
Strangely enough, when the State Fencibles visited Providence,
Rhode Island; in New England, the home of the abolition movement, Johnson's band was not allowed to provide the music. A
contrasting side of this band's musical efforts is suggested by their
playing for musical soirées at the Philadelphia Museum at Ninth
and Sansom Streets. Their series of soirées during Christmas week
of 1838 were widely advertised as being "on the plan of Musard's
concerts in Paris."

The hop waltz was a new dance evidently of great popularity
in the years 1820-1850. There were numerous compositions that
bore that cheerful name, among them *The Vigilant Hop Waltz*,
dedicated to the Vigilant Society, The *Philadelphia Hop Waltz*,
played by Hemmenway's Band [3] and many others. Septimus Winner's diary mentions numerous balls, hops, and lodge programs at
which he played a variety of instruments between the years 1842
and 1855. Even the august Carl Lenschow deigned to compose
the *Bachelors' Polka*, dedicated to the Young Bachelors' Association, and published by Lee and Walker. The polka was introduced
in America at the middle of the nineteenth century, having been orig-
inated in Bohemia about 1830, introduced into western Europe in
1841, and into America soon thereafter. Lenschow's *Bachelors'*

---

[1] These manuscript arrangements are in the Rush Collection at the Ridgway Library in Philadelphia.

[2] A military company still in existence, with present headquarters at their
Armory, 1615 Summer St.

[3] This noted popular ensemble played, as a rule, at Washington Hall,
3rd Street near Spruce, in the years after the Musical Fund Hall was built
(1825- *c.* 1835).

Polka was very probably composed in 1848, since that year marks
the regrettably unsuccessful series by the Germania Orchestra in
Philadelphia under Lenschow's direction; and it was also the first
year of the existence of the publishing firm of Lee and Walker.

Among the lighter phases of Philadelphia music of this period,
we must not neglect the tremendous popularity of the minstrel
troupes. John Clemens wrote operas which bridge the gap between the eighteenth century ballad works and the operettas of the
period after the Civil War. His *Coal Black Rose* has been called
America's first popular song. It was certainly one of the most
successful among the early negro songs. *Coal Black Rose* was composed in 1829. Clemens' *Justina* was produced in Philadelphia
during the 1829-1830 season; his *The Fiend and the Fairy* was
given in 1832. These works are somewhat more ambitious than
the *Cossack and the Volunteer,* ascribed to Clemens by some authorities, and mentioned above as having been called the first opera
by a Philadelphian.[1] None of Clemens' works could be considered
seriously as the first American opera. The popular *Coal Black
Rose* was made famous by George Washington Dixon in Philadelphia and elsewhere. Dixon introduced *Zip Coon* at the Arch Street
Theatre in 1834.

James Sanford, a native Philadelphian, was active in popular
music a little later than Clemens and Dixon. He was a noted composer and singer of Negro songs. Sanford's *Lucy Neale,* written
in 1844, is his best known work. Sam Sanford took the older
minstrel's name, although he was no relation of James Sanford.
The first permanent "'minstrel opera house" was opened by Sam
Sanford on 11th Street above Chestnut, in 1855.

One more popular furore should be recorded in the middle
years of the nineteenth century. The rage for Fanny Elssler in
Europe and America is reflected in the popular music of about
1841.[2] *The Fanny Elssler Quadrilles, 'La Sylphide,* as danced by
Fanny Elssler,' the Mazurka, or the 'Galloupe' was danced by
Fanny Elssler—these and similar tributes are paid to her in the
editions of popular music of the day.

---

[1] Cf. *supra,* p. 54. The Bureau of Music *Survey and Directory,* p. 6,
calls the *Cossack and the Volunteer* the first American opera.

[2] *Old Philadelphia Music,* Jane Campbell, p. 195.

VIII

As new and important developments are noted in this and the following chapter, we must not forget the continuing vitality of old musical institutions. While we trace with some detail the activities of the Musical Fund Society from the year of its founding until 1858, we should not neglect to mention the many older music clubs and societies that continued to exist for many years in the same period. Some of these societies are briefly discussed in alphabetical order in the following paragraphs.

The Amateurs of Music, organized in 1809, concerned themselves with chamber music rehearsals and 'Quartett Parties,' the latter being a series of subscription concerts. Their membership suggests that their organization led to the founding of the Musical Fund Society. Gillingham, La Folle, Hommann, and Schetky were the usual performers, while Charles F. Hupfeld often assisted "making quintets possible." [1]

A later group was also called Amateurs of Music. They gave a series of vocal concerts at Musical Fund Hall in 1849 and 1850. Signor Perelli, of operatic fame, directed this chorus, which numbered about seventy. Perelli's *Belschazzar*, a lyric tragedy in four acts, was given its first performance at an Amateur Musical Soirée on January 3rd, 1850. A small professional orchestra accompanied this group.

The Anacreontic Society, organized in 1833, seems to have remained active until 1860. Franklin Peale, Benjamin Cross, Elijah Dallett, William Norris, and W. H. W. Darley were among its members. Musical gatherings in the members' homes constituted the activity of this select club. W. Armstrong, writing in 1884 sums up the sad end of this society: "They were all elderly gentlemen. They have all passed away." [2] The same fate has been shared by most of the musical organizations included in this list.

In 1830-1836 an Apollo society gave concerts. Press notices mention a series of chamber music programs in 1833, and a Soirée Musicale by Hupfeld, Reinhard, Schmitz, and B. Cross on December 30th 1836. An earlier club, the Sons of Apollo, was organized in

---

[1] *Poulson's American Daily Advertiser*, July 6, and 7, 1810.
[2] *Record of the Opera in Philadelphia*, p. 248.

1807. This group had both amateur and professional members, and met at the Shakespeare Hotel. This early Apollo Club held its first rehearsals in 1809, giving nine concerts that year, and many each season until 1818. Six parties were scheduled for Tuesday evenings in July and August, 1810, at Mr. Auriol's room,[1] 64 S. 4th Street.

The Catch Club sang at Hardy's hotel, on Thursdays at 7 p.m., according to the newspapers of 1801 and several following years.

A Handelian Society, founded in 1814, gave vocal concerts from that year. It is interesting to note that the venerable Handel and Haydn Society of Boston was begun the following year, 1815. The Philadelphia Haydn Society was founded in 1809, but of course neither Handel nor Haydn choruses in this city had the long life of the Boston society. The earliest concert by the Handelian Society chorus was given in May 1814.[2] The Philadelphia *Aurora* of January 9th, 1815, announced a concert of sacred music on January 12th. There were fifteen numbers on the program, ten of them by Handel. Taylor was the organist at this concert. At a later program during the same season,[3] the Handelian Society sang what appears to have been a cantata by Taylor. Mr. S. Dyer, the society's leader, announced[4] that the *Morning Hymn* by Raynor Taylor, consisting of "solos, duetts, airs and chorusses" would be introduced at their next concert. It was repeated at their last regulaar concert of the season, on April 13th, 1815. At a sacred concert two weeks later, the Harmonic Society assisted Dyer's chorus.[5] There was

---

[1] A leading dancing studio of the day.
[2] Scharf and Westcott, *op. cit.*, p. 1088.
[3] A special concert on March 21, 1815.
[4] Philadelphia *Aurora* for March 15, 1815.
[5] The Harmonic Societies in the early nineteenth century were far too numerous to discuss in this brief resumé. The group that assisted at the Handelian Society concert was connected with the English Lutheran Church of St. John. Reverend Andrew Law organized a Harmonic Society in Philadelphia in 1802, which gave annual concerts. A rival Harmonic Society was begun in 1807, a third at St. John's Lutheran Church (*c.* 1815). St. John's Harmonic Society was organized in 1819 according to Scharf and Westcott's *History of Philadelphia*, p. 1089, which mentions several Harmonic Societies. Between 1820 and 1825 there were The Independent Union, the Associate, and the Germantown Harmonic Societies, in addition to whatever may have survived from the earlier groups of the same name. Near the end of our period, 1855, the first oratorio by a Philadelphian, *The Cities of the Plain*, was produced by the Harmonic Society. Just which of the many Harmonic Societies produced this oratorio, we do not know; but the composer of *The Cities*

organ accompaniment, according to the press notices, although at
their January concert, Mr. Gillingham is said to have led a band—
we should call it an orchestra—in addition to Raynor Taylor's
organ playing. The Handelian Society seems to have had a short
life, while the Harmonic Society continued at least until the beginning of the Musical Fund Society. Meetings in June and
October are mentioned by the *Daily Advertiser* of 1820.

A Haydn Society, mentioned above, existed from 1809 until
after 1820. Weekly meetings at 4th and Vine Streets were "to be
resumed," according to the *Daily Advertiser* of October 5th, 1820.

The Junto was a society of thirty members. All were strictly
amateur musicians, including their leader. Opera choruses were
their specialty, which may surprise us less when we learn that their
period of greatest activity was in the years 1848-1849, at a time of
great operatic popularity in this city. Of about sixty choruses sung
during that season, over twenty were taken from operas never
produced in Philadelphia.[1]

A Philadelphia Glee Association and a Philadelphia Sacred
Music Association gave concerts in the 1830's. A St. Cecelia Society, organized in 1824, sang several programs in the seasons between that year and 1830. Thomas Carr conducted the St. Cecelia
Society at their regular rehearsals in South Fourth Street. Thomas
Carr has been mentioned above as the less known brother of Benjamin Carr. He organized the St. Cecelia Society less than a year
after his arrival from Baltimore.

Two groups have been omitted in the above alphabetical summary of early nineteenth century organizations. Their importance
is greater than the choruses mentioned in that summary; at least it
spread over a longer period of years, extending beyond the limits of
this chapter. One of these groups was the Philharmonic Society,
an amateur instrumental group. This orchestra played an overture

---

of the Plain, F. T. Sully Darley, became an important figure in later musical
developments in Philadelphia. Darley was a descendant of the famous opera
singers in early Philadelphia productions, as well as of the painter and
amateur musician Thomas Sully. He became one of the most active promoters of Music in Philadelphia throughout the late nineteenth century,
closing his influential career with an active part in the founding of the
Philadelphia Orchestra in 1900.

[1] The above claim for the Junto's operatic catholicity and research is
made in W. G. Armstrong's *Record of the Opera in Philadelphia*.

by William Fry in 1833, at one of the orchestra's and Fry's earliest public appearances. For about forty years the Philharmonic Society exerted considerable influence on Philadelphia music. Nor did they confine themselves to orchestral concerts, for we read [1] that *The Seasons* was given on January 29, 1835; and Ole Bull, Benjamin Cross, Camillo Sivori, Amalia Patti, Henry Herz, and many other noted soloists appeared before the Philharmonic Society between 1844 and 1856. The Steyermarkische (Armstrong's spelling) Orchestra played at a Philharmonic concert on January 26th, 1848. Musical Fund Hall housed most of their concerts, although the Chinese Museum, at 9th and Sansom Streets, was also popular with this society.

The second society is still active. It is the Männerchor of Philadelphia, founded in 1835 by Philip Wolsiefer. The Old Männerchor, as it is now called, is Philadelphia's oldest choral group, and the oldest German singing society in America. Their music, and their organization, have changed only slightly in their over one hundred years of singing—possibly a static order of procedure, but surely one which reflects a remarkable amount of stability in musical service. The Männerchor still meets weekly, and still sings mainly, but not exclusively, in German. Their meeting places have varied in the long period of their existence; for many years they sang at Broad and Oxford Streets. At present the group rehearses under the leadership of John Kramers every Wednesday at 7th Street and Girard Avenue.

Two other German groups are scarcely less venerable than the Männerchor. The Junger Männerchor and the Arion Singing Society, founded in 1850 and 1854 respectively, are both nearing their hundredth anniversaries as continuously active choruses. Each of these German groups consists of about sixty men. They stage two concerts a year, the Junger Männerchor usually giving several extra smaller concerts. Leopold Syre is the present conductor of the Junger Männerchor; Herbert Fiss leads the Arion Singing Society.[2] Two concerts a year are also given by the Harmonie, a

---

[1] In Armstrong, *Record of the Opera in Philadelphia*.
[2] Not to be confused with the Arion Society of Germantown, a group conducted by Michael Cross in the 1870's. David Bispham sang in this later Arion club, which rehearsed in St. Luke's Church, Germantown, and gave many concerts between 1870 and 1890.

mixed chorus of over one hundred voices. This German group
was founded in 1855, and still rehearses regularly and gives concerts.

The four German choruses described above and the Musical
Fund Society appear to be the only Philadelphia groups founded in
the early nineteenth century that still contribute actively to Music
in Philadelphia. In the later 1800's there will be seen to have been
many groups organized that still have an important share in present
day music matters.

Among older music that continued while new societies came
and went, none is older than that of the church. There is less to
record concerning church music in 1800-1860 than there would be
for any other sixty year period. We could of course say that it was
a continuing and a growing field of Music in Philadelphia, that it
touched a large number of people profoundly, and that as newer
sections of the city were built the churches that arose vied with each
other in providing the most elaborate music and the finest organ.
The few books on Philadelphia church history that emphasize these
years say little about the music that was used during the services.
Benjamin Dorr's *A Historical Account of Christ Church*, and
Abraham Ritter's *History of the Moravian Church in Philadelphia*,
devote a small amount of space to the music of those churches in
the early nineteenth century. Their opinions agree with the rather
gloomy picture gained by study of the music in old choir libraries.
One feels less restrained in condemning what seems to have been
the dark ages of religious music in this city, possibly in the country
as well. This does not mean that new publications of sacred music
are wanting, but rather that they seem to hark back to the older
church musicians in an unoriginal and unprogressive way. Thus,
the *Philadelphia Harmony, or Adgate's Music Improved*, was published by M. Carey in 1801.[1] Benjamin Carr seems to have monopolized the editing and arranging of music for Episcopal services, as
already suggested earlier in this chapter. This was fortunate considering his musicianship, but Carr's influence seems to have caused
a fixed tradition in his denomination that was never altered until
the days of David Wood and Kendrick Pyne. His *Masses, Vespers
and Litanies*, 1805, *Collection of Chants*, 1816, and *The Chorister*,

---

[1] *American Daily Advertiser*, April 4, 1801.

1820, were highly influential for many years.[1]   Carr published a
collection entitled *Episcopal Music* in January 1820, consisting of
'Chants of Morning and Evening Prayer and Communion Service
as sung at St. James' Church.'   This is interesting as containing an
early reference to St. James' Church, which was a member of the
'United Parish' from 1809 to 1829, and since that time has been
an important church in Philadelphia music.   Carr directed a program of sacred music at St. Luke's Church, Germantown, on May
22nd, 1820.   This was to aid both the female benevolent society and
the church building fund, according to the *Daily Advertiser* for
May 18th, 1820.   Charles Taws had already played a recital at
St. Luke's Church before Carr's concert.   These references to St.
James' and St. Luke's in connection with Carr and Taws should be
interesting since they connect present day churches far from the
original city area with musicians who were very early in Philadelphia's history.   Such notices and events suggest the spread of the
city's finest musicianship to a wider, suburban area, a development
that has characterized church music in Philadelphia throughout the
hundred and twenty years since such early evidences of it in 1820.

The Moravian, Lutheran and Catholic musical programs are
frequently alluded to as elaborately worked out from early days.
In the *History of the Morvian Church in Philadelphia,* by Abraham
Ritter, we have a full account by an ex-choirboy and former organist, who was also a member of the church.   Since Christ Church
has been discussed under the colonial period, and St. Luke's will
be mentioned later in this book, let us choose the book by Ritter for
its particular appropriateness to the years under discussion.   The
time of his connection with the Philadelphia Moravian Church
almost coincided with the years of this chapter, 1800-1860.   His
history of the church was published in 1857.   One of Abraham
Ritter's earliest recollections concerns an aged amateur violinist
who played during some of the services at the Moravian Church.
His frequent and audible tuning impressed the choirboys, as did

---

[1] Particularly the last collection, whose full title was *The Chorister, a
Collection of Chants and Melodies adapted to psalms and hymns of the
Episcopal Church*.   Published by S. Potter Co., Phila., 1820, press notices
appeared in the *Daily Advertiser*, Aug. 15, 1820.   Potter published a sacred
collection *Songs of Judah* a few days earlier than *The Chorister*, Aug. 10,
1820.

his constant "stringy squeak" in the choral parts of the service. Since this man was not a usual Moravian affliction, "the elder brethren compassionating his infirmity, rubbed their ears to mitigate the pain" [1] when he played. The use of other instruments, beyond the usual organ and occasional violin, was limited to festival days. They were used for voluntaries, and accompanied the singing on occasions selected for their assistance. Boys provided most of the singing in the Moravian choir. Some girls were admitted later (1808), but boys and girls were "kept apart by our guardian of peace and order," the organist.[2]

Hymnology constituted a real part in the Moravian service, the hymns and sermon being worked out on a common theme. The organist was also expected to suit this central idea in his opening and closing instrumental music. Evidently the Moravians practiced what Francis Hopkinson preached [3]—a unified emphasis in every service. Anthems were occasional rather than regular features in the Moravian Church's order of service.

Ritter served as organist at this church from 1811 to 1843.[4] He and his predecessors played without salary. A new organ was installed in 1823; the church had erected a new building in 1820. It was built by E. N. Scherr of Philadelphia. Its eleven stops comprised:

Pedal organ—16' diapason, 8' diapason.
Great organ—16' Bordun ("very heavy").
        8' Open diapason, 8' Stopped diapason,
        8' flute, 8' Principal, 8' Trumpet.
Swell organ—Stopped diapason, Flute,
        Dulciana and Principal, all of 8 foot, or normal, pitch.

This instrument cost $1200, plus the value of an older organ that had cost $400. The absence of four foot tone (i.e. stops which sound an octave above the note played) is noteworthy. Mr. Ritter

---

[1] Ritter, *History of the Moravian Church in Philadelphia*, p. 152.
[2] *Ibid.*, p. 154.
[3] In his *Letter on the Conduct of a Church Organ.*
[4] He lists, on p. 165, his predecessors—somewhat vaguely—as: George Peter and John Peter, jointly from 1785, Frederick, John, and Jacob Boller successively up to 1811.

declared that the whole organ, as well as the "bordun," sounded very heavy.[1] He had retired as the church's organist for over twelve years when the next organ was purchased, yet he assisted John C. B. Standbridge, its builder, in designing it.[2] This later organ was installed in 1856, the year that the Moravian congregation moved into their new building at Wood and Franklin Streets.[3] This Standbridge instrument had twenty-one stops and couplers, and nine hundred pipes.[4]

This same period of years (1800-1860) witnessed the installation of the first organ in the First Presbyterian Church in Philadelphia. It is interesting to note that Christ Church had been using its third organ for eleven years before the First Presbyterian congregation could bring themselves to use an organ in the church. They decided in 1846 to substitute the organ for the stringed instruments which had been used since before the Revolutionary War. Evidently this decision was considered to be a momentous one. Estimates were received from Philadelphia, New York, and Boston firms, the contract for the organ being awarded to the Messrs. Hook of Boston. They provided "three sets of keys and four organs" totaling 31 stops and 1502 pipes, for the sum of $4300, exclusive of building alteration in the church.[5] Mr. John Welsh was engaged as organist and director of music, and the *Parish Psalmody* was selected for use in the services in 1847. When we consider the

---

[1] *Op. cit.*, p. 168.

[2] The new organ at Christ Church had been installed while this same J. C. B. Standbridge was organist there in 1836. This organ, built by Henry Erben, of New York, was the third to be used in that historic building. There were 13 stops on the Great organ, 9 on the Swell, 7 on the Choir, and 3 on the Pedal; 1809 pipes in all, and three couplers. With but slight addition and improvement, the 1836 organ continued in use for one hundred years.

[3] The First Moravian Church is now located on Fairmount Avenue near Seventeenth Street (1940).

[4] Russell King Miller, one of Philadelphia's most distinguished organists until his death in 1939, studied on a J. C. B. Standbridge organ installed in 1852 at Calvary Presbyterian Church, 15th and Locust Streets. This organ had many more than the twenty-one stops recorded by Ritter for the Moravian organ, yet it was pumped by hand.

[5] The other estimates may prove of interest to some readers: Thomas Appleton of Boston, 34 stops, 1912 pipes $4000. Thomas Hall of New York, 26 stops, 1609 pipes $4500. Henry Erben of New York, 29 stops, 1907 pipes $4000. J. C. B. Standbridge, Philadelphia, 29 stops, 1756 pipes $5000. Henry Corrie of Philadelphia, 31 stops, 1860 pipes $4700.

antiquity of that church, the lateness of their use of an organ is surprising. The use of organs in Presbyterian churches in Scotland dates from the same period. The Moravian congregation installed their third new organ only a few years after 1847.

IX

It has been stated that the older theatrical music continued to exist for many years after the introduction of more serious operas. In fact, ballad opera had declined in popular favor for only a few years in leading theatres before it arose again in the form of light opera, and it has continued to flourish under various names—comic opera, operetta, musical comedy, revue—ever since. The early nineteenth century was a period of Philadelphia's earliest enthusiasm for grand opera; hence that form receives the main share of our discussion for this period.

Secular and sacred concerts were surprisingly similar in character during this period. In 1801 the first complete oratorio performance in Philadelphia illustrates this fusion of sacred and secular elements to perfection. Dr. Shaw, wishing to produce *the Messiah* in its entirety at the hall of the University of Pennsylvania, 4th Street below Arch, secured both his soloists and his chorus from the theatrical company in Philadelphia. John Darley, Darley Junior, Mrs. Oldmixon, and Miss Broadhurst, sang the solos at this early oratorio performance, which took place on April 9th.[1] Gillingham conducted the orchestra, Taylor played the organ, and Dr. Shaw led the singers.

In the concert field, both the sacred and secular had been well launched prior to 1800. The emphasis seems to have been on the serious, the "grand," in concert programs as well as in theatrical productions. A concert programmed as a *Grand Selection of Sacred Music* at St. Augustine's Church, June 20th, 1810, is an outstanding event of this typically ambitious nature. The program consisted of 37 vocal selections sung by a large chorus and accompanied by a "full band." Carr and Schetky directed the chorus while Gillingham led the band. Raynor Taylor assisted at the organ. Part one

---

[1] Scharf and Westcott, *op. cit.*, pp. 1077-1078.

consisted of 7 numbers from Haydn's *Creation*, 3 from Pergolesi's *Stabat Mater*, and 3 from Graun's *Te Deum*. Part two contained 15 selections from Handel's *Messiah*, and part three consisted of 9 numbers by Carr, Taylor, and Dr. Arnold. Tickets cost two dollars, and were sold by Matthew Carey and the C. A. Conrad company. The *Daily Advertiser* contained five notices of this *Grand Selection of Sacred Music*, four of them giving the program, and one containing suggestions for the regulation of traffic.[1]

Many ambitious though less noted sacred concerts were given in the years under discussion. At a program in 1820 the promoters declare that four Handel oratorios would be represented in a style not heard in the city for many years. Another in the same year contained 46 selections given in morning and evening sessions. Handel, Boyce, Haydn, and Pergolesi composed the music. Mrs. De Luce, Mr. Brennan, Mr. Sidebotham, 130 amateurs, and an orchestra of 20 were directed by Charles Hupfeld. This program was given on April 11th and 13th at Washington Hall. Notices including the lengthy program lists were given in the *Daily Advertiser*.

A brief digression to quote some early Philadelphia musical journalism might be of interest. The concert of April 11, 1820, was given the added encouragement of a 'card' in the *Daily Advertiser*, three days before its performance. An admirer writes of the participants:

> The principal vocal participants, De Luce, Brennan, and Side-botham, are of the highest rank in the country; the choristers are in full practice and numerous. The orchestra is well filled with the best talent in the state; all the parts . . . are calculated to produce the sublimest effect. . . . How heavenly it is to see one hundred and thirty ladies and gentlemen chanting their songs of praise and thanks-giving to that Omnipotent Being, who looks down upon us with parental tenderness and affection cannot but encite the most pleasing sensations. I conclude by wishing that their exertions may be crowned with success and induce them to go on in their labour of love.
>
> April 8, 1820. An Admirer.

---

[1] The last was mentioned above under the account of Benjamin Carr, p. 52, which also contains some discussion of the concert itself.

This press notice is rather publicity than music criticism. The same might be said of the following account of Victoire Boudet's playing the harp and singing. Miss Boudet was a pupil of H. Gilles, of the Paris Conservatoire, possibly the father of Philadelphia's P. Gilles. Miss Boudet appeared on several programs from 1815 to 1824, playing and singing works of her own composition as well as 'music by the greatest masters.' Labbe's Hall and Masonic Hall seem to have been the scenes of her concerts, with various Philadelphia artists assisting. While the *Daily Advertiser's* editorial seems to have been a somewhat reproachful message to an unappreciative public, their author had heard her on several occasions. His remarks are more than mere advertisement, for they contain real criticism of Victoria Boudet's previous performances.

> December 14, 1820: It affords us unfeigned pleasure that Miss Boudet is again willing to exhibit her uncommon talents to a Philadelphia audience. As a native of this country, and a female, she has a right to expect something more *in this city* than cold neglect. We venture to assert that were Miss Boudet's very superior talents of exotic origin she would not be under the chilling necessity of waisting her voice on a beggarly account of empty benches. It is a melancholy fact that we are too dubious of our indigenous talent; if a European audience awards the palm of merit to a performer he at once receives in the United States an introduction to the Temple of Fame, but if a native genius attempts to raise his head he is doomed to buffet with storms of adversity and neglect, until retribution approaches to smooth his passage to the tomb. That Miss Boudet may experience a speedier and more agreeable expression of the public liberality, we hope; because it will be an earnest of better feeling for native talent; and because filial affection will receive its due reward. Miss Boudet's unremitted efforts to render the declining years of her parents happy are of highest merit, and were she not able to afford the most ample satisfaction by her musical powers, might well plead her excuse before an enlightened audience. To a mellifluous voice of fullest compassion, she unites talents of chastest discipline. May she realize the munificent reward to which her amiable deportment justly entitles her.

Lewis's Lovely and Interesting Children far outshone Victoria Boudet in the matter of tender ages. *The Daily Advertiser* of November 9th, 1820, devotes nearly a half column to a glowing criticism of their musicianship and charm. The author, signing himself "Merit," recounts the excellences of Master J. Lewis aged ten, who played the pianoforte, violin, and pedal harp, while his younger brother played the violoncello. Two Miss Lewises, the younger but three years of age, "inspired the audience with pleasure amounting to a degree of rapture and enthusiasm." The four lovely children were pronounced "literally phenomena in musical execution, never before equalled, and exhibit a precocity of genius as well as an example of persevering industry . . ." Their concerts, for a week only, took place at Washington Hall.

Other examples of early music criticism have already been quoted in the accounts of the performances of the Musical Fund Society. Their hall at 8th and Locust Streets, Washington Hall at 3rd Street above Spruce, and the Philadelphia Museum, or Chinese Museum, at 9th and Sansom Streets,[1] seem to have been the favorite auditoriums for musical affairs. The Chestnut Street, and after 1820 the Walnut Street and the Arch Street Theatres were the leading theatrical edifices until the opening of the Academy of Music in 1857. Press notices containing considerable sincere criticism along with their usually enthusiastic tone, appear in the *Daily Advertiser* and *Aurora* for many musical functions at all of these old Philadelphia halls.

One 'card,' or editorial in the *Daily Advertiser*, contains criticism of music, though hardly exemplifying our local beginnings as music journalists.

SWEET HARMONY

June 28, 1820.

The neighbors in the vicinity of ————— and ————— Streets take this method to tender their thanks to the young gentleman, Dilletante Horn blower, for his strenuous obstrepero-harmonious and *well tuned* efforts to contribute to their pleasure and repose. As he is evidently a young beginner, they beg leave, with the utmost delicacy and deference, to suggest the advantage of his taking some *private* lessons before he again "comes out."

---

[1] Masonic Hall, Labbe's Hall, Mr. Auriol's room, Mr. Quesnet's room (the latter three were dancing academies), were also used for musical gatherings.

One of the good effects likely to result from [this] would be, to silence the clamour of those tasteless cavillers who "having no music in their souls" nor fear of the fashion before their eyes, express themselves on the occasion, with much impatience and indignation; and even dare to say, that they would rather have their rest disturbed by the sound of [a] Conch-shell.

It is however fondly anticipated, that by his attending to the above friendly hint, these very hypercritics will, in a few months, in spite of their teeth, be compelled to express their satisfaction and delight at having their peaceful slumber interrupted by him, at *one or two o'clock in the morning.*

Of course, articles on music frequently appeared in magazines of this period. The national song contest organized by the *Portfolio* in 1814 reflects the patriotic zeal aroused by the progress of the war of 1812. The *Portfolio*, a Philadelphia monthly magazine, offered fifty dollars to the writer of the best national song. An early example of failure to award the stipulated prize is provided by this competition. The best words, submitted by "'Henry C. Knight of Massachusetts" were considered worthy of insertion in the *Portfolio* of July, 1814,[1] as were the verses by Edwin C. Holland of Charleston, South Carolina,[2] and an anonymous set published in December, 1814. There were many patriotic songs in the *Daily Aurora* in the year 1815.

A much more elevated sample of a magazine's featuring music than the above possibly spurious song contest, is found in the writings of James Maxwell, editor of *The Literary Gazette*. The February 17, 1821, issue [3] of that magazine contains a striking article on music and art:

The strong analogy between these [music and painting] is very manifest. . . . Some German pieces of music which introduce a deep and growling base in order to set off a gay air, remind us of a picture by Rembrandt, where a small light peeping out of broad shadows of surrounding darkness, brings to view a little old woman spinning by a small window in a very large room.

---

[1] P. 118.
[2] September issue, p. 332.
[3] P. 112.

The tendency toward the huge or spectacular that existed in concert and theatrical music is illustrated in both sacred and secular programs. Close similarities in these musical fields are not surprising when we realize that the same performers gave Philadelphia its finest concerts in all kinds of music at this period.

The Havana opera company's performances of *Moses in Egypt* at both the Philadelphia Museum and the Musical Fund Hall in 1847 merely followed the example of the earlier Montressor troupe and the 1801 pioneer performance of the *Messiah*—sung by Wignell-Reinagle theatre musicians. Benjamin Cross and Benjamin Carr could still be church organists, noted orchestra leaders, composers and opera singers. The Musical Fund group decided to put on an opera, staging the American première of *The Magic Flute;* and according to the press, did it very well. The musical specialization that produces men like Leopold Stokowski, Rollo Maitland, and Joseph Hofmann, among modern Philadelphians, had not progressed very far prior to 1860.

X

Leopold Meignen was probably the most influential teacher of the years that close our early nineteenth century period. Thomas à Becket, who arranged the music to *Columbia the Gem of the Ocean,*[1] taught his son, and presumably many others, in the years immediately preceding the Civil War. Charles W. Jarvis was an English pianist and teacher who came to Philadelphia c.1835 and was active in the same years as were Meignen and à Becket. For many years he managed high grade concerts in Philadelphia. His son's even more famous series of concerts and recitals were outstanding in the late ninetenth century. Jarvis senior published the opera *Luli, or The Switzer's Bride* in 1846. *Deign O Heavens,* a recitative from this opera, shows interesting use of a minor ninth chord.[2] Jarvis published a successful instruction book in 1852. If the teaching of à Becket and Jarvis are to be estimated by the talent and influence of Thomas à Becket Jr. and Charles Jarvis Jr., these earlier pedagogues must have been experts in their musical

---

[1] Cf. Index.
[2] Upton, *Art Song in America,* p. 36.

field. Professor Leopold Meignen, however, was very probably the teacher and guide of a larger number of talented music students than any other man of the day. His pupils included William H. Fry, Michael Cross, Charles H. Jarvis, and Septimus Winner. The period of his greatest musical influence in Philadelphia was from 1830 to 1860. Dr. Meignen was a graduate of the Paris Conservatoire. The productions of *Leonora* in 1845 were under the direction of Leopold Meignen. His varied musical activities included regular conducting of the Musical Fund orchestra from about 1846 to 1857. He has already been mentioned, in the account of that organization, as having introduced both the Beethoven Second and Third Symphonies to Philadelphia audiences in 1846 and 1847. The Handel and Haydn Society engaged him as their conductor during the 1850's. Meignen composed a great deal of music, notably the *Grand Military Symphony*, which was produced at a Musical Fund concert in April 1845, and an oratorio, *The Deluge*. L. C. Madeira characterizes the former as naive in his account of the Musical Fund Society.[1] The works of his better known pupil William Fry often earn the same doubtful praise. Meignen outlived Fry by nine years.[2] In both chronological and artistic classifications they were true contemporaries, much more so than one would suppose from their original relation of teacher and pupil. Both men lived in Paris for many years, and appear to have acquired an Italian manner of composition colored by French influences of the early nineteenth century. Meignen was much more the professional musician than Fry, who was primarily a journalist. His publishing business was considerable, the firm of Fiot-Meignen being active from 1834 to 1855. The influence of his leadership and long years as a teacher of Philadelphia's most gifted music students make Dr. Leopold Meignen an important figure in the middle of the last century. From the little that existing records can tell us, Meignen remains a shadowy figure for one who taught so many noted musicians. His reputation for profound musical knowledge, while based on recollection and legend more than preserved evidence, made an indelible impression on the best musical minds of Philadelphia over a considerable period of years.

---

[1] Madeira, *op. cit.*, p. 145.
[2] Leopold Meignen was born in 1793, and died at Philadelphia in 1873.

XI

The advances in instrumental music by the members of the Musical Fund Society have been discussed rather fully under the account of that organization. It is a long way from the chamber orchestras that offered concert series to city subscribers to the large American orchestra assembled by Theodore Thomas in 1861. This distance was bridged in the years under discussion, and it should be reiterated that the Philadelphia organization having the largest share in this development was the orchestra of the Musical Fund Society. There were many concerts given by that orchestra in which over a hundred men participated. The Philharmonic Society Orchestra extended its influence in this great advance over many years in the same period.

In addition to the above two groups, there were other orchestras composed both of local members and visiting players that exerted a powerful influence in raising the standard of orchestral performance. The Steiermärkisches Orchestra was the first noted visiting orchestra to play a series of concerts in Philadelphia. They appeared before the Philharmonic Society on January 26th, 1848. Henry Riha conducted this orchestra. Greater fame was earned by the Germania Orchestra, under the leadership of Carl Lenschow. Both of these organizations made Philadelphia a stopping place on their extended tours of eastern cities in this country. The length of such visits was conditioned by the warmth of their reception and the financial success in each city. It is sad to have to record that both of these companies stayed a very short time in Philadelphia; in fact, the Germania Orchestra disbanded after their lack of success in this city in 1848. They were reorganized under the leadership of Carl Bergmann during the same year, however. Their influence in Philadelphia was deeper than the apparent failures indicated; for a Philadelphia instrumental group instituted in 1856 revived the name Germania Orchestra and played with considerable artistic and financial success for forty years after that date. The conductors of that Philadelphia Germania Orchestra were Carl Sentz, Charles Schmitz, and William Stoll, Jr. While the work of these men and of the orchestra they conducted lies mainly in the late nineteenth century, we should note that the beginning of this highly important instrumental organization was an event of the period under discussion.

Anton Philip Heinrich (Bohemia, 1781-1861 New York), settled in Philadelphia at about 1817. Heinrich was a colorful if somewhat legendary figure in Philadelphia and elsewhere in Europe and America from 1805 to about 1835, when he settled in New York. Sharf and Westcott's history states that he was a Bohemian, a former man of wealth,[1] who came to Philadelphia in 1805, later wandering over the country. The same history declares that Heinrich was the composer of over a hundred works, oratorios, symphonies, overtures, and songs, many of them very original.[1] He conducted the orchestra at the Southwark Theatre for at least a year after 1817.[2] A few years later Heinrich composed an "American National dramatic divertissement," entitled *The Treaty of William Penn with the Indians, Concerto Grosso.* This work, dedicated to the Musical Fund Society, must have been very grand, although for some reason the word *grand* does not appear in its title. A. P. Heinrich has been noted above as a violinist in the orchestra of the first concert given by the Musical Fund Society.

A later visiting conductor, Louis A. Jullien, brought his own orchestra for several concerts in 1853 and 1854. November 15, 1853 was advertised as Beethoven night, December 2nd, as Grand Mozart night. Jullien's orchestra engaged first rank soloists, among them Bottesini on the bass viol; in fact their concerts in Philadelphia seem to have been of a better and more restrained order than most of their programs in American cities. The famous *Fire Engine Quadrille* was played by this orchestra, but is in no way the finest work they did, or even typical of their Philadelphia concerts. This Quadrille represented the gradual approach of the fire engine company. When it has—musically—arrived near the hall, bells were rung and the firemen rushed down the aisles, in full uniform and armed with hoses. Jullien was certainly erratic; yet he was an important figure in raising orchestral standards in this country in the 1850's.

---

[1] Cf. Scharf and Westcott, *History of Philadelphia,* p. 1079.

[2] Julian's *Dictionary of Hymnology* states, in the article on W. B. Tappan, that Anton Heinrich of Philadelphia set *There is an hour of peaceful rest* to music in 1819.

The *Express Train Galop* might be considered an insult to the
musical maturity of our 1858 audiences, yet Musard insulted Paris-
ian audiences with the same and similar orchestral music in those
years. Musard's orchestra played several concerts at the Academy
of Music in Philadelphia. His *Cattle Show* and *Express Train
Galop* were featured in the five programs by Musard's orchestra in
May and June of 1858. The train-noises machine was advertised
as an importation from Paris for the concert of May 31st. This
machine had been completely reconstructed to "follow local truth in
locomotive effects." Messrs. Legendre and Moreau were noted
French soloists on the newly adopted cornet-à-pistons and ophicleide
respectively, who appeared as soloists with this organization.
Musard's programs were a strange combination of childish descriptive works and standard symphonic music.[1] We must not forget
the raising of standards by both Jullien and Musard in our amaze-
ment at their spectacular devices. Theodore Thomas was assistant
conductor to Musard; Carl Formes, Caroline Richings, and other
noted performers were regular soloists with this orchestra. The
performances showed the Philadelphia audiences what a large professional orchestra could do with the standard orchestral literature.
They paved the way for the Theodore Thomas orchestra founded
a few years later than the Musard appearances in Philadelphia. It
is interesting to note that Thomas himself shared in the conducting
of Musard's concerts so near the close of our 1800-1860 period.
The Father of American Symphonic Music, Theodore Thomas, was
only twenty-two years old at these early concerts in Philadelphia's
new Academy of Music. His great work, in Philadelphia and elsewhere, lies in the next period, that of the late nineteenth century.

If we balance our backward look into the eighteenth century
—with which this lengthy chapter began—by a glance ahead as we
leave the 1800-1860 period, we shall find that much of the development of the later years is begun or prophesied by concluding events
in this earlier time. The Germania Orchestra, the Academy of

---

[1] The first Musard concert in Philadelphia included: Overture to William Tell, Rossini; Aria, Ray of Hope, Bishop (Clarionet obbligato) ; Celes-
tine Polka; Irish Ballad (Kate Kearney) ; Cuckoo Polka, Herzog; Scotch
Fantasia, Cooper; Grand Descriptive Galop (The Express Train), Musard;
Grand Battle Scene (Les Zouaves), Musard. This last composition featured
the firing of heavy artillery.

Music, the Musical Fund Society, the Männerchöre, are but a few of the institutions that began in the early period and continued their activities well into the years after 1860. The spread of the city districts from the few squares by the Delaware to the banks of the Schuylkill River, and the official extension of the city boundaries to their present limits were civic developments well within the 1800-1860 period. Fine church music in many sections of the city, and public school music in quantity resulted from the spread and growth of Philadelphia's population in those years.[1] As previously mentioned, the persons active in the early nineteenth century were often the parents or teachers, or both, of later musicians who dominated the following period.[2] Many of these descendants and pupils are still important in Music in Philadelphia in 1940.

---

[1] The population of Philadelphia was 28,522 in 1800, and 563,529 in 1860.
[2] Cf. *supra*, p. 80 for a list of the more important among them.

CHAPTER FOUR

MUSIC OF THE LATE NINETEENTH CENTURY

I

Two very different men were active in Philadelphia music during the years after the Civil War. That Septimus Winner and David Wood had little in common as musicians in spite of their chronological identity, the following biographical sketches will make plain.

David Duffle Wood was born in Pittsburgh in 1838. He became totally blind at the age of two, and entered the Pennsylvania Institution for the Instruction of the Blind in Philadelphia as a child of five. The journey of five days and five nights was made by David Wood at the age of five. He made the journey by stage, canal, and train, and made it alone. As a young student at the School for the Blind, Wood learned to play violin, flute, and piano without any formal instruction. His organ instruction consisted of only six months' lessons with Wilhelm Schnabel, principal instructor at the school. Schnabel's pupil of one-half year became Philadelphia's greatest organist in the mid-nineteenth century, excelling in the interpretation of the works of Bach, many of which he played for the first time in Philadelphia. For about thirty years Dr. Wood played four services each Sunday, all of elaborate musical form, and all, of course, from memory. Statements like that concerning Wood's journey to Philadelphia, or the mastery of Bach almost without organ instruction, or even the extended period of memorized Sunday services, challenge belief. Yet plentiful evidence of their truth is to be found in Philadelphia today. His many pupils reverence his abilities with a well-nigh superstitious awe. Of thousands who heard him play, there are hundreds still living who are eager to testify to the outstanding quality of his muscianship. The late J. Fred. Wolle who made the Bethlehem Festivals in Pennsylvania internationally famous, was a pupil and friend of

Wood. He attributes his knowledge and love of Bach to Dr. Wood's teaching.[1]

David Wood's activities were nearly as incredible as his musicianship, if we bear in mind the handicap of blindness. He became organist at St. Stephen's Church in 1864, and choirmaster there in 1870. Dr. Wood's service at St. Stephen's lasted exactly forty-six years, for he began on Easter Day, and died a few hours after the Easter services of 1910. The Baptist Temple secured him as their organist and director in 1884, which position he filled until 1909, less than a year before his death. Wood played only the evening service at the Temple. He was, concurrently, director of music at the School for the Blind, for twenty-three years, 1887 to 1910. He had taught at that institution since 1853. The total service there was thus of fifty-seven years duration, that at St. Stephen's forty-six years, and twenty-five years at the Baptist Temple. David Wood taught organ at the Philadelphia Musical Academy for thirty years, and had a number of private pupils. A reader who knows the locations of these institutions in Philadelphia will wonder how a blind man got to all of them several times each week, while any one who remembers the city before there were any automobiles, or electric trolleys, must again say 'Incredible' at this point!

The outstanding achievement of David Wood's work at the School for the Blind was a series of oratorios produced at Musical Fund Hall with accompaniment by members of the Philadelphia Orchestra. Beginning in 1904 with Mendelssohn's *Hymn of Praise*,

---

[1] Philip Goepp's account of Dr. Wood quotes Wolle's letter to his former teacher, written immediately after the first Bach festival at Bethlehem: "Mar. 29, 1900, . . . Your kind letter touches me too deeply for expression. Coming from you who embody Bach's spirit, and have Beethoven's head, the letter is the greatest treasure I possess. . . . It was your masterful inspiration which led me to the study of Bach. Very affectionately, Fred." In Wolle's letter to Mrs. Wood after David Wood's death, he declares: "If I have accomplished anything, or if I ever do anything worth while, may it reflect all the glory back to my dear old friend and teacher." Since this letter was written in 1910, Fred Wolle had surely 'done something worth while,' and was destined to do even more in the Bethlehem festivals organized and directed by him from 1900 to 1932.

A later pupil, scarcely less distinguished, Rollo F. Maitland, has been Philadelphia's leading authority on Bach organ music and the city's most noted interpreter of that supreme musical literature since the death of Dr. Wood in 1910. The late Philip Goepp was a third famous pupil of David Wood.

these oratorio concerts were annual affairs. *The Seasons, The Creation, Samson, Judas Maccabaeus, Acis and Galatea,* and *My Spirit was in Heaviness,* were all sung. The precision of the blind chorus's attack and release amazed leading musicians of the day, Fritz Scheel among them, since they realized the importance of the baton, especially in the performance of memorized music.

Space forbids the listing of oratorios and cantatas produced at the Baptist Temple and at St. Stephen's church. An all-Bach program for Wood's recital at the Church of the New Jerusalem on May 8th, 1894, was preserved by Dr. Rollo Maitland, the present organist at that church.[1] Wood played the following numbers:

> Passacaglia and Fugue in C minor.
> Chorale Prelude, "Schmücke dich, O liebe Seele."
> Prelude and Fugue in E flat.
> Recitative,[2] (He will not speak) and Aria[2] (Behold how still, how calm) from the St. Matthew *Passion.*
>
> Pastorale (four movements).
> Toccata and Fugue in D minor.
> Chorale Prelude, "Herzlich thut mich verlangen."

David Wood was known for his authoritative playing; his clarity, unusual for the period; and his gifted contrapuntal improvisation. The character of the man impressed all he met. He was a religious musician. There is something deeply touching in the well known anthem by this blind organist: "There shall be no night there and they need no lamp nor light of the sun, for the Lord God shall give them light." His religion was a firm and dignified influence however, as we should expect of the organist at two of Philadelphia's leading churches, and as befitted a man who had made such a large part of himself out of the great thoughts of Haydn, Mozart, Beethoven, and above all, J. S. Bach.

Very nearly the same years are covered by the Philadelphia activities of Septimus Winner. Winner may well be contrasted

---

[1] 1894 is very early for an all-Bach organ recital in Philadelphia. Wood's pupil, Fred. Wolle, is known to have given such a recital in 1893 at the Chicago World's Fair.

[2] Sung by Mme. Emma Suelke, soprano soloist at St. Stephen's at that time.

with David Wood, and with the older colleague of both, William H. Fry.

Septimus Winner is in many ways Fry's exact musical opposite. William Fry aimed at greatness, in fact he was a great personality. Septimus Winner was of a much humbler cast, both in his nature and in his musical activities. As fiddler in dance groups, and the proprietor of a music printing establishment and store, Winner exemplifies the successful professional musician of an intensely practical order. His compositions and books on music were unpretentious, but very well executed and highly successful. It is typical of the two men that Fry is best remembered for his 'first American grand opera' *Leonora*, and Winner for the simple ballad *Listen to the Mocking Bird*.

Septimus Winner was born in Philadelphia, May 11, 1827. He came of old Pennsylvania stock, and of a gifted musical family as well. His father, Joseph E. Winner, was an expert instrument maker, particularly apt in violin craftsmanship. His artistic nature sometimes got the better of him, particularly when under the influence of alcoholic stimulants. The story of his literal interpretation of the command of an officer in the Civil War, who told him to whitewash his entire room, is too good to be omitted here. Joseph Winner proceeded to whitewash all walls, then the bed, the stove, and other furniture. He finished by whitewashing the officer's boots. This humor grew out of a natural affability which Septimus seems to have inherited. His diary [1] is full of humorous touches, and the poetry of a far seeing practical man. The name *Septimus* suggests a humorous regard for the seventh child of Joseph Winner, while Septimus' older brother *Sivori* reflects the violinistic leanings of their father.

Winner graduated from the Philadelphia Central High School. Very early in life he became identified with Music in Philadelphia. His diary mentions his frequent participation in the Musical Fund Society rehearsals, the Philadelphia Brass Band functions, the Cecillian [*sic*] Musical Society meetings and the various balls and lodge programs at which he played his various assortment of musical instruments.

---

[1] Quoted in *The Mocking Bird* by C. E. Claghorn (Philadelphia, 1937).

From 1850 we find Septimus Winner more devoted to composition and less to teaching and performing. His first publication of music, *Village Polkas,* dates from 1850. His study of composition under Leopold Meignen at about 1853 shows his sincere interest in that field.

Listen to the Mocking Bird was written in 1854. The melody was credited to Dick Milburn, a colored street musician who whistled it as he played the guitar. Septimus Winner adapted and arranged Milburn's melody, and gave the ex-beggar a job in his store.[1] Soon after copyrighting *The Mocking Bird,* Winner sold the rights to Lee and Walker for five dollars. The story ran true to type—the publisher made a fortune out of it.[2] However, the fame of Alice Hawthorne, Winner's pseudonym, helped the humble composer to become a prosperous musician and publisher very quickly. Less desirable was the notoriety Winner received as the author and composer of the Civil War song, *Give Us Back Our Old Commander.* This song reflected popular sentiment in favor of the restoration to command of General George B. McClellan. The War Department and President Lincoln did not favor 'Little Mac, the People's Pride,' and considered this Winner song high treason! Septimus Winner was promptly arrested, and only released when he protested innocence of treasonable motives and promised to destroy all remaining copies of the song. Eighty thousand copies had been sold within a few days after its issue. This song was later revived when General Grant was running for a third term as President of the United States in 1880, the old commander obviously being Ulysses S. Grant in those years.

Two other songs should be mentioned among the more than two thousand published works by Septimus Winner. *Whispering Hope* is his most loftily aimed effort, while the *Deutcher's Dog* is one of his humblest. We are apt to recall that Alice Hawthorne (Septimus Winner) was responsible for the harmonization of such insistent thirds and sixths under the melody of *Whispering Hope—*

---

[1] A copy of the first edition kindly furnished by Mr. Joseph L. Armstrong ascribes the melody to Milburn, and its arrangement to Alice Hawthorne (Septimus Winner.)

[2] *The Philadelphia Press* declared that twenty million copies of this song had been sold between 1855 and 1905, nearly fifteen million in the United States.

which melody, however, suggests such a sugary alto all too inevitably. How many of us realize that the same 'Sep. Winner' wrote the words for *O Where O where ish my little dog gone?*[1]

Winner's *Eureka Methods* were the most popular of his books on learning to play musical instruments. He wrote over two hundred instruction books, for more than twenty-three instruments. There are also about two thousand arrangements for piano and violin. The sheer size of this composing, arranging, and publishing business was remarkable even in the period when all of Philadelphia, and all of the United States, found large numbers and mammoth sizes quite the order of the day. Winner's years of professional music activity were 1850 to 1902.

The diary of Septimus Winner, for November 22, 1902, closes with this locally interesting entry: "A fine beautiful day, a nice parade with President Roosevelt to open the new High School, at Broad and Green."[2] Mr. Winner died that same afternoon. "In his poems he will live long after more ambitious celebrities have ceased to be remembered" is the opinion of Alexander J. Drexel Biddle.[3] *The Philadelphia Inquirer* shortly after Winner's death made the penetrating observation, "He deserves more of his countrymen than he is ever apt to receive." This has been true, possibly because of a definite lack of maturity in the musical style and in the sentiment of the text of his many works. Instead of ridiculing the naïveté in much of the music by Winner, we should recollect that as a writer of popular songs he could succeed only through reflecting and reproducing the adolescent quality of the period in which his music was written.

It is extremely unlikely that Septimus Winner and David Wood were acquainted with each other. Wood's great preoccupation with serious things, and his social handicap of blindness prevented his knowledge of a sufficiently inclusive circle of musical friends for his humbler colleague to be among them. Winner, on the other hand, was equally busy in Philadelphia music, but his

---

[1] Winner arranged the German folk song *Im Lauterbach hab'ich mein' Strumpf verlorn* to the *Deutcher's Dog* words. His simple words are so wedded to this German tune that many may express surprise that they are not a translation of a German text.

[2] Claghorn, *op. cit.,* p. 57.

[3] Quoted in Claghorn, *op. cit.,* p. 60.

interests lay in far different fields from those of the retiring organist and great teacher, David Wood. That it was possible for the two professional musicians to be active and prominent for the same fifty years and not to know each other, possibly not to be informed about each other's musical work, testifies to a great growth in Music in Philadelphia. At the beginning of the period of the last chapter, 1800, these two fields would not have been covered by two unacquainted persons. The probability is that there would not have been two men at all, but one man active in the sacred, the secular, and the commercial phases. The increase in the size of the city and in the amount of its music was definitely causing specialization among musicians in the years after 1860. No two men illustrate this divergence of musical interests earlier and better than Winner and Wood.

II

The Academy of Music is an institution that has been important in Philadelphia since before the Civil War. While it has in no way lost its importance down to the present year, 1940, its rise to prominence occurred in the 1860 to 1900 period. Although its remarkable planning and construction will be seen to have been completed before 1860, and its latter end far in the future, an account of its musical events must be included in any discussion of late nineteenth century Music in Philadelphia. The following story of the Academy of Music includes references to most of its years as the city's leading music hall, many allusions being made to periods beyond the avowed temporal limits of this chapter.

There can be no doubt that among Philadelphia buildings, the Academy of Music stands first historically and artistically in any account of music in that city. The Musical Fund Hall is its closest rival for historical primacy. For a long course of musically notable performances, the Academy of Music has no competitors in Philadelphia, probably none in America. A detailed discussion of its history, while other Philadelphia buildings are dismissed with but a brief mention, is no more than a true reflection of the outstanding importance that this old theatre has achieved in Philadelphia's musical life. Seldom can such agreement among performers, producers, and auditors be discovered on any musical question as exists in their unanimous opinion concerning the varied excellences of this building. Its location, architecture, capacity, furnishings, decorations, and especially its acoustics, have never ceased to be marvelous to persons interested in those various fields. Even the dispatch with which audiences can get out of the building is dwelt upon as a remarkable feature. Early programs [1] contain glowing accounts of safety devices and air cooling machines,[2] declared to be the finest in existence—and certainly among the earliest of their kind. Americans are said to love superlatives: it is not surprising that so many are lavished upon the "Old Academy." Among the interesting superlatives are those which deal with the Academy Bat. Records are scarce, but recollections are plentiful, concerning this greatest of theatrical bats. No bat ever caused so much distraction at so many operas, concerts, and lectures, nor annoyed so many performers, nor caused so many jewelled ladies to sparkle with fright. Its powers of eluding hundreds of pursuers for such an extended period of time were declared to be phenomenal. Entire seasons elapsed without the bat's contribution to the Academy spectacle, but the identical creature is said and sworn to have reappeared after more than a year's hibernation.[3] This greatest bat on earth spread its activity over the years 1857 to the present.

Leaving the superlatives, it may be interesting though not equally amusing to consider the facts of the history of the Academy

---

[1] Of the 1860's.

[2] The summer programs of 1859 state that "The house will be kept perfectly cool by an immense REVOLVING Fan in the Cellar, worked by a steam engine of 10-horse power, which is placed outside the building."

[3] The late Howard E. Keiser, manager of the Academy of Music, stated with both reason and knowledge that 'the bat' has been several bats. Each has paid its series of visits, heard its fill of music, and departed. Some have been captured for a price by Academy employees, at least the supposition has always been that the bat slain was the bat wanted, but subsequent appearances have caused question to be raised as to certainty of this. Edward Bok is known to have paid the assistant electrician, John Flynn, $50.00 bat blood money in 1932. The Evening Bulletin of February 18, 1933, related that another Academy bat was killed. "Their repeated appearances after long periods of absence suggests that they are not one bat, as many ladies have insisted, or even one family; but any bat who wishes an evening of excitement or culture."

of Music. Shortly after 1850, Philadelphia had outgrown Musical
Fund Hall. City traffic and noise were approaching uncomfortably
close to 8th and Locust Streets—although in 1820 this Musical
Fund Hall location had been far west of the civic center. Fifth
Street was becoming quite a main artery, and traffic west of Washington Square was growing heavier and noisier. The fine residen-
tial section near Broad and Locust Streets was thought to be an
ideal quiet spot for a new and larger temple of music. The lot on
the southwest corner of Broad and Locust Streets—the "far side of
Broad Street"—was accordingly purchased for $88,360 in 1854
(June 3rd). The building was begun in 1855 (July 26) and
finished in 1856. Its construction was actually very rapid—the
length of the period being caused by the fact that it was allowed to
stand for a year without its roof.[1] The heat and cold, and various
other atmospheric conditions caused the walls to settle so completely that no cracks have appeared in the almost one hundred
years of the building's existence.[2] The architects, Napoleon Le
Brun and Gustavus Runge, were responsible for this excellence and
for the acoustical research that have made the building celebrated
down to the present day. The first board of directors,[3] elected
June 2nd, 1856, raised $225,000 which paid for the ground, and
for most of the construction of the building. This low cost is surprising unless the reader recalls the startlingly inexpensive cost of
the ground and building of the Musical Fund Hall thirty-five years
earlier.[4]

A gala opening performance, February 25, 1857, featured the

---

[1] Most of the historical data are from a booklet, "The Story of the
Academy," published by the corporation of the Academy of Music in 1920.
Charles W. Duke, of the *Philadelphia Ledger,* assembled the facts for that
work.

[2] Two subways have been dug, one on Broad Street, the other on Locust
Street, since 1925. The record of the Academy walls is the more remarkable
in the light of their old type of construction and the surface and underground
traffic that has surrounded them.

[3] John B. Budd, President　　　　John P. Steiner
　　George S. Pepper　　　　　　　James C. Hand
　　Fred Graff　　　　　　　　　　Charles H. Fisher
　　Samuel Branson　　　　　　　　Isaac S. Waterman
　　Lyon J. Levy　　　　　　　　　James Traquair
　　F. J. Dreer　　　　　　　　　　Fairman Rogers
[4] $23,500 in 1820.

opera *Il Trovatore* sung by distinguished soloists. The theatre achieved national fame in a night. *Lucrezia Borgia, Traviata, Ernani, Barber of Seville, I Puritani, Linda,* and *Luisa Miller*,[1] were produced during the balance of the season, February to April, 1857. In June of the same year a German company gave twelve performances of opera. *Freischütz, Fidelio,* and *Martha* were among their offerings. Theodore Thomas led the orchestra, probably from the first violin desk.

Nightly promenade concerts by the Germania Orchestra and assisting soloists were given from July 1 to September 1 in 1857. Ambitious productions of *Faust,* managed by Maretzek and danced by the Ronzani troupe, were given daily from September 16 to October 3. The opera season began on October 5. Surely the Academy was used and appreciated from its first days.

The operatic performances starring Adelina Patti in 1860, were noted for the unusual enthusiasm of the audiences; while the Prince of Wales Box in the theatre commemorates the presence of Edward VII at what was called the most brilliant performance in America.

To bring together some of the outstanding names of musicians and others who have appeared on the stage of the Academy of Music would be tantamount to listing the noted musicians and orators of the past hundred years. Ole Bull, Anton Rubinstein, von Bülow, Moreau, Legendre, Vieuxtemps, and Mahler were among the nineteenth century instrumental soloists to play there. Most of the opera singers of the day have acted there. Dramatic occasions, and political meetings at the Academy of Music do not concern us here; but it may be interesting to note that every President of the United States since 1856, Dom Pedro, Emperor of Brazil, Clay, Webster, Garrison, Beecher, Ingersoll, and Blaine, are among the distinguished speakers of the past who have been heard from the Academy stage. Tschaikowsky and Strauss have conducted their symphonic works there; Victor Herbert played his own 'cello concerto there also. Since 1900 the list of soloists and com-

---

[1] *Luisa Miller,* according to programs of March, 1857, was an opera by Verdi written especially for Mme. Gazzaniga. It was given ten times in a few weeks' time by the Maretzek Opera Troupe in the Philadelphia Academy of Music's first opera season.

posers to be heard, containing as it does most of the musically famous of the world, could hardly be condensed into this short account.

American premières have been numerous at the American Academy of Music in Philadelphia. Prior to 1900 these first performances consisted mainly of operatic productions. *La Traviata, Aida, Hamlet, Faust,* and *Lohengrin* were among acknowledged masterpieces in a long list of such American premières. Since the founding of the Philadelphia Orchestra there have been many first performances in America and many world premières of symphonic works from the Academy stage.[1]

The actual events of musical importance from 1857 to 1939 are covered under various headings elsewhere in this book. It has been already stated that the Academy of Music has housed a large share of the city's musical productions during that entire period of years. Today (1940) its main hall or its smaller auditorium, the foyer, form the background for nearly all of Philadelphia's finest music.

The main hall has been in very constant use, although the success and brilliance has varied according to local economic conditions. Thus 1928, one of the most extravagant years in our country's history, saw a large number of opera performances at the Academy of Music. The Metropolitan Opera Company of New York staged its usual weekly productions, the Philadelphia Civic Opera Company put on sixteen operas; The Philadelphia Grand Opera Company, ten; the Pennsylvania Grand Opera Company, ten; and the Philadelphia Operatic Society, three. In 1930 Cyrus H. K. Curtis was announced to have donated a large site at Nineteenth and Race Streets for the erection of a new Music Hall. *The Inquirer* of June 20, 1930, featured a picture of this future building, with the statement that it would be used for opera, orchestra, recitals and the Philadelphia Forum—in other words the same performances as those currently held at the Academy of Music. This same question was revived as recently as 1937.[2] The lovers of the old building may thank Napoleon Le Brun for the acoustical excellence of the Academy of Music, and for its continued use as a result.

---

[1] They are listed at the end of the chapter on the Philadelphia Orchestra, cf. *infra* pp. 190-194.
[2] Cf. *The Inquirer* for February 14, 1937.

Appended lists show the musical occasions for which the Academy of Music was used in its first two years, 1857-1858, and in one recent year, 1937.[1]

1857:—

> January 20, Inaugural concert and ball. Doors open at "7½", music at 8½, dancing at 10.
>
> February 25, *Il Trovatore,* Maretzek Company.
>
> February 25-May 25, Season of Italian Operas, including the debut of Adelaide Phillips as Rosina in *Barber of Seville,* and ten performances of *"Louisa Miller"* with Mme. Gazzaniga.
>
> June 15, Musical Jubilee of the Middle States, followed by a Pic Nic at Lemon Hill.
>
> June 8-27, Season of German opera.
>
> July 1-September 1, Nightly promenade concerts by Germania Orchestra.
>
> September 16-October 3, Fifteen performances of Ballet, mainly *Faust.* Maretzek agent, Ronzani dancers.
>
> October 5-24, Twelve Italian Opera performances, Maretzek Company.

1858:

> January 22-February 6, Opera series conducted by Carl Anschutz. "Leader Theodore Thomas."
>
> March 16-May 17, Thirty opera performances by Maretzek Company, sixteen works in repertoire.
>
> May 20-30, Operatic fragments, included request selections sung by Gazzaniga, and Caroline Richings' greatly admired singing of *The Mocking Bird.*
>
> May 31-June 11, Five concerts by Musard's Orchestra, assisted by Formes, Pickaneser, and Richings, soloists.
>
> June 26-July 10, Twelve promenade Concerts by Germania Orchestra. The Junger Maennerchor sang on the programs of July 8, 9.
>
> November 1-30, Strakosch Opera Company.

1937:—

> January 2-December 18, Philadelphia Orchestra, about 100 concerts.
>
> January 11, Trudi Schoop Ballet, music by Paul Schoop.
>
> January 18, José Iturbi.

---

[1] These old programs, as well as those more recently filed, were made available through the kindness of the late Howard E. Keiser, while he was manager of the Academy of Music.

January 22, Moritz Rosenthal.

January 5, Metropolitan Opera Co., *Samson and Delilah.*

January 8, Princeton Triangle Club, Operetta.

February 2, Elizabeth Hipple, pianist (Foyer).

February 2, Civic Opera Co., *Aida.*

February 4, Milstein, violinist.

February 12, Philadelphia Ballet, American premiere of *The Sleeping Beauty* (Tschaikowsky).

February 15, Shan-Kar, Hindu Ballet.

February 16, Metropolitan Company, *Lakmé.*

February 17, Orpheus Club Concert.

February 26, Samaroff-Tureck lecture recital.

March 1, Sidor Belarski, bass (Foyer).

March 3, Philadelphia Award, Three orchestra numbers by Philadelphia Orchestra.

March 9, Metropolitan Opera Company, *La Bohème.*

March 11, Nelson Eddy.

March 12, Jubilee Concert of Freiheit Gesang Verein, with orchestra from the Philadelphia Music Center.

March 17, Civic Opera Company, *Mme. Butterfly.*

March 31, Boston Symphony Orchestra.

April 1, Curtis Opera Company *Le Pauvre Matelot,* American première, and *Amelia al Ballo.*

April 5, Samaroff-Anderson, Lecture Recital.

April 6, Civic Opera Company *Tristan and Isolde.*

April 9, University of Pittsburgh Glee Club Concert.

April 12, Franz Philipp Opera Company, *Traviata.*

April 13, Louis Kazze, Sylvia Noble. Two-piano recital (Foyer).

April 15, Curtis Symphony Orchestra.

April 18, Magic Key Radio Broadcast concert.

April 20, Civic Opera Company *Tosca.*

April 22, Helene Diedrichs, piano recital (Foyer).

April 23, 24, Schoop Ballet.

April 27, Catholic Girls' Spring Music Festival.

April 28, Orpheus Club.

May 1, Fortnightly Club Concert.

May 8, Marian Anderson, recital.

May 10, Jubilee of Children's Schools (I.W.O.) with Children's chorus and orchestra.

May 12, Celebration of the Coronation of George VI, with orchestra, anthems, pageants, etc.

May 13, University Glee Club of Philadelphia, concert (Foyer).

May 14, 15, Savoy Company; *Iolanthe.*

June 1, Pennsylvania College of Optometry Commencement (4 orchestral numbers).

June 4, Jefferson Medical College Commencement (musical preludes of one-half hour).

June 22, West Philadelphia High School Commencement (Orchestral and choral music).

June, Musical Art Studios Annual Recital.

September 16, Police and Firemen's Band of Philadelphia, in celebration of Constitution Anniversary.

October 11, Jooss Ballet (two-piano accompaniment).

October 14, Flagstad recital.

October 15, Hammond Organ and Westminster Choir, in Centennial of Foreign Mission Board of Presbyterian Church.

October 23, Kreisler recital.

October 26, Robert Elmore, piano recital (in Foyer).

November 3, Rudolph Serkin, pianist.

November 8, Jooss Ballet.

November 15, Salzburg Opera Guild, *Cosi fan tutti.*

November 20, Rachmaninoff recital.

November 22, Jessica Dragonette, benefit recital.

November 23, Civic Opera Company, *Carmen.*

November 29, Italian play, with three orchestral numbers as prelude.

November 30, Metropolitan Opera Company, *Norma.*

December 1, Richard Crooks recital.

December 6, Civic Opera Company, *Mme. Butterfly.*

December 8, Orpheus Club.

December 10, 11, Shan-Kar Hindu Ballet.

December 14, Metropolitan Opera Company, *La Traviata.*

December 16, Menuhin recital.

December 17, 18, 22, Catharine Littlefield Ballet with Philadelphia Orchestra. Music by Bach, J. Strauss, Ravel (*Daphnis and Chloe*), and first performance of Gabowitz' *Parable in Blue.*

December 20, Princeton Triangle Club.

December 21, Metropolitan Opera Company, *Tristan and Isolde.*

December 27, Carlo Buti, vaudeville.

December 28, Civic Opera Company *Hänsel and Gretel.*

Add the one hundred concerts given in the Academy by the Philadelphia Orchestra to the above sixty-five varied musical events in 1937, and a long and active musical season will be seen to have been staged in this theatre.

III

Opera and concert life in Philadelphia from 1860 to 1900 are so inseparably linked with the history of the Academy of Music that were it not for the excessive length of the combined subjects they should all have been treated in one section. The following performances are selected as being important landmarks in the advancement of Philadelphia music—regardless of whether the Academy of Music or any other theatre provided the staging for them. When not otherwise specified the reader should assume that concerts and operas of this period were produced at the Academy of Music.

The opera performances did not stop or even abate during the Civil War period. The Academy of Music was evidently a great drawing card to professional companies. They followed Barnum's lead [1] in the matter of advertising—though with less flamboyant success. With three thousand possible paying customers instead of the preceding theatres' two thousand, the Academy of Music became a great center for professional musicians of all kinds. It becomes increasingly difficult to summarize the varied offerings of the late nineteenth century opera companies. New works were presented—many Philadelphia premières and a few American premières among them. In addition to William Fry's two operas (*Leonora* and *Esmerelda*), J. H. Bonawitz's operas, *The Bride of Messina* and *Ostralenka*, were given as world premières, in 1874. Armstrong found them fine musically but lacking in dramatic action.[2]

French and German companies; Miss Richings and her company; Miss Kellogg, Bellini and others; Zucchi, Miss Phillips and others; are among the opera companies most frequently found on

---

[1] P. T. Barnum was responsible for the furore caused by Jenny Lind in 1850. This statement is in no way intended to suggest that Mme. Goldschmidt (Jenny Lind), was not a great person and singer, but the unparalleled success of her appearances was largely due to Barnum's business management.

[2] *Op. cit.,* p. 179.

the programs at the Academy of Music.[1] Such operas as *L'Afri-caine, L'Etoile du Nord, La Forza del Destino, Mireille, The Grand Duchess, The Prophet, Aïda, Mignon, Lohengrin, Rienzi,* and the *Flying Dutchman,* were introduced into Philadelphia between 1860 and 1880, as were indeed many more whose careers were of less importance in subsequent opera history.

Mme. Parepa's first appearance in Philadelphia was with the Strakosch opera company in 1867 (April 8). The names of Maret-zek, La Grange, and Gazzaniga, still appear frequently upon the programs up to 1870, with such artists as Brignoli,[2] and Amodio singing main roles of their operatic troupes.. The famous baritone Del Puente began his long series of Philadelphia opera appearances on December 8, 1873, in *Traviata,* with the Strakosch troupe. As new names appear in great numbers during the last quarter of the nineteenth century, it is interesting to note the survival of the name Seguin [3] as late as May, 1880, while George Werrenrath, the father of Reinald, appeared in *Der Freischütz* in 1876. The great majority of the Philadelphia opera singers cannot be individually discussed in this chapter.[4] It may be sufficient to say that when the Royal Italian Opera company was formed in London (1847), seven of the nine principal singers were former favorites in Phila-delphia opera companies. Eight of ten soloists in the Royal Italian Opera and Her Majesty's Theatre—a joint British company formed in 1869—had been heard regularly in Philadelphia Opera perform-ances.[5]

The period about the year 1880 saw the rise of the operetta to greater popularity. Historically the operetta precedes grand opera

---

[1] The Academy of Music Programs are preserved in the Pennsylvania Historical Society, 13th and Locust Street, Philadelphia; and (in part) at the Academy of Music, Broad and Locust Street.

[2] "Fat Brignoli ate too much and died" (1884) is Huneker's summary treatment of Pasqualino Brignoli's latter end. (*Steeplejack,* Vol. II, p. 34.) Brignoli was active as an operatic tenor in New York and Philadelphia from 1855 to 1884. His portrait hangs in the Green Room of the Academy of Music.

[3] Zelda Seguin, in *The Bohemian Girl,* was the daughter-in-law of Arthur and Anne Seguin.

[4] Many others are mentioned in the index to this book. For a full listing, the Academy of Music programs should be consulted; also W. G. Arm-strong's *Record of the Opera in Philadelphia.*

[5] Armstrong, *op. cit.,* pp. 227, 228.

in Philadelphia annals, for the ballad operas resembled operettas very closely. The performances of *Bohemian Girl, Chimes of Normandy, Giroflé-Girofla,* and the *Grand Duchess,* were favorite light operas on the programs of 1875 to 1880. *Her Majesty's Ship Pinafore* was given two productions in the 1878-1879 season, one by professionals [1] at the Broad Street Theatre and one by amateurs at the Academy of Music. In the renascence of operetta such works as *Boccaccio, Fatinitza, Mascotte, Fortunio, Rip Van Winkle, A Night in Venice, The Queen's Lace Handkerchief, Iolanthe,* and many more were given in Philadelphia (1880-1885).

The parallel existence of grand and comic opera from 1880 to the present, becomes less surprising when we study the development of a strong tradition of both amateur and professional opera productions extending all the way to Civil War times.

Signor Perelli conducted his own opera *Clarissa Harlowe* at the Chestnut Street Concert Hall on February 6, 1866. Several grand operas were produced that spring at the same hall, among them *Lucrezia, Maria di Rohan, Linda, La Favorita.* A more extended series, of less ambitious music, began in 1868 at the Amateur Drawing Room. Thirty-five light operas were given in a period of less than four years. The names of many of the singers will be familiar to a large number of Philadelphians today. Among them were "The Three Misses Durang of the Philadelphia Opera Company," Mr. and Miss Gilchrist, Messrs. C. N. Drew, Bishop, Barnhurst, Bradshaw, à Becket (Jr.), Madame Schimpf, and the Misses Gregory, Barrett and Poole. Mrs. Galton was a member of several casts in the above series, later forming "The Susan Galton Operatta Company" (1872).

The Church Choir Company made a wise choice in their selection of Gilbert and Sullivan's *Pinafore* as their main operatic offering. The performances in the spring of 1879 at Philadelphia's South Broad Street Theatre were so successful that the company was taken to many nearby cities to give the work. The name "Church Choir Company" had been chosen to attract Philadelphia's non-theatrical element to their light opera productions. Not least among their attractions was a fine orchestra directed by John Philip

---

[1] The Church Choir Company.

Sousa, who was a resident of Philadelphia in the five years following the Centennial exhibition of 1876. Sousa's connection with Philadelphia seems to have begun with his engagement as a member of Offenbach's orchestra at the Centennial. For about two years after the exhibition Sousa played in the orchestra at the Chestnut Street Theatre. Simon Hassler, the leader of that group, is known to have asked Sousa to do the first orchestral transcription in the latter's long career as composer and arranger. The Hasslers, Simon and Mark, were Philadelphia's leading conductors during the years that Sousa made that city his home.[1] In discussing the popularity of operetta, the Church Choir Company, and its twenty-four year old leader, John P. Sousa, we find that the music lies between the high ground of grand opera and the average plain of theatrical and popular music. The same may be said of Sousa's own compositions. Many of his marches and operettas were composed while Sousa lived in Philadelphia. The premières of most Sousa works took place in the Abbey's Theatre on Arch Street, or in the South Broad Street Theatre. Reading, Pottsville, Wilmington, and Trenton were frequently visited by J. P. Sousa and the various theatrical companies that he directed. In 1879 the Church Choir visited several New England cities as well as those near Philadelphia. On this tour *Pinafore* and a rearranged version of Sullivan's *The Contrabandista* were given. The later trips by Philadelphia theatre companies featured works by Sousa himself. Of his eleven comic operas *The Smugglers, The Queen of Hearts, El Capitan,* and *The Charlatan* were the most popular. In 1879 Sousa married Jennie Bellis of Philadelphia, a young understudy in the cast of *Pinafore*. In 1880 this march king renewed his connection with the United States Marine Corps, and conducted its band for the twelve years following. Sousa had previously been a marine from 1867 until about 1875. *Marching Along,* his interesting autobiography,[2] contains a full account of his travels as the director of Philadelphia operetta troupes, of the Marine Band, and of Sousa's Band from 1892 until 1926. In all of these years Philadelphia was an important stopping place for the Sousa organizations,

---

[1] Cf. *infra,* pp. 153-4 for account of the Hasslers.
[2] J. P. Sousa, *Marching Along.* (Boston 1928, Hale, Cushman and Flint.)

since it was Mrs. Sousa's home, and as nearly a home as the writer of *Marching Along* ever knew. Probably Willow Grove Park, a few miles north of Philadelphia, is more closely identified with Sousa's band and Sousa marches than any spot in the world. The first season of concerts by this band at Willow Grove was that of 1901, the last closed the summer concerts of 1926.[1] The Wanamaker music festival of 1908 secured Sousa as a judge; the music festival at the Philadelphia Metropolitan Opera House, November 6, 1916, was given in honor of Sousa and his band; the band gave several concerts in Philadelphia in 1917 for the benefit of the Red Cross; and so the record goes, as Sousa became an international figure in the world of band music and the composition of marches, and toured literally around the globe with his noted musicians. His death, in Reading, Pennsylvania, in 1932, makes him appear to be quite a recent figure, which indeed he is as the renowned march king; but his most intimate connection with Philadelphia lay in the years of the Church Choir Company of 1878-1879, and the other theatrical experiences of his youth.

The Emma Abbott Grand English Opera company gave a long series of performances at the Chestnut Street Opera House in the spring of 1883. The *English Opera* section of this company's title was the more authentic, since their repertoire consisted mainly of operettas. The company had given performances in New York and Philadelphia since 1878, the season of 1883 being their first extended visit to the latter city.

Three American operatic premières belong to the decade that followed the Centennial. Performances of Wagner's *Flying Dutchman* were given in 1876 and 1883. The former was the first American performance of that opera, or of *Il Vascello Fantasma* as it should be called since the work was sung in Italian. The 1883 performance, starring Mme. Emma Albani as Senta, was given on April 16th—also in Italian. The second was a world première of *Uncle Tom's Cabin,* opera seria by Caryl Florio. Florio, who conducted many opera performances in New York and Philadelphia, wrote both words and music for this work, and conducted its first performance, which took place at the Academy of Music in 1882.

---

1 Cf. *infra*, pp. 195-6, for Sousa's Band and other music at Willow Grove Park.

Edward E. Hipsher, who records this event in his book on *American Opera and its Composers*,[1] states that the music for *Uncle Tom's Cabin* is of considerable merit.   In the following year, March 25, 1883, *Fortunio*, a comic opera by F. T. S. Darley, was produced. Darley's cantata *The Cities of the Plain* was one of the last works to be given by the Musical Fund Society in 1857.   His operetta *Fortunio* placed him again in the musical limelight in the chronological center of the late nineteenth century period.   The founding of the Philadelphia Orchestra in 1900 was greatly aided by the interest of F. T. Sully Darley whose influence and activity is thus seen to have extended over a long period of time.[2]

Maurice Grau brought a French opera company to Philadelphia in the autumn of 1883.   Comic opera seems to have dominated the field in the years between 1876 and 1890.   The appended list of first performances in America shows that no new works of the first rank seem to have been performed in this city during those years.   The Aimée opera company had been managed by Grau in some of their operas at the Academy of Music, which extended from 1872 to 1879.   Their repertoire was made up of French and a few Italian operas.   The troupe was named for its principal soprano, Mlle. Aimée.

Maurice Grau also managed the Kellogg opera company for some of its later appearances in Philadelphia.   Clara Louise Kellogg first sang in Philadelphia on April 17, 1861, as *Linda of Chamounix*. Her success in this city and elsewhere seems to have been enormous. In 1862 the company, already known as the Kellogg Troupe, gave several operas in Philadelphia.   From 1874 the company was reorganized as a native grand opera troupe—the first important group to be so constituted.   Miss Kellogg was not a Philadelphian, having been born in South Carolina in 1842, but for the long period between 1861 and 1882 her many operatic performances centered in that city and in New York.   A fine performance of *Faust* on April 14, 1882, at the Philadelphia Academy of Music, signalized Kellogg's farewell to the operatic stage.   She appeared in concert for a few additional years, married Max Strakosch, one of her managers, in

---

[1] P. 182.
[2] Darley was the first vice-president of the Philadelphia Orchestra, and one of its original guarantors.

1887, and soon retired from musical activities. Clara L. Kellogg was the first of the long line of American singers to win international fame. She is said to have known forty leading operatic roles, and to have sung many of them on one hundred and twenty-five nights of the 1874-1875 season.

David Bispham was also managed by Maurice Grau for many years. Grau's main importance in Music in Philadelphia was his connection with the lengthy series of visits by the Metropolitan Opera Company of New York to Philadelphia. From 1891 until 1903 the newly organized New York company gave many operas in Philadelphia under Grau's management. More must be said concerning Bispham, and the Metropolitan Opera Company, in later periods of Philadelphia's musical history.[1]

Two musical Heinrichs and one Hinrichs should next claim our attention. All of them wandered as much as their eccentric namesake Anton Philip Heinrich, but there is no room for skepticism concerning their real musical excellence as there seems to be in the case of the earlier A. P. Heinrich. Max Heinrich came to Philadelphia in 1873, where he settled [2] as a teacher and concert baritone. He married Annie Schubert, the daughter of a violinist in the Germania Orchestra. Their daughter, Julia Heinrich, became a noted concert and opera soprano between 1900 and 1919. She sang in concert with her father, and in German and American opera companies, notably the Metropolitan Company, from 1915 to the year of her death. Julia Heinrich is said to have been better equipped vocally than her father, while inheriting his musical memory and his special art of playing accompaniments.[3] She was killed by a train in 1919; the death was believed to have been suicidal.

Max Heinrich accepted a teaching position in Judson College, Alabama, which he held from 1876 to 1882. He then returned to Philadelphia, resuming his private teaching and singing as baritone soloist at the Cathedral of S.S. Peter and Paul, and at Rodeph

---

[1] Cf. *infra*, pp. 133-4 for Bispham, and pp. 231-2 for the Metropolitan productions in Philadelphia.

[2] The home of Max Heinrich still stands on Cherry Street below Twentieth. James G. Huneker describes it fondly as "his little house with a garden" full of babies sprawled everywhere, landscape paintings and birds. (*Steeplejack*, Volume I, pp. 148-152.)

[3] Huneker, *Steeplejack*, volume I, p. 159.

Shalom Synagogue. In 1882 he sang *Elijah* under Leopold Damrosch in New York. Shortly thereafter his popularity in New
York caused him to move to that city. From 1888 to 1893 Heinrich was vocal instructor at the Royal Academy of Music in London.
He returned to Philadelphia in 1893, moved to Chicago in 1894,
thence to Boston, and finally settled in New York (1910-1916).
Throughout his wandering life Max Heinrich composed, edited,
and translated songs. He is the author of *Correct Principles of
Classical Singing*. As a thorough musician—he usually played his
own accompaniments—and the possessor of one of the finest voices
in the country, Heinrich met with success wherever he travelled.
The leading orchestras secured him as assisting soloist; he also
sang in opera for some years. Less dramatic than his Philadelphia
contemporary David Bispham, yet a more thoroughly trained musician, Heinrich was at his best in lieder concerts and informal programs.[1] His final public appearance was in New York in 1915, a
year before his death.

Gustav Hinrichs was born earlier than either of the two Heinrichs, Max or Julia, but has outlived them by many years. Born
in Germany in 1850, Hinrichs came to San Francisco in 1870. Here
he played in orchestras and later (1875-1885) conducted operas
and concert programs. From 1885 to 1888 he assisted Theodore
Thomas in conducting and managing the American Opera Company. This group was an early company to give "opera in English
by American singers." Some fifteen years later the Philadelphia
Operatic Society aimed at the same objective. Though less pro-
fessionally managed than the American Opera Company, the Philadelphia group gave their productions over a much longer period of
years.[2] Gustav Hinrichs came to Philadelphia in 1888, and from
that year until 1896, the most important opera productions of his
long career were staged in this city. The new Grand Opera House
on Broad Street at Montgomery Avenue had just been completed

---

[1] Emma Schubert Brister, Heinrich's sister-in-law, has included a great
deal about Max in her autobiographical book *Incidents* (Private printing,
Phila. 1935). On page 23 of *Incidents*, Mrs. Brister declares Heinrich to
have been America's finest baritone in his day. James Gibbons Huneker
declares that Heinrich's solo work in classical oratorios was unapproachable.
Steeplejack, volume I, p. 150.

[2] Cf. *infra*, pp. 241-2.

by John F. Betz, a wealthy brewer. Hinrichs opened this new theatre with the first of a three weeks' season of operas. The skill of his management and directing was so great that the success of grand opera, and the new opera house, was immediate. Del Puente was a regular artist with Hinrichs; Minnie Hauk [1] and Emil Fischer [2] appeared as guest soloists with his company. The ambitious seasons features nightly productions of opera, fifty-eight different works being given in the seven seasons of the company's existence. American premières included *Pagliacci* and *Cavalleria Rusticana* (1891), *L'Amico Fritz* (1892), *Pearl Fishers* (1893), and *Manon Lescaut* (1894).[3] *Onteora,* Hinrichs' own opera, was given its world première at the Grand Opera House in 1891.

At the beginning of the season of 1895-1896 several wealthy opera patrons became dissatisfied with certain eccentricities of Metropolitan Opera Company singers, and transferred their support from the well-nigh distracted Behrens [4] to Hinrichs. A season of operas conducted and managed by Hinrichs was accordingly produced in the Academy of Music. *Hänsel and Gretel* was given in December, 1895, its first American performance. The *Memoirs* state sadly that a trolley strike and severe weather ruined the season. The star system of opera casting did not prevail, although the singers were declared easily adequate for their parts. Then too, there were about three operas each week, a larger number than Philadelphia's opera public would support.

San Francisco and New York secured Hinrichs as a conductor in subsequent seasons, although he did not manage the finances for any more operatic ventures. Occasional performances of opera were conducted by Hinrichs in London, Boston, and Chicago. His conducting of *Ben Hur* (1906-1912) was noted in many cities. In

---

[1] Minnie Hauk is called "the greatest contralto of them all" by J. G. Huneker (*Steeplejack,* Volume II, p. 34; Volume I, p. 42), possibly since she was the first singer he heard as Carmen.

[2] Emil Fischer, noted Wagnerian bass, a member of the faculty of the National Conservatory, founded by Jeannette M. Thurber in New York, in 1881.

[3] While Gustav Hinrichs' *Memoirs* mention these busy and important seasons at some length, and duly note the works introduced to America, the memories of countless older music lovers in Philadelphia also retain glowing pictures of these performances.

[4] Siegfried Behrens had been agent for the Metropolitan Company's Philadelphia performances since 1890.

1930 the Philadelphia Operatic Society dedicated its performance of *Il Trovatore* to "Gustav Hinrichs the Father of Opera in Philadelphia." Hinrichs was the guest of honor on that occasion. Four years later the production of *Martha* by students of the Olney High School was assisted by the experienced advice of this octogenarian conductor. At present he lives in retirement at Mountain Lakes, New Jersey. Beyond question no man can so justly be called the father of opera in Philadelphia. His conducting and managing of over eighteen hundred nights of opera in that city coupled with his constant conscientious efforts toward the best in opera productions have earned him that title, and also the admiration and respect of all Philadelphia opera goers.

Gustav Hinrichs was a lover of Philadelphia, despite his wandering life and notwithstanding his financial losses at the Academy of Music. He calls it fondly the city of his adoption, and as such he regards its musical past with far more loyalty than that shown by many native musicians of Philadelphia who have found the city of their adoption elsewhere. Hinrichs' *Memoirs* declares that the history of Philadelphia opera from 1750 to 1850 is the history of opera in America for that period. His most appreciated managing and conducting was that of the years at the Grand Opera House in Philadelphia. He also considered those seasons to have been the most successful from an artistic viewpoint.

In 1896, shortly after Hinrichs had left this city, Philadelphia witnessed the farewell appearance of one of the greatest nineteenth century impresarios. J. Henry Mapleson had brought an English troupe, Her Majesty's Opera Company, to Philadelphia each season from 1878 to 1896. Mr. Mapleson produced in October of that year the American première of *André Chenier*. This performance must have been notably forward looking for a final production by Mapleson, who was sixty-six years old at the time. An amusing incident took place before the opera. Mme. Bona Plata-Bau, who had been engaged by Mapleson to sing the role of Madeleine, sent word on the day of the performance that she must be paid in advance or she would not sing. Mapleson did not acknowledge this message, but immediately communicated with the Metropolitan Opera offices in New York to find whether another soprano could be found. The reply stated that Mrs. Graham of Philadelphia had created the role in its Italian production under the guidance of Giordano himself. Having been so fortunate as to find a substitute living in Philadelphia, Mapleson sent for the luckless Bona Plata-Bau, and informed her that she was not to be permitted to sing in the opera, that Philadelphia's discriminating audience would not be satisfied with any soprano but the one who had created the role in Italy. Persons who witnessed this eclipse of one of our earliest variable stars, declare that Mapleson's grand manner on that occasion alone would easily justify the title Colonel which he had assumed some years previous. Mrs. Graham, or Mme. Chalia, as she was also called, is said to have been the possessor of one of the largest vibrati among operatic soprani.

The Metropolitan Opera Company of New York has provided Philadelphia's longest continuous stream of fine opera. This company has given regular opera seasons in Philadelphia since 1889. Occasional seasons have passed with but few Philadelphia performances; in fact certain years have seen few operas by any professional company. With all of the Metropolitan's variation as to the number and excellence of works produced, its record remains remarkable for the regularity and number of its visits to Philadelphia.

The name of Siegfried Behrens is inevitably associated with the early visits of the Metropolitan Opera Company to Philadelphia. Mr. Behrens was Philadelphia's most famous impresario of the late nineteenth century. He had come to Philadelphia as an operatic conductor for some of our greatest singers, Patti, Parepa-Rosa, Piccolomini, and Gerster among them. His arranging for other companies' visits to Philadelphia constitutes his greatest claim to musical importance. Behrens was lessee of the Academy of Music and local agent for many musical companies. The newly organized Metropolitan Opera Company was the most noted visiting troupe to be brought to Philadelphia under Behrens' management. When we consider the vast importance of the operas given in Philadelphia by this New York company for a period of over fifty years, the mere agency for their early visits becomes a noteworthy item. Behrens' home on Locust Street near Eighth was the meeting place of many world famous musicians from about 1885 to 1905. He was the original conductor of the Behrens Opera Club, which group was the predecessor of the Philadelphia Operatic Society, famous in later years of Music in Philadelphia.[1]

By far the largest part of the significance of the operas by the Metropolitan Opera Company lies in the years after 1900, and hence it is given a fuller account in later pages of this book.[2] Some particularly noted productions of their early years are chronologically within our late nineteenth century period. They are significant for their own musical values, and also because they are the beginning of the long series of operas that is still providing Philadelphia's finest music in that form.

The first performance in Philadelphia of the Wagner tetralogy, *The Ring of the Nibelungen,* was given by the Metropolitan Opera Company in 1889. The soloists for these Ring operas included Lilli.Lehmann, Emil Fischer, and Max Alvary; the conductor was Anton Seidl. This noted visit by the New York company gave Philadelphia a première of the Wagner Tetralogy immediately after its introduction to America in New York, March, 1889. In the winter months of the early 1890's, this company visited Philadelphia once a week giving works from their large repertoire [3] with considerable success. In 1895 the season of operas conducted by Hinrichs at the Academy of Music caused the abandonment of Metropolitan visits for that year. The failure of Philadelphia patrons to support the Metropolitan Opera Company seems to have influenced that organization to outdo itself in an opera festival at the close of Hinrichs' 1895-1896 season. In the spring of 1896, seven operas were given in one week. This operatic orgy included all of the well known Meyerbeer works except *L'Etoile du Nord,*[4] and the American première of Reyer's *Sigurd.* This gesture was timed to perfection and executed with great brilliance. The 'star system,' i.e. the securing of the country's leading singers for solo parts, had conquered. Hinrichs, opera in English, productions with merely adequate casts, all had been proven not good enough

---

[1] Cf. *infra,* p. 241 for the history of the Philadelphia Operatic Society.
[2] Cf. *infra,* pp. 231-235.
[3] The Metropolitan Company had given eighty different operas in the first fifteen years of its existence (1883-1898).
[4] I.e., *The Prophet, Dinorah, Robert le Diable,* and *Huguenots.*

for the main season of operas at the Academy of Music. The Metropolitan Opera Company had shown what its large organization could do; but Philadelphia had also gained the privilege of hearing only the best that the Metropolitan had to offer.

Walter Damrosch led many of Philadelphia's most important operatic performances in the 1890's. This Damrosch Opera Company visited Philadelphia in 1894, the first year of its existence. The first week in April, 1894, found this company in Philadelphia, staging a Wagner festival consisting of *Die Walküre, Götterdämmerung, and Tannhäuser.* The newspapers were full of advertisements and accounts of the performances. The *Public Ledger* of April 1 included in the advance notices the promise that "Outgoing trains will be held until after the performances." The great length of Wagner scores made a deep impression in 1894. The Damrosch Opera Company later became the Damrosch-Ellis and finally the Ellis Opera Company. One of their noted productions was a very early and well staged performance of Damrosch's *Scarlet Letter,* 1896. The cast included David Bispham and Johanna Gadski. During the same week the Damrosch-Ellis Company gave *Tristan and Isolde* for the first time in Philadelphia, and other well selected operas. This company seems to have provided the last serious rivalry to the leadership of the Metropolitan Company until the spectacular productions managed by Hammerstein in New York and Philadelphia in 1907 and 1908. Walter Damrosch's visits as the conductor of his own opera company continued until 1899, when he gave up the enterprise to devote more time to composition. In the years after 1900 he resumed his conducting of the New York Symphony Orchestra and became conductor for German operas of the Metropolitan Opera Company.

A stellar performance of *Tristan* in March 1898 stands out as exceptional even in the series of operas given by the Metropolitan Opera Company. The singers were:

Jean de Reszke .... Tristan
Edouard de Reszke .... Mark
David Bishpham .... Kurwenal
Schumann-Heink .... Brangäne
Lillian Nordica .... Isolde
Conductor—Emil Pauer.

The name of David Bispham, appearing in both the *Scarlet Letter* Philadelphia première and the notable performance of *Tristan,* suggests that as a Philadelphian his biography might well be included in this period. Bispham's activity as singer and teacher extended so far into the twentieth century that many of his friends would be surprised to discover how large a part of his contribution to Music in Philadelphia was made before 1900.

David Scull Bispham was born in Philadelphia in 1857 and died in New York in 1921. His father was a strict Quaker but played the flute and was otherwise "original." [1] His grandfather Bispham even had a piano which neither the Sculls nor the Lippincotts, his other relatives, were broadminded enough to possess. While a student at Haverford College and for about six years afterward, Bispham was subject to all of the musical influences in Philadelphia. This period of his life falling in the years 1876-1886, David Bispham may be said to have been a product of Music in Philadelphia of the late nineteenth century. Max Heinrich was a lifelong friend of Bispham, Michael Cross was another great vocal influence on the young Friend in his early years in Philadelphia. Cross conducted the choir of Holy Trinity Church, the Orpheus Club, and the Arion Singing Society of Germantown. Bispham sang in all of these choruses under Cross's direction. Ole Bull, Zelda Seguin, Clara Louise Kellogg, and Giuseppe Del Puente were among the great artists whom he admired. Del Puente was one of the first to prophesy Bispham's unusual success as a dramatic soloist. [2] St. Mark's choir succeeded that of Holy Trinity as a sacred musical influence on Bispham. He became precentor there, and a soloist in the many musical clubs to which he belonged.

Shortly after 1886 Bispham resolved to devote his life to music, and went to Europe to finish his musical education. After several years of study, chiefly in England and Italy, Bispham's professional operatic début was made in London in 1891. He returned to America in 1896 the master of several major operatic rôles. The part of Falstaff and certain Wagnerian parts were said to be his

---

[1] The term is David Bispham's, in his book, *A Quaker Singer's Recollections,* New York, 1921, the MacMillan Company.

[2] Less musical but cultural influences of the time were the acting of Edwin Booth and John Drew, and the distinctive environment of the Mercantile Library.

finest operatic rôles. Two of Bispham's outstanding Philadelphia appearances have already been mentioned. He became a favorite soloist with the Metropolitan Company, the Worcester Festivals, and in concerts in this country, many of the last being sung at the Philadelphia Academy of Music. The Orpheus Club elected him an honorary member in return for his great interest and frequent assistance at their concerts. Like certain other noted Philadelphians, David Bispham was a strong advocate of opera in English. His dramatic recitations were nationally famous. The Mendelssohn Club of Philadelphia engaged him for a performance of Sophocles' *Antigone* for chorus, orchestra, and speaking voice. The music for this performance, which was given February 8, 1908, is a composition of Mendelssohn.

David Bispham's writing on the subject of the voice, and his numerous editions of song collections, spring mainly from the years after 1910, which he devoted to vocal teaching. Bispham was Philadelphia's most widely beloved singer. Two singers of today, Nelson Eddy and Marian Anderson, may well rival David Bispham in international popularity, but up until such time as their careers shall have progressed much farther the claim made above for the Quaker singer and teacher cannot well be disputed.

IV

The year 1876, while a decidedly backward step from the later events in the life of David Bispham, is a long remembered one in Philadelphia annals. Philadelphia's most successful exhibition, the Centennial, was held in that year. The main musical efforts of the Centennial Exhibition seem to have been expended on its opening ceremonies.

National hymns by the Centennial Orchestra under Theodore Thomas began the inaugural program of May 10, 1876. The American, Austrian, French, and German songs were played, also the Brazilian in honor of the Emperor and Empress of Brazil who were present. Wagner's *Centennial Inauguration March,* composed for the occasion, was played at the arrival of the President of the United States. James Gibbons Huneker, outstanding music critic,

„Nur der verdient sich Freiheit wie das Leben,
Der täglich sie erobern muss."
Goethe

Grosser Festmarsch

zur Eröffnung

der hundertjährigen Gedenkfeier der Unabhängigkeits-Erklärung

der vereinigten Staaten

VON NORDAMERIKA.

Dem Festfeier-Frauenverein

gewidmet von

Richard Wagner.

Für das PIANOFORTE übertragen

von

JOSEPH RUBINSTEIN

Eigenthum der Verleger Eingetragen in das Archiv der Union

Mainz, bei B Schott's Söhne

Brussel, Gebrüder Schott   Paris, Schott,   London Schott & Cⁱᵉ
45 Montagne de la Cour   6 Rue de Hazard Richelieu   159 Regent Street

Vollständiges Aufführungs-Lager,
LEIPZIG, C. F. LEEDE.
Propriété pour tous pays.
Tous Droits Reserves
22107. 22138.
22141.

THE CENTENNIAL MARCH BY WAGNER

gives the usual verdict about the Wagner march: "I heard Richard Wagner's $5000 Centennial March played by the Thomas orchestra, and wondered how so much money could have been wasted on such commonplace music." [1]   (Huneker was born in Philadelphia in 1860, and lived there until 1900.)   After the Wagner came a long prayer, which was followed by John K. Paine's setting of Whittier's *Centennial Hymn.* "The music for this poem . . . was exceedingly beautiful, though not of striking individuality." This criticism [2] was an apt comment for a rather unmusical historian to have made—especially in 1876, when Paine was considered America's leading composer.   The effect of the choral work is somewhat less penetratingly criticized: "The voices of the chorus were particularly full and strong in every bar, and some of the higher chords could be distinctly heard for a great distance."   The account continues with the words of Whittier's poem, obviously an occasional effort, which begins:

> "Our fathers' God from out whose hand
> The centuries fall like grains of sand."

Next on the program was a short address by the chairman of the board of finance, followed by the *Centennial Cantata.* This work, consisting of Lanier's words and Dudley Buck's music, seems to have been better received than any of the preceding music of the day.[3]

The speeches by the President of the Centennial Commission and President Grant, which followed the cantata, were surprisingly short.   The music of this program was truly its noteworthy feature, a wise plan considering the open air scene of the ceremonies and the crowd of over 100,000 persons that was attempting to hear them.   The final musical number of the opening program followed Grant's speech.   Orchestra, organ and chorus combined in Handel's *Hallelujah Chorus,* followed by chime ringing in Machinery Hall and a salute of 100 guns, from George's Hill.   Four thousand

---

[1] *Steeplejack,* vol. 1, p. 122.
[2] By James D. McCabe, in his *History of the Centennial Exhibition,* p. 293; National Publishing Co., Philadelphia, 1876.
[3] Lanier's poetry (Meditation of Columbus) is quoted on p. 297 of the *History of the Centennial Exhibition;* Whittier's poem on p. 294.

invited guests then formed in a long procession, which passed through Memorial Hall and into the Main Building.[1]

Let us remain in the main building to inspect the large organ which had provided accompaniments for the Centennial Chorus of 1000 voices. Hook and Hastings of Boston had erected this instrument at a cost of $15,000. There were four manuals and pedals, 59 stops and couplers, and over 2700 pipes. This organ's three bellows were blown by a hydraulic motor. A Roosevelt organ was in the New York section of the main building. Although somewhat smaller than the Hook and Hastings instrument, the Roosevelt organ had many novel features. Included among them were two echo organs, one connected by a wire cable of two hundred feet in length. Both hydraulic and electric engines provided the power for this modern organ. This organ cost $20,000 to build. There were several organs in the main building at this exhibition.

Many piano makers displayed their instruments at the Centennial. "Steinway, Chickering, Weber, Knabe and a score of well known names greeted us at every turn. . . . Several of the leading firms engaged distinguished performers to show off their instruments, and one was sure of always hearing some brilliant pianist while lingering in this department." [2] Wood, and Mason and Hamlin exhibited cabinet organs near the piano displays, but the chief exhibitor of these instruments was J. Estey of Vermont. The C. F. Albert Company of Philadelphia exhibited a case of string instruments: the illustration on the following page is reproduced from the 1876 account of the Centennial.

Horticultural Hall was provided with music by a mechanical Orchestrion, the invention of Wm. F., and H. Schmoele of Philadelphia. This instrument was also named an Electro Magnetic Orchestra. It used paper rolls similar to the later music for player

---

[1] While the Order of Procession is not musically significant, it is interesting to consider how many notable men were in it. Among them were President Grant and his cabinet, the Chief Justice and Supreme Court, the Senate, led by the Vice-President, the Governors of States and territories, the House of Representatives, the General of the Army and Staff, the Admiral of the Navy and Staff; and a similar array of Pennsylvania and Philadelphia officials. President Grant and Dom Pedro II of Brazil divided the honors of starting the wheels in Machinery Hall, hence symbolically, the active operation of the Centennial.

[2] McCabe, *History of the Centennial Exhibition*, p. 379.

pianos, and complicated processes of impulsation into twelve instruments "besides the drums" were electrically operated.[1]

The opening program has been recorded above in some detail. Theodore Thomas, the general director of music for the Centennial, had commissioned the best known poets and musicians to produce appropriate material for those inaugural exercises. Whittier, Lanier, Wagner, Paine, and Buck had been secured through Thomas's efforts. There were other occasional programs throughout the summer of 1876, with their own specially composed odes and hymns. The performance of July 4th at Independence Hall vied with the opening program for actual musical success, although it did not number so many famous men among those commissioned to compose words and music for the occasion. The Centennial Musical Association began the Independence Day program with Helfrich's *Centennial Triumphal March*. Thomas later declared that Wagner's *Centennial March* was so bad that it was an insult to the exhibition. Even the serious Richard Wagner permitted himself the levity, "The best thing about that composition was the money I got for it." [2] Some of this money was rather questionably procured through the sale of a German edition of the march which Wagner's publisher had stocked in New York music stores. The Women's Centennial Committees had been granted exclusive American rights to publish this Centennial March, but before they could do so the work was on sale through New York firms and their agents. It is possibly just as well that Mrs. E. D. Gillespie, the head of the women's committees, was thus prevented from publishing and marketing the work, since it was a complete failure so far as the American public was concerned.

We could hardly say that Helfrich's *Centennial Triumphal March* was any finer than Wagner's, but we may be sure that it was less expensive. Whittier's *Centennial Hymn,* music by Paine, and *The Voice of the Old Bell,* a Centennial Ode, were sung by a chorus of one hundred and fifty voices. A second *Centennial Hymn,* by C. S. Upham, was sung on this program. The band played *God Save America* and several other patriotic airs during the affair.

---

[1] *The History of the Centennial* describes this as "one of the most remarkable machines to be seen in the Exhibition," pp. 572-574.

[2] Quoted in *Wagner and His Works,* volume II, p. 509, by H. T. Finck.

George F. Bristow of New York arranged an overture, *The Great Republic,* for this occasion, basing it on *Hail Columbia,* which song rivalled *The Star Spangled Banner* as this country's national anthem in 1876. The orchestra, or band as it seems to have still been variously designated, was led by Mr. P. Gilmore.

The July Fourth celebrations were attended by notables nearly as distinguished as those at the Exhibition's opening. General Sherman reviewed the troops, assisted by Prince Oscar of Sweden, several governors, and foreign officers. Our historian somewhat too frankly states, "General Grant declined the invitation to be present, and remained in Washington, preferring his selfish ease to a little patriotic exertion and exposure to the heat on this grandest of his country's festivals." [1]

Musical awards were received by many American exhibitors. Medals were given to the piano firms of Steck, Decker, Bacon and Karr, Weber, and Steinway, all of New York; Chickering of Boston, and Knabe of Baltimore. Mason and Hamlin; Burdett, Erie, Pennsylvania; and Peloubet, Pelton, and Company, received awards among reed organ exhibitors.

The closing ceremonies were planned to be as impressive as possible. A company of notables was assembled, including President Grant, and most of the men who had assisted at the opening exercises in May. "Professor Wagner's" march was again used to begin the program. It was considered more effective when heard on the closing day, due partly to the fact that the stormy weather had made it necessary for the program to be staged indoors. Other musical numbers were a Chorale and Fugue by Bach, played by the orchestra; a "Te Deum by Dettingen [!] rendered with fine effect by the orchestra and chorus" [2]; Beethoven's Sixth Symphony; the *Hallelujah Chorus;* and *America.*[3]

The actual fair thus officially ended, the permanent exhibition committee announced that the main building would continue to house a large collection for some years. The Centennial organ was allowed

---

[1] McCabe's *History,* p. 750-751, published in 1876.

[2] McCabe, *op. cit.,* p. 872.

[3] The Centennial far surpassed any previous European or American Exhibition both as to the number of visitors (9,789,392) and receipts ($3,813,750). Paris and Vienna exhibitions had exceeded the Centennial in the number of exhibitions, however.

AN EXHIBIT OF STRING INSTRUMENTS AT THE CENTENNIAL.

to remain in a transept section of the building large enough to seat an audience of 8000. This use of the main building as a permanent museum was abandoned after four years, due to financial difficulties. The Memorial.and Horticultural Halls are still maintained as permanent buildings in Fairmount Park.

One loftily aimed musical feature should be mentioned before we leave the account of the Centennial. The Peerless Summer Nights' Concerts were conducted by Theodore Thomas, musical director of the.exhibition. This concert series seems to have been Mrs Gillespie's peculiar pride, her partiality to Thomas being so great that she believed that crowds would journey to Broad Street above Master to hear an orchestra amid quieter surroundings than were available at the exhibition grounds.[1]

Thomas's outstanding music library was sold under the hammer of the Sheriff of Philadelphia to pay for the summer concerts. Fortunately wealthy friends bought it, and it was again made available to Thomas at a fraction of its true value. The failure was due to the remoteness and inaccessibility of Broad and Master Streets in the year 1876. Thomas's being permitted to pay for deficits, or pocket profits, reminds us that the specialization of present day musical organization did not exist in those years. The orchestra was the Theodore Thomas Orchestra, and its finances must have been merely another side of their affairs which he was expected to manage.

For once we·need not berate Philadelphia audiences for their unappreciative response to the highest in musical art. The fact that Offenbach's concerts at the Centennial grounds, and at Broad and Cherry Streets, drew crowds, while Thomas's heavier programs were almost without any audience, reflects our national musical inertia more than any local lack of appreciation. The location was

---

[1] McCabe's *History of the Centennial* contains a full page illustration of the 'Women's Centennial Concert Garden, Broad Street,' p. 750, but maintains a discreet silence concerning the unsuccessful concert series staged there. Thomas's biographies do not avoid this unpleasant chapter. The concerts were not patronized, and Theodore Thomas assumed all responsibilities for the deficit rather than go bankrupt to escape them. "Twelve years of sheriffs and scoundrels" resulted from his decision to pay what seemed to be his just debts. (Quoted from a letter by Thomas in *Memoirs of Theodore Thomas* by his widow, Rose F. Thomas. New York, Moffatt, Yard and Co., 1911.)

poorly chosen for the Peerless Summer Nights' Concerts, as has been stated above; but had Offenbach's orchestra played there the probability is that the concerts would have been well attended. The gestures toward the heights seem to have evoked the few unsuccessful features of the fair—the Wagner *March* and the Thomas concerts provide musical examples of this sad fact.

The Centennial Exhibition provides a mirror of the nation's interests, both musical and general. Beyond question the 1876 World's Fair was a conspicuous success and its music was greatly admired by most of the ten million persons who visited Philadelphia during the six months of its duration. Yet we must admit that the mechanical ingenuity of Hilburne Roosevelt's organ and Schmoele's Electric Orchestrion, and the huge size of orchestras and choruses created the strongest impression on the many visitors who remember this exhibition.

Philadelphia musicians were surely not in evidence at the fair grounds. Offenbach was truly a greater musical figure than either Simon or Mark Hassler, yet either of the Hasslers could have appeared as conductor of a Centennial program in place of their more noted French colleague without appreciable musical loss. The Hasslers did direct some of the less publicized concerts of this exhibition. Friends of the late Albert H. Rosewig delight to relate how he led the Thomas orchestra and Centennial chorus of a thousand voices to that eminent gentleman's evident satisfaction. The matchless organ playing of David Wood is not mentioned in any account of the many organ programs in the Centennial main building.[1] Yet Wood had been organist at St. Stephen's church for twelve years before the Centennial year. Michael Cross did not

---

[1] Henry Gordon Thunder, Sr. (Ireland 1832-1881 Philadelphia) was the official organist of the exhibition. He was a Philadelphian by adoption, but seems to have secured his post at the Centennial as a New York organist, since he was organist at St. Stephen's church in New York in 1876. Thunder Sr.'s Philadelphia positions included that of accompanist for the Handel and Haydn Society of Philadelphia and organist at St. Augustine's Church. The latter post he filled from 1855 to the year of his death, with the exception of about five years as organist at St. Stephen's, New York. Henry G. Thunder, Jr., Philadelphia's present dean of choral conductors, played at both the Centennial and the Sesqui-Centennial exhibitions. His father took him to the Centennial on many occasions as a boy of twelve while the Sesqui-Centennial secured his services as a noted organist in 1926.

participate as conductor in any of the choral programs at the exhibition. Yet he had been a prominent organizer and leader of Philadelphia choral groups for many years, and was closely identified with Music in Philadelphia as the son of Benjamin Cross and in his own right, for a very long period of time. There are doubtless reasons for this searching far afield for conductors and soloists, which do not appear in the musical records of the *History of the Centennial.*

V

The important topic of choral music demands separate consideration in the period of the late nineteenth century. Closely associated with this field, or, as it must be subdivided in these later years, these fields, were two important Philadelphia musicians. Michael Hurley Cross and William Wallace Gilchrist were, successively, the dominant figures in chorus conducting during this period. The connections of Cross with bygone eras of Music in Philadelphia have already been suggested. His father's activities and his own training and early musical life were all bound up with early nineteenth century Music in Philadelphia. Cross's own large influence lay in earlier years than that of his colleague W. W. Gilchrist.

Michael H. Cross was born in Philadelphia in 1833 and died there in 1897. His life was a sequence of learning and teaching, of following and leading. He was an assiduous pupil and a noted teacher. As pupil he studied piano with his father, Benjamin Cross, theory with Dr. Meignen, violin with Charles Hommann and Charles Hupfeld, and 'cello with Leopold Engelke. Cross spoke several languages fluently and played several musical instruments well, surely proof positive that he was a great student. This diverse array of musical influences on the pupil is matched by the varied assortment of private pupils and choruses Cross in turn guided as a teacher. The Orpheus Club is the most important of the many groups which he conducted.[1] He preceded Hugh Clarke as leader of the Abt male chorus, and conducted the Arion men's

---

[1] Cf., *infra* pp. 258-262 for an account of this venerable organization.

singing society of Germantown. The Euridice chorus of women [1] and the Cecelian mixed chorus were led by Cross from their first years. The latter group supplanted the Beethoven Society as Philadelphia's leading choral group, in 1875. The Beethoven Society had been founded by Carl Wolfsohn in 1869. Wolfsohn left Philadelphia in 1873 and organized and directed a Beethoven Society in Chicago (1873-1884). The Cecelian's first concerts consisted of miscellaneous numbers, but later such works as *The Messiah, Israel in Egypt, Elijah, St. Paul, The Creation, Samson,* and *Judas Maccabaeus* were sung by groups of over 400 voices. Gounod's *Redemption* and *Mors et Vita* were introduced to Philadelphia at concerts by the Cecelian Society. Both the Germania and the Theodore Thomas Orchestras provided accompaniment for many of these concerts directed by Michael Cross. His pupils included such diverse musicians as Henry Keely, a pioneer exponent of junior choirs in Philadelphia; James Gibbons Huneker, art and music critic; Adele Gilpin Yarnall, Philadelphia's leading manager of chamber concerts, and David Bispham, who was at one time a member of three choruses under Cross' direction. Michael Cross as a teacher was an early advocate of worthy musical content for study material. He may have slighted technical matters—compared with the mechanically flawless Charles Jarvis he surely neglected technique—yet his musicianly nature forbade the tolerance of incorrect as well as inartistic performance. The smooth lyricism of Mozart was more his passion than the rugged intellectuality of Bach. When transferred to piano pupils, or even to the many choruses directed by him, this neglect of technical interest constituted a weakness in his work as teacher and conductor.

Even the numerous churches at which Cross was organist suggest a pleasing variety that might arouse envy in the heart of many who have led a less varied life in the field of church music. Yet Philadelphia's George A. A. West or John McE. Ward has each

---

[1] A concert given by the Euridice Chorus at Musical Fund Hall was heartily praised by an article in the *Evening Ledger* of Apr. 23, 1894. The singing by the chorus, the directing of M. Cross, and the accompaniment provided by Stanley Addicks were all commended. The concert, on Apr. 21, 1894, was given in the eighth season of the chorus's existence; hence the Euridice chorus must have been organized about 1886. Cf. *infra,* p. 267 for the later history of the Euridice chorus.

contributed more in one church than the versatile Michael Cross
in many. At fifteen he was appointed organist at St. Patrick's
Church. Later posts included St. John's, the First Baptist, the
Cathedral of SS. Peter and Paul, 1862 to 1880, and Holy Trinity,
1880 to 1897.

Cross was deeply interested in chamber music. This form of
musical art being notable for social and intellectual expression, it
is not surprising that the sociable and gifted Michael Cross delighted in it. He played violin, viola, and 'cello, having studied the
last named under Engelke at the age of forty. The Saturday evening quartet parties at Cross' home extended over many years of
the late 1870's and early eighties. Carl Gaertner[1] and William
Stoll[2] alternated as first violin, Simon Stern played second, Mr.
Roggenberger viola, and Mr. Cross 'cello. When Engelke or
Charles Schmitz could be secured as violoncellist, Cross played the
viola. The piano was seldom used in chamber ensembles at the
Cross home.

In Michael Cross' later years he was recognized as Philadelphia's outstanding conductor. He added to his general busyness by
leading societies in New York and Brooklyn. The epithet "musician of the old school" fitted him particularly in his contempt for
musical specialists, virtuosi, and stars. He was one of the latest
musicians in Philadelphia to achieve conspicuous success in varied
fields in a period of growing musical specialization. Not many subsequent men have attempted such an inclusive mastery in music,
few if any have achieved such varied musical success as did Michael
Cross. A tablet in his memory was placed in the lobby of the
Academy of Music in Philadelphia. Cross' influence and musical
style were diametrically opposed to those of his contemporary

---

1 Carl Gaertner was a drummer under Carl Sentz, later a violinist who
gave chamber music concerts in the Academy of Music Foyer. J. G. Huneker,
his pupil, states (*Steeplejack,* vol. I, p. 145) that in the Gaertner studios
there were three busts: Mozart, Beethoven, and Gaertner. Carl Gaertner
played poorly but with enthusiasm—most important of all, he knew the best
in music, and played it with excellent musical judgment.

2 William Stoll was a prominent concert violinist and an influential figure
in chamber music in Philadelphia. Stoll directed the Germania Orchestra in
many of its promenade concerts at the Academy of Fine Arts between 1888
and 1895. Stoll's own ensemble, called the Beethoven Quartet, consisted of
William Stoll, Edward Brill, Richard Schmidt, and Rudolph Hennig. This
was a later and more expert group than that of the Cross parties.

Charles Jarvis.[1] His pianistic god was Rubinstein. Though not a virtuoso on any instrument, the piano was the one he played best. His admiration for the musical playing of Rubinstein is understandable when we realize the technical feats and heavy touch of many "modern virtuosi" of his day.

The biographical account of William W. Gilchrist has been placed in a later chapter, that dealing with Twentieth Century Singing Societies. Gilchrist's conducting and composing extended for fifteen years after 1900, and the Mendelssohn Club, founded by Gilchrist, being still a leading mixed chorus, his life and works are discussed in the account of that group.[2]

One of Dr. Gilchrist's most ambitious ventures lay in the choral field in the years under discussion. The Philadelphia Music Festival Association was a large combination of several vocal choruses. Three of Gilchrist's vocal groups held joint rehearsals and gave a four-day festival at the Academy of Music on May 9, 10, 11 and 12, 1883. The Gilchrist groups were *The Amphion,* of Germantown, *The West Philadelphia Choral Society,* and *The Arcadian.* Other singers were added to this already huge choir ; probably certain German groups were well represented. The conducting was shared by Gilchrist and Charles M. Schmitz. The chorus numbered 540, the orchestra 100. While the first festival was considered a successful one, an 1884 attempt was not carried through. Most of the chorus members continued to meet as a large group known as The Philadelphia Chorus. As late as February 28, 1888, we find that the Philadelphia Chorus was one of the participating societies in an ambitious concert for the benefit of the Beethoven Memorial Association. Other societies in this amalgamated vocal ensemble were the Orpheus Club, Germania Glee Club, Harmonie, Young Maennerchor, United Singers of Philadelphia, and the Philadelphia Quartette Club. Some of the former members of the Music Festival Association, and the Philadelphia Chorus, later joined the Philadelphia Choral Society, organized by Henry Gordon Thunder in 1897. This choral group still plays an active part in Philadelphia's vocal music.[3]

---

[1] Cf., *infra,* pp. 158-160 for account of Jarvis.
[2] Cf., *infra,* pp. 250-51.
[3] Cf., *infra,* p. 254 for an account of the Philadelphia Choral Society.

Church choirs seem to have been the only choruses to have led a continuous existence in nineteenth century Philadelphia. Even in the secluded music of the church the worldly adulation of great musical artists is reflected in the quartet movement. This popularity of a soloist, or of music by four soloists, resembles the current operatic and concert star system, and constitutes its counterpart in sacred music. There is no exact limit to the beginning or the ending of the substitution of church quartets for chorus choirs. The height of the quartet movement is difficult to date, since like most cultural episodes it was a wave of influence rather than a definitely set change. The middle of the years of this chapter saw the quartet choir in leading churches of Philadelphia. Quartet choirs are still present in many Philadelphia churches, but the movement was on the wane in this city long before Pope Pius X officially discouraged their presence in Catholic services.

The most significant development in church music of the 1860-1900 period was a raising of the standards of choral singing. A finished production sung by a large choir was well-nigh unheard of in Philadelphia before 1860. Yet David Wood came to St. Stephen's church in 1864 as organist, and in 1870 became its choirmaster. Henry J. Keely did his noted work with the junior choir and the large chorus choir at Gethsemane Baptist Church in 1872-1908. Kendrick Pyne made the boy choir of St. Mark's church a wonder of the eastern states in 1875,[1] while Minton Pyne maintained the standards of that chorus from 1881 to 1905. Charles N. Boyd in an article on "Choir Development since 1876"[2] states that the three outstanding Episcopal choirs in 1876-1878 were those of Trinity Church, New York, St. Mark's, Philadelphia, and Church of the Advent, Boston. This article mentions the fine work done by the celebrated director-organist combination of Gilchrist and Goepp, during the same years. Similar results to those of the Pyne brothers were accomplished for the choir of St. Clement's Church by its choirmaster J. Benton Tipton, who was organist there from 1888 to 1894.[3] Hugh A. Clarke seems to have begun the tradition

---

[1] Kendrick Pyne was called back to England in 1876 to become the organist at Manchester Cathedral, a position he held until 1938.

[2] From the *Proceedings of the Music Teachers National Association,* 1928.

[3] Tipton was called to New York to become organist at Albany Cathedral in 1894.

of fine choral music at the Second Presbyterian Church shortly after 1870. Clarke's most celebrated pupil, William W. Gilchrist, has already been mentioned as one of the outstanding men in vocal music of the late nineteenth century. His influence as choir director in St. Clement's Church, prior to Tipton's tenure there, and in the Church of the New Jerusalem belongs to the same general stream that made these years so important in the rise of chorus choir music.

Toward the close of this same forty year period several organists came to Philadelphia from England. George Alexander A. West came to St. Luke's Church, Germantown, in 1890, and is now finishing his fiftieth year there as organist and choirmaster. The contributions of Harry Alexander Matthews are somewhat more varied than those of West, but the main work of both men lying in the twentieth century, further mention will be made of it in a later chapter.[1] H. A. Matthews' older brother, J. Sebastian Matthews, came to Philadelphia in 1891 to become organist at St. Martin's Church. Walter Henry Hall was organist at St. Luke's, Germantown, from 1884 until 1890. J. S. Matthews and Hall left Philadelphia in 1901 and 1890 respectively. The number of right notes played, composed, and arranged by these well-trained English organists, and sung by choruses under their direction, is enormous. The work of these later choir directors was added to earlier influences exerted by the Canadian, Hugh Clarke, the Englishmen, Minton Pyne, and James E. Ackroyd, and the home trained David Wood, Michael Cross, William W. Gilchrist, Henry J. Keely[2] and George F. LeJeune.[3] Hence improvement in chorus choirs in

---

[1] Cf. pp. 317, 255, 263-4.

[2] Henry J. Keely was born in Reading, Pa., in 1839, and died in Philadelphia in 1926. He sang in St. Clement's choir as a boy, and studied organ with Michael Cross. Keely taught piano, organ, and voice for about fifty years. The choirs at Gethsemane Baptist Church were directed by Henry Keely from 1872 to 1908. His adult choir was considered a fine chorus in its day; his junior choir of 150 voices was probably the earliest such children's group of note. The Lyric Choral Society was also directed by Keely. From three to five concerts were given annually by this chorus between 1878 and about 1890. Abbie Keely, one of Philadelphia's most popular sopranos from 1890 to 1920, was the daughter and pupil of this noted organist.

[3] George F. LeJeune lived in the same house with Kendrick Pyne during the latter's short stay in Philadelphia. LeJeune was the organist at St. Luke's Church at that time (1875), and became a follower of Pyne's system of choir training at St. Luke's and at St. John's Chapel in New York.

Philadelphia is a striking feature in its church music of the years 1860 to 1900.

The liturgical accomplishments of Henry Gordon Thunder, Sr., belong to this same epoch. His stay at St. Augustine's began a few years before the Civil War, and, with the exception of about five years in which he was organist in St. Stephen's, New York, extended up to 1881. Huneker mentions Thunder's organ playing in his autobiography. He recalls that it was "A Sunday morning treat to go with my father to High Mass at St. Augustine's Church, to the choir, there to hear Henry Thunder, Sr., play the organ of which he was a master." [1] The two sons of Henry G. Thunder are still "masters," and remain active in many musical matters, as our pages on the twentieth century will substantiate.

Let us conclude this section on choral music with a brief mention of two men who exerted considerable influence in both nineteenth and twentieth century music in Philadelphia. The activities of Albert Rosewig and Hugh A. Clarke included as varied an assortment of musical fields as did those of Cross or Gilchrist.

Albert H. Rosewig was born in Germany in 1846, and came to Philadelphia before he was ten years of age. For about fifty years, 1865 to 1915, he was an active person in that city. In his younger days Rosewig composed a few pieces of secular music. A song, *Maid of Athens Here We Part,* was composed by him at the age of 12. William R. Smith published this early work, paying the composer twenty-five copies for it. Smith made thousands of dollars from this song, and sold it to F. A. North for $1,400 when North bought out the Smith publishing firm.

Rosewig devoted his mature interest to composing and studying vocal music of the Catholic Church. The music of the Catholic Church of St. Charles Borromeo was directed by him for more than thirty-five years. His extensive music publishing was done at 133 South 11th Street.[2] Rosewig died in Philadelphia in 1929.

Rosewig was a distinguished and picturesque figure among Philadelphians of the early twentieth century. If Willard Spenser outlived his artistic generation, we should surely say that Rosewig did the same. His last years were spent recalling occasions long

---

[1] James G. Huneker, in *Steeplejack,* vol. I, p. 188.
[2] Joseph L. Armstrong is the successor to the Rosewig publishing firm.

past, such as the conducting of the Thomas Orchestra and the Centennial Chorus in 1876, or the Damrosch Orchestra and a festival chorus of 600 voices in 1894. Rosewig knew Reginald De Koven and Victor Herbert intimately, and was acquainted with Arthur Sullivan. The latter he met on the occasion of his acting as a pirate-copyist for Lee and Walker. Rosewig had been sent by that publishing firm to copy the melodies of *Pinafore* and *Mikado* during performances of those operettas at the South Broad Street Theatre. Among the European acquaintances made by Mr. Rosewig on his many trips abroad he counted such musicians as Gounod, Massenet, and Berthold Tours. D'Oyly Carte was also a friend of this inveterate traveller. One of the hardest ambitions for Albert H. Rosewig to realize was that of hearing his name correctly pronounced. Church musicians who may have been puzzled by the apparent typesetter's error in RoSEWIG publications are hereby notified that this small "o" was merely a device to get the public to pronounce his name in three syllables ROS-EWIG.

Hugh Archibald Clarke was a much greater man than his wealthy contemporary Rosewig. They are similar in their long career in Philadelphia music, Dr. Clarke having been active in its various phases for sixty-five years. Hugh Clarke was born in Canada, near Toronto, in 1839, and died in Philadelphia in 1927. His father, James P. Clarke, organist (and an Oxonian Mus. Doc.), was Hugh Clarke's only teacher. Clarke came to Philadelphia at the age of twenty, and soon began his long career as organist and teacher in that city. His most notable work as organist was done at the Second Presbyterian Church soon after that congregation had occupied their new building at 21st and Walnut Streets (1872). The tradition of fine music that still makes this church outstanding among Philadelphia Presbyterian churches was begun by Hugh Clarke.[1] His connection with the University of Pennsylvania is even more noted. Dr. Clarke shares with J. K. Paine of Harvard the distinction of being the first professor of music at a university in this country. His lectures at the University of Pennsylvania extended from 1875 to 1925. Productions of Clarke's

---

[1] Subsequent organist-directors have been Henry G. Thunder 1899-1912, Harry A. Matthews, N. Lindsay Norden, 1916-1927, and Alexander McCurdy, the present organist.

overture and choruses for Aristophanes' *The Acharnians* moved the University authorities to confer upon Hugh Clarke the degree of Doctor of Music in 1886.

Clarke succeeded Michael Cross as director of the Abt Male Chorus in 1871. He gave up this position shortly after his engagement at the University of Pennsylvania.

Compositions by Hugh Clarke include an opera *Iphigenia in Tauris,* an oratorio *Jerusalem,* chamber music, and many shorter works. His greatest importance lay in his fifty-one years of teaching at the University of Pennsylvania and in the textbooks and other works on music that he wrote. Among the latter are *The Scratch Club,* 1888, *A Dictionary of Musical Terms,* 1896, *Music and the Comrade Arts,* 1899, and *Highways and Byways of Music,* 1901.

The vitality of Hugh Clarke was an obvious characteristic to his many students and friends. During his early years in Philadelphia Clarke was a noted amateur boxer. Even in his eighty-fifth year he remained active and interested in all musical developments. He conducted the Jenny Lind Concert at Musical Fund Hall [1] at the age of eighty-one. As an impersonator of Maurice Strakosch at that concert, Hugh Clarke was declared the life of the anniversary program.

VI

The final section of our late nineteenth century discussion centers around the development of orchestral playing. It will be remembered that in the last pages of the preceding chapter many visiting orchestras were described, Steyermark and Germania (1848), Jullien and Musard among them. The Germania orchestra, not from Berlin, but organized in Philadelphia by Carl Sentz, was the only local orchestral group that existed for any long period of years in the late nineteenth century. Its beginnings go back to 1856, and they were accordingly mentioned in the preceding chapter. Its incorporation took place in 1860. The existence of the Germania Orchestra, Inc., beginning in 1860 and ending in 1895, is almost chronologically coextensive with the limits of the present chapter. The fact that about one-half of the members of Henry Thunder's

---

[1] Cf., *infra,* p. 356.

orchestra of 1895-1899 were taken from the recently disbanded Germania Orchestra, carries their influence throughout the years 1860-1899. And the incorporation of the entire Thunder Orchestra into the Philadelphia Orchestra under Scheel is noteworthy in connecting the Germania Orchestra with the famous Philadelphia group of the present day.

The concerts by the Germania Orchestra provide a stable and reasonably musical background for the visiting conductors and their more spectacular programs. It played concerts in Musical Fund Hall, even before the cessation of that society's own orchestra in 1857. The first season of summer concerts at the Academy of Music is worthy of notice among the early accomplishments by the Germania Orchestra. From July 1 to September 1, 1857, this group played nightly promenade concerts at the new Academy. The following years they gave concerts from June 26 to July 10. As the Germania Musical Society the group led by Carl Sentz played on many occasions. They gave open air concerts in the Männerchor Garden at Franklin Street and Fairmount Avenue in the years after the Civil War. Their many seasons of indoor programs under the leadership of Charles M. Schmitz and William Stoll, Jr., at the Academy of Fine Arts were among the first concerts to be given in an art museum in this country. These programs were entitled Promenade Concerts, and were given from 1888 to 1895. Well-written program notes were prepared for the Promenade Concerts, many of them containing abundant thematic illustrations in music notation.

Press announcements of the Germania Concerts are plentiful, some giving the program numbers for a coming event, others mentioning the success of a preceding concert. The *Philadelphia Ledger* for April 7, 1894, mentions that the concert for the afternoon of April 12th would include a Minuet by Boccherini, the Mendelssohn Wedding March, and the Andante from Beethoven's Pastoral Symphony. The program of April 19, 1894, was announced as a concert devoted to the works of "Spohr and Italian composers."

The fame of Theodore Thomas among American conductors rests on his achievements in Philadelphia only slightly less than those in his native New York. His early visits to Philadelphia were devoted to orchestral and chamber music engagements. As a member of string quartets, Thomas played in concerts and soirées in New York and Philadelphia for at least five years after the founding of his own celebrated orchestra. The beginning of these visits to Philadelphia is difficult to trace. He played as an orchestra member in opera and concert programs from about 1855. As early as 1857 he is called leader of the orchestra in some of the first season's programs of the Academy of Music. Since Carl Anschütz was styled conductor for these same performances, the probability is that Thomas was concertmaster of the orchestra. He was only twenty-one years old at the time, the programs being the German operas of June, 1857, already mentioned. In the 1858 Musard Concerts, Thomas was called assistant conductor to Musard. He was designated as concertmaster of the Philadelphia orchestra in 1860.[1] This may mean an orchestra more or less regularly associated with the Academy of Music for the accompaniment of various operatic troupes. Thomas and Anschütz are mentioned as conductors of the nine farewell appearances of Marietta Gazzaniga (May 2-17, 1859). The Strakosch or Strakosch-Ullman Italian Opera Company was directed and conducted by Sig. Muzio, "leader Theodore Thomas." Whatever Thomas may or may not have accomplished in the line of leadership when a director and conductor were also present, we learn that he directed, conducted, and led the performances of *Notre Dame de Paris* in 1864. These productions of Fry's last opera took place about two years after the organization of the Thomas Orchestra. This orchestra was founded in 1861, and played its first Philadelphia program on May 13, 1862. It also provided the instrumental music for *Notre Dame de Paris*. The orchestra paid frequent visits to Philadelphia as accompanists to opera, and as a featured symphonic organization, between the years 1862 and 1878. The account of the Centennial has mentioned his general musical direction and his disastrous Summer Nights' Concerts.[2] Theodore Thomas had to spend twelve years to get out of debt after 1876. The women's committees started this process

---

[1] By Marian B. Good, in *Some Musical Backgrounds of Pennsylvania,* p. 92.

[2] Cf. *supra,* p. 139.

of debt payment by organizing a series of ten Festival Concerts at the Academy of Music in 1876, September 20 to November 4.

Theodore Thomas realized the necessity for placating audiences with dance tunes just as singers of the period advertised themselves as freaks in order to secure an audience.[1] In our admiration for his large achievements and the serious music played by his orchestra we must not forget the great practicality of his scheme of concert management. The lessons learned as member of Jullien's orchestra, as assistant conductor to Musard, and as leader for popular-priced opera performances, were applied in his own program building with notable success.

Philadelphians had never forgotten the high artistic level reached by the Thomas orchestra when in the late 1890's a Philadelphia orchestra was contemplated. Mrs. E. D. Gillespie, who had helped to assist Thomas to get out of debt by the Festival Concerts of 1876, was the most persistent and influential advocate for his engagement as conductor of such an orchestra. In fact she refused to support or even attend the concerts of the Philadelphia Orchestra because Scheel and not Thomas had been secured as its conductor.

There is a similarity in the orchestral contributions made in 1857 to 1878 by Theodore Thomas, and the operatic contributions made later by Gustav Hinrichs. Both men were actually visitors in Philadelphia, yet each was far more important in his musical field than any native of the city. Thomas and Hinrichs were closely associated in New York in the year before the latter's seasons of operas in Philadelphia.[2] As the Father of the American Symphony Orchestra, Theodore Thomas both perfected his art and lived his musically influential life in Philadelphia, as well as in New York, Chicago, and Cincinnati.

The leading 'cellist in the Thomas Orchestra from 1872 to 1879 was Rudolph Hennig. Born in Germany in 1850, Hennig came to America as a young man. He was a 'cellist at the Walnut Street Theatre in the years after the Civil War, and was one of the founders of the Philadelphia Musical Academy in 1869.[3] After his years as first 'cello with Thomas, Rudolph Hennig returned to

---

[1] *Steeplejack*, vol. II, p. 32.
[2] Cf. *Memoirs of Theodore Thomas*, by Rose F. Thomas, pp. 279-296.
[3] Oliver Hopkinson was a pupil of Rudolph Hennig.

Philadelphia, shortly after 1880, and became an important teacher and participant in chamber ensembles for many years. He died in Philadelphia in 1904, and was one of the few men to be honored by a memorial tablet in the Academy of Music.

A different type of orchestral music was being conducted by the brothers Simon and Mark Hassler. The Hasslers provide a notable musical exception to the statement made earlier that no musician of the third generation has appeared in a given family despite so many musical fathers and sons. Simon and Mark Hassler were sons of Henry Hassler who came to Philadelphia in 1842 as a violinist and conductor. The original Henry Hassler led orchestras in various theatres and gardens from 1842 to 1855. The Musical Fund Society elected him to membership in 1847. It is an odd coincidence that exactly ninety years later, April 13, 1937, his grandson Arthur Hassler joined the Musical Fund Society. Henry Hassler's theatrical work included regular engagements as conductor of the orchestras at the Arch Street Theatre, 1844; the Chestnut Street Theatre, 1845; and the Walnut Street Theatre, 1846 to 1855. Several concerts at Peale's Museum during the above years were conducted by Hassler. When we recall the nature of the music staged at these theatres, in the years before the Academy of Music was built, the importance of this earliest Hassler is very evident.

Simon Hassler was the better known of Henry Hassler's sons, although persons who remember concerts directed by Simon and Mark Hassler are in doubt as to which of the two was the better conductor or had a finer orchestra. Simon Hassler was born in Germany in 1832, came to Philadelphia in 1842, joined the Musical Fund Society in 1854, and conducted orchestras in Philadelphia from 1850 to 1894. The direction of certain Centennial concerts, the conducting of part of the 1891 concert on the occasion of the remodelling of Musical Fund Hall, and the leading of various festival concerts are among Simon Hassler's special achievements. His more regular positions consisted of conducting the orchestra at the Walnut Street Theatre 1865-1872, the Chestnut Street Theatre 1872-1882, and the Chestnut Street Opera House 1882-1899.

Mark Hassler was two years younger than his brother. He died in Philadelphia in 1906. He seems to have had an ability similar to that of Simon as a theatre orchestra leader, and a special aptitude for conducting at exclusive balls in Philadelphia, Baltimore, and Washington. The finest parties from about 1870 to 1900 secured the services of Mark Hassler's Orchestra. He is said to have been the first to use the waltzes of Johann Strauss at dances in America. As to the theatre conducting which constituted the Hasslers' main musical claim to fame, Mark seems to have alternated with Simon Hassler in the duties at leading performances. Mark Hassler was officially the musical director for Mrs. John Drew at the Arch Street Theatre, but this being more an honorary than a musical distinction, he seems to have filled his brother's engagements in other theatres, and travelled with a large orchestra of his own to provide music for the very wealthy.

An interesting comment on the orchestras of the period, and on Mark Hassler in particular, is provided among the *Recollections of a Happy Life* by M. F. Egan.[1]

> "The orchestra of Mark Hassler and his brother held undivided supremacy and there were occasionally good concerts of chamber music. We younger people all loved the Hasslers because they played for the dances, or rather the 'hops' in Congress Hall during the season at Cape May. But personally I felt for some time a grudge against them, as a part of their orchestra always supported the annual concert given by the pupils of La Salle College, and as I was one of the unwilling bassos unfortunately placed too near the director's baton and justly mistreated during rehearsals, it was some time before I could hear them without having a temptation to duck, such as I am told the old fashioned canal captain felt when the pilot called 'bridge!' . . . ."

The flutist of the Hassler orchestras was a legendary figure named Lipschutz. He is said to have been the only first class flutist who had two complete sets of false teeth. Koch and Zilenziger were other noted local orchestra men. The former was a barber who played the horn with various visiting opera companies which brought only some of their orchestra members with them in former years. This William Koch was the father of a horn player in the later Philadelphia Orchestra. Mr. Zilenziger obliged in a similar manner on the bass drum in the same years (1875-1885).

---

[1] Maurice Francis Egan, *Recollections of a Happy Life*, p. 85. (New York, Doran and Co., 1924.)

The third generation of the Hassler family contains four children of Mark Hassler who were all musicians. One daughter, Harriet, was a vocal teacher in New York, a second, Rosalie, is a pianist and graduate of the music school of the University of Pennsylvania. The older son, Herbert, directed the music at the Chestnut Street Opera House for many years. Arthur Hassler, Mark's younger son, was associated with his father in the management of dance and concert orchestras, and later (1935-1939) held several positions in the directing of Federal Music Projects. Carl Buchman, a great-grandson of Henry Hassler, plans to continue in the family's line of orchestral conducting. Mr. Buchman graduated from the Curtis Institute conducting course in May, 1937. He is the composer of orchestral works that have been played in Cleveland and Paris, and is also a professional pianist, accompanist, and coach.

The activities of Willard Spenser lie in the humble but very large field of popular music. Spenser succeeded Septimus Winner as a writer and composer of popular songs. The successors to Spenser in this field have been residents of other cities, chiefly New York. While Winner and Spenser were national figures through their popular songs, the leadership in this voluminous field passed away from Philadelphia at about the middle of Spenser's career (c. 1905).

Willard Spenser was born in Cooperstown, New York, in 1852, while his parents were paying a visit relative to his father's illustrations for Cooper's novels. The senior Spenser was a prominent steel engraver in Philadelphia, and had designed the current five and ten dollar bills. His wife was gifted with a fine voice. William Fry had offered her the part of Leonora in his opera productions. Willard Spenser states that she played the Sonata Pathétique beautifully at the age of ninety-five.[1]

At the age of seven Spenser composed a waltz which was "buried under the tolerant criticism of his family." [2] The firm of Lee and Walker published another waltz, written in 1867, when Willard was fifteen. His childhood was spent in Philadelphia, his

---

[1] This claim is advanced in Spenser's (unpublished) autobiography, *The Wheel of Memory.*

[2] According to a lengthy article in the *Philadelphia Public Ledger*, Dec. 17, 1933, a few days after Spenser's death.

boyhood and young manhood in New York. His memoirs testify to his eclectic musical upbringing. Minstrel troupes of all varieties alternated with Gerster, Campanini, Calve, Patti (his favorite), and the Thomas Orchestra in the musical environment of Spenser's youth.

Spenser's earliest operetta, *The Little Tycoon,* was the first successful comic opera by an American. After a three years' search for a producer, *The Little Tycoon* was given in the Temple Theatre in 1885. William Singerly, the proprietor of the *Philadelphia Record,* was the far-sighted producer who backed this highly successful operetta. Over 2,600 professional performances of *The Little Tycoon* were given by the companies under the original management, and as later managed by Spenser himself in a coast-to-coast tour. Willard Spenser had taken over the management of this play when both New York and Philadelphia managers had insisted on introducing vulgarities into its lines. The amateur performances of *The Little Tycoon* have exceeded six thousand. The *Evening Bulletin* for December 19, 1933, admits that "Willard Spenser outlived his artistic generation" but claims that "to match this kind of popularity it is necessary to turn to Gilbert and Sullivan." Spenser had been accused of turning to Gilbert for his libretto for *The Little Tycoon,* which contains marked similarities to that of *The Mikado.* If any plagiarism occurred it was on the part of Gilbert, since Spenser showed his manuscript for *The Little Tycoon* to Colonel Morse, the Gilbert and Sullivan manager, three years before *The Mikado* was first produced in London.

His next operetta, *The Princess Bonnie,* was managed by its author and composer from the start. The Chestnut Street Theatre housed its opening performances, beginning on March 26, 1894. This play, and *The Little Tycoon,* are still being given (1940), *Princess Bonnie's* total of performances now approaching the 3,000 mark, while *The Little Tycoon* is nearing its 10,000th performance.[1] The *Ledger* of March 31, 1894, says of *The Princess Bonnie's* opening performance: "Mr. Spenser has written in a popular vein. ... The production was handsomely staged and the cast is a fully

---

[1] According to a careful count made by Willard Spenser, Jr., who has continued to handle copyrights and editions of his father's sensational operettas.

competent one." Eleanor Mayo became famous as the Princess Bonnie—in fact, her fame as an actress in light opera rests almost entirely on the interpretation of that part, for James Elverson, Jr., the proprietor of the *Philadelphia Inquirer,* married Miss Mayo while the professional performances of *Princess Bonnie* were still in progress. Among such personal items we might mention the fact that one of the chorus girls of *The Little Tycoon* married Lord Hope, or possibly the Hope Diamond.

Miss Bob White, Spenser's third successful operetta, opened at the Chestnut Street Theatre, April 15, 1901. There have been over 3,000 professional and amateur performances of this play to date. Raymond Hitchcock, who had played a minor part in earlier Spenser productions, became famous as one of the tramps in *Miss Bob White.* The management of this play was in the hands of Zimmerman and Nixon. The composer wished to have more leisure for creative work, and retired from the strenuous managerial field. His memoirs relate with feeling how *Miss Bob White* was nearly ruined because one of the managers had cast a matronly soprano opera singer as Miss Bob White. Beyond question the failure of Spenser's last two operettas, *Rosalie* and *The Wild Goose,* was brought about in large measure by poor casting and inept management. Willard Spenser's gift of simple and charming melody is freely spread throughout all of his works. The naive plots and the perfectly matched music did not fail in the later works. But we do not know a "Heel and Toe Polka" nor yet a "Love Comes Like a Summer Sigh" from either of them. The polka is mentioned in Mark Sullivan's *Our Times* series [1] as belonging to a folk music strain to which the words, if any, did not matter. Sullivan classifies *Heel and Toe Polka* with Fisher's Hornpipe and Rochester Schottische.

It is hardly an exaggeration to say that Philadelphia's rivalry with New York as the home for the most important light opera productions of the late nineteenth century rests largely upon the twenty years of nearly continuous success achieved by Spenser's music. Of course the operettas made fortunes for the author-composer-manager himself, as well as for many persons associated with him

---

[1] Vol. II, p. 162, Scribner, New York, 1927.

in their long professional runs throughout the country. Willard Spenser devoted his later years to supervising the many performances of his operettas, and to the pursuit of his sporting and social hobbies and clubs. He died at Wayne, Pa., a Philadelphia suburb, in 1933.

We shall attempt an outline of chamber music in the twentieth century chapters devoted to Instrumental Groups. That section will include a historical review of some leading ensembles of our present epoch. However, we cannot omit consideration of Charles H. Jarvis in the late nineteenth century, the period to which he so completely belonged. The musicales at Cross's home and the Gaertner and Stoll chamber concerts have already been mentioned. Charles Jarvis was even more significant than these men in the development of chamber music in Philadelphia.

Charles H. Jarvis was born in Philadelphia in 1837, the son of an English pianist and teacher, Charles W. Jarvis, who had settled there a few years before that date. Charles H. Jarvis acquired his remarkable piano technique at an early age through study with his father. His first public appearance as a pianist was made at the age of seven. Leopold Meignen taught Jarvis the theory of music, which branch never rivalled technical proficiency in his interests or among his abilities. Charles Jarvis appeared as soloist with noted orchestras, the New York Philharmonic and the Theodore Thomas among them. The Classical Soirées, instituted in 1862 and continued for more than thirty years, constitute Jarvis" most important activity in Philadelphia music history. The Natatorium at Broad and Locust Streets was frequently used for these programs of chamber music. The Horticultural Hall, Broad Street below Locust, the New Century Drawing Room, and an auditorium at the Academy of Fine Arts were also used for some of Jarvis' concerts in this lengthy series. Over 800 compositions were presented at the Jarvis concerts. Since the main organizer and star of the Classical Soirées was a pianist, the chamber music had an unduly large share of works in which his special abilities were featured. "All of the great piano concertos from Bach in D minor to Henselt in F minor were given in a finished manner. Profound interpretation was absent however." James G. Huneker so characterizes

the main fare of the Classical Soirées.[1] Huneker had been a piano
pupil of Michael Cross, that versatile instrumentalist. He regrets
that Jarvis was not engaged to teach him, for the specialization in
the technical side of piano playing which was Charles Jarvis's greatest asset, was not possessed by Cross. The two men were rivals,
insofar as Cross trespassed on Jarvis's special field of chamber music
concerts. Yet we should say today that the occasional chamber
music series given at Cross's, or under his management at Horticultural Hall, possessed more of the fine qualities inherent to good
chamber music than all of Jarvis's piano-dominated Classical
Soirées.

As a musician Charles H. Jarvis was a thorough technician on
the piano, and specialized in that type of activity. He did not
memorize his tremendous repertoire of concertos and other difficult
selections. A certain lack of emotional background in Jarvis's playing caused his audiences to feel oppressed by monotony at the end
of a long program. At the end of thirty years of long programs,
Philadelphia audiences must have welcomed the more musicianly
interpretation of later pianists such as the Philadelphians Sternberg
and Ezerman, or the visiting Godowsky and Hofmann.

David D. Wood's account of Philadelphia music from 1860 to
1909 [2] mentions the Classical Soirées as among the most important
events in the late nineteenth century. One of the latest programs
in Jarvis' series is thus recorded in the *Philadelphia Public Ledger*
of April 9, 1894:

> Charles Jarvis closed the thirtieth season of chamber music
> concerts, in the New Century Drawing Room, April 7. Mr. Jarvis
> played two solos, the Bach C minor Toccata and Fugue, and the Raff
> Suite in D. He was assisted by William Stoll, Jr., E. A. Brill, R.
> Schmidt, and Rudolph Hennig. They presented two quintettes for
> piano and strings,—Spohr in D minor and Dvořák in A. major.
> "The interest of each was heightened by the other of these most
> unlike compositions. The performance individually and generally
> throughout the evening was of the high order so often before
> commended."

---

[1] *Steeplejack*, vol. I, p. 143.
[2] Prepared for the Musical Art Club, December 8, 1909. Manuscript
kindly furnished by Mrs. Wood.

When concertos were given the assisting quartet played a reduction of the orchestral score. The aggregate educational influence of Jarvis's concerts is difficult to estimate. Beyond question his programs, in spite of artistic limitations, developed an acquaintance with chamber music and piano works that prepared the way for later instrumental ventures.

Charles H. Jarvis died in 1895. A tablet to his memory is located in the lobby of the Academy of Music. Jarvis's library of 1,700 volumes of chamber music forms a part of the large library of the Curtis Institute of Music.

An early example of telephonic transmission from New York to Philadelphia is suggested by the pianistic chamber music of Charles Jarvis. Since it occurred in 1877 it antedates the telephone operas recounted above [1] as heard by Edward Fry in 1883. "Mr. Boscovitz the renowned pianist" played, no louder than normal, *Home Sweet Home* with variations, *Swanee River,* and other airs, in New York. The audience heard this program via telephone at the Academy of Music in Philadelphia. The critics of the day considered the achievement a scientific marvel rather than a musical one. One writer declared that the tone received sounded like a hand organ; to another it resembled the music of a calliope. Professor Elisha Gray, an important scientist in the development of the telephone, was responsible for this demonstration. A grand concert conducted by Strakosch was heard at the Academy of Music on the same night that the telephoned piano numbers were introduced (April 13, 1877).

As a final thought on nineteenth century music, let us consider some of the distinguished visitors who participated in orchestral music during its closing years. In 1891, the year in which Philadelphia's perennial visitor Theodore Thomas was engaged as conductor of the Chicago Symphony, there was a notable concert by the Boston Festival Orchestra. The *Philadelphia Public Ledger* will tell in two brief quotations the story of this visiting orchestra's plans and accomplishments.

> The Boston Festival Orchestra, Victor Herbert, conductor, will
> be heard in the Academy of Music Monday evening, May 18th,

---

[1] Cf. *supra*, p. 76,

Notable artists will take part, including Peter I. Tschaikovsky; Miss Adele Aus der Ohe, soloist in the piano concerto in B flat minor; Miss Rose Stewart, soprano; Myron Whitney, basso; Felix Winternitz, violinist; and Mr. Victor Herbert in 'cello numbers. The concert is of importance because it is Tschaikovsky's only appearance here. —Public Ledger, May 1, 1891.

A few days before the concert, May 15th, the *Ledger* repeated the substance of the above article, and added that Tschaikovsky would conduct two numbers. Press notices of May 18th added that S. Behrens was the Philadelphia manager for this visit of the Boston Festival Orchestra.

The criticism of the concert is contained in the *Ledger* of May 19.

"Tschaikovsky made the occasion remarkable by conducting two of his own compositions; a suite for string orchestra. . . . Badly placed at the close of the program . . ."; and his B flat minor concerto for piano and orchestra. . . . "He is an energetic and authoritative conductor, and under his direction the men felt the spirit of his music, as they could not have felt it under any other leader. . . . The orchestra, organized on a basis of three double basses, and six violins, was notably well balanced and satisfactory in volume and quality of tone, except in Tschaikovsky's Suite, when the principal and another first violin dropped out for some reason not readily apparent. . . . With Miss Adele Aus der Ohe at the piano . . . the concerto had unsurpassable interpretation . . . with the composer to emphasize its character and bring out the innermost beauties. Miss Aus der Ohe . . . and Tschaikovsky were called before the house three times."

An earlier visit, 1875, by the composer-pianist von Bülow is described in *Steeplejack,* the autobiography of James G. Huneker. Benjamin J. Lang of Boston conducted for von Bülow's tour in 1875-1876. In the Philadelphia concert of December 17, 1875, Tschaikovsky's First Piano Concerto was played. "Things were soon at sixes and sevens. . . . The solo performer was white with rage." [1] Von Bülow's sure but heavy manner of playing was admired by Charles Jarvis, but not by Michael Cross.

---

[1] *Steeplejack*, vol. I, p. 247.

Ferruccio Busoni was the soloist with the Boston Symphony Orchestra at a concert in Philadelphia on April 27, 1894. The French organist Alexandre Guilmant and his greater contemporary Camille Saint-Saëns paid visits to Philadelphia in the later years of the nineteenth century. In spite of all the effort and ability of Siegfried Behrens as Philadelphia agent for visiting orchestras, and opera companies, the years prior to 1900 cannot boast so numerous an array of leading instrumentalists as participate in the present yearly series of Philadelphia's orchestra concerts.

Perhaps the most effective series of programs by visiting orchestras in the 1890's was that begun at Willow Grove Park in 1896. This was our final instrumental development of importance in the nineteenth century. The importance of Willow Grove as a summer musical center became more marked after 1900, but it was organized and many of its concerts were given during the closing years of the nineteenth century. This music center, destined for many seasons to be the summer capital of American music, is described in the accounts of the twentieth century.[1] The Philadelphia Symphony Society, 1893-1900, and the Thunder Orchestra, 1895-1899, have also been mentioned as immediate predecessors of the Philadelphia Orchestra in the introductory sections of the chapter devoted to that orchestra. The Symphony Society was a predecessor in point of time, while the Thunder Orchestra was a connecting link in personnel as well, for, as will be seen, it was incorporated into the Philadelphia Orchestra at the beginning of that organization.

---

[1] Cf. *infra,* pp. 195-6.

PART II

CHAPTER FIVE

INTRODUCTION TO THE TWENTIETH CENTURY

Up to the year 1900 the panorama of Philadelphia music has been unfolded as a continuous historical representation. Sometimes a topic was followed for a few years, or a man's life was traced over a considerable span of time, making it necessary for us to retrace our steps in order to catch up in the general chronological sequence. This topical method, which was the exception in the historical chapters, must become the accepted rule in the twentieth century sections of this book.

The necessity for presenting a complete account of the musical affairs of the present day arises from the fact that no attempt at any comprehensive account of Philadelphia musical organizations is available for reference purposes. Many large and flourishing choirs, choruses, and orchestras, and many no less significant smaller vocal and instrumental ensembles, are leavening the lump of the city's widespread life. Their number and diversity has been seen to have increased during the preceding periods already considered. It is this large growth of music—seldom rising above mediocrity perhaps, but surely not meriting the complete lack of mention that most music histories have accorded it—that becomes particularly rapid near the year 1900.

A realization that Chicago had permanently secured Theodore Thomas may have caused concert goers, who had heard what the Thomas Orchestra could do in the late nineteenth century, to discover that Philadelphia had lost the opportunity of engaging this greatest of early American orchestral conductors to direct regular seasons of orchestra concerts in that city. Indeed, several music lovers were so intent on having Thomas return east for a Philadelphia Orchestra that they refused to attend concerts directed by Fritz Scheel—possibly a greater (though less American) conductor

than Theodore Thomas.[1] A belated recognition that New York
had unquestonably surpassed Philadelphia in matters artistic as
well as commercial may have stirred other civic minded individuals
to hazard some daring innovations in our local musical life. Frank
Damrosch's success as leader of the Orpheus Club (1897-1905)
showed that the New York Damrosch family could perhaps best
carry on what Benjamin and Michael Cross had done for Philadelphia for so many years. The advocates of Walter Damrosch [2]
for the position of conductor of the newly founded Philadelphia
Orchestra were nearly as numerous—and from all accounts, as
noisy—as those favoring Theodore Thomas.

Of course the records and recollections of the spur of such
provincial rivalries give only a small part of the reason for the vast
spread of musical activities around the year 1900. Deeper causes
lay in Philadelphia's great geographical expansion from 1875 to
1900. The area of its built-up sections increased rapidly during
these years, the people moving out from the center of the city in
large numbers. It was in 1854 that the Philadelphia city limits
were extended to the boundaries of what had been Philadelphia
County. Many schools and churches were built in suburban and
remote urban sections of the city. Philadelphia church music of
artistic as well as devotional excellence had ceased to be confined
to about a dozen central city churches, and spread to the many large
and active institutions built mainly from 1875 to 1910 outside of
the central district. The music of the public schools had probably
been introduced with the beginning of public school organization in
1836, but it was in 1897 that the music department now in existence
was created as a part of the Philadelphia school system. The growth
of interest in orchestral concerts in the late nineteenth century was
followed by the founding in 1900 of the present Philadelphia Orchestra. Singing societies also increased and multiplied during the

---

[1] The previously mentioned story of Mrs. Edward D. Gillespie's boycott
of all Philadelphia's Orchestra concerts because Theodore Thomas had not
been engaged to conduct them provides a sad commentary on the intense feeling about who should be awarded the important post of the first conductor
of the Philadelphia Orchestra.

[2] Brother of Frank, and son of Leopold Damrosch—Walter Damrosch
became conductor of the New York Symphony Orchestra which position he
filled with distinction until 1927. He is today undoubtedly the best known
and best loved radio lecturer on the appreciation of music.

last decade of the nineteenth century. Many of the important vocal groups of the present day were founded near the year 1900.[1]

So many varied groups still active in their chosen spheres demand a series of topical accounts, if for no other reason than the need for an available source for reference purposes. A few representative organizations of each nature will be treated with some degree of completeness, a few more will be mentioned in the text; and many which had to be omitted from the topical chapters which follow will be found in the index-dictionary at the end of this book.

Hugh A. Clarke, William Wallace Gilchrist, David D. Wood, Philip Goepp, D. Hendrik Ezerman, Richard Zeckwer, Gilbert R. Combs, were among the leaders who did most to organize this growing, spreading musical life. Beyond the limits of their actual directing, teaching and composing, the example of their high standards reaches throughout Philadelphia and beyond. Younger men who are still active in the city's musical life, and who made large contributions to musical developments near the year 1900 include Henry Gordon Thunder, William Sylvano Thunder, Thaddeus Rich, David Edgar Crozier, H. Alexander Matthews, Ralph Kinder, J. W. F. Leman, George A. A. West, and Leopold Stokowski. These lists, which are perhaps too long to be readable, and certainly too short to contain even the important names of the musicians of the beginning of the century,[2] are given here because the topical nature of the following pages prevents any impressive array of leading names in different musical fields.

---

[1] The Orpheus Club was organized in 1872, the Mendelssohn Club in 1874, the Fortnightly Club in 1893, the Matinee Musical Club in 1894, the Philadelphia Choral Society in 1897, and the Philadelphia Music Club in 1911. The Manuscript Music Society, the Musical Art Club and several other music study and musical-social organizations date from the same years.

[2] An account of each will be found in the sections following, or in the index.

Chapter Six

THE PHILADELPHIA ORCHESTRA

I

Probably no musical venture demands the interest and cooperation of more patrons than does a large symphonic orchestra. The opera is more expensive for each performance, but it has been such a popular musical form in the period of Philadelphia's history that it has come closer to paying for itself than has a professional orchestra of symphonic dimensions. Within the past decade, from the depression period of 1930, to the present, 1940, a slight waning in public appreciation of opera seems to be causing the companies to adopt policies of private and public patronage that have been characteristic of the Philadelphia Orchestra management from its inception. It has been said that Philadelphia's especial apathy to fine orchestral entertainment is partly due to a survival of early policies of repression, still lingering in the consciousness of wealthy descendants of the Quaker tradition. Ronald F. Eyer [1] illustrates this very natural view in an interesting quotation, "Just why one of America's earliest centres of civilization should have been so tardy in symphonic culture is a little difficult to understand, but some light may be gained from this missive of Justus Falckner, written in 1701: 'The Dancing School, Assembly, and Concert Room have been shut up, as inconsistent with the Gospel: and though the gentlemen concerned caused the door to be broke open again, we are informed that no company came to the last Assembly night.'" Falckner was not unusual among early leaders in Philadelphia in expressing this sentiment, as our chapter on Colonial Music made plain in many instances.

---

[1] *Musical America*, January 25, 1937, article *America's Notable Orchestras.*

If such opposition and resultant apathy had been typical of the entire period of Philadelphia history until the founding of the orchestra in 1900, the subsequent achievements of that group would have been far too miraculous. Obviously this was not the case, for though the principal credit for the rapid rise of the Philadelphia Orchestra in its early years belongs to Fritz Scheel, its first conductor, a considerable amount of orchestral experience was available to Philadelphia musicians—both amateur and professional—throughout the period 1760-1900, in spite of both apathy and opposition in influential quarters. Some of the preceding orchestral groups of historical importance have already been discussed, but the few important and relatively immediate predecessors to the Philadelphia Orchestra should be mentioned here.

The orchestra of the Musical Fund Society was the earliest of the ninteenth century groups that can be said to have been an ancestor of the Philadelphia Orchestra. Their concerts from 1820 to 1857 have been discussed [1] in an earlier chapter. Their courteous assistance to the Germania Orchestra from 1856 to 1895, and to the Thunder Orchestra in 1896-1897, makes the Musical Fund Society the sponsor of almost all of Philadelphia's ninteenth century orchestral music. The Germania Orchestra gave most of its concerts in Musical Fund Hall, as did Dr. Thunder's group during its first season.

A Germania Orchestra from Berlin gave six concerts in Philadelphia in 1848. This series was a disastrous failure, although the orchestra met with fair success in other cities. This is possibly just another example of musical difficulties in Philadelphia. A Philadelphia orchestra named *Germania* had a long career (1856-1895) of considerable local success. These two symphonic organizations, the German one and its German-American namesake in Philadelphia, are widely recognized to have been the most important influences in the city's musical history during the middle and late ninteenth century.[2] The Offenbach concerts of 1876 and the concerts by the Thomas Orchestra in the late ninteenth century have been described in an earlier chapter.

---

[1] Cf., *supra*, pp. 57-68.
[2] See Chapter VI (pp. 149-150) for a fuller account of these orchestras.

The Philadelphia Symphony Society (1893-1900) was led by William Wallace Gilchrist. Though entirely an amateur organization, this society was an immediate predecessor in point of years of the present Philadelphia Orchestra. It was one of the important organizations that bridged the gap between the various nineteenth century groups and the present noted orchestra.

During these same years a group of professional musicians was led by Henry Gordon Thunder. This Thunder Orchestra gave concerts from 1896 to 1899, continuing to a great extent the professional traditions of the recently disbanded Germania Orchestra.[1] While the Symphony Society aided the Philadelphia Orchestra at its inception in matters of organization, and provided a group of enthusiastic music lovers (not to mention a large orchestral library, a set of music stands and kettle drums), the Thunder Orchestra was incorporated to a man in Scheel's group of 1900. Only ten of these Thunderers were retained in 1901, however, and it is remarkable to observe that five of these ten are still (1940) members of the Philadelphia Orchestra.[2]

II

Fritz Scheel was conducting an orchestra at Woodside Park in 1899 when Mrs. Frederick N. Innes and later Dr. Edward I. Keffer were deeply impressed by his unusual abilities. He was engaged to conduct the Philadelphia Symphony Society's three annual concerts, with the understanding that he would also conduct a spring concert with professional musicians only. The Symphony Society programs gotten out of the way, the problem of an audience for his professionals presented itself. The idea of a benefit concert for widows of soldiers and sailors killed in the Philippine War proved so popular that eight hundred patrons were secured, and two professional concerts were presented. Due to the excellence of the orchestra and the wise selection of assisting soloists (Vladimir de Pachmann, Edouard de Reszke) the concerts were a

---

[1] About twenty-five members of the Germania Orchestra were later in Dr. Thunder's Orchestra.
[2] P. Lotz, C. E. Gerhard, D. Bove, W. Schmidt, A. Horner.

tremendous success. The city-wide interest of musical organizations may be noted from the promptness with which Philadelphians met to organize a permanent orchestra with Scheel as conductor. The Orpheus Club rooms were used for the meeting; Dr. Dunglison, president of the Musical Fund Society, issued invitations to members of many other organizations, the press, and persons of civic prominence. A fund of $15,000 was raised, and the first performance of the Philadelphia Orchestra was announced for November 16, 1900—both being direct results of that musically important meeting.

The programs from the orchestra's beginning were of the highest musical order. However, without the benefit motive of the first concerts to help sell tickets, the deficits mounted from the start.

Scheel was more willing to conduct popular and lighter concerts than some who remember only the strictness of his orchestral discipline will admit. Nor did he fail to provide novel attractions on the orchestra programs of those early years. The invasions of New York and Boston (1902 and 1904) were daring and successful ventures. So, too, were a Beethoven cycle of five concerts in 1903, and special engagements whereby Richard Strauss conducted his own works in 1904 [1] and Weingartner his own second symphony in 1905. But special activities, including annual tours to cities in the Middle Atlantic States made Scheel busier than his health would permit. He was conducting the Orpheus and Euridice clubs in the later years of his connection with the Philadelphia Orchestra, and leading an opera class as well. His chamber music programs, special concerts, and arrangements for visiting conductors and orchestra tours in 1904-1906 are said to have caused his death in 1907 at the age of fifty-five.

On the occasion of Strauss' conducting—which was also connected with the orchestral tour of 1904—the newspapers were full of highest tributes to the distinguished visitor. The following comments are taken from a large collection contained in Frances Wister's book.

---

[1] For a complete account of the appearances of R. Strauss as conductor of the Philadelphia Orchestra and friend of Fritz Scheel, see Frances Wister's *Twenty-five Years of the Philadelphia Orchestra*, pp. 37-42.

Philadelphia Inquirer, March 5th, 1904:

"RICHARD STRAUSS AT THE ACADEMY
"FIRST APPEARANCE OF THE FAMOUS COMPOSER
MADE YESTERDAY AFTERNOON. HE CONDUCTS
A FINE PERFORMANCE OF HIS OWN 'DEATH
AND TRANSFIGURATION' AND HIS WIFE
SINGS FOUR SONGS

"There was a very large audience at the Academy of Music yesterday afternoon, when the Philadelphia Orchestra gave its last Friday afternoon performance for the current season. The occasion was made notable by the first appearance in this city of the famous composer, Richard Strauss, who had arranged to guide the orchestra through the mazes of the tone poem entitled, 'Death and Transfiguration,' one of his best and most characteristic works; and it was rendered additionally interesting and important by the Philadelphia debut of Mme. Strauss-de Ahna, who has the reputation of being an exceptionally skillful and sympathetic interpreter of her distinguished husband's songs."

*   *   *   *   *   *

"After his wife had finished her group of songs, and the enthusiastic and long continued applause which her work had elicited had died away, Mr. Richard Strauss returned to the platform to conduct his own 'Tod und Verklaerung.' He is a singularly modest and unobtrusive looking man, with an appearance more suggestive of a school teacher than of a musician, and with nothing about him to betray any large estimate of his own consequence, but there can be no question as to his ability as a conductor. That had already been indicated in the manner he played the accompaniments to his wife's singing, but it was conclusively demonstrated by the way in which he conducted the orchestral feature of the programme. In its lucidity and balance, in its delicate sense of proportion; in its wide and pregnant variations of light and shade; in the splendor of its climaxes and the salient force with which each detail was projected and each nuance given its proper value, his performance of 'Death and Transfiguration' has certainly never been equalled in this city. It was a very great achievement and the audience rightly recognized it as such."

Philadelphia Ledger, March 5th 1904:

"STRAUSS CONCERT A GREAT SUCCESS
WARM GREETING FOR THE COMPOSER AND HIS WIFE

* * * * * *

"Strauss has a very precise beat, ordinarily quiet and undemonstrative and making very little use of his left hand; but when he wants a big climax for the brasses—and he is not afraid of noise—he conducts with his whole person. The orchestra knew the music perfectly and was absolutely responsive to every nuance."

City and State, March 10th, 1904:

"The highest point, not only of the winter, but in a certain sense of all previous musical seasons was reached last week. To have the most eminent musician—we use the word advisedly in the strictest sense—interpret his compositions with our own orchestra in two concerts, certainly marks Philadelphia as one of the self dependent musical centers of the world. But it was much more significant to hear the unstinted praise which Mr. Strauss bestowed on the orchestra after the concerts. On Friday, after the exalting performance of 'Death and Transfiguration,' the composer seemed to forget his audience in the heartiness of his acknowledgments to the orchestra."

The monthly concerts at the Academy of Music required more interest and support than the concert goers of Philadelphia were willing to provide. Officers and other financial backers have maintained a constant stream of contributions to keep the orchestra running. A new departure was found to be eminently successful,—the women's committees which provided further financial assistance, particularly in the period before the present endowment policy was inaugurated. The first Women's Committee for the Philadelphia Orchestra was organized in 1904.

Scheel was adamant in refusing to include lighter music for more popular appeal in his regular concerts, but he did rehearse and conduct additional concerts, benefit performances and the like, which included lighter works and netted considerable profits. His first program as conductor of the Philadelphia Orchestra is given in full because of the significance and obvious worth of the music he selected.

THE PHILADELPHIA ORCHESTRA

MR. FRITZ SCHEEL, *Conductor*

FIRST CONCERT

Friday, November 16, 1900, at 8:15 P.M.

Program

Carl Goldmark ....Overture, In Spring, Op. 36

Ludwig van Beethoven ....Symphony No. 5, C minor, Op. 67

    I. Allegro con brio 2-4

    II. Andante con moto 3-8

    III. Allegro 3-4

    IV. Allegro 4-4

Intermission of ten minutes.

Peter Ilich Tschaikowsky..................Concerto for pianoforte, No. 1

    in B flat minor Op. 23

    I. Allegro, non troppo e molto maestoso 3-4

    II. Andantino semplice 6-8

    III. Allegro con fuoco 3-4

Carl Maria von Weber.................."Invitation to the Dance," Op. 65

Richard Wagner ....Entry of the Gods into Walhalla

Soloist, Mr. Ossip Gabrilowitsch

When we note the soloist and date of this concert, the thought occurs that this Philadelphia concerto performance was Gabrilowitsch's American debut, rather than a later New York appearance generally considered to have had that honor.[1]

It is hardly surprising that Scheel was fully informed concerning the best music of the day, since he had known von Bülow, Brahms, Tschaikowsky, and Rubinstein intimately, and must have had a slight acquaintance with many other famous musical personages in a long and brilliant series of musical positions in Germany. In the United States he had conducted concerts at the World's Fair in Chicago (1893), as well as having been the first conductor of the San Francisco Orchestra (1893-1897).

---

[1] It is noted in Miss Wister's book (*Twenty-five Years of the Philadelphia Orchestra,* Stern and Company, Philadelphia, 1925) that the same program as Scheel's opener was given by the orchestra under Stokowski, with the same soloist, in 1925 (November 13 and 14). Although the celebrations of a successful start could not be indulged in, there were numerous appropriate demonstrations at the organization's Silver Anniversary.

Scheel's ability to imitate the tone of missing instruments by combinations of instruments that were available has become a legend in Philadelphia amateur music circles. One writer, a friend of the conductor who remembers Scheel as a leader of various amateur groups, recalls his "using the French horn and the 'cello together to play the third bassoon part.'" [1] This "peculiar faculty" may not strike modern musicians as a phenomenal musical gift, yet they must all agree as to Fritz Scheel's resourcefulness in making the substitution at all, and his conscientiousness in working out the details necessary to play it.

The second, third and fourth programs will further show better than any attempt at descriptive words the immediate high level of Fritz Scheel's accomplishment.

SECOND CONCERT
Friday, December 14, 1900, at 8:15

Beethoven .... Overture, Leonore, No. 3
Brahms .... Symphony No. 2, D major (Op. 73)
Ambroise Thomas .... "Mad Scene" (Hamlet)
Tschaikowsky .... Serenade for Strings Op. 48
Songs —
      Spring Has Come (Hiawatha) .... Tyler
      Skylark .... Handel
      An April Birthday .... Ronald
Bedrich Smetana ...."Vltave" (From the Symphonic Poem "My Country")
Madame Lillian Blauvelt, Soloist
Selden Miller, Accompanist

THIRD CONCERT
Friday, January 18, 1901, at 8:15

Wagner .... Faust Overture
Beethoven .... Symphony No. 4, Op. 60
Intermission
Vieuxtemps .... Concerto No. 2, Op. 19
Engelbert Humperdinck .... Moorish Rhapsody
      I. Tarila (Sunset Elegy)
      II. Tanger (A Night in a Moorish Café)
      III. Tetuan (A Ride in the Desert)
Soloist—Fritz Kreisler

---

[1] *Twenty-five Years of the Philadelphia Orchestra*, F. Wister, p. 29.

FOURTH CONCERT
Friday, February 8, 1901, 8:00 P.M.

William W. Gilchrist ....Symphony in C
    I. Introduction. Vivace impetuoso—Allegro molto
    II. Adagio, Andante moderato
    III. Scherzo——Vivace
    IV. Finale—Molto allegro
Edward MacDowell ....Concerto for Piano No. 2
Carl Maria von Weber................................Overture, Oberon
Edvard Grieg ....Berceuse for Strings, from Op. 68
Heinrich Hoffman ....Elves and Giants, Op. 22
Anton Dvořák ....Slavonic Dances III and IV
Soloist—Edward MacDowell

    Without danger of appearing maudlin or even insincere, one can say that these concerts would possess true musical interest to present day orchestral connoisseurs. The orchestral music before 1900, even from their most worthy programs, seems of rather antiquarian and pioneering significance when compared to the initial Philadelphia Orchestra programs quoted above. One can say not only historically but musically, it would be good to have been at these first concerts under Fritz Scheel.[1]

    The well merited admiration which the first conductor of the Philadelphia Orchestra has ever been accorded must not obscure the names of other important persons who made his accomplishments possible. The Philadelphia Orchestra Association, formed May 17, 1901, and incorporated in 1903, consisted of the following men and women:

---

[1] One of the best qualified judges of the solid and scholarly foundation of the Philadelphia Orchestra, Leopold Stokowski, is quoted (in Frances Wister's *Twenty-five Years of the Philadelphia Orchestra,* p. 85) in the following tribute to Fritz Scheel: "The man who really made the Philadelphia Orchestra from a musical standpoint, is Fritz Scheel. . . . He must have had very high musical ideals. They are evident in everything he did. Also he must have had a wonderful faculty for choosing the highest type of artists for the orchestra; he set a standard then which has been difficult to live up to musically. Such artists as Rich, Horner, Schwar—to mention only a few who are remaining (1925) in the Philadelphia Orchestra from Fritz Scheel's time—are absolutely in the first rank for their instrument, not only in America but in the whole world. It was Scheel's vision that laid such a wonderful foundation for this orchestra . . . we can never sufficiently recognize the debt we owe to Fritz Scheel: the good work he did and the influence of his ideals seem to live on forever."

George Burnham, Jr. John H. Ingham Richard Rossmassler
A. J. Cassatt Oliver B. Judson Edgar Scott
John H. Converse Edward I. Keffer Anne Thomson
Eckley B. Coxe, Jr. C. Hartman Kuhn Simon A. Stern
William L. Elkins Edward G. McCollin Alexander Van Rensselaer
Mary K. Gibson Thomas B. Newbold Henry Whelen, Jr.
Clement A. Griscom James W. Paul, Jr. P. A. B. Widener
Mrs. Alfred Harrison Mrs. Frank H. Rosengarten

The officers and executive committees were responsible for the orchestra's continuance during the least successful period of its history. Alexander Van Rensselaer, President; F. T. Sully Darley, Vice-President; John Hall Ingham, Secretary; and Henry Whelen, Jr., Treasurer, carried the burden of the orchestra management and support from 1900 to 1905.

III

Unfortunately Scheel died in 1907 (March 13) and others less noted finished that season's concerts. His successor, Carl Pohlig, was a master of conducting,[1] and led the Philadelphia Orchestra for about the same space of time as did Scheel. Yet he seems to have occupied a position somewhat analogous to that of Mendelssohn's father—who dubbed himself the son of Moses Mendelssohn and the father of Felix Mendelssohn. Like this modest middle Mendelssohn, Pohlig followed Scheel and preceded Stokowski. Like him, also, he was much appreciated at home,[2] that

[1] The *Neue Musik Zeitung* speaks thus of Carl Pohlig as conductor, "Pohlig directs with fire and deep feeling, and with a certain clearness that can only spring from a quiet insight into the innermost content of the music, into the finest fibre of its design." From the same journal: "In the symphony concerts he directs with equal fervor the works of Beethoven, Mozart and Haydn, as well as the creations of the later masters. It goes without saying that Liszt is especially dear to him."
[2] The Philadelphia *North American*, October 19, 1907, says, "Conductor Carl Pohlig came, waved his baton, and conquered at the Academy of Music yesterday afternoon—the first concert of the Philadelphia Orchestra's regular season. The new musical director's local début was a brilliant success and an artistic triumph."

is to say, by the Philadelphia audiences; but did not rise to widespread fame. In fact his visit with the orchestra to New York was received without much acclaim.[1] Financially the orchestra seemed to depend on the officers and members of the Philadelphia Orchestra Association, and especially on the women's committees. These committees assisted in securing concerts in nearby cities and in the financial support of the orchestra. Of course a regular and uniformly worthwhile series of concerts preserved a technique and ensemble which Scheel had organized and developed. Yet there seem to have been relatively few introductions of new music, though music by Philadelphia composers is found on several of Pohlig's programs. The three recorded first American performances under Pohlig (none of which seems to have had any permanent importance) appear meagre when compared to the fifteen introduced to America by Scheel. Scheel's premières included two D'Indy symphonies, Rimsky-Korsakof's C♯ minor Piano Concerto, and the Glazounov *Scènes de Ballet*. Stokowski produced ten major symphonic works for the first time in America in 1916 alone—among them the celebrated performances of Mahler's Eighth Symphony.

Pohlig's resignation was due to personal difficulties with the management and with some of the orchestra members themselves. It might be interesting to speculate as to just what quality made Scheel an important legend among Philadelphia music lovers, and will in all probability make Stokowski an even more striking figure in years to come, leaving Carl Pohlig as the man who came between them. The Bohemian origin of Pohlig matched the romantic glamor of the court of Württemberg at which he had been Kapellmeister before coming to Philadelphia. He had both operatic and symphonic experience abroad, and finally as pupil and friend of Franz Liszt there seemed to be the full quota of training, interest and ability that would have made him a great musical figure. It may have been a lack of showmanship that caused his downfall, or it may have been that imponderable element—personality.

---

[1] See quotation (Frances Wister, *Twenty-five Years of the Philadelphia Orchestra*) of New York reviews, from Philadelphia papers, Nov. 7, 1907; and Philadelphia's impassioned defense of Pohlig.

IV

The third chapter of the Philadelphia Orchestra is considerably longer than the total of both preceding ones. It begins with the engagement of Leopold Stokowski as conductor in 1912 [1] and extends to the present, 1940, when Stokowski is co-conductor with Eugene Ormandy. Hence it extends over a period of twenty-eight years, a little more than twice the length of the previous years of the orchestra's existence. That the period is more than twice as significant in musical accomplishment would probably be a well-nigh unanimous conviction of Philadelphia concert goers at this time. It is hardly necessary to admit that a contemporary judgment on such an artistic and extended question is worth very little, in the long history of musical development. Present-day enthusiasms are apt to assign a great deal of importance to the Stokowski years of the Philadelphia Orchestra. Whether the future will confirm current opinion on this matter, the future alone will tell.

Nineteen-twelve to 1940 was characteristically a period of regular growth and cumulative progress, as opposed to the more or less chequered career of Philadelphia instrumental music in all the previous periods. There were, however, some outstanding events which command particular mention during the many years that Stokowski has conducted the orchestra. First let us note the musical ventures of especial importance. Stokowski aimed, from early days with the Philadelphia Orchestra, to make the spectacular the usual. It seems to have been one of the secrets of his phenomenal success with, and real power over, the orchestra audiences that he knew how often the new could be introduced and still be novel. A large share of the finest standard works has always been retained on the programs, not so much to pacify a less advanced element among the subscribers, as to set forth adequately the new compositions in a consciously achieved balance in program building. Many conservative concert goers will still remember their horror at some of the more extreme manifestations of musical modernism, only to

---

[1] The engagement of Stokowski was brought about by a committee consisting of Andrew Wheeler, Harvey Watts, and Charles A. Braun.

admit that hearing these same compositions ten years later has become a distinctly pleasant experience. Appended lists will show that Stokowski was not the first conductor to introduce new instrumental compositions to America in Philadelphia performances. They will also show how great an increase in that very introductory process took place from the year of Stokowski's arrival (1912). For example, not a year passed without the first American performance, or world première, of some major works, with the exception of 1917, the year of the World War. There seems to be a truly educative impulse, which conservatives are apt to call spectacularism, at work in the policy adopted by the orchestra under Stokowski's leadership. This very charge of *spectacularism* has been levelled at the Philadelphia Orchestra for some years by many who are a bit jealous of its success, and by some who certainly have no such motive. Daniel Gregory Mason [1] calls the preponderance of Wagner on Philadelphia Orchestra programs an evidence of sensationalism. Such programs are more sensational than those specializing in Haydn and Mozart to be sure, yet much less so than the numbers suggested by well-wishing friends, who advocated "something more popular, like the *Fire Engine Quadrille* or the *Express Train Galop*" in the early days of building up an audience for the Philadelphia Orchestra. The program building with its "preponderance of Wagner" (Mason's phrase) has never ceased to be fine music, and has never caused the orchestra to play to empty seats—since Stokowski's advent at least. Fritz Scheel used to say that he was thankful that he conducted with his back to the audience, so that he could forget how few people were present to hear the music. It was quite usual for only 600 seats to be occupied in the Academy of Music at the orchestra's regular concerts from 1901 to 1906. Neither Stokowski nor his co-conductor, Eugene Ormandy, need hesitate to gaze upon the large audiences who attend the Philadelphia Orchestra concerts of today. The first program directed by Leopold Stokowski as conductor of the Philadelphia Orchestra and a few excerpts from the press concerning it are here reproduced for their artistic and historic interest:

---

[1] *Tune in America,* by Daniel Gregory Mason, p. 41.

THE PHILADELPHIA ORCHESTRA ASSOCIATION
(Incorporated)
Maintaining
THE PHILADELHIA ORCHESTRA
(Founded 1900)
LEOPOLD STOKOWSKI, *Conductor*
First Pair of Symphony Concerts
Friday afternoon at 3.00   Saturday evening at 8.15
October 11th and 12th, 1912
Programme

1. Ludwig van Beethoven ....Overture, "Leonore No. 3"
   (1770-1827)
2. Johannes Brahms ....Symphony No. 1, in C minor, Op. 68
   (1833-1897)
      I. Un poco sostenuto; Allegro (6/8)
      II. Andante sostenuto (3/4)
      III. Un poco allegretto e grazioso (2/4)
      IV. Adagio-piu andante; allegro non troppo, ma con brio (4/4)
3. Michael Ippolitow-Iwanow ...."Sketches from the Caucasus"
   (1850-   )
      I. In the Mountain Pass
      II. The Mountain Village
      III. March of the Sirdar (First Time at These Concerts)
4. Richard Wagner ....Overture "Tannhäuser"
   (1813-1883)

Public Ledger, October 12th, 1912:
New Conductor of Philadelphia Orchestra
Tendered Ovation in Academy

Leopold Stokowski made his début yesterday afternoon at the
Academy as conductor of the Philadelphia Orchestra, in the opening concert of its thirteenth season.   Every seat was taken and the
extra chairs had been placed within the orchestra rail.   There was
much enthusiasm, manifesting itself at the beginning in prolonged
applause as Stokowski came forward with bowed head, evidently
pondering the content of his musical message.   Those who went
forth to see a hirsute eccentricity were disappointed.   They beheld a
surprisingly boyish and thoroughly business-like figure who was sure
of himself, yet free from conceit, who dispensed with the score by

virtue of an infallible memory, and held his men and his audience from first note to last firmly in his grasp.

Mr. Stokowski has known the players, and they have known him, for only four days of actual rehearsal, and it was not to be expected that the organization at the outset would manifest the homogeneity to be expected later. Yet in this brief time the new leader has been surprisingly successful in welding the several choirs into a single coherent entity. They played yesterday with a unity of purpose—particularly among the first violins—not usually attained until mid-winter. They brought out the full value of the lights and shadows. The climaxes were duly accentuated, the pianissimos with the utmost delicacy and refinement were contrasted with the full throated polyphony.

Methods of Conductor

Mr. Stokowski's conducting is after the order of Nikisch, whom he frankly admires. He does not tear a passion to tatters. He holds his thunders and the winds of Aeolus in a leash. His gestures are graphic, the arc and parabolas he describes tell of a kind of geometrical translation going on in his mind, whereby he visualizes the confluent rhythms in outward action. At impassioned moments his movements have the freedom of a violinist's bow arm; at other instants he brings his fists against his shoulders with vehement concentration, or his uplifted eloquent left hand pleads with some suppressed choir to come forward and assert itself in power. There is, from first to last, no languor or slackened moment; he directs with a fine vigor and intensity that mounts to ecstasy yet does not lose its balance or forget its sane and ordered method.

Tribute Presented

At the close of the symphony a laurel wreath was laid on the dais ere Mr. Stokowski found his way to the footlights in response to the tumultuous applause. The wreath was so large that he stood in it while he called upon his musicians to rise, himself applauding their efforts and modestly disavowing his leonine share of the credit.

The Mahler Eighth Symphony was the largest achievement of Stokowski's early years with the orchestra. One of my own early recollections is that of singing in the chorus as a member of the Knabenchor, which participated in this work. Not a distinctive privilege, since the chorus numbered almost 1,000, but a great one, none the less. The many performances of this herculean work [1] in Philadelphia, and the trip to New York to give the symphony at the Metropolitan Opera House are notable facts in the history of the orchestra, and of Music in Philadelphia as well. The financial obstacles to these productions are not so widely known as the acclaim which Philadelphia and New York accorded them. The directors considered the $14,000 asked by Stokowski to produce this work as a staggering sum. Yet they raised this, and more, for the nine Philadelphia performances. The symphony made money for the Orchestra Association. The single New York performance cost the New York management $12,000. The press representatives far surpassed their previous superlatives (quoted above) in writing of the enthusiasm evoked by these performances. Even the New York papers ceased to be cool in regarding the visiting Philadelphia Orchestra.[2]

A buffet dinner was given to the chorus, orchestra, and soloists of the Mahler Symphony performances, by Alexander Van Rensselaer at Horticultural Hall on March 16, 1916. The drum solo played by Oscar Schwar (on about ten drums) was a notable bit of dexterous nonsense, well remembered by those present. The program notes for this affair constituted a needed comic relief to the sustained high seriousness and difficulty of Mahler's music. Hans Kindler and Thaddeus Rich were among the notable members of the 1916 Philadelphia Orchestra who were featured at this humorous "Mahler-ia concert." The note concerning "Herr Schwer's" (Schwar) drum selection shows that the naïveté of nineteenth century musical taste had gone for good.

"Tausend Kunstler" ....Schreiner
                                                    Bavarian
(First time in America)
"This work really requires 'more men,' but Herr Schwer thinks he can handle it alone. The principal theme is of a martial and military nature. Mr. Schwer only had one rival, and that man died long ago. You will not have much difficulty in following Mr.

---

[1] The Mahler Eighth Symphony for orchestra, soloists and chorus consists of but two movements, yet requires a full evening for its performance.
[2] Quotations of press eulogiums too lengthy to be even paraphrased above may be found in *Twenty-five Years of the Philadelphia Orchestra* by Frances Wister, pp. 105-110.

Schwer, for in this work the performer is very much in evidence at all times. He is very familiar with all of the instruments required for this composition. He has 'hit them' very often and possesses an unusual amount of originality. 'TO SEE IT IS TO APPRECIATE IT.' Mr. Schwer will depict thunder claps, echoes, bombardments, combats, cavalry charges, charge accounts, railroad wrecks, and many other scenic effects while performing this work." [1]

These program notes and many more like them show that the earlier "bombardments" of Hewitt's *Battle of Trenton,* as well as the 1860 *Express Train* effects of Musard, would be regarded as humorous rather than musically interesting in the twentieth century.

The fact that the Mahler Symphony was such a success financially after the long debated expenditure of the $14,000 asked by Stokowski to produce it led the managers of the Philadelphia Orchestra to realize with particular clearness that the investment of capital would produce income for musical ventures, as well as for the more directly commercial enterprises with which they were intimately connected. Endowment funds had been discussed for some years by the board of directors. The international publicity of the Mahler productions and the ever increasing difficulty of securing an annual guarantee fund combined to make 1916 seem a good year to begin an Endowment Fund Campaign. A mysterious element was injected into the campaign by a contributor who signed himself "The Unknown Donor." This anonymous person offered to pay the deficit for five years provided the Orchestra Association would raise $100,000 each year for an orchestra endowment. This scheme worked so successfully that it was continued for two additional years; hence the name the Seven Year Endowment Fund. Nearly $800,000 was raised during these years. The committee knew that this shadowy figure must be well informed concerning their financial problems, since they hesitated to ask patrons to give for an endowment fund when current deficits required generous gifts at the same time.

The Unknown Donor turned out to be Edward W. Bok, himself a member of the endowment committee of the Orchestra Asso-

---

[1] *Twenty-five Years of the Philadelphia Orchestra* by Frances Wister, pp. 111, 112.

THE PHILADELPHIA ORCHESTRA AND CHORUS OF THE MAHLER SYMPHONY

ciation. The other members of this highly active and successful group were Alexander Van Rensselaer and Frances A. Wister.

Mr. Bok's generosity and interest were an example of just the sort of "elevation of public taste" desired by the Musical Fund Society since 1820. His early partiality to opera and indifference to symphony concerts were typical of most social leaders in the early days of the Philadelphia Orchestra. The story is told that when one of the active promoters of the orchestra in 1901 sought to interest Mr. Bok in the concerts Mrs. Bok replied that she was very interested indeed, but "You know how Teddy is. If you could get Mr. Scheel to put on the *Pathétique* by Tschaikowsky, I might be able to get him to come to a concert." While there is nothing scandalously low in Mr. Bok's earlier taste, as revealed by his wife's remark, it is far from the later position assumed by the "Unknown Donor" who was mainly responsible for the success of the Endowment Campaign.

While speaking of improvements in taste, it might be interesting to recall Alexander Van Rensselaer's original reaction when offered the presidency of the Philadelphia Orchestra Association in 1900. That distinguished gentleman burst into a prolonged laughing fit at such an idea. Dr. Keffer and Mr. McCollin having succeeded in rousing him from this seizure, Mr. Van Rensselaer told these two that he had never attended a symphony concert in his life. Mr. Van Rensselaer, once persuaded, made an admirable president for nearly the entire history of the orchestra up to the present day (1900-1935).

Mr. Bok and Mr. Van Rensselaer were responsible for the inauguration and organization of a second Endowment Campaign in 1919. This fund was quickly oversubscribed—the goal of a million dollars being reached in November of that year. The Women's Committees secured over half of this money, and thus assumed a financial leadership in Philadelphia Orchestra affairs which they have retained to the present year.

A phase of the life and contribution of this orchestra that often escapes notice in consideration of its work is the spread of its influence beyond the regular Academy of Music audiences. It would be logical to deplore the narrowness of its sphere, were the subscribers the only ones to hear its music. Six thousand listeners, that is, a maximum audience for two Academy Concerts, seems to be a large audience for weekly orchestral music, when compared to the small groups assembled to hear even the best instrumental programs of the nineteenth century. The same six thousand seems small when related to a population of two million in the city—three million within its "metropolitan territory." The 1919 endowments were contributed by more than 13,000 persons, suggesting that at a time midway between the orchestra's organization (1900) and the present (1940) there were already more than twice as many music lovers interested in Philadelphia's orchestra than could have heard its concerts in the Academy of Music. This wide interest and financial support is the more remarkable when we remember that the radio had not been used at all by the orchestra at that time, and that orchestral recording for phonographs was in its infancy. The fact is that many extra appearances by the orchestra have spread its influence in nearby cities, and recently throughout the United States. At least a dozen singing societies have participated in regular orchestra concerts, in addition to the Philadelphia Orchestra Chorus, organized during the production of Mahler's Eighth Symphony, and the additional tremendous vocal aggregation required by that symphony itself.

Popular concerts have been given at various times since 1902, with admission prices of from ten to fifty cents.[1] They never were financially self-supporting, of course, and never seem to have been continued for more than a few seasons consecutively. A permanent organization of summer concerts did not occur until the building of the outdoor concert auditorium in Robin Hood Dell, Fairmount Park. Since 1930, this ambitious series of "pop" concerts has been a regular feature of Philadelphia's musical life. As will be mentioned in the account of the Musical Fund Society,[2] which contributed generously to the Dell Concerts, the music of these summer programs is, in the opinion of many, the most far reaching musical influence in Philadelphia. The prices are twenty-five cents to fifty cents ; the concerts are nightly affairs including a week in June, all of July and half of August (a season of eight weeks) ; the soloists

[1] A series of free concerts at the Metropolitan Opera House were given on Sunday afternoons of the season 1917-1918.
[2] Pp. 356-7.

and conductors are of the first rank.[1] These summer programs provide an opportunity for an eclectic musical environment—long an ambition of the Philadelphia Orchestra Association—and an opportunity for the public taste to be improved in musical matters— still one of the purposes of the Musical Fund Society.

A further spread of influence is provided by the special concerts for young people, originally financed by Cyrus H. K. Curtis in 1915. From that year to the present these educational concerts have been a regular series in addition to the usual concerts by the Philadelphia Orchestra. They have been variously organized as Public School Concerts, Children's Concerts, and Youth Concerts, with the slight shift of musical emphasis connoted by the age of the young people they were intended to serve.[2] Thaddeus Rich, Ernest Schelling, Eugene Ormandy, and particularly Leopold Stokowski have been gifted in selecting suitable compositions and explaining them in picturesque language to the young audiences. A few letters are reproduced from those collected by Frances A. Wister [3] to testify in youthfully charming phrases to the children's appreciation of the concerts.

"I want to tell you the lovely time I had at the concert. I want to thank you for sending the tickets. I adored the beautiful light in the Academy of Music. The conductor's name was Mr. Stokowski and he was a very nice man. I liked the part when the little boy only seven years old played the violin. He looked like Jackie Coogan. He watched the leader all the time he played. I wonder how long it took him to learn to play the violin so well.

"Mr. Stokowski is a very pleasant man. He conducted very well. He told a story of a little goat boy who played on Sand Pipes. He asked the people to sing Auld Lang Syne."

---

[1] The 1938 Robin Hood Dell prospectus announced as conductors: Ormandy, Smallens, Caston, Goossens, van Hoogstraten, Wallenstein, Hilsberg, and O'Connell; as soloists, Swarthout and Castagna, contraltos; Zimbalist, violinist; Gieseking and Rosenthal, pianists; the Littlefield and Montgomery Ballets; the Hall Johnson Choir; and four operas featuring Metropolitan Company guest artists.

[2] Fritz Scheel had three seasons of Young People's Educational Concerts (1902 to 1906). These were given in the Broad Street Theatre. Many similar programs were led by Thaddeus Rich and Leopold Stokowski in various public school buildings, also at the University of Pennsylvania and at Princeton.

[3] Op. cit. pp. 146-147 contain a fuller account of the children's programs played by the Philadelphia Orchestra, in addition to the above letters.

"I thought the concert was fine. I think the little boy played a good piece of music when he played his violin. I would like to play a drum, because my brother plays a drum, and I could easily learn. He used to play in a band called the 'Ardmore Band.' He was the best drummer they had. People could hear him far away."

"I enjoyed the concert so much. The orchestra was the largest I have ever seen. It seemed as if there were at least a hundred men on the stage. Mr. Stokowski looked very gay in his medium blue suit. I liked to watch his hands.

"He said anyone could learn to play in an orchestra if he wanted to because it was up to the person himself."

The obvious spread of both musical influence and civic fame through the medium of orchestra tours need hardly be treated here. The trips throughout the United States are recent accomplishments of the orchestra. Of long standing has been the practice of less extended journeys, and regular series of concerts in eastern cities.[1]

The Philadelphia Orchestra has been very active in recording the masterpieces of instrumental composition. While Stokowski has been deeply interested also in instrumental broadcasting, and the orchestra has appeared on many radio programs, few of the regular concerts have been broadcast. The summer programs are available to radio listeners, however. Thus the widest spread of music may again be seen to be an objective of the extra appearances rather than of the regular concerts at the Academy of Music.

From a vast array of names of patrons and performers who have made the Philadelphia Orchestra what it is today, a few may be singled out as particularly important. Dr. Edward I. Keffer was the leading spirit in the founding of the Philadelphia Orchestra, in which project his main assistant was Edward G. McCollin. Alexander Van Rensselaer has been discussed as the most influential person in the orchestra's history. He was President of the Orchestra Association from its founding until his death in 1935. Edward Bok has also been credited above with being the financial

---

[1] Boston, Baltimore, Washington, Pittsburgh, New York and Toronto, are the larger cities to be so visited.

adviser and main contributor in the endowment programs of the orchestra. The name of Henry Whelen, Jr., must be preserved as that of a man who was most active in the organization of the orchestra, serving as treasurer from 1900 to his death in 1907. He advanced upwards of $40,000 to the orchestra association, which sum was definitely responsible for the continuation of the orchestra in the period of its hardest struggle (1902-1904). The three conductors should be mentioned next; the period and contribution of each has already been stated. Dr. Eugene Ormandy, although still called a co-conductor with Stokowski, was named musical director of the orchestra in September, 1938. The Women's Committees have exerted an increasing amount of influence in orchestra affairs since the founding of the first committee in 1904, a logical concomitant to their having secured so large a share of endowments and subscriptions for the orchestra's financial success. The name of Frances A. Wister is inseparably linked with the organization and management of the Women's Committees. Miss Wister has been a director of the Philadelphia Orchestra Association since 1905, and since 1912 has been president of the Women's Committee for the Philadelphia Orchestra. Mrs. Edward G. McCollin, who first had the idea of forming the women's committees, and Mrs. Alexander J. Dallas Dixon, the first president of this group of women, were of great importance in saving the orchestra in 1904, and in assisting it thereafter. The long term of Arthur Judson as manager, and the longer period in which Louis Mattson has assisted the manager (1907 to the present, 1940) should be mentioned. Mr. Philip Goepp's composition of the program notes for Philadelphia Orchestra concerts from 1900 to 1930 implies a herculean amount of labor. Mr. Goepp frequently appeared as guest conductor of the orchestra. Dr. Thaddeus Rich links management, men, and soloists, since he has acted so often in all of these capacities. As concertmaster throughout the larger part of the orchestra's existence (1906-1926), as soloist with the orchestra every season from 1906 to 1926, and as conductor of over sixty concerts by this entire organization, Dr. Rich's contribution to the proficiency and musical excellence of the Philadelphia Orchestra is inestimable. Marcel Tabuteau, oboe, and William M. Kincaid, flute, are two distinguished

woodwind soloists, both of whom have been with the Philadelphia
Orchestra for a very long period, Tabuteau twenty-five years, and
Kincaid nineteen.   The names of five men who were members of
the orchestra conducted by H. G. Thunder, and have remained with
the Philadelphia Orchestra from its founding to the present day
have been previously mentioned.[1]   Oscar Schwar and Emil
Kresse, timpani; Joseph La Monaca, flute; Richard Kruger, bassoon; William A. Schmidt, 'cello; and Otto Henneberg, horn, are
men who have held important posts in the Philadelphia Orchestra
for such unusually long periods of time that an account of the
organization should not fail to mention their notable contribution
to their respective instrumental sections.   The guest conductors and
visiting soloists have been far too numerous to attempt to list them
here.[2]   The most frequently heard assisting soloists and the period
in which they made numerous Philadelphia appearances are: Harold Bauer, 1902 to 1931; Mischa Elman, 1909 to 1917; Ossip
Gabrilowitsch, 1900 to 1931; Florence Hinkle, 1910 to 1922; Joseph
Hofmann, 1901 to the present; William Kincaid, 1922 to the present; Hans Kindler, 1915 to 1932; Fritz Kreisler, 1901 to the
present; Daniel Maquarre, 1911 to 1918; Serge Rachmaninoff, 1909
to the present; Thaddeus Rich, 1906 to 1926; Olga Samaroff, 1905
to 1931; Herman Sandby, 1902 to 1916; Ernestine Schumann-
Heink, 1902 to 1916; Marcel Tabuteau, 1915 to the present; John K.
Witzemann, 1902 to 1916; and Efrem Zimbalist, 1912 to the present.   It is not so difficult as it is dangerous to pick these most
popular soloists out of a list that includes hundreds of the greatest
twentieth century names in music.   The above list simply states
that those soloists were the ones most frequently heard with the
Philadelphia Orchestra.   A few splendid artists who have not yet
piled up the impressive list of performances, but will in a few years
quite surely have as many solo appearances with the Philadelphia
Orchestra to their credit are: Agnes Davis, Kirsten Flagstad, Jascha
Heifetz, Vladimir Horowitz, José Iturbi, Yehudi Menuhin, Lily
Pons, John Charles Thomas, and Lawrence Tibbett.

---

[1] P. 168.
[2] Pp. 216-227 of *Twenty-five Years of the Philadelphia Orchestra* by
Frances A. Wister, contains a complete list for 1900-1925.

The rather lengthy account of this relatively recent musical organization should not close without bringing the story up to the present. Unfortunately the present as mentioned in books can never even approximate the present of absolute fact. By the time an account is printed the most modern may be just a bit passé: thus the present state of a musical organization as conscientiously recorded today will cease to obtain when it is read tomorrow. Important changes may be made suddenly in an orchestra, for the conductor must be permitted to act quickly, and autocratically also, when the good of the group demands it. Selecting January, 1939, as an arbitrary present point, let us conclude by considering the main divisions which current policies suggest as the probable sphere of future Philadelphia Orchestra activities.

A summer of elaborately planned Robin Hood Dell concerts and operas has been successfully completed. The uncertainties of the weather—which bothered the outdoor impressarios at Bush Hill and Vauxhall Gardens one hundred and fifty years ago—constituted the only bad feature of the season's music. The fourteen cancellations due to rain were unfortunate, and the many evenings when the audience was small due to the threatening weather must have been equally discouraging.

The winter concerts from October, 1938, to April, 1939, show a slight departure from the usual policy of numerous home appearances and few concerts outside of the Philadelphia Academy of Music.[1] A rather noticeable lack of touring has been characteristic of the orchestra as a rule. Two conspicuous exceptions to the stay-at-home policy were the transcontinental tours made by the orchestra in 1936 and 1937. During five weeks (April 19 to May 23, 1937) thirty-seven concerts were played in eighteen states and in Canada. These long journeys were entirely occasional, and there is no reason to suppose that similar trips are anticipated for the future.

The conductors and soloists are interestingly varied in each winter season. Opera has been produced occasionally in recent

---

[1] 68 concerts in Philadelphia, at the Academy of Music; 13 concerts in New York; 5 concerts in Washington and 5 in Baltimore; 22 concerts in other cities in Eastern United States.

years, and ballets have been given ambitious staging,[1] both as items included in the subscribers' regular series. Yet the related muses beyond the strictly instrumental—or the instrumental and vocal of the concert calibre—have been increasingly slighted of late. The orchestra management is committing itself to a consistent program of the best in the playing of new and old orchestral literature. Guest conductors and assisting soloists provide variety, and as such furnish what little additional attraction the orchestra itself might need. The potpourri of choruses, operas, ballets, soloists, and widely varied leadership belongs more logically to the somewhat lighter programs of the summer concerts. Philadelphians should be proud of their continued support of one of the finest orchestras and of the uniform excellence of its programs as arranged for the regular concerts at the Academy of Music.

Appendix: World and American Premières by the Philadelphia Orchestra

First performances in America by the Philadelphia Orchestra have not been named in the text of the preceding account. The following list, while possibly incomplete, will show why it was found impractical to include any chronological mention of these works in a chapter intended to remain at all readable. The list is given as an appendix to this chapter, rather than relegated to the end of the book—with most of whose pages it bears no relation in any case.

---

[1] Between 1925 and 1935 several operas and ballets have been given under the Philadelphia Orchestra management. The Metropolitan Opera House (in Philadelphia) was used for some of the more spectacular productions during those years. *Wozzeck,* and *Oedipus Rex* among opera premières, and *Parsifal* and *Meistersinger* among standard operas were outstanding productions between the years 1930-1936. *H.P., The Age of Steel, The Rite of Spring,* are recent American premières in the field of orchestra and ballet productions by the Philadelphia Orchestra and various dancing groups.

A festival of the Monte Carlo Ballet Russe, and the Philadelphia Orchestra was featured during the first week of March, 1938. The following six ballets were among the dances given in this extended series of performances.

Aurora's Wedding .... Tschaikowski
Jeux d'Enfants .... Bizet
Choreartium .... Brahms, *Fourth Symphony*
Prince Igor .... Borodine
Sheherazade .... Rimsky-Korsakof
Prélude à l'Après-midi d'un Faune .... Debussy

1901 Dvořák—Heldenlied.

1903 F. G. Kauffman—Salambo.   D'Indy—Wallenstein Symphony.
Sibelius—Swan of Tuonela.

1904 Boehe—Wanderings of Odysseus.   Schilling—The Witches' Song.
D'Indy—Symphony in B flat.

1905 Converse—Incidental Music to Joan of Arc.   Liadov—Baba Jaga.
Leps—Andon.   Rimsky-Korsakof—Piano Concerto in C sharp minor.
Converse—The Mystic Trumpeter.   Glazounov—Scenes de Ballet.
Magnard—Chant Funèbre.

1907 Juon—Fantasie (Watchman's Son).   Reger—Variations and Fugue.

1908 Wagner—Christopher Columbus Overture.

1910 Volbach—Symphony in B minor.

1912 Schelling—Legende Symphonique.

1913 Rabaud—Symphony in E minor.   Paderewski—Symphony in B minor.
Hausegger—Wieland der Schmied.   Arbos—Guajiras (Violin and orch.)
Schmitt—Rhapsodie Viennoise.

1914 Busoni—Indian Fantasy.   Roussel—La Ville Rose.

1915 Schoenberg—Kammer Symphonie.   Sandby—Violin Concerto in D.
Skriabin—Symphony No. 3, Le Divin Poème, and Symphony No. 5 in
B flat.

1916 Strauss—Alpensymphonie.   Zeckwer—Sohrab and Rustum.
Mahler—Symphony No. 8 for orchestra and chorus, and Das Lied von
der Erde (Symphony for Solo Voices and Orchestra).
Elgar—Le Drapeau Belge.   Mason—Symphony in C.
Granados—Intermezzo and Epilogue from Goyescas.
Bruch—Concerto for two pianos (World Première).

1918 Gardner—New Russia.   Chausson—Symphony in B flat.
Hadley—Othello Overture.   Griffes—Notturno, The White Peacock,
Clouds, Bacchanale.   Pizetti—Fedra, prelude to act 1.
Dvorsky—The Haunted Castle.

1920 Carpenter—A Pilgrim Vision.   Elgar—Enigma Variations.
Rachmaninoff—Symphony No. 3 (The Bells).   Scott—Piano Concerto
in E, played and conducted by the composer.   Scott—Two Passa-
caglias.

1921 Fitelberg—Polish Rhapsody. (Bach Passacaglia and Fugue, transcribed
by Stokowski).   Sibelius—Symphony No. 5 in E flat.
Braunfeld—Fantastic Variations.

1922 De Falla—Excerpts from El Amor Brujo.   Stravinski—Rite of Spring.

1923   Stravinsky—Symphony for wind instruments, in memory of Debussy.
        Auric—Nocturne. Rimsky-Korsakof—Excerpts from Kitesch.
        Stravinsky—Chant du Rossignol.

1924   Purcell—Trumpet Prelude. Medtner—Piano Concerto in C minor.
        Szymanowski—Piano Concerto.

1925   Bliss, *Mêlée fantastique.*
        Ornstein, *Second Concerto* for Piano and Orchestra.
        Tailleferre *Concerto* for Piano and Orchestra.
        Leps, *Loretto.*
        Gilchrist—*Symphony No. 1.*

1926   Albeniz—*Fête-Dieu a Seville.*
        Berners—*Fantasie Espagnole.*
        Szymanowski—*Symphony No. 3.*
        Debussy—*La Cathèdral Engloutie.*
        Respighi—*Old Dances and Airs for Lute.*
        Sibelius—*Symphony No. 6.*
        Sibelius—*Symphony No. 7.*
        Miaskovsky—*Symphony No. 6.*
        Bach-Stokowski—*Toccata and Fugue in D Minor.*
        Varese—*Ameriques.*

1927   Varese—*Les Arcanes.*
        Rachmaninoff—*Concerto No. 4.*
        Carillo—*Concerto* for Quarter-Eighth-and-Sixteenth-Tone Instruments. World première.

1928   Copland—*Scherzo* from Symphony with Organ, World première.
        Farwell—*Once I Passed through a Populous City.* World première.
        Gilbert—*Nocturne.*
        Shostakovitch—*Symphony No. 1.*

1929   Stravinsky—*Les Noces,* opera and ballet, given in New York by Philadelphia Orchestra (and cast).

1930   Stravinsky—*Le Sacre du Printemps,* with ballet.
        Schoenberg—*Die glückliche Hand.*
        Chasins—*Piano Concerto,* composer at piano.

1931   Stravinsky—*Oedipus Rex,* puppet opera.
        Prokofieff—*Age of Steel,* ballet.

1932   Zimbalist—*Daphnis and Chloe* (Symphonic Poem). World première.
        Malipiero—*Concerti.* World première.
        Shostakovitch—*Symphony No. 3* (May Day).

1933 Schoenberg—*Pierrot Lunaire*, given by the Philadelphia Orchestra in New York.

1934 Walton—*Belshazzar's Feast*.

1935 Gluck—*Iphigenia in Aulis*, in French.
Gabowitz—*Parable in Blue*. World première.

1936 Bartók—*Hungarian Sketches*.
Strauss—*The Silent Woman*.
Harris—*Prelude and Fugue* for String Orchestra. World première.
Deutsch, *Scottish Suite* (Orchestra and Bagpipes).
McDonald—*Three Aramaic Poems*. World première.
Barlow—*Babar*. World première.

1937 Serly—*Symphony*.

1938 Hill—*String Suite*.
Bennet—*Orchestral Etudes*.
Gliere—*Second Symphony*.
McDonald—*Fourth Symphony*. World première.
McDonald—*Lament for the Stolen*. World première.

1939 Gretchaninof—*Fifth Symphony*. World première.

A list of world premiéres of transcriptions by Lucien Cailliet follows. Such transcriptions or arrangements were omitted from the preceding list, which was already a voluminous one. Mr. Cailliet had been a general utility player on various clarinets and saxophones with the Philadelphia Orchestra for over twenty years when he accepted a musical engagement in Hollywood in 1938. His transcriptions were played in the years since 1933, and when their number is considered it will be evident that a large share of the orchestra's première selections were found among these transcriptions.

    Transcribed from Bach—Prelude and Fugue in F minor
                    Prelude in E
                    Nun freut euch lieben Christen gemein
                    Prelude and Fugue in B minor
                    Herzlich thut mich verlangen
                    Fugue a la Gigue
                    Air, from Suite in G
                    Jesu, Joy of Man's Desiring
                    Pastorale, from Christmas Oratorio

Buxtehude—Passacaglia in D minor
Debussy—"General Lavine"
Handel—Fantasia in C
Andante in B minor
Moussorgsky—Pictures at an Exhibition
Purcell—Suite from *Dido and Aeneas*
Rachmaninoff—Prelude in C sharp minor
Three Preludes
Rimsky-Korsakoff—Church Scene
Rameau—Suite
Turina—Sacro-Monte
Wagner—Excerpts from *Siegfried, Die Walküre* (Act
III), *Götterdämmerung,* and *Rheingold.*

CHAPTER SEVEN

OTHER INSTRUMENTAL GROUPS

I

No more fitting beginning to a chapter on various instrumental groups could be found than the musical programs at Williow Grove Park. Chronologically these concerts, beginning in 1896, antedate our arbitrary starting point for this section, the year 1900. They are the true predecessors of the Robin Hood Dell concerts, dating from 1930, since the ambitious arrangements for Willow Grove music stopped but a few years before the concerts at the Dell began.

The first musical organization to be heard at the new Music Center at Willow Grove was the Innes Band, in May and June, 1896. Sousa's band played there in 1901, giving an annual series of concerts, with few omissions, until 1926. At about 1900 the arrangements were made for the country's finest orchestras and bands to appear at Willow Grove each season. Walter Damrosch led the New York Symphony Orchestra there for two or three week periods during several summer seasons.

Orchestra leaders who have taken part in the summer concerts at Willow Grove were enthusiastic about the accomplishments of this "music center of America from May to September." [1] Frederick Stock who led the Theodore Thomas Orchestra of Chicago [2] at Willow Grove for many years said, "It is in reality the greatest out-of-door summer school of music in the whole world, a blessing for the multitude of people who take advantage of having offered to them a liberal musical education at nominal expense." Many Philadelphians, as well as persons who journeyed to Willow Grove

---

[1] Arthur Pryor describes it as such in 1909, in a pamphlet *Musical Offerings at Willow Grove Park*. The above statements by Stock, Sousa, and Herbert are quoted from this 1909 publication.

[2] The Chicago Symphony Orchestra was so described until 1912.

from greater distances, will remember being a part of this "multitude." The musical events became leading social occasions; hundreds donned formal attire to attend these concerts.

"Tschaikowsky and Wagner, Mendelssohn and Bach, Beethoven and Brahms find here a multitude of admirers as discriminating in musical taste as the most intellectual of conductors could ask in listeners." This is the glowing, though somewhat involved, tribute paid by Victor Herbert, who adds: "With an enterprise like Willow Grove Park, which has no counterpart anywhere else in this country, the setting up of a healthy musical force may be assuredly looked for, if not, indeed, prophesied as an inevitable outcome." Herbert's Orchestra was second in popularity only to Sousa's Band in a long series of summer engagements at Willow Grove. For example, in the summer of 1909, from whose reports the above tributes are quoted, Victor Herbert and his orchestra provided the music nightly from July 11 to August 14.

John Philip Sousa, who conducted more Willow Grove Concerts than any other person, declares: "The yearly schedules of the symphony and eclectic concerts, grand and light opera, oratorio, cantata and recitals are matters of the deepest interest to the music lover. . . . The concerts have become a public necessity. . . . Poet and painter, novelist and historian, maid and matron, youth and man pay willing tribute to music; and there is no fairer shrine for the devotee of melody than Willow Grove Park." The concerts of other than symphonic nature, mentioned by Sousa, included programs by the Strawbridge and Clothier Chorus, the Junger Männerchor, and the German Saengerfest. Numerous individual soloists have appeared in opera and concert performances. Noted conductors in addition to those already mentioned included Patrick Conway, Nahan Franko, Henry Hadley, Guiseppe Creatore, and Wassili Leps.

These entire cycles of summer concerts were provided and managed by the Philadelphia Transportation Company. In recent years this transportation company has maintained a considerable interest in music, although its Willow Grove programs have become occasional and less ambitiously conceived since 1926. The Philadelphia Transportation Company band was organized in 1919, and received first prize among bands at the Sesqui-Centennial Exposition. It now numbers 145 men, and is directed by Albert W. Eckenroth, president of the Pennsylvania Bandmasters' Association.[1] There is also a Scotch Bagpipe group, a harmonica unit, and a negro band of fifty members. No small part of the success of the musical work among employees has been due to the interest and assistance of its president, Ralph T. Senter. Mr. Senter is an amateur painter and musician, and a firm believer in musical organization among the employees as a humanizing medium, and hence a real business asset.

Instrumental groups have been organized in other business concerns, although the vocal chorus has been favored by commercial and industrial companies, as being more easily organized and more rapidly successful. The Wanamaker Store has featured instrumental music since its earliest days. The orchestrion and various organs are discussed in a later chapter devoted to church music and organs.[2] The Wanamaker employees' bands, field music, and bagpipe group are the most important instrumental groups connected with a Philadelphia store. Arthur A. Rosander has been conductor of the Wanamaker bands, and in general charge of instrumental music[3] at that store since 1914.

The Frankford Symphony Society occupies an odd chronological position in Philadelphia music. It was not organized before 1900, so does not belong to the historical chapters of this book. It stopped its activities four years ago, hence it could not properly be classified as a current musical organization. Its influential position among amateur orchestras from 1909, the year of its first concerts, to 1935, when its active program was indefinitely suspended, makes the Frankford Symphony one of the most important among Other Instrumental Groups since 1900. This Symphony Society developed from musical gatherings among men in the vicinity of Frankford. In 1908 Julian T. Hammond and T. Worcester Worrell conceived the idea of forming a larger group of both professional and amateur musicians. These two men, and Dr. Mark

---

[1] The P.T.C. band and the musical interests of Ralph Senter are fully described in the *Etude* for February 1938.

[2] Cf. *infra*, pp. 317-9.

[3] Except the music of the famous Wanamaker Organ, which is managed by Mary E. Vogt.

Bradner and H. G. Bradner, had all been members of Gilchrist's Philadelphia Symphony Society of the 1890's. William Jefferson Guernsey, M.D., was appointed business manager, and a board of trustees was chosen. Dr. Guernsey remained the guiding personality for the society's finances for nearly twenty years. Various halls were used for rehearsals and concerts. Eighteen men were in the orchestra at its first concert, May 10, 1909; while in 1924 the orchestra membership had grown to seventy-seven. Among the five conductors the longest and most successful tenures have been those of Hedda van den Beemt, 1916-1925, and J. W. F. Leman, 1925-1935.

Most of the Frankford Symphony Society's concerts have been given in the auditorium of the Frankford High School. One of the outstanding programs, the first to be given in the new high school building, is quoted in full.

CONCERT BY THE

FRANKFORD SYMPHONY SOCIETY

HEDDA VAN DEN BEEMT, *Conductor*

HANS KINDLER, *Soloist*

Auber ....Overture to Masaniello
Boellmann ....Symphonic Variations

'Cello and Orchestra

Gade ....Symphony No. 4, in B♭
Grieg ....Two Melodies for Strings
    Hjertesår
    Våren
Handel ....Minuetto
                                                          Scherzo

Hans Kindler, 'Cellist

Meyerbeer.........................Coronation March from *The Prophet*

Many fine programs were given by this organization. Among the noted assisting soloists, besides Kindler, were Katharine Meisle, then a resident of Frankford, and Nelson Eddy, then a resident of Philadelphia.

The cessation of rehearsals and concerts in 1935 was due to the gradual lack of community support for the enterprise. The new elevated railway had made the central city more accessible for many years; the popularity and use of the automobile, the moving picture theatre, and particularly the radio, all combined to make it impossible for their concerts to continue to be self-supporting. They had never inaugurated any other means for serving Frankford than the policy of the concerts' paying their own way each season.

Like the Brahms Chorus, the Frankford Symphony Society has postponed further activity, but has not ceased to exist. There is some possibility, according to J. W. F. Leman, its conductor, that rehearsals may be resumed.

An unusual group in Philadelphia is the Women's Symphony Orchestra. Founded and organized by Mabel Swint Ewer in 1921, this orchestra has given annual concerts since that year, and many sectional concerts as well. J. W. F. Leman has directed the Women's Symphony Orchestra since its inception. The seventy members of this group represent all instruments of a standard symphonic orchestra. Weekly rehearsals are held at Bethany Presbyterian Church. The concerts have been given mainly in the Bellevue-Stratford Ball Room. Women's clubs, schools and other organizations have engaged the Women's Symphony Orchestra, or sections of its membership, for many concerts in Philadelphia and nearby cities and towns. The Philadelphia Music Club has been the principal financial backer for this orchestra.

Important concerts were given between 1919 and 1926 by the Philadelphia Philharmonic Society. This group revived the purposes of the earlier local group of the same name [1] in securing a variety of musical attractions for a series of Sunday evening concerts. The Philharmonic Society was the first musical organization successfully to withstand local opposition to Sunday concerts for which there were paid admissions. A series of from six to eight concerts was given, and each subscriber received tickets in advance. Thus there was no technical charging of money at the time of the Sunday concert. Subscriptions for Sunday programs of chamber music and vocal concerts on a less public and widely advertised scale had been sold in a similar fashion for many years.

Their programs were given in the Forrest and Shubert Theatres from 1919 to 1921, and in the Academy of Music from 1921

---

[1] Cf., *supra*, pp. 89-90.

to 1926. The usual orchestra was made up of Philadelphia Orchestra men under the direction of Joseph Pasternack. Noted occasional conductors were Leopold Stokowski, Fritz Reiner, Alexander Smallens and Hans Kindler. Reiner, Smallens and Kindler did their first conducting of a large orchestra at concerts of the Philharmonic Society. Paul Whiteman repeated his historic program of symphonic jazz for this society, George Gershwin appearing as soloist in the concerto version of the *Rhapsody in Blue*. Igor Stravinsky, who played his own piano concerto, Olga Samaroff, and Florence Easton were among other noted soloists to appear at their concerts. Marian Anderson made her first appearance with orchestra at a Philharmonic concert. The first broadcasting of a symphony orchestra in Philadelphia was done by this Pasternack orchestra, Miss Anderson's debut being broadcast from the Academy of Music on January 16, 1923.

The guiding personality of the Philadelphia Philharmonic Society was its treasurer and manager, Charles G. Hirsch, M.D. Its main financial backer was the late Jules Mastbaum.

The vicinity of the first Philadelphia orchestra—that of the Hermits of the Wissahickon in 1694—is blest with two of its newest community orchestras. Roxborough and Germantown have organized instrumental groups within the past ten years.

The Roxborough Symphony Orchestra began its career on August 29, 1932. Several of the members of the new group had played with a small instrumental ensemble since 1910, and the present orchestra has developed from that previous organization. The first president, elected in 1932, still heads the Roxborough Symphony Orchestra. This leading personality, Ernest F. Miller, was active in the older groups since 1910. The first concert was given on October 2, 1932, at the Roxborough High School. There were three concerts the first season, and each succeeding year a like number has been played. Weekly rehearsals were held in Turner's Hall until 1937; since that year the Kendrick Recreation Center has been used. The concerts are given in the High School Auditorium. Henry Gurney, Louis Angeloty, and Henri Scott were the soloists at the three concerts of the 1932-1933 season. Stanley Hart Cauffman conducted the concerts of that first year. Mr. Hayden Marriott led the orchestra from 1933 to 1935; from the latter year Leonard DeMaria has been its conductor. The five seasons of Mr. De Maria's directing have witnessed the growth of the society's library, the increased aid of the newly formed women's auxiliary, the enlargement of the list of patrons from about fifty to one hundred and fifty, and a natural and encouraging advance in orchestral technique and improvement in instrumental balance. The orchestra now has fifty members. This orchestra's serene progress, both artistically and financially, shows us that music can flourish in depression years, and that an orchestra can be organized and succeed in such a difficult period.

The other recent orchestra to echo the early instrumental work of the Wissahickon Hermits is the Germantown Orchestra directed by N. Lindsay Norden. Mr. Norden and Samuel B. Scott have been responsible for this new instrumental venture's promising start. These two men were on the board of directors of the Musical Art Club during the period of that organization's lamented lingering demise. In March, 1936, the project of an orchestra for Germantown was launched, the rehearsals began in the following autumn, and its first concert was performed in March, 1937. Three concerts were given in each of the following three seasons. This orchestra, while lacking the preceding instrumental organizations that helped the Roxborough group in its first years, has nevertheless embarked immediately on an ambitious series of rehearsals and concerts. Many standard symphonies and overtures are already in their repertoire. The membership includes forty-five players, all instruments being well represented except the elusive bassoon.

While Norden's chief musical field has been the organization and conducting of choral groups, the Germantown Orchestra seems to be his first activity to be mentioned in our arrangement of Music in Philadelphia. N. Lindsay Norden was born in Philadelphia in 1887. His musical education was gained in New York, as were his early positions as organist and choirmaster.[1] The Æolian Choir of Brooklyn was the first non-ecclesiastical chorus to benefit from Norden's skill in the interpretation of Russian works.

---

[1] Norden studied with Spicker, Rybner, Weld, and F. W. Robinson in New York, and is a graduate of Columbia University. His early appointments included that of Chapel Organist at St. Bartholomew's in New York, and St. Mary's and All Saints' churches in Brooklyn.

The earliest Philadelphia musical activity of N. L. Norden was the conducting of the Mendelssohn Club. His years as leader of that historic organization (1916-1926) are described in the account of Philadelphia Singing Societies.[1] At the conclusion of this engagement as Mendelssohn Club conductor Norden led a vocal concert of the festival variety at the Sesqui-Centennial Exhibition in Philadelphia. The Mendelssohn Club, the Reading Choral Society, and the Strawbridge and Clothier Chorus combined as a chorus of seven hundred voices, with the assistance of the Philadelphia Orchestra. Mendelssohn's *Hymn of Praise* was sung by the chorus with marked success. The *Public Ledger* declared in describing the instrumental sections of this concert, which took place on June 17, 1926:

> Mr. Norden gave a superb reading of the rather banal Finale of Tschaikowsky's *Fourth Symphony*, and his own *Silver Plume*. There is much good work in the [latter] composition, both from the standpoint of composition and orchestration.

In 1919 Mr. Norden was engaged as conductor of the Reading Choral Society, a vocal group only a few years younger than the Mendelssohn Club.[2] He filled this position with distinction for twenty years.

The choir of the Second Presbyterian Church was directed by N. Lindsay Norden from 1917 to 1927. This mixed chorus excelled in a cappella Russian music, of which Norden has ever been a prolific editor and ardent exponent. Their singing in Æolian Hall occasioned the most enthusiastic New York newspaper comment accorded to a Philadelphia chorus since Stokowski staged the Mahler Eighth Symphony in 1916. The verdict of the *Musical Courier* was: "The work throughout the concert was of an exceedingly high order, and technically speaking, well nigh flawless. The pitch of the choir was excellent, and the attacks and releases were extraordinarily clean."

An organization founded largely through Mr. Norden's effort is the Brahms Chorus of Philadelphia. From 1926 until about 1935

---

[1] Cf. *infra*, pp. 249-254.
[2] The Reading Choral Society was founded in 1880.

this large ensemble provided some of the finest choral concerts in the city. The group has not ceased to exist, but has found it necessary to discontinue rehearsals during the past few seasons. The larger compositions by Bach, and a cappella singing, constituted the high points of the artistic accomplishments of the Brahms Chorus.

Since 1922 N. Lindsay Norden has been organist and director of music at the Temple Rodeph Shalom, and from 1927 has held these same positions at the First Presbyterian Church in Germantown.

In addition to the tremendous importance of the guidance and stimulation of such a large share of Philadelphia's choral music, Mr. Norden's theoretical researches and numerous compositions are noteworthy. He hopes to climax a lengthy series of articles on acoustics with a theoretical work to be entitled *The Untempered Harmony of a Cappella Music*. The Germantown Orchestra is Mr. Norden's most recent musical activity, although it is the first connection in which his contribution to Music in Philadelphia appears in this book. As theoretician, composer, conductor, and organist, N. Lindsay Norden is making a significant contribution to many phases of Philadelphia music.

An unusual organization among Philadelphia's instrumental groups is the Society of Ancient Instruments founded by Ben Stad in 1924. Concerts by such rare instruments as the viol, viola da gamba, viola d'amore, oboe d'amore, harpsichord, clavichord and recorder are frequently played by members of this group. Eleven annual festivals have been held by this society, those since 1937 have been national in scope. The third national festival was held March 29 and 30, 1939, at the Ritz Carlton Hotel in Philadelphia. Musical numbers for various combinations of the instruments named above were supplemented by vocal solos and dances from the sixteenth and seventeenth centuries. The Society of Ancient Instruments plays about five concerts a year, mainly in Philadelphia and New York. They provided the music at the dedication of the Folger Shakespearian Library in Washington. This group has made three albums of records for the R.C.A. Victor Company.

One of the oldest amateur orchestras in Philadelphia is that of the Symphony Club. This society was founded by Edwin A.

Fleisher in 1909. Its original and main activity is orchestral playing. The orchestra of their first season contained sixty-five boys from seven to seventeen years of age. The club's present headquarters at 1235 Pine Street were occupied in 1911, at which time the orchestra became limited to string players. In 1915 William F. Happich was secured as conductor of the Symphony Club. There have been two string ensembles and one full orchestra ever since Mr. Happich's engagement as director. These orchestras rehearse twice a week, and give concerts yearly. One half of each rehearsal is devoted to sight reading. This excellent practice accounts for the club's need for such a tremendous library of music for string and symphonic orchestras. The generosity of the founder has made the noted collection of orchestral works available for the use of the Symphony Club. A special room in the Free Library of Philadelphia houses this large "Fleisher Collection." Standard and modern scores are present in great number, as are many manuscript and photostatic copies of unpublished works by recent composers.[1] A glowing account of the Symphony Club appeared in the *London Musical Times*.[2] This article mentions the orchestras, chamber groups, theory classes, and piano instruction of the club, and concludes by saying:

> England has a good many admirable organizations for developing music among young people . . . but there is nothing on so comprehensive a scale as this Philadelphia enterprise.

A new and original method of giving orchestra concerts is being used at the Philadelphia Music Center, 310 S. Juniper Street. The Music Center is in reality a social service club whose main feature happens to be a symphony orchestra. This group, of full symphonic dimensions, has given Sunday evening concerts for the past six seasons (1933-1940). The audience usually begins by joining in mass singing, which is followed by a brief lecture on the music that is to follow. Then the orchestral music is played, after which the audience is encouraged to ask questions about the concert

---

[1] A summary of the Symphony Club by Edwin Fleisher, containing the above facts and many further details, may be found in the catalogue of the Fleisher Collection (publ. by Stern and Co., Phila. 1933).
[2] September 1, 1929; pp. 791-3.

in particular, or music in general. The new in music alternates with Beethoven and Brahms Cycles or works by Bach. The entire organization is run in an unconventional but highly educational manner. The Music Center has a People's Chorus directed by Mendy Shain which participates in some of their concerts. Classes in practically every phase of music are taught by well qualified instructors at the Center Music School. Chamber music has been fostered since the beginning of the Philadelphia Music Center's existence. One of the early seasons of their activity included ten concerts devoted to a historical survey of chamber music. The first program of that series, October 11, 1936, exemplifies the care and thoroughness with which the subject was approached.

PROGRAM

I. BYRD
   Fantasia—for string sextet
II. PURCELL
   a. Fantasia—Three part
   b. Fantasia—Four part
   c. Fantasia—Five part
III. J. C. BACH—String Quartet
   1st movement—Allegro
IV. DITTERSDORF—String
   Quartet in E♭
   Allegro
   Andante
   Minuetto
   Finale

PROGRAM

V. BOCCHERINI—String Quintet
   Andante con moto
   Menuett
   Grave
   Rondo
   Performers

VIOLINS
   Leon Zawisza
   Arthur Cohn
   Sam Savar
VIOLAS
   David Marsh
   Morris Sutow
CELLI
   Herman Gordon
   Jules Drossin

Commentator—ARTHUR COHN

A string orchestra preceded the present symphonic group. Arthur Cohn and Joseph Levine conduct the orchestra of this Music Center, Sidney Fox is its president. The concerts and the activities of the school are offered at very low cost, the Music Center having realized that only by such a policy could good music be made available to the people. Other musical objectives are the revival of chamber music, and the encouragement of contemporary composers.

The last named objective suggests the Philadelphia Simfonietta; indeed, several works for string orchestra that had been played by that more finished group were also included on the programs at the Center. This duplication should not imply that there has been any lack of first performances by the musical groups at the Music Center. Premières of works by recognized composers and students of composition have frequently appeared on their programs.

The logic of the views expressed by the founders of this new organization can hardly be refuted. They saw that hundreds of musicians needed employment and thousands of Philadelphians needed music—*i.e.*, actual and not reproduced music. Success, which seems to have crowned their efforts from the start, should long remain with this useful and altruistic organization.

Philadelphia's instrumental activities have left little room for visiting orchestras in recent years. Particularly since the beginning of the depression period, from which the city and country are still emerging after ten years (1930-1940), the lack of support for musical organizations from other cities has discouraged their attempting many concerts in Philadelphia. Thus the New York Philharmonic Orchestra, which had given regular series of concerts in Philadelphia for many years (even those in which the Philadelphia Orchestra played as many as one hundred concerts), discontinued them in 1933. A different factor seems to have crowded out the Boston Symphony Orchestra. That group had played monthly concerts, usually for the five winter months, since about 1890. In 1900 these visits were increased to ten, the purpose being to capitalize on the local interest in concerts stirred up by the start of the Philadelphia Orchestra under Scheel. After 1905 the concerts by the Boston Symphony were again reduced to five or six a year. From 1915 their Philadelphia appearances became even less frequent, this city becoming merely a stopping place on their tours through the East, or an additional trip after one of the regular concerts in New York. The New York and Brooklyn programs by the Boston Orchestra have continued with great regularity from 1887 to the present day. Their Philadelphia concerts stopped in 1926, and have only recently been resumed as an annual appearance before the audience of the Philadelphia Forum. These Forum programs are held in the Academy of Music, and have included the single yearly concert by the Boston Symphony since 1934.

The influence of the Philadelphia Orchestra and its success in the last twenty-five years has been the main factor in reducing or eliminating that city's need of concerts by visiting orchestras. Single appearances by outside orchestras provide welcome variety in instrumental fare; but the day of extended series of concerts by orchestras from other cities seems to have been ended by the increased activity of the Philadelphia Orchestra. The support for even that local group has been somewhat reduced in the past few seasons. The increased number of radio concerts and a general improvement in radio broadcasting and reception of musical programs have contributed to this slight falling off in attendance, as has the long period of financial depression.

Community orchestras, local developments in school and college instrumental groups, and the increasing recognition of the excellence of the Philadelphia Orchestra both as a unit and as a source of small instrumental combinations, all make it seem unlikely that Philadelphia will again be dependent on orchestras from other cities or countries for any considerable share of its instrumental music.

II

The Philadelphia Federal Symphony Orchestra is exerting a tremendous influence on music in Philadelphia. If we could but assume that its organization and its remarkable work are to endure for as many years as the Philadelphia Orchestra has been with us, there would need be no apology for placing the Federal Symphony in a leading position among the city's instrumental groups. An unfortunate parallel in the brilliant but erratic career of the Philadelphia Civic Opera Company cautions us to wait and to see whether through many years a seasoned ensemble of the first rank develops from the auspicious beginnings of the past five years.

A report on the purposes and activity of the Civic Symphony Orchestra from January, 1936, to August, 1937, provides the following account of the orchestras which preceded the Federal Symphony.

In Philadelphia, the local Federal Music Project was established in October, 1935. Preceding that time there had been other music projects, the first, formed in February, 1934, operating under the Civil Works Administration, and the second under the Local Works Division of the Philadelphia County Relief Board of the State Emergency Relief Administration. One of the first results of the initial project was the formation of a symphony orchestra, known as the City Symphony Orchestra of Philadelphia, which was conducted by Dr. Thaddeus Rich, former concertmaster and assistant conductor of the Philadelphia Orchestra, as well as a distinguished solo violinist. Dr. Rich, since October, 1935, has been one of the principal assistants to Dr. Nikolai Sokoloff, National Director of the Federal Music Project. During 1934 and part of 1935, the City Symphony Orchestra gave many concerts throughout the city, winning public and critical acclaim. In the spring of 1935 the orchestra was disbanded as a result of drastic curtailment in project personnel. However, the musicians laid off faced the unemployment problem anew, many being forced on the relief rolls. When the Philadelphia project of the W. P. A. Federal Music Project was established in October, 1935, the majority of the musicians who had constituted the personnel of the City Symphony Orchestra were still unemployed and recipients of relief. Given employment by W. P. A., these instrumentalists and others were combined in a newly formed symphony orchestra—the Civic Symphony Orchestra—which made its initial appearances before the public in January, 1936. The Civic Symphony Orchestra, therefore, while newly organized, had the advantage of beginning its musical life with a membership made up largely of musicians who had formerly been associated in rehearsal and performance as members of the City Symphony Orchestra.

The Civic Symphony Orchestra gave more than 130 concerts from January 1, 1936, to August 31, 1937,[1] reaching thousands of Philadelphians with fine music during this period of eighteen months.

In the course of these months many reviews of the concerts of the Civic Symphony Orchestra have appeared in the columns

---

[1] These dates limit the period covered by the report mentioned above as the source of most of the facts in this account.

of the Philadelphia newspapers. Quotations from several of these reviews are given. *Evening Ledger:* "An interesting and well-performed program"; "An excellent reading and performance"; "Commendable playing in various solo passages by 'firsts' of ensemble." *Evening Bulletin:* "Admirable response from the instrumentalists"; "Orchestra played with spirit and zeal. . . . Listeners responded with much enthusiasm." *Philadelphia Record:* "Civic musicians gave fine account of themselves"; "An especially interesting and well-played program"; *Daily News:* "Tone quality and proficiency were effectively displayed"; "The W.P.A. Civic Symphony Orchestra marked up another pleasing concert to its credit."

The Civic Symphony Orchestra's personnel comprises many musicians who were formerly associated with the Philadelphia Orchestra, the Cleveland Symphony Orchestra, the Chicago Symphony Orchestra, and other symphonic organizations in this country and abroad. Other members served as musicians in opera houses, theatres, and moving picture houses. Still others are young musicians who graduated from music schools and conservatories during the depression period and found an outlet for their skill through the W.P.A. Federal Music Project. These elements have been welded into an excellent symphony orchestra through constant rehearsal and performances since January, 1936, under J. W. F. Leman and other conductors. Previous to that time many members of the orchestra, as stated previously, had been associated with the City Symphony Orchestra.

It is the policy of the W.P.A. Federal Music Project of Philadelphia to have soloists, choral groups, and other organizations participate in concerts of the Civic Symphony Orchestra frequently, with special consideration for Philadelphia vocalists, instrumentalists, and ensembles. The project has as one of its important functions the providing of the opportunity for talented musicians of this area to appear as soloists with a large orchestra. Applicants for solo appearances are heard by an audition committee which determines whether or not the respective singers or instrumentalists possess the qualifications for successful and artistic performances before the public. From January 1, 1936 to August 31, 1937, seventy-three soloists have been featured on Civic Symphony

Orchestra programs. Of these, fifty-eight were Philadelphians. Their names are listed below:

> Pianists: LeRoy Anspach, Walter Baker, George F. Boyle, Pearl Applegate Boyle, Marion Dougherty, Richard Goodman, Henry Harris, Louis Kazze, Joseph Lockett, Guy Marriner, Harry Mayor, Phyllis Moss, Ruth Oehler, Rose Subell, William Sylvano Thunder, and Josef Wissow.
>
> Violinists: Raymond Brown, William Carboni, Armand DeCamillo, Frank Gasparro, Jack Gorodetzky, Sacha Jacobinoff, Sidney Katchurin, Julius Kunstler, Wilhelm Kurasch, Alvin Rudnitsky, Albert Sonder, Nathan Snader, Jacob Stahl, and Isadore Schwartz.
>
> Other Instrumentalists: Dr. Rollo F. Maitland, Organist; Erwin Groer, Violist; Waldemar Giese, Contrabassist; Leslie Flounders, Saxophonist; Michael Dell'Angelo, Trumpeter.
>
> Vocalists: Sopranos—Selma Amansky, Tilly Barmach, Riva Bercova, Mary Black, Mildred Faas, Ruth Freiberg, Caroline Wagner Green, Wilburta Horn, Elsa Raspa, Louise Rich, Bertha Schlessinger, Dorothy Schoenfeld, Helen Stearns, Elizabeth Jane Taylor, and Cecelia Thompson. Contraltos—Virginia Kendrick, Marie Stone Langston, Marguerite Barr MacClain, and Katherine Welsh. Tenors—Joseph Amato, George Lapham, and Ottone Tamini. Baritones and Basses—Eric Belar, Clinton A. Miller, Edward Rhein.

There were also about twenty-five soloists with the Civic Symphony Orchestra from cities other than Philadelphia.

Choral organizations from the Philadelphia area which have appeared with the Civic Symphony Orchestra during the period covered by this report include: the Palestrina Choir, Nicola A. Montani, conductor; the Junger Maennerchor, Leopold Syre, conductor; the Bach Society of Delaware County, James Allan Dash, conductor (an all-Bach Program); the Hoxter Jubilee Choir, Franklin Hoxter, conductor; and the Philco Men's Glee Club, Joseph Smith, conductor. The roster of concerts also included an orchestral-choreographic program, with the Mary Binney Montgomery Dancers of this city participating. A visiting choral organization was the Reading Choral Society of Reading, Pa., which sang Bach's great B minor Mass with accompaniment by the Civic

Symphony Orchestra, N. Lindsay Norden, conducting. The orchestra also presented two children's operas by Leon Lewin, Philadelphia composer and W. P. A. musician, these sung and acted by the Philadelphia W.P.A. Children's Operatic Ensemble.

The resident conductor of the Civic Symphony Orchestra since January 1936 has been J. W. F. Leman, a Philadelphia musician who has been prominent in the city's musical life for many years. A student of eminent teachers in Philadelphia and New York during his youth, an alumnus of the University of Pennsylvania, and experienced both as a violin soloist and orchestral player through personal recitals and several years service (1908-1918) with the Philadelphia Orchestra under Carl Pohlig and Leopold Stokowski, Mr. Leman has a definite background both as theoretical and practical musician. He resigned from the Philadelphia Orchestra to devote his energies to conducting and musical pedagogy and has since been active in these fields. Other groups that have been conducted by Mr. Leman include the Apollo Orchestra, 1909-1918; the Junior League Ballet-Pantomine, 1912-1918; the Wanamaker Orchestra, 1905-1935; and the Women's Symphony Orchestra, 1921 to the present. He has also conducted five seasons of the Philadelphia Music Club's Operatic Society, and four annual productions of the Savoy Opera Company. Mr. Leman has taken time to do considerable composing and arranging for vocal and instrumental combinations.

Among visiting conductors have been such celebrated men as Nikolai Sokoloff, Eugene Ormandy, Thaddeus Rich, and Arthur Fiedler.

Works by more than 150 composers were played by the Civic Symphony Orchestra in 1936 and 1937. Forty-seven American composers, twenty Philadelphians among them, have been represented on their programs, many of such American works being played for the first time at these concerts. In addition to new music by Philadelphia composers which was played, the Civic Symphony Orchestra at rehearsals tried out many other works by local musicians, the authors often being present to hear the "reading." The Philadelphia composer of one hundred years ago, William Fry, should have lived to see this fulfilment of his dream of an opportunity for a hearing of orchestral music by local composers.

Standard works were of course played in large numbers, sixteen symphonies and thirty-three concertos being noted in the period from January 1936 to September 1937. American and world premières by Federal groups, from 1936 to the present year, 1940, can merely be summarized. Full lists were preserved in reports and files kindly made available by W. E. Smith, assistant head of the Philadelphia Federal Music Project. The Orchestra and the Composers' Forum-Laboratory have performed publicly over fifty world premières since January 1936. The Composers' Forum-Laboratory is a division of the Federal Music Project planned and operated solely for the playing of music by local composers. Again, the long lists must be merely summarized. One hundred and thirty-two works by American composers have been played at concerts given by this division, over one hundred of them having been written by Philadelphians. The Rittenhouse Concert Orchestra, while not organized primarily for the introduction of American music, has performed over forty compositions by Philadelphians, and about one hundred American works. Other Works Progress instrumental groups, the Penn and the Sylvania concert bands, have performed thirty-four compositions by Philadelphia musicians.

This bewildering array of Philadelphia musicians whose compositions are given public performance by the Federal groups marks the most significant development of Music in Philadelphia during the past five years.

The most recent developments in the active program of the Works Progress Administration Music Project have been a new name for the orchestra—the Philadelphia Federal Symphony Orchestra—and a new home for some of their concerts, the historic Walnut Street Theatre. Concerts are also held at the Irvine Auditorium of the University of Pennsylvania and the Mitten Hall of Temple University. It is interesting to find that the most recent phase of Philadelphia's newest large music organization is staged in its oldest theatre. Their first concert at the Walnut Street Theatre was given February 26, 1939.

In conclusion, two programs are given. They are typical of all concerts given by the Philadelphia Federal Symphony Orchestra—or, as it was then called, the Philadelphia Civic Symphony

Orchestra. Both programs show the introduction of Philadelphia artists, the production of modern American music, and a worthwhile selection of standard compositions from orchestral literature.

1.

WORKS PROGRESS ADMINISTRATION, PENNSYLVANIA
J. BANKS HUDSON, *State Administrator*
MITTEN HALL, BROAD AND BERKS STREETS,
PHILADELPHIA, PA.
SUNDAY AFTERNOON, JUNE 12, 1938
AT 2:30 O'CLOCK
Auspices of Temple University

THE PHILADELPHIA CIVIC SYMPHONY ORCHESTRA
ISADORE FREED, *Guest-Conductor*
Participating Artists, The Guild Singers

PROGRAM

CONCERTO GROSSO IN B-FLAT, FOR STRINGS AND WOODWINDS ....*Handel*
    Allegro moderato—Largo—Allegro
             (A Cappella Group)
    Laudate Dominum ....Pitoni (1657-1743)
    O Vos Omnes ....Vittoria (1540-1608)
    Canzone ....Provenzale (17th Century)
             (The Guild Singers)
SYMPHONY NO. 3, IN E-FLAT, THE "RHENISH" ....*Schumann*
    Allegro
        Scherzo: Allegretto
        Moderato
        Grave ("The Cathedral")
        Finale: Allegro

Intermission

TWO NOCTURNES FOR ORCHESTRA ....*Debussy*
      "Nuages"   "Fêtes"
"PASTORALS," NINE PIECES FOR ORCHESTRA ....*Freed*
            (First Performance)

1. "The Bells"	4. "The Country Cart"	7. "Gray Skies"
2. "The Mill"	5. "The Shepherd's Pipe"	8. "The Village Band"
3. "The Hidden Brook"	6. "At the Fair"	9. "Country Revel"

Polovetzian Dances from "Prince Igor" ....*Borodin*
(The Guild Singers and Orchestra)
This Concert Is Presented by the Federal Music Project of the
Works Progress Administration
Division of Women's and Professional Projects,
Ellen S. Woodward, *Assistant Administrator,*
Federal Music Project
Dr. Nikolai Sokoloff, *National Director*
Dr. Thaddeus Rich, *Assistant to the Director*
Next Concert—Irvine Auditorium, 34th and Spruce Streets
Sunday Afternoon, June 19th, at 3:30 O'Clock
Antonio Ferraro, *Guest-Conductor*   Soloist, Jack Gorodetzky, *Violinist*
Radio Broadcasts by the Orchestra—Station KYW
Monday Evenings at 10:30 O'Clock

2.
IRVINE AUDITORIUM, UNIVERSITY OF PENNSYLVANIA
34TH AND SPRUCE STREETS, PHILADELPHIA, PENNA.
SUNDAY AFTERNOON, OCTOBER 16, 1938
AT 3:30 O'CLOCK
Auspices of the University of Pennsylvania School of Fine Arts

PROGRAM
Overture to "La Clemenza Di Tito" ....*Mozart*
Symphony No. 2, in D Major ....*Beethoven*
Adagio molto—Allegro con brio
Larghetto
Scherzo
Allegro molto
Intermission
Overture to "Le Caid" ....*Thomas*
Aria "Le Tambour Major Tout Gallone" from "Le Caid".......*Thomas*
Soloist, Leonard Treash
Hungarian Dances, Nos. 5 and 6 ....*Brahms*
Excerpts from the Music-Drama "The Valkyr" ....*Wagner*
"The Ride of the Valkyrs"
Finale—"Wotan's Farewell" and "Magic Fire" Scene
Soloist, Leonard Treash
Next Concert—Sunday, October 23, at 2:30 P.M.
Mitten Hall, Broad and Berks Streets
BACH—BEETHOVEN—BRAHMS—PROGRAM

CHAPTER EIGHT

CHAMBER MUSIC IN PHILADELPHIA

I

"It is better to be inside of bad music than outside of good music," said Thomas Whitney Surette. This may help to explain why amateurs have performed such a large share in music's most difficult sphere—that of chamber music. The instrumental music for small combinations has been divided into two contrasting sections since about 1800. The good chamber music requires an overwhelming majority to be 'outside of it,' that is, its auditors. The bad chamber music invites all to participate, amateur and professional often playing in the same trio or quartet. It is good to be in any form of chamber ensemble, so we may question whether any of it is properly called *bad*. A few examples of both expert and average Philadelphia Chamber music have already been noted in our historical chapters. The Hermits of the Wissahickon played in a small orchestra in 1700 when such an accomplishment would have been unheard of in Philadelphia proper.[1] Hopkinson organized one of the first chamber orchestras in the city, between 1760 and 1770. Palma, Bentley and Gualdo were actually leading small instrumental groups in the colonial years of Philadelphia. It was not until about 1780 that we find instrumental ensembles that had passed the numerical limit that separates chamber music from what would be termed a small orchestra. Reinagle led an orchestra in the concerts and theatrical programs between 1780 and 1800. There was a recognized difference between the musical groups at the homes of Dr. Adam Kuhn and Joseph Hopkinson and the concert orchestras—termed 'full bands'—of the late eighteenth century.

Kuhn's descendants maintained the custom of providing frequent evenings of the instrumental music at their home well into the nineteenth century. The descendants of Francis Hopkinson

---

[1] Cf., *supra,* p. 4.

preserved the same tradition for a still longer period of years. Oliver Hopkinson (1812-1905), grandson of Joseph, was a capable violinist, having studied in Paris with Vieuxtemps. His former teacher participated in the Hopkinson amateur chamber music parties when he visited Philadelphia in 1844 and 1857. Ernesto Sivori was also a friend of Oliver Hopkinson. When Sivori gave his concert in Musical Fund Hall in 1846, Mrs. Joseph Hopkinson was too ill to attend. Oliver brought his friend home, and he obligingly repeated most of the solos for the invalid's private ear.[1] Theodore Thomas was a frequent visitor at the Hopkinsons' house on Spruce Street. Oliver Hopkinson Jr., born in 1857, now living in Merion, Pennsylvania, played violoncello in many amateur quartets. Carl Wolfsohn, Michael Cross, Charles Jarvis, Massah Warner and Thomas à Becket, Jr., were among the professional musicians of note who joined with the Hopkinsons in producing chamber music in the years between 1875 and 1900. Leopold Engelke, a 'cellist who had come to Philadelphia with the Germania Orchestra in 1848, was one of the teachers of Oliver Hopkinson, Jr., and often joined in the musical soirées. Brau and Hennig also taught Dr. Hopkinson. This last of the musical Hopkinsons recalls playing a 'cello sonata by Michael Cross with the composer at the piano, and many other interesting incidents he experienced in his years of participation in amateur chamber ensembles. Some of the earliest musical programs at the University of Pennsylvania after that institution had moved to its present site in West Philadelphia were greatly furthered by Oliver Hopkinson, Jr. An orchestra of seven members was organized there by Hopkinson and directed by Engelke in 1877. In 1878 this group abandoned its original chamber orchestra organization and was increased to about twenty members. Upon being requested to cease and desist in the College Hall the orchestra met at 21st and Walnut Streets, in the home of Dr. Hewson. Hopkinson played violoncello in this early university orchestra, and also assisted as 'cello soloist at glee club concerts between 1878 and 1885. A piano quartet of which Oliver Hopkinson was a member played in a semi-professional manner at benefit concerts and soirées between 1878 and 1880. Dr. Hopkinson kindly

[1] Ernesto C. Sivori was one of the world's greatest violinists, and was said to be Paganini's only pupil.

furnished the program of a concert given April 27, 1878, at St. George's Hall, Thirteenth and Arch Streets. The program contained both vocal and instrumental numbers, the latter being:

Beethoven—Quartet in B flat (the "Grand B♭")
Schumann—Quartet in E flat (Op. 47)
Mendelssohn—Sonata for 'Cello and Piano (First Movement).

The quartet members at this concert were J. Nurick, G. Guhlman, A. Kellner, and O. Hopkinson.

Thomas Sully was an amateur flutist as well as a noted painter. An earlier Philadelphian, Gustavus Hesselius (1682-1755), also excelled in the same two artistic media.[1] Hesselius's son John Hesselius was an early teacher of Charles Wilson Peale (1741-1827), a distinguished portrait painter of revolutionary days. His son Rembrandt Peale, 1778-1860, was scarcely less noted as a painter. Thomas Sully, 1783-1872, who was a contemporary of both Peales, united his musical and artistic interests in a series of nine portraits of noted members of the Musical Fund Society. The connection of Thomas Sully as a member and officer of the Musical Fund and as host to its early orchestral meetings has been previously discussed.[2] There were many evenings of music at Thomas Sully's home in the early and middle nineteenth century.

Descendants of William and John Darley were active in art and music throughout the nineteenth century. J. C. Darley painted Carr and Schetky's portraits for the Musical Fund Society, the first of the series continued by Sully. John Darley, possibly a son of J. C., has been mentioned as one of the principal actors in the American première of *Der Freischütz* in 1825. W. H. W. Darley was a member of musical clubs between 1825 and 1850, an organist and composer of church music. Several references were made to F. T. Sully Darley, composer of the first oratorio by a Philadelphian,[3] the opera *Fortunio,*[4] and vice-president of the

---

[1] John Henderson, organist at old St. Paul's Church, Philadelphia, was a grandson of G. Hesselius.

[2] The preliminary instrumental groups rehearsed at Earle and Sully's galleries of paintings. Cf. *supra*, p. 56.

[3] *The Cities of the Plain*; cf., *supra*, p. 88, footnote 5.

[4] *Fortunio* was produced at the Academy of Music in Philadelphia, March 25, 1883.

Philadelphia Orchestra Association in 1900. F. T. S. Darley was a member of the Musical Fund Society, and also carried on the artistic traditions of the Sullys and Darleys.

The fortnightly musicals at the home of Franklin Peale suggest to us another example of an amateur interest in chamber music present in several generations of the same family. Mr. and Mrs. Peale were both accomplished musicians themselves, according to Armstrong's *Records of the Opera in Philadelphia* (p. 9), and invited both professionals and amateurs to play at their musical gatherings. Franklin Peale is a musical and artistic descendant of Gustavus Hesselius, through Charles and Rembrandt Peale. His descendant Franklin Peale Patterson, born in 1871, studied under Clarke at the University of Pennsylvania, and composed three operas, *Mountain Blood, The Echo,* and *Beggar's Love.* Study in Munich and a position on the staff of the *Musical Courier* have made Patterson give up his residence in Philadelphia since the closing years of the nineteenth century. He is the author of books and articles on music as well as the operas named above.

The 18th Street home of John Converse boasted a family trio, as did many others whose members happened to have escaped mention in any public manner. Mrs. Converse played the piano, John Sr. the violin, and his son the 'cello. The Hopkinsons and Converses often combined forces in musical gatherings of the late nineteenth century.

II

The Philadelphia Art Alliance, a group of the present day with interests encompassing all the arts, may be said to follow in the line of Sully, Darley, and Peale in their interests in painting and music. From its organization in 1915 the Art Alliance has fostered all forms of musical programs. Members' music hours have been held monthly since 1937. Recitals, chamber music, and concerts of all description have been given at the Art Alliance for many years. All of these programs have stressed the new in music, as have several lectures on musical topics. The Euridice award of one hundred dollars is offered every three years by this society for an original composition for women's chorus.

Music at the Art Alliance is generally of the "good" variety, the kind in which most amateurs are not permitted to participate. Chamber music produced by professionals, or amateurs of unusual skill, has developed beside the various informal meetings of trios or quartets which certain families have fostered in Philadelphia since 1760. Let us call such more expert ensembles professional chamber music groups, since their performances usually included some professional members, and always reached a high level of artistic, or at least technical, accomplishment. In the early nineteenth century chapter many clubs and quartet parties were recorded.[1] Hupfeld(t), Homman(n), Schetky, Gillingham, and Gilles are musicians who may be remembered as participants in small instrumental groups of expert or professional calibre.

Among the earliest programs of chamber music in the Academy of Music were four concerts by a piano quintet and eight male voices, in the foyer during February and March of 1859. Henry Gordon Thunder was the pianist for these concerts. Among the instrumental works played were the quartet in B, and the piano quartet in F by Beethoven, a string quintet by Mozart, and the "Hayden" D major quartet. In this same year, 1859, the celebrated Mendelssohn Quintet, organized in Boston in 1849, played its first Philadelphia concert.

November 17th 1859, was announced in the *Philadelphia Evening Bulletin* as the date for the first classical soirée of that season. The Schumann piano quintet in E♭ was announced for this performance. Carl Wolfsohn and Carl Hohnstock, both pianists, were assisted by a violin, viola and 'cello at this concert. The influence of Wolfsohn in recitals and chamber ensemble programs was important in Philadelphia from 1854 to 1873. In the latter year Wolfsohn went to Chicago. He is mentioned elsewhere as the founder and director of the Beethoven Society of Philadelphia, 1869-1873.

The period after the Civil War included the chamber music programs of Cross and Jarvis as the most influential series of chamber music of the expert variety. William Stoll's Beethoven Quartet and Carl Gaertner's chamber ensemble have also been

---

[1] Cf. *supra*, pp. 86-87.

mentioned as professional organizations of importance. The later years of the nineteenth century brought many fine teachers of string instruments to the new music schools that had begun and prospered between 1870 and 1900. The faculty chamber music concerts at various conservatories have provided many well played programs of this difficult field of our art. Heman Allen was active in such groups between 1862 and 1867. Gustav Hille remained an important teacher and member of chamber ensembles from 1880 to 1910, in which year he returned to Germany. Henry Schradieck, at the Broad Street Conservatory 1898-1912, and Hedda van den Beemt and Boris Koutzen at the Philadelphia Conservatory in more recent years, have continued the faculty, or teacher and student, chamber ensembles down to the present day.

The activities at the Philadelphia Musical Academy in the production and composition of chamber works are noteworthy. Burnett C. Tuthill mentions only two Philadelphia items in his article on *Fifty years of Chamber Music in the United States.*[1] He refers to the melodious and scholarly chamber compositions by Camille Zeckwer, graduate, teacher, and later director of the Philadelphia Musical Academy. The auditorium at the academy, often known as the Zeckwer-Hahn conservatory, has been the scene of much original chamber music as well as standard compositions for small instrumental groups. The other Philadelphia chamber music item in Tuthill's article concerns the 1928-1929 season of chamber concerts at the Art Museum, described later in this chapter.

The longest period of influence in such faculty and student chamber ensembles was that exerted by Gilbert R. Combs. From the year of the founding of the Broad Street Conservatory, 1885, until shortly before his death in 1934, Combs was an active participant and consistent patron of instrumental groups. He was a founder of the *Sinfonia,* a musical fraternity, and was twice its president.[2]

In the years immediately preceding and following 1900 the many visits of the Kneisel Quartet revealed the possibilities and beauties of this most frequently played form of chamber music.

---

[1] *Fifty Years of Chamber Music in the United States,* by Tuthill is included in the 1928 Proceedings of the Music Teachers National Association.
[2] Cf. account of Combs Broad Street Conservatory, pp. 301-2.

The influence of the Philadelphia Symphony Society, particularly the interest and financial assistance of its concertmaster Edward I. Keffer, brought this Boston quartet to Philadelphia in 1896. Witherspoon Hall was used for the programs by the Kneisel Quartet. This outstanding chamber ensemble played several concerts in Philadelphia each season for over twenty years. Public support for the Kneisel concerts was considered good, but not quite sufficient to operate the concerts without a fairly constant annual deficit.

Dr. Edward I. Keffer, the concertmaster of the Philadelphia Symphony Society, the leading person in the organization of the Philadelphia Orchestra, and the main backer of the Kneisel Quartet, was also an enthusiastic performer in chamber ensembles. From 1900 to 1928 he held weekly "quartet parties" in which the finest musicians of the city participated. Among the quartet and quintet members were Philip Goepp, Hendrik Ezerman (whose tragic death occurred while returning from one of these affairs), Johan Grolle, Thaddeus Rich, and Hans Kindler, and of course Keffer himself. Distinguished visitors were also present for many of these programs, Kreisler, Gadsky, Bispham, and De Pachmann among them. Some of the regular quartet members at the Keffer musicales belonged also to an ensemble that was active between 1906 and 1910. Quartets, piano quartets, and piano quintets were played by this group, which consisted of Johan Grolle, Hedda van den Beemt, Samuel Laciar, D. Hendrik Ezerman, and Philip Goepp.

III

The recent growth and artistic development of the Philadelphia Orchestra has provided a large number of fine string players and woodwind soloists that are available for any desired form of chamber ensemble.

Fritz Scheel conducted seven programs of House Music at the residence of Mrs. Spencer Ervin in the seasons of 1904-1905 and 1905-1906. These chamber music concerts were given as a compliment to the women's committees in the early years of their activity. This same chamber orchestra played at the White House for President and Mrs. Theodore Roosevelt on January 29, 1906, to the great admiration of all present, particularly the President.

One of the finest and most permanent organizations of Philadelphia Orchestra men was the Rich-Kindler-Hammann trio. This group was active in Philadelphia and throughout the eastern states from 1915 to 1929. A Rich Quartet [1] gave concerts during these same years. Emma S. Brister mentions the trio[2] in connection with the appearances made by her niece Julia Heinrich at their concerts. Mrs. Brister expresses the sentiment of many an admirer of chamber music when she states: "It was a real loss to music lovers when this trio disbanded, for a similar organization equally talented has never succeeded them."

Among the many connections in instrumental music of Thaddeus Rich, none is closer to his own heart than the field of chamber music. A short biographical account of this dean of Philadelphia instrumentalists is accordingly inserted here. Thaddeus Rich was born in Indianapolis in 1885. His father, William S. Rich, was an accomplished amateur violinist, and gave Thaddeus his first lessons on the instrument on which he later specialized with such unusual success. Rich studied with Indianapolis teachers until 1896, in which year he entered the Leipsic Conservatory. He graduated from this famous institution with highest honors, at the age of fifteen, and was appointed a member of the Gewandhaus Orchestra under Nikisch. William Bachaus and Thaddeus Rich gave joint recitals, consisting mainly of violin sonatas, before their Leipsic friends, including Arthur Nikisch and Max Reger. In 1902 Rich settled in Berlin, where he became a pupil of Joachim, and in the same year concertmaster of the orchestra at the city opera—the youngest man to hold such a position in the history of that organization.

Thaddeus Rich had been a celebrated soloist since the age of nine. His violin technique and general musical powers vastly enlarged by the years of European study and experience, Rich returned to America in 1905. He immediately began an ambitious series of recitals in this country, seventeen of them being given in New York during the 1905-1906 season. Fritz Scheel secured Thaddeus Rich as concertmaster for the Philadelphia Orchestra in 1906, a post which Rich filled with distinction for over twenty

---

[1] T. Rich, H. Aleinikoff, E. Ferier, H. Kindler.
[2] *Incidents*, pp. 56-57.

years.[1] He has directed many programs by that orchestra, and
has conducted at various eastern music festivals.[2] During the period
of Rich's connection with the Philadelphia Orchestra, he became
one of that city's leading teachers of violin, and was appointed
Dean of the School of Music at Temple University, a position which
he still holds (1940). The university awarded the degree of Doctor
of Music to Thaddeus Rich in 1913. Dr. Rich resigned from the
Philadelphia Orchestra in 1926 to become curator of the Rodman
Wanamaker collection of instruments and musical advisor to that
eminent business executive.

In recent years Thaddeus Rich has acted as a member of many
musical boards. He has served as a director of the Presser Foundation, and as a judge in many contests and auditions. Dr. Rich's
main activity at present lies in the Federal Music Project of the
Works Progress Administration. He conducted the City Symphony
Orchestra in 1934, later becoming State Director of Music for
Pennsylvania. Late in 1935 the Federal Music Project was organized in its present form, and Dr. Rich was appointed an assistant to Nicolai Sokoloff, its national director.[3] He is regional
director for the section including Pennsylvania, New Jersey, Delaware, Maryland, West Virginia and the District of Columbia. As
the preceding pages have testified, the activities of the Federal
Music Project are among the most important developments in
American music during the past four years.

A larger chamber ensemble made up entirely of Philadelphia
Orchestra members was known as the Philadelphia Chamber Ensemble. Its ten instruments consisted of the first five string players
and the first five woodwinds of the Philadelphia Orchestra. This
group gave concerts between 1915 and 1926.

Still another chamber group consisting of Philadelphia Orchestra members was the Schmidt Quartet. This ensemble had a
long career of considerable success in the Philadelphia area. From
1909 to 1922 the Schmidt Quartet maintained a fairly constant
personnel, gave a series of two or three public concerts a year, and

---

[1] Cf., *supra*, pp. 187-8 for Rich as member and assistant conductor of the
Philadelphia Orchestra.
[2] Worcester, Asheville, and Winston-Salem.
[3] Cf., *supra*, pp. 207-214 for account of Rich and other Philadelphians
connected with the W.P.A.

made additional appearances at various functions. The members during the season of 1916-1917 were Emil F. Schmidt, Louis Angeloty, Alfred Lorenz, and William A. Schmidt. The violins and 'cello were played by these same men throughout the 1909-1922 period, but there were several violists besides Mr. Lorenz.[1]

The Guarnerius Quartet, consisting of Alexander Hilsberg, David Madison, Samuel Lifschey, and Willem Van den Burg gave programs of chamber music from 1932 to 1934. In their concert (March 25, 1934) devoted to the works of Samuel Laciar this quartet was assisted by Leon Frengut, viola, and Frank Miller, violoncello.

There have been other groups made up in part or altogether of Philadelphia Orchestra members, as there will almost certainly be many more in years to come, but the few mentioned above have been the most widely known up to this time.

IV

Besides the Orchestra as a source for the best chamber music in Philadelphia we must not omit to record the activities of the Philadelphia Chamber Music Association. From 1916 to 1932 this association was responsible for weekly concerts given in the ballroom of the Bellevue-Stratford Hotel. At these programs, which were performed on Sunday afternoons, a bewildering assortment of the finest chamber ensembles were heard. The original purpose of the group was the creation of an opportunity for local and visiting ensembles to be heard in chamber concerts. A few Philadelphia groups played on these programs, but the vast majority of the concerts were given by famous quartets from remote places. The Rich Quartet, the Rich-Kindler-Hammann Trio, the Philadelphia Chamber String Simfonietta, the Philadelphia Orchestra Ensemble (in their first appearance, October 28, 1928) and the Schmidt Quartet were among the local chamber ensembles that played at these concerts. The increasingly cosmopolitan nature of the concerts sponsored by the Philadelphia Chamber Music

---

[1] Johan Grolle, J. W. F. Leman, William Happich and Samuel Belov played viola at various concerts, or seasons, of the Schmidt Quartet. A more recent group (Zenker, Bancroft, Elkan, Schmidt) still is known as the Schmidt Quartet.

Association is marked by their engagement of a large number of soloists and ensembles from other cities, and from Europe as well. Among these non-Philadelphia chamber groups were the Flonzaley, Kneisel, Lener, New York, London, Budapest, and Hart House [1] quartets. Jacques Thibaut and Alfred Cortot performed a notable concert of violin sonatas in this series at the Bellevue-Stratford Hotel. The Elshuco Quartet played in several series; the Pro-Arte Quartet of Brussels made its first Philadelphia appearance at one of the Chamber Music Association concerts. This same association offered a prize of $500 for a work for chamber ensemble by an American composer. The award was won by Sandor Harmati with a string quartet.

Mrs. Harold E. Yarnall as founder and president of the Philadelphia Chamber Music Association has been the outstanding person in arranging for all of their concerts. As Adele Gilpin, Mrs. Yarnall was a popular soprano from 1885 to 1890. Michael Cross taught her from 1880 to 1882 and secured her first important engagement as soloist at a concert by the Orpheus Club. Mrs. Yarnall's former husband, Spencer Ervin, was a member of that chorus, and a wealthy musical amateur. Max Heinrich and Mrs. Spencer Ervin were the soloists at a concert by the Orpheus Club and the Philadelphia Orchestra led by Fritz Scheel. Mrs. Ervin was also an active member of the women's committee for the orchestra, and the hostess to their chamber concerts, directed by Scheel from 1904 to 1906. A long series of Monday morning musicales paralleled the Sunday chamber concerts. These Monday programs were also managed by Mrs. Ervin, later Mrs. Harold Yarnall, and were given from 1917 to 1930. An array of soloists as imposing as the chamber ensembles listed above gave recitals at Mrs. Yarnall's Monday programs, which were also held at the ballroom of the Bellevue-Stratford Hotel. To name only the most noted among them requires a long list: Cortot, Bachaus, Kindler, Garden, Bori, Garrison, Schelling, Chaliapin, Onegin, Flesch, Landowska, Gauthier, Thomas, Melchior, Szigeti, Giannini, Horowitz, and Braslau. Ensembles were also presented, but a solo recitalist was the usual attraction at these performances.

---

[1] A quartet associated with the Hart House, a hotel in Toronto.

The concerts managed by Mrs. Harold E. Yarnall provided a great part of the early success of the Simfonietta. This rather large chamber ensemble is made up of eighteen members of the Philadelphia Orchestra. It is officially named the Philadelphia Chamber String Simfonietta, usually referred to simply as the Simfonietta, and was fondly styled the 'little brother of the Philadelphia Orchestra' by Leopold Stokowski. Fabian Sevitzky founded the Simfonietta in 1925. This ensemble gives three public concerts, and one children's program each year. As conductor of the Indianapolis Symphony Orchestra, Sevitzky continues to follow in the footsteps of his noted uncle Serge Koussevitzky. He arranges the Philadelphia Simfonietta appearances so that both rehearsals and performances take place when the Indianapolis position does not require his presence in that city. The Simfonietta has inspired many compositions by well known musicians and has also provided an opportunity for student pieces of exceptional merit to receive public performance. These factors have combined to make the world and American premières by the Simfonietta an important part of their contribution to Music in Philadelphia. Many works by Arcady Dubensky have been given their first performance by Sevitzky's group, among them *In Memory of Old Moscow, Gossips, Anno* 1600, *Soldiers' Song,* and *Children's Alphabet.* The Philadelphia musician Frances McCollin [1] is the composer of four works for string orchestra, given their world première performance by the Simfonietta: *Adagio, Two Chorale Preludes, Scherzo* (*Heavenly Children at Play*), and *Prayer. The Sea,* a composition for chorus and string orchestra by the Philadelphia composer Harl McDonald, was given its first performance by the Simfonietta and the Chorus of the University of Pennsylvania. World premières

---

[1] Frances McCollin, born in Philadelphia 1892, is the daughter of Edward McCollin, an active figure in the Orpheus Club, the Musical Fund Society and one of E. I. Keffer's ablest assistants in the founding of the Philadelphia Orchestra. Miss McCollin's lectures on musical subjects, particularly her hundreds of talks on the current programs by the Philadelphia Orchestra, are well known to musicians in that city. Her study with Dr. Gilchrist and Dr. H. A. Matthews seems to have equipped Frances McCollin to inherit what John Tasker Howard calls Gilchrist's 'uncanny faculty for winning prizes.' (*Our American Music,* p. 321.) Ten national awards for choral compositions have been won by this Philadelphia composer. She has also written many works for orchestra and chamber groups.

by this string orchestra of less local interest include *Gods,* by Blitz-stein, *Four Songs* (vocal quartet and Simfonietta) by Gretchaninoff, *Four Indiscretions* by Gruenberg, and *Recreations* by Wall. Among many works performed for the first time in America are: Fuleihan, *Piano concerto* (composer at the piano); Britten, *Variations on a Theme by Bridge;* Stutky, *Salt of the Sea;* Menotti, *Pastorale and Dance* for piano and strings (composer at the piano); and *Radiations,* by Whitmer.

When we list the objectives and the accomplishments of the Simfonietta we have reached a present point in the consideration of Philadelphia chamber music. The small combinations of instruments that exist in schools, conservatories or in private homes in present day Philadelphia could not be discussed or listed in this book. The Curtis Institute of Music has staged many concerts of chamber music in the fifteen years of its existence. A Curtis String Quartet made up of former students of this school has become internationally noted through its successful tours abroad, and gives concerts in many American cities as well as in the Curtis Institute at Casimir Hall. This ensemble played forty-three concerts in thirty-three American cities during the season of 1938-1939. The members of the Curtis Quartet are Jascha Brodsky, Charles Jaffe, Max Aronoff, and Lucius Cole.

One of the most interesting series of local chamber concerts was given in the spring of the current season at the Ethical Society Auditorium. The four programs were composed entirely of modern works for instrumental groups. The final concert April 3, 1939, contains the most novel combinations of the series, and is reproduced in full below.

HONEGGER ....Three Pieces
            For Piccolo, Oboe, Violin, Violoncello
   Prelude
      Choral
        Canon
*DeFalla ....Seven Popular Spanish Songs

---

* The accompaniment originally for piano has been transcribed for two harps by Carlos Salzedo.

For Soprano and Two Harps

El Pano Moruno   Jota

Seguidilla Murciana   Nana

Asturiana   Cancion

Polo

HINDEMITH ....Sonata for Viola and Piano

Fantasie

Thema mit variationen

Finale (mit variationen)[1]

PROKOFIEFF ....Sonata for Two Violins

Andante Cantabile

Allegro

Commodo (Quasi Allegretto)

Allegro Con Brio

SANDERS ....Sonata for Violoncello and Piano

(In One Movement)

DeFALLA ....Concerto

For Piano, Violin, Violoncello, Flute, Oboe, Clarinet

The credit for the public presentation of this Modern Chamber Music Series belongs to the Philadelphia Conservatory of Music. Of twenty-six soloists required to perform the extremely varied compositions, nearly half were members of the faculty of that conservatory.

One of the most noted composers to appear as a member of a chamber ensemble in Philadelphia was Richard Strauss. On November 1, 1921, Elizabeth Schumann and Strauss performed a concert consisting mainly of songs by the latter at the Academy of Music. They were assisted by a violin and violoncello. Dr. Strauss obliged both as accompanist for Miss Schumann and as pianist for the assisting trio. That concert, which would have greatly excited an orchestra audience, seems to have been taken by the devotees of chamber music all in their pride, and without undue betrayal of emotion.

---

[1] The 'variation' here announced was a little too marked, for this Hindemith sonata was not performed at all. The piano sonata by the same composer was played by Paul Nordoff in its place. Nordoff was born in Philadelphia in 1909, and studied in that city and New York. He is a gifted pianist and composer, and a member of the faculty of the Philadelphia Conservatory of Music.

Chamber Music programs have had a difficult time to fill halls large enough to make them self-supporting. The Academy Foyer, the New Century Club, the Academy of Fine Arts, Horticultural Hall, the Bellevue-Stratford Ballroom, Witherspoon Hall, the Penn Athletic Club, the Art Alliance, and the Ethical Society Auditorium have all presented ideally located and planned rooms for the chamber orchestra. Yet their offerings have received meagre support in prosperous years, and their members have feared to attempt performances for profit in depression years. One answer to the problem seems to be the civic sponsoring of advanced student ensembles, or of chamber groups that will perform for a modest fee in public buildings. Several series so organized were given at the Art Museum on the Parkway. Tuthill's review of chamber music [1] mentions the throngs that heard these free concerts as evidence of popular approval of chamber ensembles. The concert of November 18, 1928, was attended by thousands of people according to Tuthill's article. The obvious limitation as to how well the music could be heard by so many listeners constituted a very real barrier to the artistic success of the Art Museum chamber concerts. Six Sunday evening programs were played by students of the Curtis Institute of Music during the season of 1928-1929. Six following years witnessed the continued free chamber music at the Art Museum. The concerts were given under the direction of Dr. Louis Bailly, who produced many novelties, premières, and works of unusual interest such as the Fauré *Requiem* for Voice, Chorus, Organ, and Orchestra (first secular performance in U. S.), the Tansman *Triptyque* for String Orchestra (first performance in Philadelphia) ; Chausson's *Chanson Perpetuelle,* Poulenc's *Rapsodie Nègre* for Voice and Orchestra, Ravel's *Shéhérazade* for Voice and Orchestra and his *Introduction and Allegro* for Harp, Flute, Clarinet, and String Quartet, Schönberg's *Verklärte Nacht* for String Sextet, the Svendsen String Octet, Op. 3, Zilcher's setting of the *Song of Solomon,* for Voice and String Quartet, and his *Marienlieder* for Voice and String Quartet.

---

[1] *Fifty Years of Chamber Music in the United States* by Burnett C. Tuthill (Proceedings of M.T.N.A., 1928).

The weekly concerts given under the auspices of the Philadelphia Music Bureau from 1929 to 1933 were devoted largely to chamber music. These programs were given at the Academy of Fine Arts each Sunday during the concert season.[1] The Philadelphia Music Center's efforts in the behalf of chamber music began shortly after the concerts by the Curtis Institute and the Music Bureau were discontinued.[2] A small fee for each performer and a larger sum of money for heating a hall and handling huge crowds would enable some of the interrupted series of chamber concerts to be resumed.

---

[1] For material on the Music Bureau cf. *infra*, pp. 351-4.
[2] The Music Center is described in the preceding chapter; *supra*, pp. 204-206.

CHAPTER NINE

OPERA IN PHILADELPHIA SINCE 1900

Many companies must be mentioned in any account of opera in Philadelphia during the past forty years. To present even the barest vital statistics of the more important among them calls for lists and facts in great number; to single out notable performances from the thousands of opera nights is interesting but dangerous to attempt; to evaluate the significance of the many companies of recent years is impossible without the perspective of time.

Let us embark on the safe course. Facts and statistics accord the Metropolitan Opera Company of New York the largest share of importance in Philadelphia since 1900. Their performances began in New York in 1883, and their first performance in Philadelphia took place on December 21, 1885. It was not until the years of Maurice Grau's management that the New York company attempted weekly operas in Philadelphia. The weekly schedule calls for about twenty-five operas in the concert season. This number may be regarded as a maximum for the Metropolitan Company's Philadelphia performances. Many years have seen this large number realized, although they were all before the season of 1932-1933, the worst depression years. From 1910 to 1925 the productions of the Metropolitan Opera Company were given in the Metropolitan Opera House at Broad and Poplar Streets. Since 1925, annual seasons of opera have been given by this company at the Academy of Music, with the exception of the 1933-1934 season. In 1934-1935 the Metropolitan resumed its Philadelphia performances, but with a small number of operas. The season 1938-1939 brought ten operas to Philadelphia by the Metropolitan, among them a performance of the complete *Ring of the Nibelungen*.[1] The management

---

[1] The complete tetralogy *The Ring of the Nibelungen* has been produced in Philadelphia nine times, as follows:

1889, 1903, 1904, 1908-1909.......The Metropolitan Opera Company of N. Y.
1923 ....Charlottenburg Company
1929-1930 ....Philadelphia Civic Opera Company
1929, 1930 ....German Opera Company
1939 ....Metropolitan Opera Company of N. Y.

of this New York company announced ten operas during the current season, 1939-1940.

Although it might be dangerous—as mentioned above—to select a few outstanding facts from the many that are significant in the long course of visits by the Metropolitan Opera Company, the following may prove of interest. In the years after 1900 when this company reigned supreme in both New York and Philadelphia such singers as Nordica, Campanari, the De Reszkes, Melba, Gadski, Homer, Schumann-Heink, Scotti, Milka Ternina, Paul Plançon, and David Bispham were frequently heard in their productions at the Academy of Music in Philadelphia. Caruso made his first Philadelphia appearance as the Duke in *Rigoletto,* a production of the Metropolitan Company on December 29, 1903. Homer, Sembrich, and Scotti were in the same cast. A slightly earlier performance, that of *The Magic Flute* on February 6th, 1902, was sung by Sembrich, Ternina, Homer, Eames, Campanari, Edouard de Reszke, and Fritzi Scheff. Alfred Hertz appeared for the first time in Philadelphia as the conductor of *Lohengrin,* on December 11, 1902. The leading parts were sung by Gadski, Schumann-Heink, and Bispham. Mancinelli and Damrosch conducted most of these Metropolitan performances early in the twentieth century. Such an array of the great singers and conductors did not stop in the early 1900's. The more remote are advisedly chosen, since their greatness loses nothing in the intervening years, while the perspective of time adds certainty to the estimates of their contemporary admirers.

The list of operas introduced to Philadelphia at the end of this chapter shows that the vast majority of such novelties were given by the Metropolitan Company. We have seen that Gustav Hinrichs rivalled the Metropolitan with regard to new works in the earlier days of the New York Company's Philadelphia visits. In the years after 1900 the Henry Savage English Opera Company produced new operas never before heard in Philadelphia; while the Hammerstein Opera Company in its brief career, 1908 to 1910, was noted for its policy of introducing new operas. The list will also reveal that for some years, 1910 to 1919, the Philadelphia-Chicago Opera Company carried on the Hammerstein tradition of producing many new works.

The Hammerstein Company, and its subsequent reorganization the Philadelphia-Chicago Opera Company, form a combination second in significance to only the Metropolitan Company in Philadelphia opera of the twentieth century. The building known as the Metropolitan Opera House, at Broad and Poplar Streets in Philadelphia, was built for productions by the Hammerstein Company. In the spring of 1908 Oscar Hammerstein and his Manhattan Opera Company produced *Louise* with Mary Garden, and *Lucia* with Tetrazzini, at the Philadelphia Academy of Music. These operas were received with such enthusiasm that Hammerstein promised to build a new opera house in Philadelphia, as a home for his productions during the following season. His promise was to open the new building by the middle of November. On November 17, 1908, the Metropolitan Opera House was opened with a production of *Carmen*. During the same week Hammerstein's company produced *Samson and Delilah* for the first time in Philadelphia, and staged a fine performance of *The Barber of Seville* with Mme. Tetrazzini as Rosina. The first Philadelphia performance of *Thaïs*, with Mary Garden in the title role, was given a week after the opening of Hammerstein's theatre, November 24, 1908. There were four operas a week for a twenty week season during the 1908-1909 and 1909-1910 seasons. These were also years of tremendous popularity of opera elsewhere in Philadelphia. Over one hundred and twenty Philadelphia productions of opera were given in the season of the completion of the Metropolitan Opera House,[1] and an even larger number were produced the following season.

The building that challenged the leadership of the Academy of Music after its supremacy of over fifty years, this theatre that is still Philadelphia's largest, is justly famous for various reasons. The many boxes were planned to please the wealthy patrons, as was the large foyer on which they opened. The main floor and a single balcony were used for the remainder of the audience, instead of the usual two balconies in other theatres, or the three in the Academy of Music. The accommodation of 4000 people with the use

---

[1] According to Joseph M. Rogers' *History of Grand Opera in Philadelphia*, Philadelphia, 1909.

of but one balcony required that the entire opera house be built on a larger scale than any theatre of Philadelphia, before or since.

Soon the Metropolitan Opera Company was attracted by the new opera house at Broad and Poplar Streets, and from 1910 to 1925 their performances were given at the Metropolitan Opera House. In this large building's brief period of musical importance, 1908 to 1931, it was used for performances by many opera companies. Visiting troupes such as the La Scala and San Carlo companies used it for many performances. Most performances of the Philadelphia Civic Opera Company in its early years of activity, 1924 to 1930, were given there. *Aïda* was given at the debut of the Civic Opera Company in this opera house on February 28th, 1924.

The 1922 productions of the Charlottenburg Company were noted performances at the Metropolitan Opera House. Friedrich Schorr, Heinrich Knöte, Alexander Kipnis, and Elsa Alsen sang in a variety of German operas with this company. Their first visit began on February 5th and lasted one week; their second engagement began on April 20th and included the performance of the entire *Ring of the Nibelungen.*

A somewhat similar festival of German Opera was given by the German Grand Opera Company at this same theatre in 1930. The troupe was managed by Hurok, and had previously sung at Keith's Theatre, Philadelphia, beginning on January 28th, 1929. Their performances at the Metropolitan Opera House opened on January 11, 1930. Both visits to Philadelphia were signalized by entire *Ring* performances. The season at the Metropolitan Opera House also included *The Flying Dutchman, Tristan,* and *Don Giovanni* in German.

The Philadelphia Orchestra gave many concerts at the Metropolitan Opera House in the years following Stokowski's engagement as its conductor. These were extra events, however; the regular series of concerts were never moved from their original home— the Academy of Music. In 1915, 1916 and 1917 the Metropolitan Opera House was used for series of free Sunday concerts by the Philadelphia Orchestra. Edward W. Bok sponsored these concerts. This orchestra has staged some of its most spectacular performances at the Metropolitan Opera House. *Le Sacre du Printemps* and *Pas d'Acier,* orchestra-ballet performances of 1930 and 1931, were particularly well suited to its large stage, as was the puppet opera *Oedipus Rex.*

Many less pretentious musical offerings have been given at the Metropolitan Opera House. School operettas, religious pageants, "The Miracle," a stirring production of the Passion Play by the Freiburg Players, and many musico-dramatic performances of varying natures have been given at this large theatre. We close our brief digression, from opera to the opera house, with the mention of two unusual occasions in the later history of this building. The first was a production of the Bach *Passion Music* according to St. Matthew, by the Philadelphia Orchestra and a large chorus made up of several Philadelphia singing societies. Nelson Eddy and Richard Crooks were among the soloists: Ossip Gabrilowitsch conducted "from the continuum"—in this case it was a harpsichord. Very different, but equally significant, was a series of rehearsals of the Sesqui-Centennial chorus, directed by Bruce A. Carey. On those occasions the four thousand seats were filled with performers; it was even necessary to place five hundred of them on the stage. The enthusiasm of this huge chorus matched, as it generally will, that of its conductor.

In 1920 the Metropolitan Opera House had been sold by Edward T. Stotesbury to the Knights of the Mystic Shrine. In the same year Edward W. Bok leased the Academy of Music for five years, and arranged for many needed repairs in that older building. Since 1925 the Metropolitan Opera Company of New York has given its productions in the Academy of Music every season, with the exception of 1933-1934, the year following the worst period of the depression. The Metropolitan Opera House is still a comparatively new building. Its eminent suitability for the presentation of the spectacular and tremendous will undoubtedly bring about needed repairs and renovations for future musical events.

Incidental mention has been made of the Philadelphia-Chicago Grand Opera Company. It has been our aim to be consistent in the order of the names *Philadelphia-Chicago* in its title, but this has not been easy since the company itself was equally careful to be

inconsistent! Notices, stationery, programs and such official literature printed for use in Philadelphia were headed 'Philadelphia-
Chicago Grand Opera Company,' while those for us in Illinois were
as carefully worded 'Chicago-Philadelphia Grand Opera Company.'
Thus one must cater to local pride. Whatever its title, this company gave five long seasons of opera at the Metropolitan Opera
House in Philadelphia (1910-1915), after which the Philadelphia
portion of its management was dropped. There were visits in 1919
and 1922, however, by the Chicago Opera Company. In the former
year Massenet's *Cleopatra* was given, which included one of Mary
Garden's last new roles. The 1922 visit included productions of
Salomé, Pelléas, and *Monna Vanna* (by Février). Clearly the
Chicago Opera Company was still producing operatic novelties.

The world première of Victor Herbert's *Natoma* must not be
omitted from any discussion of the Chicago-Philadelphia Opera
Company and the Metropolitan Opera House in Philadelphia. This
American Opera was given for the first time on February 25, 1911.
Mary Garden and John McCormack were in the cast of this Philadelphia first performance. The Chicago-Philadelphia Opera Company gave *Natoma* thirty-five times. Nicholas Slominsky quotes
press criticisms of the opening performance in his book on *Music
Since 1900*.[1] The New York Sun spoke rather doubtfully of how
"Philadelphia certainly did enjoy itself at *Natoma's* Irish-American
World Première." Excerpts from the *Evening Transcript* are more
positively negative: "A dull text set to mediocre music. . . . Natoma
was a comparative failure at its first performance in Philadelphia,
in spite of an able cast and thorough preparation." Critic H. T.
Parker continues with some mention of the vivid pictorial side of
the opera and of Miss Garden as an Indian girl.

The Philadelphia Civic Opera rose to prominence nine years
after this city relinquished its share in the management and performances of the Chicago company. W. Atmore Robinson, its
artistic director, and Mrs. Henry M. Tracy, its president and general manager, were the chief sponsors for this new company. It
was organized as a "professional opera company but not for profit,"
and as such deserved more generous support than it ever received.

---

[1] N. Slominsky, *Music Since 1900;* New York, Norton, 1937.

The chorus and minor soloists were not paid, with the exception of certain members who participated in a large number of performances, and were therefore paid some such nominal fee as five dollars an opera. The money was supposed to be used for vocal lessons, in the case of these regular chorus members. The main solo parts were sung by young artists, following the custom of the Philadelphia Operatic Society,[1] or by established singers who had ceased to command huge fees for public performances. In its first organization the Civic Opera Company was partially subsidized by the city of Philadelphia, but this arrangement soon failed to operate in the manner of civic opera systems of certain cities in Europe on which it was to have been modelled.

The opening performance was *Aïda,* given at the Metropolitan Opera House February 28, 1924. *Faust* was produced later the same spring. Among several operas given the following season *Madame Butterfly,* and *The Love of Three Kings* were the most unusual. In 1925-1926 *The Jewels of the Madonna, La Navarraise,* and *Gianni Schicchi* were added to the repertoire of this company. The next season *Romeo and Juliet, Lohengrin,* and *Die Walküre* were sung, in addition to performances of the company's other operas. Four American premières were given in 1927 by this company: Korngold, *Der Ring des Polykrates;* Gluck, *The May Queen;* Strauss, *Feuersnot;* and De Falla, *El Amor Brujo.* The American première of Strauss's *Ariadne auf Naxos,* November 1, 1928, and the first performance in Philadelphia of *Le Chemineau* by Leroux, December 7, 1928, were notable achievements of the 1928-1929 season. During that year *Manon Lescaut* and *Prince Igor* were also sung by the Philadelphia Civic Company as additions to their previous operatic repertoire. In 1929-30 the entire Wagner *Ring* was given, as were *Magic Flute,* and *Marriage of Figaro,* and other operas more commonly heard in Philadelphia. Alexander Smallens trained the chorus and acted as general director and conductor for this company.

If other operatic patrons had been able to cooperate with Mrs. Tracy and Smallens instead of organizing competing troupes, the course of opera in Philadelphia would have been a far steadier

---

[1] The Civic Opera Company included many singers formerly with the Philadelphia Operatic Society.

one. Unfortunately within three years after the organization of the Civic Opera Company two operatic groups were organized in this city. The first of these was the Philadelphia Grand Opera Company, founded in 1926, with Mrs. Joseph Leidy as president. This company also chose *Aïda* for its opening performance, Oct. 28, 1926. A somewhat similar career to that of the Philadelphia Civic Opera Company marks the various seasons of this newer organization. Their productions did not share the Civic Opera's aim of "professional performances, but not for profit," however, and the entire career of the Philadelphia Grand Opera Company was more in the manner of the usual course of professional opera. There were several noteworthy achievements in the course of the five years of this company's activity. The first performance in America of Goossen's *Judith* and the Philadelphia première of Mozart's *Il Serraglio* were given on December 26, 1929. A year later Mary Garden made her last Philadelphia appearance in *The Juggler of Notre Dame,* October 23, 1930. This same Philadelphia Grand Opera Company collaborated with Stokowski and the Philadelphia Orchestra in the American première of *Wozzeck* on March 19, 1931. A later performance in 1931 reflects the affiliation of the opera department of the Curtis Institute of Music with the Philadelphia Grand Opera Company, and of their respective financial backers, Mrs. Bok and Mrs. Leidy. Three of the leading artists in the performance of *Elektra,* October 29, 1931, were students at the Curtis Institute.[1]

The repetition of Wozzeck on Nov. 19, 1931, was the last outstanding production by this company. Fritz Reiner, a member of the faculty of the Curtis Institute of Music since 1931, conducted this performance.

The Pennsylvania Grand Opera Company was organized in 1927. Francesco Pelosi managed this company, which was unfortunately the third competing Philadelphia opera company in its years of activity, the other two being the Philadelphia Civic Opera Company and the Philadelphia Grand Opera Company. There

---

[1] Helen Jepson, Rose Bampton, and Virginia Kendrick. Nelson Eddy was in this same cast. His operatic training had previously been secured under Smallens in the Philadelphia Civic Opera Company. Matzenauer sang the part ef Elektra.

was also a surviving section of the Philadelphia Operatic Society which existed (and still lives in 1940) as a separate operatic venture. The Pennsylvania Grand Opera Company produced Rubinstein's opera *The Demon* in its second season, November 7, 1928, a work seldom sung. Arthur Rodzinski conducted *The Demon,* and the company's production of *Manon* in the same season.

In the season of 1934-1935 a series of operas was produced by the Philadelphia Orchestra management. The twenty-one performances between November and April included eight operas, two of them being given for the first time in America (*Mavra,* by Stravinsky, Dec. 28, 1934, and *Iphigénie en Aulide,* Feb. 22, 1935). Katharine Meisle made her operatic debut in *Hänsel und Gretel,* on Dec. 28, 1934, with the "Philadelphia Orchestra Opera." Other works given were *Falstaff, Marriage of Figaro, Die Meistersinger,* and *Boris Godounof.*

Before bringing our account of opera to its present period, 1940, there are several companies that should be at least mentioned for their occasional contribution to opera in Philadelphia during the past forty years. The Sembrich Opera Company visited Philadelphia in January and February 1901. Mascagni brought an opera company from Italy in 1902. From October 13 to 20 this Mascagni company gave performances of its conductor's operas in the Academy of Music. *Zanetto, Iris* and *Cavalleria Rusticana* were produced. The Henry Savage opera company gave the first Philadelphia performance of *Parsifal* in 1904. This advanced work was given for two weeks at the Chestnut Street Opera House. *Parsifal,* sung by Alois Pennarini, was a striking success, as was *Madame Butterfly,* introduced by Savage in 1906. In May 1904 the stock company of Forepaugh's Theatre, 8th Street above Vine, gave a week of performances of *Parsifal* as a play. These productions, which did not include any of the Wagner music, testify to the local popularity of the story, although they are said [1] to have been of doubtful artistic significance.

The production of *Cassandra* by Vittorio Gnecchi, an American première by the Chicago-Philadelphia Opera Company, caused

---

[1] By H. T. Craven who has a complete file of music programs since 1900, and a remarkable memory for their peculiarities.

quite a scandal after its opening performance in Philadelphia, 1914. Fifty themes were identical with melodies contained in Richard Strauss' *Elektra*. A Boston Grand Opera Company gave short seasons of opera in the seasons of 1915 to 1917. The brief visit of the Russian Grand Opera Company April 24-30, 1922, provided a well staged series of Russian works. Among them were *The Czar's Bride*, by Rimsky-Korsakoff, produced for the first time in Philadelphia by this company; *Pique Dame* by Tschaikowsky, *The Mermaid* by Dargomizky, and *The Snow Maiden* by Rimsky-Korsakoff.

One of the most recent operatic groups is the Philadelphia-La Scala Company, organized in 1938, with Pelosi as its manager. Their first appearance was on December 10 in a well produced *Rigoletto*. Their second opera was Camille de Senez's *Horus*, given its first performance by Pelosi's company January 5, 1939. Fritz Mahler conducted both *Rigoletto* and *Horus*, in the latter production "doing his best to make something musical out of material which provided virtually no opportunity." [1] Current newspapers, March 21, 1939, announce the withdrawal of Philadelphia-La Scala's third opera of this season, and contain the information that a reorganized company would be presented in the autumn of 1939.

It may be but musical justice that Pelosi's Philadelphia-La Scala company had hardly finished its opening performance when a new Philadelphia Opera Company was organized. The reader may recall that Francesco Pelosi was the manager of the third competing company at the time of his organization of the Pennsylvania Grand Opera Company in 1927. The new Philadelphia Opera Company resembles the earlier Philadelphia Civic Opera Company in that young singers from the vicinity of the city are given positions in the chorus and solo roles. In fact it went further in its initial performance, *La Boheme*, January 19, 1939, by selecting a complete cast of Philadelphia singers. Henry Pleasants, one of Philadelphia's most discriminating music critics, wrote with great enthusiasm concerning the performance of *La Boheme*, suggesting that successful grand opera is possible with local singers

---

[1] *Musical America* for Jan. 25, 1939, p. 28.

provided the staging and acting have life and vigor, and adding that

"Last night's production was an impressive demonstration [of this]. It was remarkable for its unity, its freshness and its vitality. The production was a fine achievement measured by any standard." [1]

For its second production this company gave on March 30 the first complete performance in English of Puccini's Trilogy, *The Cloak, Sister Angelica,* and *Gianni Schicchi.* C. David Hocker, president, and Sylvan Levin, musical director, deserve credit for a successful start for the new Philadelphia Opera Company. It is still true that three companies are now competing in a field that could well be covered by one. The third company, mentioned last since it has been in a quiescent state since 1935, is the Philadelphia Operatic Society. With the account of this operatic society and the Savoy Opera Company, the complicated list of the leading opera productions in Philadelphia is completed.

Among amateur organizations devoted to operatic work, there are two outstanding Philadelphia companies. The Philadelphia Operatic Society and the Savoy Company are quite different in their methods and repertoire but both are amateur theatrical companies in a broad sense. No narrow amateur standing could be applied to many of the leading singers in either group, but in a broader sense they are non-professional organizations in that members are not paid for their participation in the productions.

The Philadelphia Operatic Society, though slightly younger as a group than the Savoy Company, produces a more ambitious series of works. It was founded in 1906 by John Curtis, and gave eighty performances up to the season of 1934-5 after which it suspended its activities. The operas chosen are extremely varied, lighter works being perhaps more numerous in the history of the company. Yet operas like *Il Trovatore* and works by Richard Wagner have been given by the Philadelphia Operatic Society.

---

[1] Henry Pleasants in the *Philadelphia Evening Bulletin* January 20, 1939. Sanborn of the *New York World Telegram* and Laciar of the *Philadelphia Public Ledger* were as enthusiastic as the article quoted from *The Evening Bulletin.*

The following lists and other data are taken from Edward E. Hipsher's account of the Philadelphia Operatic Society in *American Opera and Its Composers*, pp. 44, 45. Its first public appearance was in a presentation of *Faust* in the historic Academy of Music, on April 16, 1907; and from the first year no season has passed without from two to four performances, though in 1913 there was a spring festival which brought that year's record up to ten. With the numbers following the name indicating the times that each work has been given, when more than once, the following remarkable repertoire has been offered: Aïda (6), Boccaccio (2), La Bohème, Bohemian Girl (6), Brian Boru, Bride Elect, Carmen (3), Cavalleria Rusticana (3), El Capitan, Faust (7), Fra Diavolo, Der Freischütz (2), Gypsy Baron, Hänsel und Gretel, Hoshi-San (world première), Les Huguenots (2), Il Trovatore (2), Jewels of the Madonna, La Sonnambula, Lucia di Lammermoor, Madame Butterfly, Maritana, Marriage of Jeannette, Manon, Martha (5), Mignon (2), Norma, I Pagliacci (3), Queen's Lace Handkerchief, Rip Van Winkle, Robin Hood (3), Secret of Suzanne, The Serenade (3), Stradella, Tales of Hoffmann (2), Tannhäuser; two dramatic oratorios—The Golden Legend and The Rose of Destiny; and four ballets—Coppelia, Dance of the Hours, Dances of the Pyrenees, and The Four Seasons.

John Philip Sousa, Reginald deKoven, and Victor Herbert have been honorary members of the Society; and when Mr. Sousa's works have been given he has conducted. The slogan of the organization has been "Opera in English by Philadelphians." . . . Among organizations of more local interest, and yet which have done notable work to promote the cause of opera in English, the palm probably belongs to the Philadelphia Operatic Society. . . . In all it has given stage experience to some two hundred and fifty of Philadelphia's leading soloists, to more than one thousand choristers, as well as having sustained a *corps de ballet*."

Such singers as Paul Althouse, Nelson Eddy, Henri Scott, and Bianca Saroya have made their débuts with this company and later gone on the professional stage. Obviously these artists were semi-professional at the time of their operatic débuts, having sung in choirs or concerts for a fee; but their operatic work was of amateur or student nature when they appeared with the Operatic Society. Philadelphia Orchestra men have provided the accompaniment for all of the productions by this group. For many years the operas of both the Philadelphia Operatic Society and the Savoy Company have been given in the Academy of Music.

Every Gilbert and Sullivan addict will know the nature of the operas produced by the Savoy Company of Philadelphia. What he may not realize is that the company has produced a longer and more inclusive series of Gilbert and Sullivan Operettas than any other amateur organization in the world. Since 1901 there has been an annual Gilbert and Sullivan light opera, this unbroken series [1] including all of these collaborations (even *Utopia Limited* and *The Grand Duke,* which their musical director, Mr. John Thoms, was obliged to orchestrate from Sullivan's piano scores.)

The founder of the Savoy Company was Dr. Alfred Reginald Allen, a graduate and teacher at the University of Pennsylvania. In memory of Major Allen, who was killed in action in France, the Alfred Reginald Allen Memorial Fund was founded at the University of Pennsylvania, for the assistance of the School of Music at that institution. Proceeds from the productions since 1921 have been donated to this fund and have been of great assistance to the University, since most of the music and musical books that have been added to its library in recent years have been purchased from this fund.

The distinctive though limited field of the Savoy company interests young singers of less ambitious views than those of the Philadelphia Operatic Society. Social as well as musical pleasures are derived from each Savoy production. Measured by the entirely logical standard of the amount of pleasure provided for performers and audiences, the Savoy Company holds a high place among musical organizations in Philadelphia.

With the Savoy Company we have reached an organization which lies between the fields of opera and musical comedy. The story of popular music as contained in musical plays and revues, while mentioned in preceding historical chapters, does not belong to so serious a subject as the history of opera. Oscar Hammerstein used to declare, "I do not give grand opera: I give great opera." We are led to wonder whether this man who was both a great doer and talker was not trying to convince himself as well

[1] Except 1919, the year following the World War.

as his public of the truth of his own epigrammatic claim. With all of the opera's most lavish accessories many musical purists declare that it is seldom if ever great. It is so universally grand, in the attempt if not in the realization, that no other term can well be substituted for that usual adjective in describing it. Lavignac calls Richard Wagner "the most discussed, most maligned, most adored of composers." [1] Wagner was the greatest of opera composers in the opinion of many, and it might be fitting to transfer Lavignac's phrase to opera itself. Opera, as the most discussed, maligned, and adored of musical forms, has received more attention than any other in Music in Philadelphia.

Two appended lists follow, one of general, the second of local interest. The former list contains the date of first performances in America that were given in Philadelphia, with the date that each opera was sung:

1825—Der Freischütz.
1827—Cinderella (Rossini).
1840—Norma (Libretto translated by J. R. Fry).
1841—Magic Flute.
1845—Leonora (W. H. Fry, world première).
1848—Maritana.
1852—Luisa Miller.
1856—Il Trovatore.
1861—Betly (Donizetti).
    Les Noces de Jeannette.
1863—Faust.
1864—Notre Dame de Paris (W. H. Fry, world première).
1876—Flying Dutchman.
1891—Cavalleria Rusticana and Pagliacci.
1892—L'Amico Fritz.
1893—Pêcheurs des Perles.
1894—Manon Lescaut.
1895—Hänsel und Gretel.
1896—Sigurd (Reyer)
    André Chenier.
1906—Les Contes d'Hoffmann.

---

[1] In *Music and Musicians*, p. 427, by Albert Lavignac, New York, Holt and Co., 1903.

1908—Hoshi-San (Leps).
1911—Secret of Suzanne.
   Natoma (Herbert).
   Quo Vadis (Noguès).
   Sarrona (Legrand Howland).
1912—Cendrillon.
   The Cricket on the Hearth.
1913—Le Ranz des Vaches.
   Noel (Erlanger).
   A Lover's Quarrel.
   Cristoforo Colombo.
1914—Cassandra.
1917—Masque of the American Drama (DeKoven).
1927—Der Ring des Polykrates (Korngold).
   Die Maienkoenigin.
   Feuersnot.
   El Amor Brujo (De Falla).
1928—Ariadne auf Naxos.
   Khovanchina.
   Verbum Nobile (Muniusko).
   Le Chemineau (Leroux).
1929—Judith (Goossens).
   Boris Godounof (first performance of Moussorgsky's original
   score).
1931—Wozzeck.
1934—Mavra (Stravinsky).
1935—Iphigénie en Aulide.
1937—Le Pauvre Matelot, and Amelia al Ballo (world première).
1939—Horus (De Senez).
1939—The Trilogy (Puccini. First performance in English in America.)

In addition to the works of the preceding list, the following
mention of the first Philadelphia performance of important operatic works should be interesting.   Some may have been American
premières as well, but conclusive evidence is not available concerning that fact.   The fact that so many lie in the period between
1850 and 1939 shows us that after the former year other cities,
Boston and then New York among them, were rivalling and outdistancing Philadelphia as centers for new opera productions.   The

date preceding each title is that of its first performance in Philadelphia.

1822	Mar.	—Barber of Seville (Henry Phillips Co.), probably its first American performance.
1832	Sept.	10—Masaniello (Mme. Feron, Mr. Sinclair).
1833	Jan.	29—Il Pirata (Montressor).
	Sept.	12—Zampa (French Co. from New Orleans).
1834	Feb.	10—Marriage of Figaro (Wood Co.)
1835	Feb.	14—Sonnambula (Wood Co.).
1857	Mar.	13—Traviata (Gazzaniga Co.)
1858	Jan.	25—Rigoletto (Gazzaniga Co.).
1863	Jan.	28—Stradella (German Co., Rotter).
1864	Feb.	12—Tannhäuser (German Co.).
	Nov.	17—Mireille (German Co.).
1865	Mar.	24—Force of Destiny (Zucchi Co.).
1866	Jan.	2—L'Africaine (Zucchi).
1868	Jan.	13—Romeo and Juliet (Hauk Co.).
	Feb.	11—Grand Duchess (Tostée Co.).
	May	14—La Belle Hélène (Tostée Co.).
1869	April	2—The Prophet (La Grange Co.).
1872	April	18—Mignon (Nilsson, Brignoli, etc.)
	April	20—Hamlet (Nilsson, Brignoli).
1873	Dec.	12—Aïda.
1874	April	16—Lohengrin (Nilsson, Campanini, Del Puente).
1875	April	21—The Talisman, Balfe (Kellogg Co.).
1876		Flying Dutchman, in Italian.
1878	Mar.	20—Rienzi (German Co., Pappenheim).
1888	May	4—Otello (Metropolitan).
1889	Mar.	25—Meistersinger (Metropolitan).
1889	Mar.	26-29—Ring of the Nibelungen (Metropolitan).
1889	Mar.	26—Rheingold (Metropolitan).
	Mar.	27—Die Walküre (3rd Phila. performance).
	Mar.	28—Siegfried (Metropolitan).
	Mar.	29—Götterdämmerung (Metropolitan).
1896		Scarlet Letter, by Damrosch, and Tristan (Damrosch Opera Co.).
	Oct.	—André Chenier (Mapleson Co.).
1898		La Bohéme (Baghetto Co. from Mexico).
1901	Jan.	22—Le Cid (Metropolitan).

1901   Feb.   —La Tosca (Metropolitan).
1904   Spring   —Parsifal (Savage English Opera Co.).
1906   Madame Butterfly (Savage).
1908   Louise (Hammerstein).
1908   Nov.   24—Thaïs (Hammerstein).
    Dec.   15—Juggler of Notre Dame (Hammerstein).
1909   Feb.   9—Pelléas et Melisande (Hammerstein).
    Feb.   16—Salomé (Hammerstein).
    Nov.   20—Sappho (Hammerstein).
1910   Feb.   5—Elektra (Hammerstein).
        Griselidis (Hammerstein).
    Dec.   20—Girl of the Golden West (Metropolitan).
1911   Feb.   14—Königskinder (Metropolitan), only Philadelphia per-
        formance.
1912   Mar.   20—Jewels of the Madonna (Chicago-Philadelphia Co.).
1913   Feb.   6—Conchita (Chicago-Philadelphia Co.).
1914   Mar.   10—Boris Godounof (Metropolitan).
1916   Feb.   19—Mme. Sans Gêne (Metropolitan).
    Nov.   21—Prince Igor (Metropolitan).
    Feb.   20—Francesca da Rimini (Metropolitan).
1917   Mar.   20—Canterbury Pilgrims (Metropolitan).
1918   Jan.   8—Saint Elizabeth, Liszt (Metropolitan).
    April   16—Le Coq d'Or (Metropolitan).
    Nov.   19—Mârouf (Metropolitan).
    Mar.   3—Cleopatra (Chicago-Philadelphia Co.).
1919   Mar.   5—Gismonda (Chicago-Philadelphia Co.).
    Mar.   18—La Reine Fiammette (Metropolitan).
1920   Feb.   3—Cleopatra's Night (Metropolitan).
    Feb.   17—Zazà (Metropolitan).
    April 20—Eugene Onegin (Metropolitan).
1922   Jan.   10—Le Roi d'Ys, Lalo (Metropolitan).
    Mar.   4—Monna Vanna (Chicago-Philadelphia Co.).
    Mar.   28—Die Tote Stadt, Korngold (Metropolitan, Jeritza's Phila-
        delphia début).
    April 24—Czar's Bride (Russian Co.).
    April 25—Pique Dame (Russian Co.).
    April 26—The Mermaid, Dargomizky (Russian Co.).
    April 27—The Snow Maiden (Russian Co.).
    Dec.   26—Loreley, Catalani (Metropolitan).

1924   Mar.   4—La Habanera, Lappara.

       Mar.   18—Le Roi de Lahore, Massenet.

       Dec.   16—Jennfa, Janachek (Metropolitan).

1925   Dec.   8—L'Heure Espagnole, Ravel (Metropolitan).

1926   Jan.   5—The Jest (Metropolitan with Gigli and Ruffo).

       Feb.   —La Vida Breve and Le Rossignol (Metropolitan).

       Nov.   30—Turandot (Metropolitan).

1927   Jan.   4—La Vestale (Metropolitan).

       Mar.   29—The King's Henchman (Metropolitan).

       Nov.   15—Violante, Korngold (Metropolitan).

1928   April   3—La Rondine (Metropolitan).

       Nov.   13—The Egyptian Helen (Metropolitan).

1929   April   2—Fra Gherardo, Pizzetti (Metropolitan).

       Oct.   29—The Sunken Bell (Metropolitan).

CHAPTER TEN

SINGING SOCIETIES

Most of the organizations which follow exist primarily for the work they do with vocal ensemble, which alone would constitute their raison d'être. Others are interested in various musical activities in addition to their singing. A few will be observed to possess almost no interest beyond their group singing program; others have such broad interests that one feels doubtful, if not a bit apologetic, about classifying them as singing societies. Thus the Philadelphia Choral Society does a great deal of singing and stops there; but the Philadelphia Music Club has so much in the way of instrumental interests, and general musical entertainments by members and distinguished guests, that the chorus is merely an outstanding feature of its manysided activity. Quite generally, it may be said that the following groups exist mainly for vocal activities, in most cases choral work, although solo performances, instrumental divisions, and sociability will be found to be part of the program of many of them.

I

Many choir directors have lightened the labors of their singers by organizing glee clubs consisting of choir members. The Mendelssohn Club merits special mention since it is one of such groups that has existed for over sixty years. Its choir origin is all but forgotten, but its founder, William Wallace Gilchrist, is well remembered in Philadelphia for his manysided musical contribution. Mr. Gilchrist organized the Mendelssohn Club in 1874 as a group of glee singers selected from his choir at St. Clement's Church.

The group remained a small male chorus for about five years; then, doubling its size, became a mixed chorus in 1879. Gilchrist led the Mendelssohn Club for more than forty years, resigning as its conductor but a year from the time of his death.

William Wallace Gilchrist seems to have been the only recent Philadelphia composer recognized as a significant figure by music historians.   Since the Mendelssohn Club was his greatest civic contribution, biographical details are given under the account of that society.

W. W. Gilchrist was born in Jersey City, January 5, 1846. He went to Philadelphia at the age of nine, beginning his music study there under Hugh Clarke.   While singing was his principal means of expression, he played piano, organ and 'cello.   His fondness for cricket and tennis helped Philadelphia to become a famous American home for these sports.   He studied law at one time but abandoned it (as did Schumann and Tschaikowsky) for music. Gilchrist's general versatility is reflected in the varied musical interests in which he excelled.   As vocal and instrumental soloist, composer and conductor, Gilchrist possessed a musical horizon as wide as the generous spread of his other interests.   He had, as most historians point out, a peculiar aptitude for winning prizes in musical composition.   Two competitions of the Abt Society of Philadelphia, three of the Mendelssohn Glee Club of New York, and the 1882 Cincinnati Festival Association prize were won by Gilchrist, all within a few years.

In later life Dr. Gilchrist devoted his time to teaching, composing, and conducting.   He held the position of choirmaster in one (or often two) of the city's leading churches for many years. Choruses in Philadelphia, Wilmington, Germantown, Harrisburg, and elsewhere, were organized and conducted by him.   The Mendelssohn Club is particularly important among the choruses founded by Gilchrist.   The Manuscript Music Society, organized in 1892, elected Dr. Gilchrist its first president.   At their first concert the orchestra of that group played Gilchrist"s Symphony in C.   Many consider this composer's instrumental works his chief claim to lasting fame.   He composed a trio and two quintets for piano and strings, and a nonet for piano, strings, horn and woodwinds.

The larger portion of his writings are for the multiform vocal combinations with which he was so familiar.   About three hundred songs, large numbers of anthems, and several cantatas were written by him.

Dr. Gilchrist's founding and conducting the Philadelphia Symphony Society (1893-1900) have been previously noted.[1] This important group should never have been discontinued in 1900: surely it never aimed at competition with the newly founded Philadelphia Orchestra. It is the writer's opinion that Dr. Gilchrist perferred the sphere of vocal work, although instrumental composition and conducting were daily duties throughout most of his life.

His compositions reveal a contrapuntal skill and a breadth of interest which was unique in his time and place. There is a remarkable rightness about his compositions which is seldom found among composers of the period who were of entirely American training. His smooth polyphonic textures have caused the adjective *cold*, or even *dry*, to be applied to some of his works. The freely inspired melody in many Gilchrist songs, and in his lesser known violin or 'cello solos, belies the term *overacademic*, which some detractors level at the music by this scholarly composer. Dr. Gilchrist died in Philadelphia, in 1916.[2]

In the long period of the club's great growth and first success (while its founder directed its activities), there was both an orchestra and a chorus made up of its members. The orchestra, begun in 1899, was heard in many of the regular concerts of the Mendelssohn Club. Since 1903, however, the Mendelssohn Club has confined its musical activity to choral work. This club shared the Philadelphia Symphony Society's interest in the founding of the Philadelphia Orchestra, and has kept up a close connection with that orchestra ever since. Three performances of the Beethoven Ninth Symphony were sung with the Philadelphia Orchestra while Dr. Gilchrist was the club's director.[3] Since the Orchestra's beginning it has called on the Mendelssohn Club to provide choral parts for many of its regular concert programs. Included in such combined concerts have been:

---

[1] P. 168.

[2] Philip Goepp's account of William W. Gilchrist, written in 1915, is the source of the facts in the above biographical sketch. Mr. Goepp and Gilchrist were close friends and musical associates for many years. A more detached, and less sympathetic, biography is contained in Rupert Hughes' *Contemporary American Composers* (pp. 196-210) ; Boston, the Page Company, 1900; revised edition (Elson) 1914.

[3] 1904, 1907, and 1914.

Henschel—*Requiem,* conducted by Henschel.

Mahler—*Eighth Symphony* (Mendelssohn Club and other choruses).

Debussy—*Les Sirenes*—Women's voices.

Honegger—*King David.*

Walton—*Belshazzar's Feast.*

Moussorgsky—*Boris Godounof* (1929), American Première of original score.

Nordoff—*Secular Mass.*

There have also been many joint performances of Beethoven's Choral Symphony since the early three mentioned above. The Mendelssohn Club has had the cooperation of members of the Philadelphia Orchestra accompanying and assisting at many of its regular concerts.

N. Lindsay Norden succeeded W. W. Gilchrist as conductor of the Mendelssohn Club in 1917.[1] His introduction of Russian works, many edited by himself, constituted a worthy addition to the club's musical program—and to the content of American choral music as well. These compositions, most of them never previously sung outside of Russia, introduced by the Mendelssohn Club, did a great deal to popularize Russian works for voices, and set a high standard of artistic a cappella singing.

Conductors since Mr. Norden have been Bruce A. Carey, 1927-1935, M. Sherwood Johnson, Harl McDonald, and Harold W. Gilbert, who directs the club at present.

The conductors of the Mendelssohn club have been discussed to the exclusion of its other important people since, in any such society, the leader's personality and musicianship become the dominating factors in its musical development. In this particular instance, however, there should be at least mention of a few members of the club who have kept up its personnel and enthusiasm. Among the officers who have given an unusually large share of time and effort to the interests of the Mendelssohn Club, Mr. Charles Bond must be recognized as outstanding. Mr. Bond became an active member of this chorus in 1893, was elected its treasurer in 1896,

---

[1] Herbert J. Tily and Charles E. Knauss had acted as assistant conductors during Dr. Gilchrist's several years of enforced absence prior to 1916. Dr. Tily conducted during the two seasons 1913-1914, and 1914-1915, Mr. Knauss during the two following.

its president in 1904. He has served as a director for thirty-seven years, treasurer for sixteen years, and president for twelve years. His contribution was probably second only to that of Dr. Gilchrist himself.

Many other members have been as active as Charles Bond, though not for such an extended period of time. Frederick K. Moore held various offices with the club over a long period of years. Mrs. William D. Gross was an active president for some years, and, for many more, assisted in the management of the club. Thomas à Becket (later a club president), Ellis C. Hammann, and Harry A. Matthews, are among many fine accompanists who served this group. The board of directors has included such noted Philadelphians as Alexander Van Rensselaer, Edward Bok, Owen Roberts, and Abbie Keeley. Had it not been for the interest and ability on the part of such members, the Mendelssohn Club would doubtless have ceased to exist shortly after the death of its founder (1916). With their help, as well as with the assistance of the subsequent conductors, this old club has maintained its position as Philadelphia's leading choral group.

The vast amount of fine music produced by the Mendelssohn Club, during its more than sixty years of continuous activity, covers a tremendous variety of style and theme. Over three hundred composers of more than twenty nationalities have been represented on their programs. At least twenty-five of these composers are Americans—several Philadelphians among them.[1] The following are famous musicians from a long list of soloists, who have assisted at the concerts by the Mendelssohn Club: Victor Herbert, Hans Kindler, Leopold Godowsky, Thaddeus Rich, Ernestine Schumann-Heink, Sigrid Onegin, Richard Crooks, Nicholas Douty, David Bispham, John Charles Thomas, Antonio Scotti, and Lawrence Tibbett. Noted organizations have played or sung on Mendelssohn Club programs. Among them are the Kneisel Quartet, the St. Cecelia Quartet, and often, the Philadelphia Orchestra.

Memories of numerous concerts, fine music, and noted soloists keep alive the activity and enthusiasm of the members of this

---

[1] Among the Philadelphians are James Bostwick, F. G. Cauffman, Nicholas Douty, Robert Elmore, W. W. Gilchrist, Philip Goepp, Frances McCollin, N. Lindsay Norden, Harl McDonald, Paul Nordoff, Herbert J. Tily, Camille W. Zeckwer.

club. Permanent and successful amateur organizations like the
Mendelssohn Club constitute America's surest guarantee that the
standards in vocal music will be raised to a high level. Dr. Gilchrist's successors may be certain that such choral development
exercises a powerful effect for good upon any community, be it
large or small.

The Philadelphia Choral Society was organized in 1897. Henry
Gordon Thunder has conducted this group in its forty-two seasons
of concerts to the present year. The annual performances of the
Messiah given in the Academy of Music have been supplemented
by additional productions until a total of sixty-six performances
of this oratorio has been sung by Dr. Thunder's mixed chorus. The
Philadelphia Choral Society does not limit itself to standard or
classic material, but has provided many novelties in its long career.
Richard Strauss's *Taillefer* (The Iron Cutter), Franck's *Beatitudes,* and Pierné's *Children's Crusade* were given their first and
only Philadelphia performance by this chorus. The *Mass in B
minor* by Bach and choral selections from Wagner's *Parsifal* were
given their first performances in this city by the Philadelphia
Choral Society. This group rehearses weekly at the Drexel Institute of Technology, and gives three or four concerts each season.

Old vocal traditions are preserved by this society. It continued the work of the Philadelphia Chorus, which succeeded the
Philadelphia Festival Association, which in turn consisted of several preceding choral groups. Through its conductor, Henry G.
Thunder, the choral society may be said to inherit very old customs
of musical organization, since his father accompanied the 'Handel
and Hayden' Society of Philadelphia for many years prior to the
Civil War. Both Henry Gordon Thunder Sr. and Jr. have been
intimately connected with choral societies and leading church choirs
in Philadelphia. Although Henry Thunder Jr. and his brother
William Sylvano Thunder were noted organ virtuosi, they have
exerted their main influence on local music through the training of
choruses and the teaching of large numbers of private pupils. The
seed of sincere musicianship has been sown by the three Thunders
in a very large field, and throughout a long period of Music in
Philadelphia.

The Choral Art Society made its first appearance in the Academy of Music on the evening of May 9, 1922. It was hailed by musical critics and friends alike as "a notable addition to Philadelphia's musical organizations" and "the most important and promising venture of some years."

It has presented a number of novelties and works never before heard in this country, one of the most notable being the mystery play, *The Coming of Christ*, by John Masefield and Gustav Holst.

The Choral Art Society had its inception in the mind of its first conductor, Dr. H. Alexander Matthews, who conceived of a virtuoso chorus made up entirely of solo voices, which would be capable of producing the same finished and artistic choral work that the great orchestras, composed of virtuoso players, are able to produce in the field of instrumental music. He further desired to end the thought that soloists could not be welded together in a body so that they would submerge their individuality in favor of the ensemble.

The society has to a large extent been supported financially by contributing and associate members during its fifteen years of existence. Since 1939 the Choral Art Society has been conducted by Clyde R. Dengler.

Henry S. Drinker conducts one of the most unusual choruses in the Philadelphia area. The members of this group are mainly amateur musicians, and practically all amateur singers. A professional piano teacher may still be an amateur vocalist, but it will be readily seen that this instrumental background will probably enable him to read vocal music as well as most professional singers and better than some of them. The title of Mr. Drinker's chorus, Accademia dei Dilettanti di Musica, described its members quite well in the first few years of its existence—it was founded in 1928 —but recent developments have made this name so modest as to become misleading. The amateur standing of many members would be difficult to establish, and the nature and interpretation of the program numbers is on a par with the most advanced professional vocal music.[1] As a vocal group the "Musical Dilettantes" are

---

[1] During the Brahms centenary year (Season 1932-1933) over fifty of Brahms' most ambitious vocal works were sung. Works by the Bach family have been the most frequently performed throughout the more than ten

strictly an amateur organization—the few professionals who have participated being considered honored guests for different occasions.

The meetings are held monthly at Mr. Drinker's home in Merion. In reading through quantities of music, as this chorus is able to do, there has necessarily been considerable repetition in the ten years of the organization's history: yet a tremendous variety of fine choral music has been sung.

Mixed choruses constitute the most numerous element among singing societies in Philadelphia. A 1917 report of the Chamber of Commerce [1] records that there were over two hundred and fifty permanent choral and operatic organizations in Philadelphia. The few leading societies mentioned in this chapter—the Mendelssohn Club, Philadelphia Choral Society, and Choral Art Society—while outstanding among mixed choruses are unfortunately far from typical of our over one hundred such groups. It would be neither interesting nor worthwhile to list all of our mixed vocal ensembles in Philadelphia. A better picture might be gained by considering some classifications into which they fall, and their usual manner of beginning.

Probably the most common origin for a vocal chorus is the personality of some musician who wishes to conduct it. The need is constant for such organizations, therefore when heaven or fate sends a man equipped to satisfy it, his activity and ability are both the cause and the limit of his chorus's success. Even the Mendelssohn Club had such a beginning in the personality and ambition of William Wallace Gilchrist; the Philadelphia Choral Society sprang from Henry Gordon Thunder's desire and ability to preserve the traditions of the recently disbanded Philadelphia Chorus; and the Choral Art Society was the product of H. Alexander Matthews' vision of a chorus made up of vocal soloists. Obviously a social-musical chorus like that led by Henry Drinker is frankly

---

seasons that this "Accademia" has held meetings. The *B Minor Mass*, the *Magnificat*, cantatas, motets have been produced on very many occasions. Mozart's *Requiem*, works by Vaughan-Williams, and Holst, compositions by the greatest Elizabethan madrigalists, are but a few of the varied program numbers frequently produced. Local composers are not slighted by this chorus, works by Harl McDonald, Alfred J. Swan, and Edith E. Braun having been given in recent years. The Beethoven *Missa Solemnis* was sung (entire) three times during the 1937-1938 season.

[1] *The Commercial Value of Music to Philadelphia.*

an expression of a fondness for great vocal music as felt by Drinker and shared by his friends.

The Guild Singers of Philadelphia have already been mentioned on the program quoted at the conclusion of the section on the Federal Symphony Orchestra.[1] This group was organized by Isadore Freed, Philadelphia composer, conductor, and pianist, late in 1935, and has been directed by him since that date. Its objective is similar to that of the Choral Art Society. The Guild Singers are a small vocal ensemble of twenty soloists that aim at artistic interpretation and perfect ensemble. This group is one of the newest among the mixed choruses that are built mainly upon the personality of one man.

James Allan Dash has developed the Bach Society of Delaware County in a similar manner. It seems that his enthusiasm for the music of Bach has been transplanted into the thought and feeling of his chorus. A Philadelphia unit has been established (October, 1938) which meets weekly at the Philadelphia Musical Academy under Mr. Dash's direction. Three performances of Bach cantatas were given jointly by the Delaware County and the Philadelphia Bach Choruses during May 1939, in the presence of audiences that more than filled St. James' Church, and similar concerts are anticipated for the future.

A second *modus incipiendi* for choruses is found in large commercial plants, banks, or stores. Here also a person leads in the movement, but the business concern is apt to give large help and encouragement to his chorus. The Strawbridge and Clothier Chorus illustrates this type of organization perfectly. Herbert J. Tily has been the conductor and guiding spirit of this singing group since its reorganization in 1904. The Strawbridge and Clothier store, of which Dr. Tily is general manager, has provided rehearsal rooms and many of the engagements for its noted chorus. The Lit Brothers' Chorus is a similar singing society, of which Henry Hotz is conductor. The Federal Reserve Bank sponsors a chorus of men and women, organized in 1938. This new group of about sixty members gives three or more concerts a year, and provides music for several functions within the bank.

---

[1] Cf. p. 213.

II

The Orpheus Club was founded in 1872 by five members of the Abt Society. When Michael H. Cross resigned in 1871 as the conductor of the Abt group, these five members also resigned, and the following season organized a new group called the Orpheus Club. A membership of twenty-one was secured, Michael Cross became conductor, and John C. Sims the first president of the club.

This club was active from its first season. Over three hundred associate members joined the club, most of them attending its three main concerts of the 1872-73 season at Musical Fund Hall. The club also gave two charity concerts, one in Philadelphia and one in Baltimore, during this same year.

The early seasons saw a steady advance in popularity and success. Regular concerts were given at Musical Fund Hall from 1872 to 1889,[1] usually three a season, and an increasing number of occasional musical evenings in Philadelphia, Atlantic City, Baltimore, New York, Washington, and many smaller cities. Among these extra functions should be mentioned the club's participation in two combined performances (1875) of Mendelssohn's *Hymn of Praise* at the Academy of Music. Theodore Thomas's orchestra provided the instrumental support on these occasions.

The music sung by this club had from its first years been taken from the works of Mendelssohn and the part songs of the English School. Contemporary journalists speak of the perfect execution of works which afforded the 'opportunity for the display of real masculine dash'.[2] Such part songs and glees have remained the major attraction at Orpheus Club concerts, although larger works have been well produced on many occasions during the long history of this men's chorus. Mendelssohn's *Sons of Art* was sung in combination with the Mendelssohn Club of New York in 1876, and his *Antigone* produced for the first time in Philadelphia (April 21, 1882) by the club, with Max Heinrich as soloist, and the Germania Orchestra accompanying. Mendelssohn's *Œdipus at Colonos* was produced under Cross in 1883, at the Academy of Music, the

---

[1] Since 1889, the Academy of Music has housed the regular concerts.
[2] From an unnamed Baltimore critic's account of the April 5, 1875 concert.

Orpheus Club and Germania Orchestra providing most of the participants. Max Bruch's *The Cross of Fire* was sung under Frank Damrosch's leadership (1903).

The Orpheus Club headquarters had been changed several times from their original location at 1415 Locust Street (1872) to their extended occupancy of rooms in the Baker Building, 1520 Chestnut Street (1883-1925). The Chestnut Street headquarters provided accommodations for social gatherings such as musicales, teas, smokers, receptions, and the like, which affairs have, since 1884, been a very important part of the life of the club. There had been a cricket eleven of Orpheans from as early as 1874.

An early instance of an attempt to enrich the literature of music for male voices is provided by the 1891 Orpheus Club competition for a men's cantata with orchestral accompaniment. Five hundred dollars was offered as the prize. This was possibly not the first cantata competition of its kind, but certainly it was far from the last. Conductors of successful male choruses have been trying this artificial method of stimulating the composition of men's cantatas ever since. Arthur E. Smith of Birmingham England, won the contest with *The Warrior's Bride*—produced in 1892 by the club, with assisting soloists and orchestra.

Three hundred and sixty solos have been included in the club's concerts, in addition to those incidental to program numbers. Among distinguished soloists who have assisted the Orpheus Club at various concerts are: Maud Powell, violinist; Evan Williams, tenor; David Bishpham, baritone (an active member of the club); Pablo Casals, violoncellist; Arnold Dolmetsch, harpsichord and clavichord; Reinald Werrenrath, baritone; Thaddeus Rich, violinist; Marcel Tabuteau, oboe; Mabel Garrison, soprano; Louise Homer, contralto; Richard Crooks, tenor; and Nelson Eddy, baritone. George P. Orr, Irene Williams, May Hotz, Arthur Jackson, and Noah Swayne are among the Philadelphia singers frequently heard on Orpheus programs.

The unusually long service of the club's accompanists deserves special mention. Thomas à Becket (1877-1898) and Ellis Clark Hammann (1901-1939), have provided nearly all of this important work throughout the club's sixty-six years of activity.

The death of Michael Cross in 1897 caused the Orpheus Club to seek a new conductor. Frank Damrosch, a famous New York choral conductor, was secured for the post. His first programs show talent in program building and wide knowledge and taste in male voice music.[1] Frank Damrosch remained as conductor for seven years. His programs introduced music of a slightly higher musical order than had previously been sung.

Many of the club's functions at this, and other, periods have been charming rather than musically significant—such as their Forecastle Night at the Corinthian Yacht Club at Essington (1899), or the concert with assistance and accompaniment of the University of Pennsylvania Mandolin club (1900). However, it should be remembered that such numbers as di Lasso's *Echo Song,* Brahms' *The Refusal,* Schumann's *Three Ritornels,* were included among the more picturesque, "dashing" majority. How the Dartmouth alumni, and New Englanders in general, would be shocked should anyone reveal that F. F. Bullard's *Winter Song* was sung first by the Orpheus Club in Philadelphia (in 1903)! The club has quite definitely stopped looking for cantatas and heavy works, which seemed to be an ambitious habit of their early years, and confine their efforts to musically fine, but light, compositions.

Damrosch's resignation was followed by a brief period in which Fritz Scheel conducted the Orpheus Club (1905-7). Dr. Gilchrist conducted the club after Scheel's illness in 1907, completing the season. Horatio Parker (1907-14), Arthur Woodruff

---

[1] Program of Damrosch's first Regular Concert (1897):
*Oh Death (in memory of M. Cross) Baritone Solo ....Brahms
In Yonder Cool Green Dell..................arranged by Horatio Parker
Old Flemish Song ....arranged by Kremser
*Three Cavalier Songs ....Stanford
               (Baritone Solo, Male Chorus, and Orchestra.)
*Six Ancient Folk Songs of the Netherlands

Part II

La Marseillaise ....Rouget de Lisle
Farewell to Minka ....Russian Folk Song
*Mandalay   }
*Danny Deever } ....[just composed by] Walter Damrosch
*Discovery ....Grieg
         (Baritone Solo, Chorus, and Orchestra)
Solos by David Bispham constitute part or all of the starred numbers.

(1914-30), and Alberto Bimboni (1930 to the present) have been the conductors since Scheel.

A list of honorary members may further show the calibre of the men associated with, and admired by, the club's active group. Among former active members David Bispham and Alexander van Rensselaer were made honorary members. Former conductors Cross, Gilchrist, Damrosch, Parker and Woodruff were later honorary members.

In addition to a continuous and consistent career of musical activity through over sixty-five years, the Orpheus Club has maintained a rich program of social functions. While they do not particularly concern Music in Philadelphia, the names of some of their regular events will shed light on the nature of the organization. "Twelfth Night Revels" and "Spring Outings," regular occasions since about 1905, have provided many amusing tales of varied good times, though athletic prowess is not claimed for many of the Orpheans by records of these affairs. Musical smokers and parties in which the members attempted to stay on the Van Rensselaer yacht, frequent cricket matches and baseball games, the latter traditionally between basses and tenors, elaborate dinner and evening programs, have always made the Orpheus nearly as much a social band as a musical organization. In 1908 the custom of serving dinner at the club rooms before rehearsals was inaugurated. Unfortunately any further account of the various Revels, Outings and other activities might be said to develop a non-musical field unduly; hence any reader who wishes to be vastly amused by a very inclusive and clever series of programs and synopses of musical and dramatic nonsense, must refer to Arthur Latham Church's account in the recently printed book "The Orpheus Club." [1]

The Orpheus Club has assisted generously in musical and financial fields. Their interest in the Philadelphia Orchestra has helped that body from its beginning; for Edward McCollin and Alexander Van Rensselaer were active Orpheans, and, as the club's records claim, they "practically founded the Philadelphia Orchestra." [2] No admission charge is made to the regular concerts of

---

[1] "Twelfth Night Revels, Outings and Other Activities," pages 99-150 in *The Orpheus Club*, privately printed, Philadelphia, 1936.

[2] *The Orpheus Club*, p. 202.

the Orpheus Club, the Academy of Music being filled with 'invited guests'—although persons interested in hearing one of these events would be certain of courteous invitation-tickets, should they request them of a member. The work of the club, musically estimated, is always most hearty and merry, well executed and of good tone. The selections will be sure to please the singers themselves and the large majority of the audience, though critics may make faint-praise condemnations of the rather easy and mainly unambitious nature of their music. The club headquarters are now at 234 South Van Pelt Street, this property having been bought and completely reconditioned in 1928.

Follows a mild parody of an anonymous verse:

> So on they sing their tuneful way;
> They're singing at this present day.
> Some people call their music strange
> To others it's a pleasant change.

One might well hesitate to re-irritate these influential musical men on the question of the high seriousness, or lack of it, in their musical work. With complete good humor and the toleration of assured courtesy, they would answer that the quotation fits them exactly, their musical work having always been, admittedly, *musical play*.

The Fortnightly Club of Philadelphia is a men's group similar in aims and accomplishment to the Orpheus Club. It was founded in 1893 and was named the Fortnightly Club due to its biweekly meetings. Like most "fortnightly" organizations, however, it did not long keep its biweekly rehearsal schedule. Instead of becoming irregular in its meetings, or inaugurating a less ambitious program, as is often the case with fortnightly recreational groups; this society meets *every* week. The name Fortnightly Club [1] has been retained although the regular weekly meetings began in very early years of the club's history.

Dr. Henry Gordon Thunder is the present director of this organization.[2] Two or more concerts are given each season at the

---

[1] Its corporate title has been The Fortnightly Club of Philadelphia since 1905.
[2] Preceding directors have been George Guhlman, Maurits Leefson, and Karl Schneider.

Academy of Music. The music is quite light in character, for the most part. Soloist members and visiting artists nearly always appear on Fortnightly programs.

The Fortnightly Club is limited to eighty active members. There is generally a waiting list of considerable size for active, or performing, membership. The officers, directors, trustees and committees present an imposing array of musical and business organization, while the lists of associate members total over three hundred names.

Unflagging interest, genuine musicianliness, and good humor have combined to make the Fortnightly Club so successful throughout nearly fifty years of continuous activity.

It would not be difficult in discussing additional male groups to parallel the general classes of mixed choruses with a similar group of examples in the field of men's choruses. The University Glee Club of Philadelphia is a recognition of H. Alexander Matthew's abilities by local alumni of the University of Pennsylvania. This group is not limited to city men, nor to the University Alumni, but consists of college graduates who are living in or near Philadelphia. There are about twenty colleges and universities represented in this glee club, forty of its seventy men being alumni of the University of Pennsylvania. This club was organized late in 1934, yet on May 11, 1938, they were able to produce the following program in the foyer of the Academy of Music with accuracy and artistry:

PART I

CLUB MOTTO: "WE MEET AGAIN TONIGHT"

1. a. Dedication ....*Robert Franz*
   b. Come Again Sweet Love ....*John Dowland* (1563-1626)
   c. The Sleigh ....*Richard Kountz*

   (The Club)

2. Piano Solos—
   a. Prelude in A Minor ....*Debussy*
   b. The Gardens of Buitenzorg ....*Godowsky*
   c. Chicks ....*Moussorgsky*
   d. Islamey ....*Balakirew*

   (Robert Elmore)

3. Gypsy Songs ....*Johannes Brahms*
    a. Gypsy, Take Thy Lute
    b. Deep Upsurging Rima Flood
    c. Know Ye When My Lassie
    d. Sweet It is to Love
    e. Sun-bronzed Lad to Tread a Measure
    f. Roses Blow All in a Row
    g. Let the Giorgio Stifle in Town
                            (The Club)

PART II

4. a. Jesu, Joy of Man's Desiring ....*Johann Sebastian Bach*
            (Flute Obbligato by Ardelle Hookins)
    b. Chorale from "Die Meistersinger" ....*Richard Wagner*
    c. Little David Play On Your Harp (Negro Spiritual)
                                    Arr. by Freeman High
                            (The Club)

5. Baritone Solos—
    a. Pilgrim's Song ....*Tschaikowsky*
    b. I'll Sing Thee Songs of Araby ....*Frederic Clay*
    c. Spanish Gold ....*Howard Fisher*
                        (Robert Carnwath, Jr.)
                        (Mary B. Worley at the piano)

6. I'm Coming Home ....*Selim Palmgren*
    March of the Musketeers ....*Rudolph Friml*
                            (The Club)
7. College Songs

The Disston[1] Male Chorus exemplifies the type of organization in which the personality of a leader, Walter H. Gebhart, is aided by the interest and cooperation of an industrial plant. This men's chorus sings without charge at worthy benefit concerts. Founded in 1937, this chorus of fifty men has given eighteen concerts in its first two years of existence.

We must remember the many ancient societies founded by groups of German-Americans from as far back as 1835, none of which seem to have stopped or taken any considerable holiday since

---

[1] Henry Disston and Sons, makers of fine saws and other metal products, are also musically noteworthy as the first manufacturers of musical saws.

their beginning. The Junger Maennerchor appears the most frequently of the various German male choruses, never failing to impress its audiences with its unusual power, spirit, and musical proficiency.[1] In addition to the choruses previously discussed in the chapter on the early nineteenth century, the Germantown Maennerchor, founded in 1867, and the men's chorus of the Philadelphia Quartet Club organized in 1878, should be mentioned as both historically significant and active in the present day. The West Philadelphia Maennerchor and the Franklinville Quartet Club are nearly as old as the two groups mentioned above. The Quartet Clubs have women's choruses also, and joint rehearsals and concerts are occasionally sung.

III

The Matinee Musical Club, for women, was organized in 1894. Its first president, Mrs. Samuel S. Burgin, served from 1894 to 1911. In early years the club met at the Orpheus Club rooms; since 1915, it has had headquarters at the Bellevue-Stratford Hotel.

A chorus was organized in 1907 by Clara Barnes Abbott. Since 1931, it has been under the direction of Dr. Harry A. Sykes. There has been as orchestra since 1911, and Junior and Juvenile clubs since 1920.

Charitable activities have been both musical and financial. Club groups have performed without charge on many occasions. During the War ten thousand dollars was raised to reconstruct a village in France where the club had engaged in relief work. Fourteen thousand dollars and over eleven thousand garments were distributed by the Matinee Musical Club's Welfare Committee during the depression (1930-33). Both a scholarship fund and a students' assistance fund have been features of the club's philanthropic program for many years.

The Matinee Musical Club was host organization to the Biennial Convention of the National Federation of Music Clubs in 1911. Hundreds of notable persons, musicians and others, have been guests of this organization.

---

[1] For a brief historical account of the German Choruses, cf. *supra*, p. 90.

There are now twenty-seven departments of activity, with distinguished Philadelphia musicians as chairmen, or directors. Among them are the above mentioned Chorus, Orchestra, Junior Divisions; also a String Ensemble, Piano Ensemble, and Harp Ensemble.

The matinee programs from which the club's name derives, continue to be held bi-weekly, on Tuesday afternoons, at the Bellevue-Stratford Ballroom. Helen Jepson, Gregor Piatigorsky, Frederick Baer, Ben Stad, Nicholas Douty, Eugene Ormandy, Arthur Rubinstein, and Rudolph Ganz, are but a few of many famous musicians who have appeared on club programs within a few months (January, February, March 1938). This club, recognized as one of the largest and most successful in the country, is headed by Julia Williams.

The Philadelphia Music Club was founded in 1911 by twenty-four women music lovers, led by Mrs. Samuel Shaw Burgin, the club's first president. The purpose was two-fold, first to further the careers of the members themselves by the production of club concerts, recitals, and other musical affairs; and second to assist, in educational and generally philanthropic ways, the careers of other Philadelphia musicians. Weekly meetings were held on Tuesday afternoons at the Orpheus Club rooms, 1520 Chestnut Street; later (from 1915) in the Bellevue Ballroom. Ambitious programs are still produced before large audiences in a continuation of this Tuesday series, now bi-weekly, in the same hall.

The Philadelphia Music Club has been active in assisting young composers and interpretative artists. Works by composer members, and other local composers, have been produced on many club programs.

Soon after the organization of the Philadelphia Music Club, a chorus was founded by the members. Today it numbers one hundred and fifty voices, and is directed by H. Alexander Matthews, Mus. Doc. There is also a string ensemble, a harp ensemble, and piano groups. A dramatic department (created in 1916) has produced many operas and plays. Most practical is the Music Club's service bureau (formed in 1917), which secures remunerative engagements for active members of ability. Philanthropically, the club members have donated their services for concerts in camps (1917-18), factories, hospitals, and various recreation centers. Junior members and men (active members) have been admitted into the Philadelphia Music Club in recent years.

The financial donations by this organization have been very large. In addition to helping their own members, the Philadelphia Music Club has donated one thousand dollars to the Endowment Fund of the Philadelphia Orchestra and a large annual contribution to the Women's Symphony Orchestra.

Club members provide most of the program numbers, but on special occasions internationally prominent musicians take part. At the April 1, 1937, meeting Madame Samaroff-Stokowski lectured, and Vronsky and Babin played several two-piano numbers.

The headquarters of the Philadelphia Music Club are at 17th and Locust Streets, at the Warwick Hotel.

The Euridice Chorus had a close connection with the Orpheus Club throughout its thirty-two years of activity, 1886 to 1918. Michael Cross was the first conductor of this group. One of many newspaper comments on a Euridice program is included in the account of Cross in this book.[1] Fritz Scheel conducted this chorus from 1900 until the year of his death. Subsequent leaders were Walter Damrosch, Horatio Parker, and Arthur Woodruff. The Euridice Award, sponsored by the Philadelphia Art Alliance, is named in honor of this women's group.

A women's chorus that had an unusually long period of musical importance was the Treble Clef Club. This group of eighty members was organized in 1884, and gave two or three concerts a season for over fifty years. The Clover Room and the Ballroom of the Bellevue-Stratford Hotel were used for concerts by the Treble Clef. Karl Schneider conducted this chorus from 1911 until 1934, the year of the club's disbanding. Ellis Clark Hammann was its accompanist for almost as long a period of years. Schneider's predecessors as conductor for this club were Samuel Herrman, William Neidlinger, and Carl Reed, their original leader.

Women's clubs have started choruses in many instances besides the two described at some length at the beginning of this

---

[1] Cf., *supra*, p. 142.

section. The Helen Ackroyd-Clare women's chorus of Germantown, and the mothers' chorus of the Edmunds School in Frankford are successful organizations of recent years. German and Welsh singing societies for women are also active as soprano and alto ensembles.

A few of the vocal-social organizations have been described at some length, and possibly a bewildering number of the less important groups have been named above. It is the conviction of many leading sociologists and psychologists that such multitudinous clubs and choruses exert a potent influence for public good. It is not to be wondered at that their significance might be overestimated by those actively engaged in music, particularly the writer, whose main interest in Music in Philadelphia has been in the choral field for many years. In defense of what may be overaccentuation of this topic, let us advance the thought that the musical leaven of many choral groups works in the loaf itself, and does not serve to decorate its upper crust. It may or may not be true that "when you attend a choir rehearsal you add a day to your life." Directors of volunteer choirs and choruses have most doctors on the side of this favorite dictum. Finally, no one can cry 'sham' nor 'charlatan' at the volunteer chorus member. The choral program is the opposite of the star system. "Pikes' Peak or bust" has been said to sum up America's chief failing in musical matters. Professional music when combined with American business methods produces a system of star worship that discourages many talented persons from participating in music. Vocal groups, ephemeral though most of them may be, provide an easy and immediate avenue for musical expression. The slightly more specialized training required for instrumental ensemble playing, and the vastly more difficult requirements for any sort of professional solo work, rise most naturally from the broader foundation of participating in a singing society.

CHAPTER ELEVEN

PUBLIC SCHOOL MUSIC IN PHILADELPHIA

I

We must again assume an early start for public school music (as was done in Chapter One for concerts in Philadelphia prior to 1757), a start far in advance of the recorded mention of school music. The record of August 29, 1848,[1] states that the newly organized Normal School taught music as one subject of its seven branch curriculum. Mr. D. P. Alden was paid in the neighborhood of $150 (annually) as instructor in vocal music. The same report gives us the information that the purpose of instruction was "the thorough training of the pupils in the branches taught in the Public Schools with reference to teaching them."[2] This establishes music as not only a subject in the Philadelphia Normal School in 1848, but as a branch of the public elementary school curriculum at that time. Indeed the great probability is that vocal music had existed as a school subject for some years before this recorded effort to train future teachers thoroughly in it, "with reference to teaching" it.

It is more likely that Mr. Alden found a more lucrative post than that he retired on savings from his salary. In any case Mr. George Kingsley succeeded him the following year, retiring a few years later in favor of William H. Fenney. When John Bower became Instructor of Music he received three hundred dollars per annum; and so the early records go, with a new incumbent every few years and an occasional increase in the salary.

Edward Shippen, President of the Board of Controllers of the First School District of Pennsylvania, advocated strongly that "those pupils commencing with the primary and ending with the high schools, who have any musical talent, should be taught at

---

[1] Board of Education Annual Report.
[2] *Ibid.*, p. 123.

least the principles and rudiments of music. . . . From year to year the Board of Controllers has applied for a small amount of money to introduce music into our schools. It is needless for me to advise you of the importance of the subject." [1] The Board of Education Committee on Revision of Studies responded promptly by urging the cultivation of vocal music. Their report (March 10, 1868) incidentally mentions that "no wiser appropriation after that necessary for the absolute support and continuance of the schools, could in their view be made by councils than a moderate one for the instruction of children in vocal music." Also, "So desirous in some of the schools are the children to receive instruction in vocal music, that each child cheerfully contributes a penny a lesson for the purpose." This constitutes the earliest reference to the penny a lesson singing teacher who flourished at least as late as the permanent adoption of music into school curricula (1897), and continued in some school organizations until well after 1900. It also shows how "City Councils" was the body who would have to appropriate the money for school music at that time.

These beginnings are important for reasons other than those of antiquarian interest. Some of the correspondence and reports defend music as a school subject, and contain suggestions as to how its benefits as an educational branch might be secured. Many of these ideas and suggestions are as modern as the present day. This same Shippen was both forward-looking and musically minded in stating ". . . The moral, social, and physical influences of music present such advantages in the training of youth, that it becomes a matter of surprise that it has been so long unrecognized as an element in our system of education. One reason, however, may be found in the difficulty of forming a simple, comprehensive, and efficient method adapted to Public School purposes, and relieved of those intricate, tedious qualities which so generally attend the study of music. To be successful, it should be adopted as a regular branch of study, *marked under examination as other studies,* and commencing as early as possible in the lower schools, be extended throughout the whole school system, with a full professorship in

[1] President Shippen's letter (p. 10) of Jan. 21, 1868, to the Board of Education.

the Normal and Central High Schools. . . . Should an appropriation be made the coming year for the purpose of teaching music, it will require great care and attention on the part of your Board, to secure proper teachers and a proper method *and thus avoid the mere teaching of tunes,* so largely practiced in our schools at this time." [1] If President Shippen was correct in this analysis of the flaws in music methods, we have here a statement of what the Normal School graduates could, and could not, accomplish in music teaching. The Normal School Principal counters with a published note asking for permission to have music "placed on the same basis as those of other departments," that is, to allot more time to its study in the Normal School curriculum. The man was rightfully anxious because the same year (1869) saw the desired "appropriation from Councils and the appointment by the controllers, of a superintendent [of music] and a corps of teachers to instruct in the Grammar and Secondary Schools of the District." [2] This newly appointed musical personage was Jean Louis, who received twelve hundred dollars a year for directing the school music in Philadelphia. He had fourteen assistants, each having an assigned list of schools to visit regularly, teaching music and supervising the musical progress made by the grade teachers in that field. The subject was surely well launched, for we read that the following year Superintendent of Music Louis had twenty-two assistants, receiving from four hundred to six hundred dollars in annual salaries.

The new President of the Board of Education in 1870 was M. Hall Stanton. He standardized the time and methods for music instruction. Ten minutes a day in Primary grades (first to fourth years) were specifically reserved for the teaching of music. [3] Mr. Stanton showed himself to be an enthusiastic advocate of music in the schools and a most appreciative admirer of the work done

---

[1] Report of January, 1869.

[2] Both the Principal's request for more time for music in the Normal School, and the list of the newly appointed Music Superintendent and his fourteen assistants, are contained in the Report of the Board of Public Education 1869, pages 26 and 34.

[3] Board of Education report of 1870. Graded course of instruction in Music, p. 81.

by Mr. Louis and his many assistants. The methods followed
recommended the use of a textbook, charts and blackboards.[1]
Singing at opening exercises was suggested at the discretion of
the teacher.

Jean Louis disappears suddenly and completely in 1873, his
place being taken by August Perrot. Mr. Perrot's success trans-
cends that of Louis, if we are to believe the reports by the Superintendent of Schools. A Board of Education Committee on Music
was appointed in 1875. Their recommendations centered around
the abandoning of the teaching of musical theory in elementary
grades. In the same report the Committee on Music announced
that "in the semi-annual examinations for promotion, music shall
be one of the subjects of examination in each school." [2] We may
suppose that the elementary children were spared this music examination, since the same report had ordered the theory of music
to be discontinued and the music period taken up by exercises and
songs. The committee's report attempted to settle questions of
salary and general organization of music work. The staff had
grown from zero to twenty-five musical specialists in five years.
If its organization was any more complicated than the committee's suggested simplification, it must have been a confusing department indeed.

In spite of the sudden triumph of music in the schools, the
special personnel was soon to drop almost to zero again. The City
Councils omitted to appropriate the salary of the Music Superintendent. The board kept Mr. Perrot on as Superintendent "pend-
ing the decision by Courts of a suit brought by that officer against
the City, for the amount of his salary."

An interesting group of professional musicians was assembled
at this time to evaluate the success of Perrot's methods in the
schools. They agreed that the system was excellent and should

---

[1] The actual contents of Professor Louis's "Manual of Music Lessons for
Primary and Secondary Schools," comprised 18 lessons for primary grades
on the fundamentals of notation, 14 lessons on notation, expression, and time;
and 60 exercises for sight reading by syllables; also 39 songs including works
by Mozart and Weber. Printed May 1, 1871, by E. C. Markley and Son.

[2] Letter to the Board of Education. May 11, 1875, from the first Committee on Music (James S. Whitney, Chairman, Andrew Nebinger, Daniel
Steinmetz, James Freeborn, A. S. Jenks).

not be subjected to the frequent changes becoming habitual in Philadelphia school music.   This committee consisted of Henry G. Thunder, Hugh A. Clarke, Francis T. S. Darley and Thomas à Becket, Jr.   They did object to a reprehensible difference in method caused by the Normal School's using a 'Tonic Sol-Fa' system entirely at variance with the Perrot-Wilhelm method.   "Even *were* the tonic sol fa a good system, it is manifestly an error of the gravest character to make use of one method in the Primary, Secondary, and Grammar Schools, and a totally different one in the Normal School, thus giving the pupils the additional task of unlearning what they have already correctly and thoroughly studied, and of recommencing at the rudiments of a method which is considered poor, and absolutely injurious, by the majority of educated musicians." [1]   (Possibly many Philadelphians share the writer's experience of meeting many Grade School teachers who are still confused concerning the music period.)   In spite of the recommendations by experts and the encomiums from school authorities, the superintendent of music and most of the salaries of special music teachers were dropped during the depression of 1877. Some schools continued to have music teachers visit them to instruct and to advise the regular grade teachers.   But when they were conscientious (or ill-advised) enough to request official permission for some voluntary-contribution music arrangement, the board flatly refused to allow it. [2]   The Superintendent of schools in 1883, James MacAlister, states in his report that the "singing of appropriate child songs by rote . . . is required in all the grades."   He advances its physical and social benefits strongly, at the same time regretting that music cannot be considered a part of the regular work of the schools.   A long stretch of years in which the music period, if any, consisted in the singing of rote songs, followed the brief technical and highly organized regimes of Louis and Perrot. Its duration (1883-1897) was about twice as long as the preceding start toward better school music, that is, from 1870-1877.

---

[1] From the report of Thunder, Clarke, Darley and Becket as contained in the *Journal of the Board of Education* (1877, Appendix 31, p. 50.)

[2] The Germantown Grammar School for Girls made such a request, to which the Board replied February 11, 1879, "Resolved that nothing shall be taught in the public schools of this district which the pupils shall be required to pay for."

One name alone stayed on—that of Professor Everest, evidently the tonic-sol-fa advocate deplored by the first music surveyors, who remained at the Girls' Normal School from 1865 to 1886. He seems to have been the survivor in the Perrot-Tonic-sol-fa dispute, whether his system was the fittest or not being difficult to say, for his position was filled by Marcia Wilson in 1886, Emily Page in 1890, Anna M. Cheston in 1891, and Joan Easley from 1926 to 1938. This ancient post—at least, ancient when compared to the short tenures and frequent reorganizations in early school music—was finally relinquished after ninety years, when as the result of a recent survey the Normal School was discontinued in 1938. Lack of funds finally overcame the Normal School as a whole, and of course the Instructor of Vocal Music lost her position—due to the same monetary deficiency that caused the early disappearance of the supervisory system under Perrot.

This period of hiatus (1877-1897), so far as organized music instruction was concerned, saw the spread of the penny-a-week music teachers. The statement of the board quoted above [1] concerning popular subscription or voluntary contribution for music teachers states clearly that such penny a week practices were far from receiving official sanction. The board committees on music often favored any scheme to secure better music instruction even though the Board of Education disapproved as a whole.[2] It is therefore not strange that schools quite generally succeeded in evading the board's more official prohibitions and the music teacher received many pennies on which the candy store proprietor had a more logical claim. The converse was often the case—the candy man getting the musician's penny, for stories are still current of many pupils who quite regularly forgot to bring their pennies for the music teacher.

---

[1] *Supra,* p. 273.

[2] See, for instance, the Music Committee's resolution of February 11, 1879, a period at the start of the disorganization of school music: "Resolved that the regularly appointed music teachers in the various sections be allowed to continue the course of instruction as laid down in the graded course of study, and permitted to receive the voluntary contributions of the various schools for that purpose. . . . In view of the fact that the action of the board at that time was decidedly contrary to the spirit of the request, your committee deem it inexpedient to make any recommendation." (*Journal of the Board of Education,* 1880, pp. 261, 262.)

II

Renewed interest in proper music instruction seems to have been due to Simon Gratz who recommended on December 31, 1895, that music be restored to the place it formerly held in the Graded Course. He includes very wise admonitions that rival methods and the advocates of different series of charts and textbooks be kept out of the school music situation.[1] The appointment of Enoch W. Pearson as Supervisor of Music in the Schools took place on April 13, 1897, a little over a year after Mr. Gratz's report. His salary 'was considered a very large one ($2000 annually), and his special assistants were again reappointed, though only six in number. These assistants constitute the body known as the music supervisors today, whose function is more advisory than instructional, and hence, whose number has never been proportionally as large as Jean Louis' twenty-two assistants. The entire system of school music today goes back to Mr. Gratz and Mr. Pearson in its essential organization and even in much of its curricular planning. The penny-a-week system was definitely discarded, although school support of a few "Professors" lingered on in certain instances.[2] Beyond question Enoch Pearson laid a sure foundation for the years of school music that have followed his coming to Philadelphia. A month of daily observation in schools, a second month of consultation with grade teachers and with his music assistants, a Summer School of Methods attended by over seven hundred teachers daily, a month spent in preparing an eighty-five page teachers' manual; all were steps accomplished between Pearson's appointment in April and the opening of the schools in September 1897. Numerous teachers' meetings and teachers' classes were instructed by the Director. This title of Director has been retained by Mr. Pearson and his successor Dr. G. L. Lindsay, to the present

---

[1] Included in the *Report of the Board of Education*, 1895. Pp. 22, 23.

[2] It is the writer's own privilege to recall Friday afternoons in a Grammar School in Philadelphia during which an assembly of an hour's duration was entertained ably and interestingly by piano solos and related talks on music appreciation by a visiting pianist. This took place as late as 1920, and while it would have been unthinkable that we would have been asked to bring pennies to pay this performer, to whom we all looked up as a great artist, the regularity and organization of these music periods was a clear survival of the unofficial music system that preceded the advent of Enoch Pearson.

time. The assistants to the directors are called Music Supervisors, a term which correctly connotes the emphasis on their advisory capacity.

The name of Dr. Edward Brooks should be linked with those of Simon Gratz and Enoch Pearson in this permanent inclusion of music in Philadelphia Schools. Brooks was Superintendent of Schools in 1897 and proved an interested and able executive in carrying out the new program of music instruction. A former music teacher himself, Dr. Brooks possessed both technical and pedagogical ability as well as insight into the value and importance of music instruction. Our present use of the movable "do" with its emphasis on scale relationships is to a considerable extent due to the opinions of Dr. Brooks, backed by quoted endorsements from Hugh Clarke, W. W. Gilchrist, David Wood, and others.[1]

The Peace Jubilee chorus of thirty-three hundred children was commended by the President of the Board of Education, Samuel Huey. Under Mr. Pearson this mammoth chorus sang patriotic selections seated in front of Independence Hall, which performance, Mr. Huey's Report of 1898 (page 25) declares "settled forever the place of this study in our Course of Instruction." The Jubilee took place on October 28, 1898. The musical contribution from the schools drew appreciative mention from President McKinley as well as from local authorities.

Mr. Pearson hastened to reestablish definite objectives for the years of music study, all of which were set down in a teachers' manual which was printed in twelve parts about the year 1900. The path of music instruction was at last a smooth one. In 1915 we read, in Mr. Pearson's own article in the *Etude,* that he and his thirty assistants supervised the music instruction of *three hundred thousand* pupils.[2] This vast organization still concentrated on vocal music exclusively. However, the same article in the *Etude* mentions some important facts concerning school instrumental music, although clearly stating that it was not under the Director's supervision. It refers to the organs used to accompany assembly singing at Central and Northeast High Schools. These

---

[1] *Report of the Superintendent of Schools,* 1897. Pp. 64-69.
[2] "Public School Music in Philadelphia," by Enoch W. Pearson in the *Etude Music Magazine,* March 1915.

THE CENTRAL HIGH SCHOOL

THE SIMON GRATZ HIGH SCHOOL

and six other high schools had orchestras of from 15 to 65 players. Two statements in the article deserve quotation: "Through assembly singing, chorus work, sight reading and appreciation lessons, the pupils of the public schools today are living in an atmosphere of music unparalleled and unprecedented in all the world. . . . In another generation, love and appreciation of that which is truly excellent in art will be acknowledged as second to none, and living in an atmosphere of good music will be as common among us as good food, pure water, fresh air, and sunlight."

The growth of the music work from 1915 to the present time has been marked by a steadily increasing staff and by introduction of considerable music study into the high schools. The seven girls' high schools all had music teachers before 1920. 1921 saw the first appointment of a music teacher in a junior high school (Holmes), also the coming of Dr. Edwin C. Broome as Superintendent of Schools. Dr. Broome's first annual report noted the deplorable lack of opportunity for music study in the higher schools. The same year, 1921, was that of a state department survey of Philadelphia schools. Hollis Dann headed the music division of this extensive survey. He admired the loyalty of grade teachers in following the director's manual, but suggested that this detailed adherence led to a unique and excessive standardization in music study. More supervisors were needed, and more minutes per day for music suggested. Twelve minutes a day had been allotted to music as opposed to Dr. Dann's suggestion, as State Superintendent of Music, of twenty minutes daily. The most significant recommendations in the survey concerned High School Music, and together with the suggestions of Dr. Broome, they may be said to have led to the shaping of our present day music curriculum in Junior and Senior High Schools. Courses of an elective nature, for school credit, in Chorus, Theory of Music, Harmony, Music History and Appreciation, and Orchestra were strongly recommended. These subjects were all introduced within a few years after the survey, even the boys' schools finally organizing classes in every branch of music.[1] A concert given in the Academy

---

[1] Detailed statement of each class as introduced into the various schools during the sessions of 1922-1923, are contained in the *Board of Education Report* of 1923; pp. 160, 161.

of Music May 14, 1923, amounted to a public demonstration of the achievements, within a year in most cases, of musical groups in high schools. Choruses and orchestras totaling over eighteen hundred high school students participated.

Leopold Stokowski's first series of three youth concerts was planned for public school pupils exclusively, and given during this same season, 1923 and 1924. A similar and equally successful series by Stokowski and the Philadelphia Orchestra was noted in Mr. Pearson's retirement report.[1] He also noted increasing popularity of four-period-a-week music courses in high schools, and a larger number of pupils receiving school credit for music lessons taken with private teachers.

III

When Mr. Pearson retired in June, 1925, Mr. George L. Lindsay, his supervisor of music in the high schools, was appointed to succeed him. Dr. Lindsay has gradually but consistently turned the focus of music study's emphasis toward a combination of sight and rote singing in elementary grades rather than the exclusive rote work (1880-97) or the overemphasized sight reading work (1897-1925) of preceding periods.[2] Pleasing tone, appreciation of good music, melodic invention, are among the new objectives sought in music periods in elementary schools, according to a revised Course of Study in Music Education (July 1926). In Junior and Senior High Schools there is much emphasis on club activities, such as orchestra, glee club, operetta and music appreciation clubs. The Normal School, admitting both men and women since 1918, was given a revised music course to fit the new school music studies.

Outstanding events in the fifteen years of Dr. Lindsay's direction, too numerous to describe, and possibly too recent to be

---

[1] Quoted in the *Board of Education Report* of 1925, p. 207.

[2] A radio address "Music in the Philadelphia Schools" (December 17, 1925) states fully Dr. Lindsay's music education philosophy, a broad one which could hardly bring about the standardization deplored by the 1921 survey, and yet which places considerable responsibility on the shoulders of often unmusical grade teachers who still must give the larger part of our music instruction.

properly estimated in importance, might well be at least named before concluding this account of Philadelphia public school music. The organization of the active "In and About Philadelphia Music Supervisors Club" (1927) ; the first of the noted All Philadelphia High School Music Festivals (1928) ; the organization of a Vocational Music Course at the Mastbaum Vocational School (opened in 1929) ; Philadelphia school musicians acting as hosts to the annual convention of the Eastern Music Supervisors Conference (March 1929) ; a steady maintenance of all music activities throughout depression years (1930-36), contrasting happily with the sad fate of Mr. Perrot and Philadelphia school music in 1877 ; the repetition of most of the seventh annual Senior High School Festival at the Municipal Auditorium as part of the celebration of the centenary of Public Education in Pennsylvania (April 28, 1934) ; the organization by the music division of five orchestras and two Bands under the CWA,[1] later LWD,[2] relief plan (1934) ; annual Junior High School Festivals similar to those of the Senior High School (since 1929) ; and numerous radio broadcasts in series and on special occasions are among the important events that the Philadelphia School Music Division has sponsored.

Such a tremendous growth in size and scope of activity has of course required the expenditure of large sums of money. The practice of buying a limited number of the non-solo instruments to enrich the orchestral texture in all of the higher schools is a particularly costly but worth while development. The carefully preserved libraries of bound and sheet music, both vocal and instrumental, are growing to impressive proportions in all the secondary and certain elementary schools. The textbooks, music books in libraries, music equipment and supplies, obviously have been enormously increased in the past twenty years.

Perhaps the most fitting manner in which to arrive at an estimate of the extent and nature of Philadelphia School Music would be to state in brief the actual subjects included in the musical life of a child in various parts of the Philadelphia School system:

---

[1] Civil Works Administration.
[2] Local Works Division of the Philadelphia County Relief Board of the State Emergency Relief Administration.

Starting with the elementary and special schools, the music work consists of daily lessons which include class and individual singing, ear training, with provision for lessons in music appreciation and melody invention. Many of these schools also have glee clubs, orchestras, and rhythm orchestras.

In the junior high school, all pupils receive one period per week in general music. Seventh and eighth grades have exploratory work in part singing and appreciation, and confirmative work in written dictation, elementary theory, and terminology. Ninth grades have mass choral work and appreciation. Music clubs for boys and girls, and mixed glees, first and second orchestras, bands, piano, violin, and wind instrument classes, operetta, appreciation, and special music groups are rostered in the club period.

The senior high school music curriculum, which begins in the tenth grade, prepares for entrance into one of the following fields of higher education: school music departments of universities and colleges as preparation for teaching and supervising public school music; fine arts departments of universities and colleges as preparation for professional or private school and college music teaching; schools of education or colleges of liberal arts and sciences for cultural education.

In addition to the music curriculum, the senior high schools provide choral singing in assembly and weekly chorus periods for all students. Music electives with full academic credit are presented in theory and practice, two terms, harmony, four terms, vocal and instrumental ensemble, each six terms. School credit is granted for private study of voice, piano, organ, and instruments of the symphony orchestra to students registered in any four- or five-period music subject. Classes in history and appreciation of music are held in all high schools.

Chapter Twelve

MUSIC IN PRIVATE SCHOOLS AND UNIVERSITIES

I

The parochial schools of the Roman Catholic Church are second to the public schools in number and educational importance. While they are far less numerous than public institutions, Philadelphia has several times as many parochial schools as there are privately operated schools of any other description. Since coeducation has not been introduced into the secondary schools managed by this church, we shall find that all-girls' or all-boys' organizations provide the only advanced music in Catholic schools.

There is a strong musical tradition in two of the girls' high schools. The Hallahan High School was slightly earlier than the West Philadelphia Catholic Girls' High School in beginning an orchestra. In 1928 a large instrumental group was started in each of these two schools. The orchestra at Hallahan now numbers 115 girls, that at West Catholic Girls' 125. Equipment was bought by the schools, and by some of the players also, until in 1940 each of these high schools boasts a full symphonic orchestra. Benjamin A. d'Amelio directs the two orchestras, while the entire project is managed by the Sisters of St. Joseph.

The success of the music at these two high schools results from the completeness of the scheme of its instruction. In addition to buying most of the instruments, the school provides weekly lessons on each under competent instructors. Many girls receive their first instrumental instruction at the high schools.[1] A combined festival is held yearly by these two associated orchestras, and the vocal groups from the same schools, at the Academy of Music. The combined orchestra has also played over radio station KYW,

---

[1] Information from Msgr. John J. Bonner, Diocesan Superintendent of Schools.

at Atlantic City and Ocean City, in the Cultural Olympics at the University of Pennsylvania, and at summer concerts in Robin Hood Dell. Each of these two high schools has a concert band and a marching band.

In an account of Nicola Montani, it is stated that Mr. and Mrs. Montani direct the glee clubs in the same two girls' high schools.[1] The Hallahan glee club was organized in 1927, that of the West Philadelphia Catholic Girls' High in 1930. These vocal groups combine at the annual festivals, and have sung jointly on other occasions as the Verse Choir.

The six boys' high schools are not so far advanced in musical work as the girls' high schools described above. Each has one or more classes in theory of music, a glee club, an orchestra, and a marching or a concert band.

In elementary grades the parochial schools follow a curriculum very similar to that of the public schools, with regard to the introduction of successively more difficult problems in the use of the voice and music notation. From grades four to eight unison and part songs are sung by all classes, and Gregorian music is also studied by the children. The words of many of the songs are religious or devotional in character, but there is also much material on nature, school life, games, and general themes of interest to children.

II

The Pennsylvania Institution for the Instruction of the Blind is in a sense a public school, since no child is refused admittance because his parents are unable to pay a set tuition fee. The State and school district of which the pupil is a legal resident appropriates about three-fifths of the amount expended on each pupil from Pennsylvania. In its special pedagogic problems and its unusual approach to musical subjects this institution has less in common with the city schools than have the many parochial schools described above. The school for the blind was begun by Julius Friedlander, its first "principal instructor," in 1832. In March,

---

[1] Cf. *infra*, p. 311.

1833, a meeting of philanthropic citizens of Philadelphia organized a board of managers and an executive committee to bring about the formal opening of the school. During the same month its first building, on Twelfth Street above Race, was occupied. In 1835 the school at 20th and Race Streets was begun, which building housed the school until 1899. In the early years of this institution Friedlander was responsible for most of the teaching. It was his influence as a thorough musician that may be said to have begun the tradition of fine musical work in the school.

The activities of men like David Wood and Adam Geibel make us feel that the blind possess musical skill in some manner compensating for their lack of sight. While it is true that hearing is sharpened through extra use on the part of blind persons, their musical powers need development just as do those of their more distracted fellows. Julius Friedlander and David Wood provided the opportunity for plentiful participation in music by all of the blind students, and for special instruction in music to the unusually gifted among them.

Other noted musicians who have taught at the Pennsylvania Institute for the Instruction of the Blind are Henry Hahn and Frederick Hahn, Adam Geibel, and Russell King Miller. The present director of music is Ralph P. Lewars, Mus. Doc.

In 1899 this school moved to Overbrook, a northwestern section of Philadelphia, and has occupied the large building and campus there since that year. The musical course of study includes much solfeggio training from kindergarten to normal school grades. Singing in classes, glee clubs, and a large chorus is an important subject throughout the school. Piano, organ, and other instruments are studied, also the theory of music, music history and appreciation. Piano tuning is also taught to students who select that subject.

It may be interesting to note that the children need not be totally blind to be admitted to this school. One tenth of normal vision is considered a maximum in selecting students. Some of the teachers are blind, more are not.

The work of David Wood as a pupil, as a teacher, and as musical director at this school is described in the account of his life.[1] Oratorios produced under Wood's direction, which constituted one of the greatest achievements of the school, are also listed in that biographical sketch.

III

A Philadelphia school that has an unusually long record for fine music work is Girard College. The musical organizations there have both a past and a present worth recording. The college is a school for boys from six to eighteen years of age, one or both of whose parents are dead. Vocal music was taught from the founding of Girard College in 1848, though in a somewhat indefinite manner, by prefects. In 1859 William G. Fischer, well known as composer of hymns,[2] became the first teacher of vocal music at this school. George F. Bishop succeeded Fischer in 1868. During the years of Bishop's tenure as teacher of singing, the Girard College Band was organized by George Bastert (1869). Bastert had been the trumpeter at the old Arch Street Theatre. Another organist succeeded Bishop as music teacher and organist at Girard College. Thomas à Becket came to this school in 1873, and for over forty years guided its musical life.

Thomas à Becket was born in Philadelphia in 1843. He studied with his father, and at the public schools. His first appearance as a pianist was made in 1855 at the Walnut Street Theatre in a flute and piano duet by à Becket Sr. In 1872 and 1873 he directed orchestras at the Arch St. and Chestnut St. Theatres. A Becket was one of the few really great accompanists that Philadelphia has produced. Bull, Schalski, Trebelli, Homer, and of course many less celebrated soloists requested à Becket's services when they were in Philadelphia. His work at Girard College lasted for the longest period of years among the many and varied musical positions held by Thomas à Becket. For forty-five years he taught music and played the organ at Girard College. He never resigned, but died after a short illness in 1918.

---

[1] Cf. *supra*, pp. 107-8.
[2] Among hymns by Fischer are: "Whiter than Snow," "I Love to Tell the Story," and "I Am Trusting Lord in Thee." William Fischer directed the chorus at the Moody and Sankey meetings in Philadelphia.

The organ played by à Becket at the college had been installed only a few years after his appointment as a member of the faculty. Mr. and Mrs. William Stoll, David D. Wood, and Thomas à Becket Jr. were among the musicians who played at its inaugural concert in 1878. In 1916 this old Jardine organ was supplanted by an Austin instrument in the newly completed high school building. Next came the rebuilding of the Chapel organ in 1924, while the most recent organ, installed in the new Chapel about ten years later, is among the few outstanding instruments separately discussed in the chapter on Philadelphia church music and noted organs.[1]

Harry C. Banks succeeded à Becket as organist at Girard College. Dr. Banks has devoted much of his time to recitals on the various new organs as they were liberally provided by the college authorities. He also directs the Glee Club, and teaches piano, organ, and theory of music at this school.

Formal classroom instruction in music began in 1896 under Jerry March. He was followed by Burton Scales who served from 1914 until his untimely death in 1922. The present director of vocal music, Bruce A. Carey, was appointed in 1922.

The instrumental work begun in 1869 has grown steadily ever since. Bastert was succeeded by his son, William D. Bastert, who led the band from 1897 until 1910. The next leader, C. Stanley Mackey, is given credit for a considerable share in the renewed success of the band.[2] A former graduate of Girard College, and member of the Sousa band, he was reputed to be the best tuba player of the time. From 1910 to 1914 Mackey trebled the size of the college band and organized a fine junior group. George O. Frey, the present director of instrumental music, followed Mackey. Mr. Frey is also an alumnus of Girard College, president of its alumni association, a former member of several noted bands, and head of the Pennsylvania Bandmasters' Association.

The appointment of Earl Pfouts as the first teacher of violin in 1922 seems a surprisingly recent addition to all of the previous

---

[1] Cf. *infra,* pp. 321-22.
[2] By Cheeseman A. Herrick, in his chapter on music in *The History of Girard College,* printed at the College, 1927.

vocal and wind instrument study. With the strong musical background and interest developed over so many years, the task of organizing an orchestra at Girard College was quickly accomplished under Mr. Pfouts' expert leadership. Shortly after the appointment of Pfouts, a new armory was completed (1924) with extensive rooms and equipment for group and individual instrumental practice.

The latest development in the musical organization at Girard College has been the beginning of intensive music study of vocational thoroughness, coupled with the granting of scholastic credit for this specialized work in music.

Girard College offers the most complete musical training of any institution in Philadelphia, except those organized primarily as conservatories or music schools. Vocal music, directed by Bruce Carey, and taught by three additional teachers, begins in the first grade. In the second year its study becòmes more formal. The boys of the fifth, sixth, and seventh grade are eligible to join the Junior Choir, which usually numbers about a hundred voices. The seventh year classes study music history and appreciation. Vocal music is discontinued in the eighth year, and resumed for the ninth tenth, and eleventh.[1] There are six large instrumental groups, three bands and three orchestras. Instrumental music is under the direction of George O. Frey. There are nine teachers of music at Girard College.

Cheeseman A. Herrick, late President of Girard College, concludes a lengthy chapter on music at that school with the following paragraph: [2]

A United States senator when visiting Girard College in 1926 asked two leading questions. The first was, "In what subject, branch of study, or activity, are the boys as a whole most interested?" The other question was, "From what subject of study or division of interest do the boys seemingly derive the largest profit?" After full consideration, the official to whom these questions were addressed answered in both cases, "music." In the later years, especially, music has loomed large in [Girard] college life. The boys have evidenced more than a casual interest, and they have realized large return

---

[1] The course of study is divided into eleven years at Girard College.
[2] *The History of Girard College*, p. 304.

from their musical studies. Music in Girard College has two functions: it contributes a cultural element to the lives of all the boys;
and it affords, in addition, to considerable numbers the opportunity
to develop themselves so that they can participate creditably in
musical activities both instrumental and vocal, and in both amateur
and professional fields. Music has in truth occupied a foremost place
in Girard College.

IV

The music at the William Penn Charter School typifies in min-
iature the larger progress of Music in Philadelphia. When this
school was founded in 1689 there was no consideration of music as
one of its subjects of instruction. In 1939, the two hundred and fiftieth anniversary of this old school, music is a prominent subject in
all the grades, and two flourishing clubs are devoted to its practice,
During the first three months of the current year the musical
clubs of Penn Charter gave ten concerts.[1] This busy schedule
marks a great change in the attitude of the authorities in an old
Friends' school. Some fifty years ago the Owls' Singing Club and
Debating Society staged a concert (April 5, 1889), which included
the following vocal music:

Eton Boat Song
The Fairy Maiden ....*A. R. Gaul*
Song of the Vikings ....*Eaton Faning*
The Hunting Day ....*Williams* [2]

To perform these works—some of them were novelties in 1889—
it was necessary to rehearse surreptitiously, with a melodeon which
was carefully hidden after each practice. The late I. H. B. Spiers,
who led this early program of music in a Friends' school, taught
at Penn Charter until 1939, and often recalled the daring required
to present this concert of the Owls' Singing Club to the Friends'
unfriendly ears.

---

[1] The Stevens, Springside, Ogontz, and Mary Lyon Schools heard these
programs. Other concerts were given at Chalfonte-Haddon Hall in Atlantic
City, the Bellevue-Stratford Hotel, at Penn Charter School, and radio
station WCAU.
[2] This program was lent by Charles T. Maclary, director of music at
Penn Charter School.

From 1899 to the present, music has been accepted by the authorities of the Penn Charter School. Burton Scales led a glee club, a mandolin club, and taught singing in the lower classes between 1899 and 1914. Richard Weaver was in charge of a similar musical program during the next seven years. He began the serious work in instrumental music at the school. The present director of music is Charles T. Maclary, whose first position on the faculty was a part-time engagement as accompanist to the music activities, in 1921.

More than eighty per cent of the boys at the Penn Charter School are in music classes or activities. Since 1926 credit toward graduation has been allowed for music study, with the maximum amount of such work set at one-fifth of the boy's school time. The choral club is a curricular subject for students in grades nine to twelve. The average attendance in this class is more than one hundred.

Music appreciation is stressed in the upper school. All boys study this cultural subject in grades six, seven, and eight. Many elect it during their three subsequent years at the school. The Carnegie Corporation gave one of its fine phonographs and a library of 600 records to Penn Charter School. This gift is placed in a special room, not used for classroom purposes, and is available to the boys at all reasonable hours. The school extends its appreciation course by subscribing to a box at the concerts of the Philadelphia Orchestra.

The instrumental activities at this school lag somewhat behind its vocal and appreciation phases. An orchestra of about twenty members plays at the musical clubs' many concerts. Individual instruction in piano and violin is given at the school. Other musical groups are a junior chorus of nearly two hundred voices, and a picked vocal ensemble of thirty older boys.

A second private school in Germantown has been the recipient of a set of Carnegie Music Appreciation Equipment. The Germantown Friends' School was much later than Penn Charter to introduce music into its activities. After five years of debating the momentous step, it was decided to purchase a piano for use in the kindergarten, in about 1914. An extra-curricular banjo club was organized in 1917. In the following year a girls' glee club was started, while the boys waited eleven years before requesting the formation of a similar group. There was an orchestra at Germantown Friends' from 1927 to 1931. The first full-time music teacher to be appointed at this school was Margaret Shane, who has directed the music there from 1927 to the present. A second teacher was engaged in 1929.

The first joint concert by the musical organizations of the Germantown Friends' School was given in the spring of 1930. Six annual operettas by Gilbert and Sullivan were produced by the vocal groups between 1932 and 1937. One or two concerts are sung each year by the students.

Boys and girls are all rostered in music classes at this school, with the exception of boys of the eighth and ninth grades. One to three periods a week are devoted to music by each student. Classroom singing for lower grades, and chorus work for older students constitute the usual musical work. A one year course in theory of music and ear training, three periods, and history and appreciation of music, two periods, may be elected by a student in his eleventh or twelfth year. Either of these two branches may be taken separately, but most musical boys and girls prefer to enroll in both of them. Germantown Friends' and Penn Charter were the first two schools in the Philadelphia area to receive the Carnegie phonograph and records.

Other Friends' schools in Philadelphia seem to be far behind the two institutions in Germantown in their musical accomplishments. All have reached the stage of introducing a piano for classroom work and assembly singing. Some limited work in music appreciation and a glee club are found in the other Friends' schools. The Frankford Friends' school introduces music for a variety of purposes in its curriculum. This school does not go beyond the sixth grade however. Even the musical Penn Charter and Germantown Friends' are weak in the instrumental side of their course of study. The orchestra at the former school is small, and that of the latter was discontinued eight years ago. If the majority of students were actually descendants of strict Quaker families, we could easily explain that an inherited aversion to instrumental music caused that side of the subject to languish in their schools. Since the majority of pupils are not of such old Quaker stock, the more likely explanation lies in the fact that instrumental music is far more costly in its equipment and in the teacher-time required to conduct it successfully than is vocal music or musical theory. The school orchestra can seldom grow from a group of instruments that gather around a piano. It must be planned and carefully prepared over a long period of time. And it must be favored and generously supported if school authorities expect it to succeed.

V

Two important dates stand out in the history of music at the University of Pennsylvania. Eighteen seventy-five was the year in which Hugh A. Clarke became its first professor of music. He shares with John K. Paine of Harvard the honor of being the earliest professor of music at an American university.[1] Music classes at the University have continued and grown from 1875 to the present year. The other important year is 1922, in which all music clubs were completely reorganized into their present form, and the music course of four years, announced in 1920, had progressed sufficiently to be a recognized department of the School of Fine Arts. Before 1922 there had been occasional clubs for many years, the Orpheus Club being in existence as early as 1759. Glee clubs, orchestras, and banjo-mandolin societies were the main divisions into which these sporadic clubs generally fell. The *Masque of Alfred,* and the organ installed in the college hall in 1760, were mentioned in the account of Francis Hopkinson.[2] Both of these early musical accomplishments were manifestations of an interest in music at the College of Philadelphia, later the University of Pennsylvania.

In 1922 the musical societies were all brought under one management and renamed the Music Club of the University of Pennsylvania. Instead of working under the usual undergraduate control, this new club was managed by George E. Nitzsche, the Recorder of the university. In 1924 Mr. Nitzsche was followed by Clayton McMichael as manager of this club. More recently the

---

[1] For an account of Dr. H. A. Clarke, see *supra,* pp. 148-9.
[2] Cf. *supra,* p. 31 and p. 18.

band and the glee clubs have again become severally independent with undergraduate government, and a newly organized Student Music Club holds public and private recitals of instrumental and vocal music performed by its more talented members.

This student management of clubs has been typical of the University of Pennsylvania.[1] It is apt to limit the correlation of the clubs with each other and with the academic work of the university. The sharp division between the student-operated clubs and classes taught by the music department of the faculty makes the work at the University of Pennsylvania very different from music in any other private or public school in Philadelphia. Two years after Hugh Clarke went to the University to become Professor of Music, we find that an orchestra was started. This 1877 University Orchestra was not directed by Clarke, however, but was managed by Oliver Hopkinson, who was then an undergraduate of the University of Pennsylvania. His teacher, Leopold Engelke, did what little coaching and directing was necessary.[2] Far from encouraging this orchestra, the college authorities felt called upon to ask them to stop meeting when their number had grown to twenty, and their noise in proportion. Occasional small orchestras were formed at various times after 1880, although the mandolin seemed to be the featured string instrument on musical programs between that year and 1910. A permanent orchestra was started in 1887. About 1890 the banjo-mandolin club combined with the glee club to form the Associated Musical Clubs of the University. An orchestra was organized in 1922 as a branch of the University Music Club. Mr. Nitzsche secured Hedda van den Beemt as conductor for this orchestra. When the management by the undergraduates was resumed in 1928, the orchestra stopped in less than a year.

The early history of the University Glee Club is hard to trace. The club now in existence was formed in 1864, but that is not the earliest glee club at this institution. A vocal group that might be called analogous to the mandolin club was active during the early

---

[1] The management by Nitzsche and McMichael was a conspicuous exception to the policy of student control. The Glee Club's selection of Harl McDonald as their director is another case in which the student members and managers have secured a faculty member to conduct their club activities.

[2] The early orchestra was mentioned in the account of Oliver Hopkinson, p. 216.

twentieth century. This club participated in the first intercollegiate contest at Carnegie Hall in the spring of 1914. Since their work had been so exclusively of the most elementary nature, the record of this glee club was never outstanding. Burton T. Scales was the director of this club from 1914 to the time of his death in 1922.

H. Alexander Matthews directed the Glee Club from 1922 to 1933. Their progress since 1922 has been rapid. The club grew from 25 members to 125 during the first year of its existence as a branch of the newly organized Music Club. Only the best choral works have been sung for many years by the University Glee Club and its associated organization for women students, the Women's Glee Club. Their tour with the Philadelphia Orchestra in 1923 was an early recognition of the artistic success of the new Glee Club. In 1925 and 1927 they participated in productions of Beethoven's Ninth Symphony by the New York Symphony Orchestra. Since 1935 the Choral Clubs of the University of Pennsylvania have been conducted by Harl McDonald. The first performance of Dr. McDonald's Third Symphony was given by the Philadelphia Orchestra with the assistance of the University choral groups and other singing societies. The symphony was given in Philadelphia, New York, Baltimore and Washington. The choral group's participation in McDonald's *The Sea* with the Simfonietta has been previously mentioned.[1] The chorus has appeared with the Philadelphia Orchestra repeatedly since 1930, a recent performance being Harl McDonald's *Lament for the Stolen* for women's chorus and orchestra, sung for the first time in 1938. An annual appearance in the series of the Philadelphia Forum, and several concerts of regular or special nature in Philadelphia and other cities, make this club an active and popular organization. Their artistic success has been permanently preserved on several Victor records.

The band of the University of Pennsylvania is another old club that became an important section of the Music Club as organized in 1922. A band was in existence at least as early as 1875, and had a continuous career between 1897 and 1922. In the latter year the band grew from 30 to 150 members. A junior band was organized the same season. Richard Weaver, Hedda van den

---

[1] Cf. *supra*, p. 226.

Beemt, and J. W. F. Leman directed the bands for short periods after 1922. Since 1926 Adolph Vogel [1] has led this branch of the Music Club. The band plays for events in Franklin Field, for two annual concerts, at three or four noon hour programs on the campus, and, in sections, at indoor games as well.

Harl McDonald, who has directed the Choral Clubs since 1933, has been a professor of music on the University faculty since 1928. Theory of music and composition are his special fields. Dr. McDonald was the chairman of the Department of Music until 1939, resigning the position after his appointment as manager of the Philadelphia Orchestra. Morrison C. Boyd, the present chairman, has been a member of the department of music since the retirement of Hugh A. Clarke in 1923. Dr. Boyd's special field lies in the history and appreciation of music, although he lectures on harmony and counterpoint also. His position as University Organist is noted in connection with the discussion of the Curtis organ in the auditorium of the University.[2] Paul Krummeich has lectured on the philosophy and history of music at the University since 1926. Since the creation of the full-time music course in 1920 there have been several part-time instructors in musical theory, history, and acoustics.

Recent developments in the School of Education at the University of Pennsylvania should be mentioned. Methods of teaching music were taught from about 1926, and have been in charge of Jesse L. Scott since 1929. This department has also engaged assistants to Mr. Scott for expert instruction in conducting, accompaniment, voice, piano, and other instruments. Even more recent has been the Cultural Olympics sponsored by the School of Education since 1937. An active program has been headed by Frederick C. Gruber during the first three years of this department. In the 1937-8 season over 6,000 contestants took part in their programs at the University. Music, dance, speech, and dramatic festivals were held; 127 awards were given that season. The musical fields of the Cultural Olympics comprise vocal and instrumental contests

---

[1] Vogel is also an active music publisher, director of the Main Line Symphony Orchestra, participant in chamber music, and a former 'cellist in the Philadelphia Orchestra.

[2] Cf. *infra*, p. 320.

consisting of performances by soloists, small ensembles, choruses, orchestras, and bands.

Bi-weekly broadcasts have been given by groups and soloists, sponsored by the Cultural Olympics, over radio station WFIL. The financial support of the entire project has been provided by George S. Johnson, president of the Lit Brothers store in Philadelphia.

Music at Temple University, though more recent in its organization than that of the University of Pennsylvania, is in some ways more complete. Thus it has very little in the way of an important musical past, but present activities are varied and flourishing. The same general divisions of music work are found in both universities—clubs, classes in Music, and in Music Education. The emphasis is different at Temple University from that at the University of Pennsylvania. Music Education and conservatory work constitute nearly the entire field of music study at Temple University. Instead of recounting a lengthy series of beginnings and reorganizations of clubs, classes, and courses of study, which have characterized the history of music at the University of Pennsylvania, we shall discuss the present organization of music at Temple University, with slight mention of its brief historical aspects.

The band and orchestra are two prominent music clubs at Temple. George O. Frey organized the band in 1926. A year later Horace E. Pike became its director. Pike has directed both the band and orchestra for the past twelve years. The band plays at autumn games, and at athletic rallies, and gives a few concerts each year in and near Philadelphia. There are sixty-four members in the Temple band, a complete and properly balanced concert instrumentation. The orchestra began as a trio in 1925, and has an average attendance of fifty in 1940. This group plays for the annual entertainment staged by the university, for the students during the school day (on occasion), and gives two or more concerts each year. The large organ installed at Mitten Hall in December, 1937, should be mentioned as a new and important addition to instrumental music at Temple University.

A men's and a women's glee club rehearse regularly and give concerts at the university and elsewhere. The Temple University

Chorus is a class in which all members of the department of Music Education are enrolled. Other undergraduates may choose this chorus and receive elective credit for membership in it. Two concerts are given each year, and a third biennially as a part of the summer session. A small a cappella choir meets as a class, and is open to music students and members of other undergraduate schools. The High School Music Festival sponsored by Temple University was omitted in 1938 and 1939, but will probably be resumed in future years. It is similar in aims and accomplishments to the choral section of the Cultural Olympics at the University of Pennsylvania.

The classes of the department of Music Education are especially complete and well planned for the preparation of teachers. Forty-six such courses are offered during the current semester. Vincent Jones, Ph.D., heads the faculty of Music Education.

The oldest division of musical work at Temple University is its School of Music, founded in 1913. This division is in reality a conservatory that is managed by a university, and is therefore placed between the colleges and the conservatories in our arrangement of Music in Philadelphia. Emphasis is placed on individual proficiency in instrumental, vocal, and theoretical music. Teachers' certificates and graduation diplomas are awarded only to candidates who have studied for two or more consecutive years at the school, and who pass the required examinations. Bachelor and Master of Music degrees are conferred by this school, and the honorary degree of Doctor of Music is also awarded.

Piano, organ, voice, harmony and composition, and nearly all of the orchestral instruments are taught at the Music School of Temple University. The arranging of music for radio programs and dance orchestras, history and appreciation of music, even the humble banjo-mandolin family is covered on the faculty of this complete school, or in its two branches in Philadelphia.

Thaddeus Rich is Dean of the Temple University School of Music. Among other distinguished musicians on its faculty are Emil F. Ulrich, William Sylvano Thunder, Henry Gurney, and William F. Happich. Recitals by faculty and student members of the School of Music are given in Mitten Hall, the auditorium of Temple University.

Some of the privately operated educational institutions began with a decided bias toward music, as did the University of Pennsylvania. Others began with the opposite attitude, among them the Friends' Schools. Mr. Ely's school, noted earlier as reciting *The Messiah* in unison at an Adgate concert,[1] was "intended solely for the improvement of church music" of the different churches in Philadelphia, according to an advertisement by John Ely in the *Pennsylvania Packet* for October 31, 1788. This was an unusual objective for a boys' school, although most girls' schools included music among the subjects taught even in those early years of Music in Philadelphia. No matter what the original or historical attitude may have been in public or private schools, it is gratifying to any music historian to find that all of them in 1940 give music a recognized or important position among their curricular subjects.

---

[1] Cf. *supra*, p. 27.

CHAPTER THIRTEEN

CONSERVATORIES AND MUSIC STUDIOS

I

The beginnings of music teaching in Philadelphia have been recorded in the chapter on Colonial Music, for Mr. Warner, Miss Ball, and others became active in that field many years before the Revolutionary War. The Uranian Academy was the first music school in this city to be organized after the manner of a conservatory.[1] Music teaching in schools is very old in Philadelphia, for Swedes and Germans like Hesselius and Dock were able musicians and are known to have taught music in their community schools.

George Gillingham was discussed, though with far less detail than his importance would warrant, in the early chapters of this book. An additional item of interest concerning this accomplished violinist is his activity in music teaching. Gillingham was one of the earliest teachers formally to announce a music school in Philadelphia. His Academy for Vocal and Instrumental Music was removed to 92 N. 7th Street in May, 1815. Announcements in the *Daily Aurora* (May 13, 19, and 24) state that lessons in singing, violin, viola, violoncello and pianoforte were given at the academy, and, by arrangement, in private homes. "A concert is held at Mr. Gillingham's every Friday evening for the improvement of Amateurs," declared the *Aurora* in several editions. Samuel Dyer, a contemporary of Gillingham, taught a singing school in Philadelphia and led the Handelian Society before leaving the United States in 1815. John Husband, Jr., the clerk of St. Paul's Church, continued "to instruct his singing school at 197 S. 4th Street in the first principles of sacred music" in November, 1820.[2] Peter Dupré reopened a New Music School at 26 Spruce Street

[1] Cf. *supra*, pp. 26-7.
[2] Poulson's *Daily Advertiser*, November 11, 1820.

on January 4, 1810. His advertisement announces that Peter Dupré "will teach from 8 A. M. to 10 P. M. except Saturday"— a strenuous schedule if he found a sufficient number of pupils to carry it out. The Christian Concert and Music School was a similar organization of the early nineteenth century. It specialized in singing for young ladies "according to the Italian school," and also had a department of piano. A concert was given at Masonic Hall on November 14, 1820, consisting of "songs and pieces from the best Italian authors." [1]

The Academy of Music of the Musical Fund Society was discussed in the account of that organization.[2] Its period of activity was from 1825 to 1832. The American Conservatorio, founded by Filippo Trajetta in 1823, had a longer career in Philadelphia. Trajetta, or Traetta, was born in Italy in 1777, and settled in Philadelphia in 1822 after brief sojourns in Boston, New York, and Virginia. His Conservatorio was a singing school which was active in Philadelphia for about thirty years. Filippo Trajetta composed many vocal works, an opera, oratorios, cantatas, and books on the voice. He died at Philadelphia in 1854.

Charles W. Jarvis, Benjamin Cross, Thomas à Becket, Sr., and Leopold Meignen have been previously mentioned as influential teachers of this period. Albert G. Emerick, organist at St. Stephen's Church, taught many pupils between 1830 and 1860. He performed and managed an important series of concerts from 1850 to about 1860, preceding those run by Michael Cross and Charles H. Jarvis. Emerick was born in Philadelphia in 1817, and was an associate of such organists as John C. B. Standbridge and W. H. W. Darley in the years before the Civil War. It would require too long a list to mention the pianists, organists, and vocalists who were important as individual teachers of music after 1850. The Germania Orchestra of 1848 and the later group of the same name, 1856 to 1895, supplied Philadelphia with many well-trained music teachers. Carl Wolfsohn, Carl Hohnstock, and Leopold Engelke were celebrated teachers of music in the middle of the nineteenth century.

---

[1] *Ibid.*, November 11 and 15, 1820.
[2] Cf., *supra*, p. 64.

II

While the years after the War between the States provided many fine teachers of music who followed the individual studio method of instruction, they were characterized by the rise of several important conservatories. The addition of these large music schools to an increasing number of independent teachers of music reflects the growth and spread of the city's population between 1865 and 1940.

Three conservatories which are still leading music schools were founded between 1870 and 1885. The Philadelphia Musical Academy, organized in 1870, is the oldest of these conservatories. The Philadelphia Conservatory was established in 1877, and the Combs Broad Street Conservatory in 1885. As each of these music schools plays a large part in the musical instruction of the present time, a short account of their history and organization is given.

John Himmelsbach founded the Philadelphia Musical Academy in 1870. When he resigned in 1876 to return to Germany, his position as head of this school was filled by Richard Zeckwer. Zeckwer was succeeded by his son, Camille Zeckwer, in 1917. The Hahn Conservatory merged with the Philadelphia Musical Academy in 1917, and since that year the conservatory has been called the Zeckwer-Hahn Philadelphia Musical Academy. Frederick Hahn, the son of Henry Hahn, who was also a noted violin teacher in Philadelphia, has been president of this school since 1924. Other celebrated musicians who have taught at the Philadelphia Musical Academy are Leopold Auer, David Wood, Maurits Leefson, Gustav Hille, Charles E. Knauss, Herbert Witherspoon, and Leo Ornstein. Their present faculty includes such noted Philadelphia musicians as Rollo Maitland, Lucius Cole, and several members of the Philadelphia Orchestra.[1] Many members of leading orchestras were students at this school. But "the school derives its greatest satisfaction from the thousands of individuals who have shared its instruction and as a result have had an abiding interest in and appreciation of music." This statement, quoted

---

[1] William A. Schmidt, Waldemar Giese, Marjorie Tyre, Jules Serpentini, Harold M. Rehrig, and Leonard Mogill.

from the 1935 catalogue of the Musical Academy, is literally true, not only of that conservatory but of several in Philadelphia.[1]

Orchestras and small ensembles, both instrumental and vocal, are part of the organization at the Philadelphia Musical Academy. Its concert hall houses many performances by these groups, and a large number of recitals by students and members of the faculty of the conservatory. Certificates, diplomas, and various degrees are awarded by this school.

The Philadelphia Conservatory, while founded seven years later than the Philadelphia Musical Academy, is the oldest chartered music school in Pennsylvania. Other conservatories now have the right to award degrees, but this music school was the first to be privileged in its charter to "grant and confer such honors, titles, and degrees as are granted and conferred by any University in the United States for proficiency in music."

The name Ezerman bears the same relation to the Philadelphia Conservatory as does Zeckwer-Hahn to the Philadelphia Musical Academy. D. Hendrik Ezerman came to Philadelphia in 1901, and taught piano at this conservatory from that year until the time of his death (1928). Mrs. Ezerman is still the managing director at the Philadelphia Conservatory. E. Brooks Keffer, the son of Edward I. Keffer,[2] grandson of Edward Brooks,[3] and president of the Settlement Music School[4] is also president of the Philadelphia Conservatory. Their faculty contains a large number of famous teachers, among them Olga Samaroff, Boris Koutzen, Susannah Dercum, and Ralph Kinder. Several members of the Philadelphia Orchestra teach at the Philadelphia Conservatory of Music.

---

[1] Grove's *Dictionary*, 1928 edition, mentions 26,000 students as the total enrollment since the founding of this conservatory. 800 pupils is an average annual total in the main school, while its three branches enroll several hundred each year.

[2] Dr. E. I. Keffer has been discussed in various connections. As chief worker for the organization of the Philadelphia Orchestra (cf. p. 168), concertmaster of the Philadelphia Symphony Society (cf. p. 168), and chamber music enthusiast extraordinary (cf. p. 221), he was one of the most influential men in Music in Philadelphia from 1890 to 1910.

[3] Dr. Edward Brooks was an unusually musical Superintendent of Schools in Philadelphia. Simon Gratz and Superintendent Brooks brought about the permanent addition of music to the curriculum of the public schools in 1897. Cf. pp. 275-76.

[4] Cf., *infra*, p. 304.

Their piano department was the special sphere of Hendrik Ezerman, and it has remained an outstanding branch of the work at this school. In addition to Mme. Samaroff, Rosalyn Tureck and Henry Harris are noted pianists among the twelve teachers of that instrument at the conservatory. Henry Albert Lang and Frederick W. Schlieder are well-known musicians who have headed the department of theory at the Philadelphia Conservatory.[1] The gifted pianist and composer Paul Nordoff has recently been appointed head of that department.

The third of the large music schools organized in the 1870-1885 period is the Combs Broad Street Conservatory. The founder of this institution was identified with Philadelphia before he established his noted music school. His biography was given in brief form in a preceding section on Chamber Music, which was always a main field in the interests of Gilbert Raynolds Combs.[2] Dr. Combs took a personal interest in each student at his school. This procedure is characteristic of all conservatories as compared with schools and colleges, but it is the more remarkable in the Combs Conservatory since it was for many years the largest music school in Philadelphia. Its buildings are the most commodious among the city's conservatories. More than 64,000 students were enrolled at Combs Conservatory between 1885 and 1932. Nineteen thousand, three hundred and fourteen of them entered the field of professional music. In addition to the usual conservatory work, with its instrumental and vocal groups, and its many concerts and recitals, the Combs Broad Street Conservatory maintains a four year college course for the preparation of teachers in the field of Public School Music. Graduates from this course are awarded the degree of Bachelor of Music Education. The degrees of Bachelor of Music and Master of Music are awarded for curricular work at

---

[1] Henry A. Lang was born in New Orleans in 1854 and died at Philadelphia in 1930. He studied and taught in Germany, and settled in Philadelphia in 1891. Between that year and 1930 Lang was an active and highly successful teacher of piano and composition in that city. From 1913 Dr. Lang headed the department of musical theory at the Philadelphia Conservatory. His compositions were both numerous and scholarly, winning several prizes of importance. He composed two symphonies, a violin concerto, much chamber music, and many piano pieces and songs.

[2] Cf. *supra*, p. 220.

this conservatory, and the degree of Doctor of Music is conferred in recognition of outstanding musical achievement.

These three schools reflect the ideals of their presidents, heads, or directors. The Philadelphia Musical Academy is generally called the Zeckwer-Hahn Conservatory, the Philadelphia Conservatory is familiarly called the Ezerman school, while the Broad Street Conservatory has never dropped the name Combs from its full title —the Combs Broad Street Conservatory, also known as Combs Musical College. Two other conservatories in Philadelphia were founded by noted pedagogues who were in Philadelphia many years before 1900.

Maurits Leefson and Gustav Hille founded the Leefson-Hille Conservatory in 1899, although both men had taught in the Philadelphia Musical Academy for some years before that time. Gustav Hille was born in Germany in 1851, came to America as a member of the Mendelssohn Quintet in 1879, and taught at the Philadelphia Musical Academy from 1880 to 1899. Hille and Leefson headed their own music school for about ten years, after which the former returned to Germany. Maurits Leefson came to Philadelphia in 1887, at the age of twenty-six, as a concert pianist. This distinguished Hollander remained active as head of the Leefson-Hille Conservatory until his death, in 1926. Leefson was an active member of several music clubs and was highly respected and greatly beloved as a teacher. Julius Leefson, a brother of the founder, has continued as director of the conservatory from 1926 to the present time. He had been a member of the faculty since 1905.

Constantin von Sternberg, a noted Russian pianist, was born in Petrograd in 1854. He studied under several noted teachers, Franz Liszt among them. After living four years in Atlanta, Georgia, Sternberg settled in Philadelphia in 1890, where he founded the conservatory that still bears his name. His many published compositions include approximately one hundred piano pieces, many of which were played by such artists as Hofmann and Godowsky. Sternberg is also the composer of six piano trios and many choral works and songs. Several magazine articles and a book on *The Ethics and Esthetics of Piano Playing* (1917) were written by Sternberg. This brilliant pianist, prolific composer, and noted pedagogue died in Philadelphia in 1924. The Sternberg

School closed six years after the death of its founder. Three branch schools have remained active since 1930, however, in West Philadelphia, Germantown, and Camden. The Sternberg School has produced an unusual number of fine pianists. The following graduates have been noted in Philadelphia, some of them throughout the eastern states: Robert Armbruster, Agnes C. Quinlan, Mary M. Mount, Harold W. Gilbert, Charles T. Maclary, Katharine O'Boyle, and Charles Dryfuse.

Several new conservatories have challenged the leadership of the three older schools in recent years. The Clarke Conservatory resembles the Leefson-Hille in that its founder, Joseph W. Clarke, was a former teacher at the Philadelphia Musical Academy. When he organized his school in 1934 several members of the older conservatory joined the new faculty. There are five branch schools of the Clarke Conservatory.[1]

Leo Ornstein, George F. Boyle and Bernard Mausert are among the many teachers who have established music schools of considerable completeness within the past twenty years. Two older conservatories, similarly organized, that have remained active down to the present time are those at the Central Young Men's Christian Association and the Hyperion School of Musical Art. The Y.M.C.A. school of music was founded in 1910, and has been directed for thirty years by Benjamin L. Kneedler. The Hyperion School was founded in 1901 by John Pommer and Franklin E. Cresson. Mr. Cresson is still director of this school at its studios in the Presser Building. Further particulars concerning the number and financial aspects of conservatories in Philadelphia are included in a later section on commercial phases of Music in Philadelphia.[2]

III

Philanthropic citizens have caused a new type of music school to develop in Philadelphia during the years since 1900. The oldest

---

[1] Germantown, West Philadelphia, New York, Wynnewood, and Drexel Hill.

[2] Cf. *infra,* p. 363.

of this endowed type of conservatory is the Settlement Music School, the most significant the Curtis Institute, and the newest the Academy of Vocal Arts.

The Settlement Music School was begun by the College Settlement of Philadelphia at their headquarters, 433 Christian Street. From 1908 to 1914 this school was a department of the settlement. In 1914 it became an independent organization, occupying the house at 427 Christian Street. In 1917 the present fine building was made available through the generosity of Mrs. Edward Bok. Branch schools have been organized by the Settlement Music School; two of them are now independent conservatories, one at the Lighthouse Settlement, the other at the Reed Street House. The advanced work of the Settlement Music School dates from 1922, the year of the establishment of their conservatory department. This group provided the nucleus for the beginning of the Curtis Institute in 1924. The Settlement Music School was active in the formation of a music division in the National Federation of Settlements. The Carnegie Corporation assists settlements through this national federation.

A rapid growth in the number of students at the Settlement Music School proclaims the people's appreciation of its musical value. There were 40 pupils in 1908, 411 in 1928, and 647 in 1934. The faculty at this school numbered 35 in 1934. A complete musical training is covered by courses there, and the related arts of drama, modeling and sketching are taught. A limited amount of dancing and large classes in social subjects are also part of the activities of the Settlement Music School. The fees for lessons range from thirteen cents to five dollars and average seventy-five cents. Mrs. Bok is honorary president of this school, and E. Brooks Keffer its president. Johan Grolle has directed the Settlement Music School since its establishment in 1908.

The Curtis Institute of Music was founded in 1924 by Mary Louise Curtis Bok. Its splendidly equipped headquarters at 18th and Locust Streets have housed this school since its establishment. Tuition is free to all students, the entire cost of running the school being covered by a generous endowment provided by Mrs. Bok. The Curtis Institute owns a complete set of orchestral instruments, many of them of great value,[1] two fine organs, and eighty-four Steinway pianos. The library at the Institute contains more than 28,000 volumes—music, scores, and books.[2] The requirements for entrance to the Curtis School are very strict. In fact, its entire purpose is the training of a limited number of particularly gifted students who already have a good knowledge of the fundamental principles in their selected musical fields. It would be difficult to name a few outstanding members on the faculty of the Curtis Institute, since nearly all of the teachers there are celebrated musicians. Dr. Randall Thompson is the director of this school, and Mary Louise Curtis Bok its president.[3] The degree of Bachelor of Music is granted to all graduates of the Curtis Institute of Music.

The Academy of Vocal Arts was founded in 1935, under the name of the School for Vocal Scholarships. The financial support

---

[1] 28 of the 46 violins used by Curtis students are old instruments, two Stradivari and two Guadagnini among them. 17 violas (two da Salo and one Amati), and 13 'cellos (nine antique instruments among them), are also used for practice and orchestral purposes at Curtis. 13 double basses, a contrabassoon, six timpani, an English horn, and the usual other instruments of a full orchestra are owned by this highly endowed school.

[2] Adam Ileborgh's book of organ preludes, dated 1448, is a rare volume in the library of the Curtis Institute. It is called the oldest book of organ preludes with pedal parts, by Jean S. Beck, a former member of the faculty. Cf. Dr. Beck's article in the February 1930 issue of Overtones, a magazine published by the Curtis Institute.

Pietro Aron's Toscanello, edition of 1529, is another valuable book in this library. It is the earliest known example of music in which the different parts were written under each other in the manner of the vertical chord writing of today.

[3] Additional faculty members, many of whom are world famous artists, include: Voice: Emilio de Gogorza, Elizabeth Schumann, Eufemia Giannini Gregory. Piano: David Saperton, Isabelle Vengerova, Rudolf Serkin. Violin: Efrem Zimbalist, Lea Luboshutz, Alexander Hilsberg. Violoncello: Felix Salmon. Viola: Louis Bailly, Max Aronoff. Harp: Carlos Salzedo. Organ: Alexander McCurdy. Accompanying: Harry Kaufman. Double Bass, Anton Torello; Flute, William Kincaid; Clarinet, Robert McGinnis; Oboe and Woodwind Ensemble, Marcel Tabuteau; Bassoon, Ferdinand del Negro; Horn, Anton Horner; Trumpet, Saul Caston; Trombone, Charles Gerhard; Tuba, Philip Donatelli; Percussion, Oscar Schwar; Conducting, Fritz Reiner (who is also the conductor of the Curtis Symphony Orchestra); Music Criticism, Samuel Chotzinoff; and Composition, Rosario Scalero. Joseph Hofmann was head of the piano department from 1924 to 1927, and director of the Curtis Institute from the latter year until 1938. There are many other faculty members for instruction in musical and academic subjects.

for the Academy, which resembles the Curtis Institute in being an endowed conservatory, has been provided largely by its president, Mrs. Clarence A. Warden. Scholarships are awarded to most of the students at this school, although rates are charged to persons who wish to enroll but are unable to win free tuition. Edgar Milton Cooke has been dean of the Academy of Vocal Arts since its first season. H. Maurice Jacquet, formerly conductor at the Opéra Comique in Paris, is the operatic director. Complete preparation for singing in opera and concert is provided by the artist-specialists who are on the faculty of this school. The Academy of Vocal Arts is located at 1920 Spruce Street. While it is much smaller than the Settlement Music School or the Curtis Institute, this new Academy is able to furnish a remarkably thorough training in voice, musicianship, languages, and dramatic work, and to assist students to secure situations in the opera and concert fields.

IV

Since 1870 there has been an increasing number of music teachers who have not founded a school nor taught in a conservatory organized by one of their more venturesome confrères. Also, most of the teachers who hold positions on faculties of one or more music schools give lessons to several private pupils not connected with the schools themselves. Their music teaching, called individual studio work, constitutes what is undoubtedly a large part of the instruction in the city, and particularly in the suburban districts of Philadelphia.

The Philadelphia Music Teachers' Association is an organization to which many of these independent pedagogues belong. The majority of the members are not connected with any music school, although some hold part- or full-time positions in conservatories, and others are music teachers in public or private schools. The Philadelphia Music Teachers' Association was founded in 1891, and is the oldest such organization in the United States. Its object is "to create better conditions for music teachers, and to foster a richer musical culture in Philadelphia and its neighboring communities." [1]   This association usually has a membership of five hundred. The main activity of this large group is the monthly meetings, at which music and speakers on musical subjects are heard. This association acted as host to the 1935 convention of the Music Teachers National Association, and has participated in other special occasions besides its long maintained series of regular activities.

The seven hundred church organists in Philadelphia include a large group of private music teachers. Some of them are members of conservatory staffs, as are H. Alexander Matthews, Alexander McCurdy, and Robert Elmore. Others have founded their own schools, as did Franklin Cresson, Bernard Mausert, and Newell Robinson. Many other organists have devoted most of their work days to private pupils, depending on the church and community to provide their students. The late Henry Keely, Henry Fry, and George A. A. West are a few of the Philadelphia organists who exemplify the continuation of the independent music teacher.

Nearly two hundred teachers and supervisors of music hold full-time positions in the public schools of Philadelphia. [2]

Musical Life in America, the recently published memoirs of Olga Samaroff, centers upon a theme appropriate to our discussion of music schools and music teachers. The improvement in American opportunities for a musical education is stressed by Mme. Samaroff in that book. [3] The financial inducements of positions in America have brought so many of the finest European musicians to the United States that it has finally become unnecessary for our students to seek advanced musical education abroad. This situation has obtained, though to a lesser degree, for a sufficient number of years for many native American musicians to be as thoroughly prepared teachers as the imported artists from Europe. The private teachers, and more particularly the music schools, described above, provide plentiful local illustrations of the consistent growth and improvement in music study in America.

---

[1] Quoted from an account of the P.M.T.A. provided by Dr. Edward E. Hipsher, the president of that organization since 1933. Previous presidents who are still active figures in Philadelphia musical life are James Francis Cooke (1910-1927) and Stanley Muschamp (1927-1933).

[2] Cf. *supra,* p. 280, for the type of teaching done by these specialists in Music Education.

[3] *Musical Life in America,* Olga Samaroff. Published by Norton, New York, 1939.

CHAPTER FOURTEEN

CHURCH MUSIC IN RECENT YEARS—NOTED ORGANS IN PHILADELPHIA

I

What is the test of whether church music is artistic? Eric Delamarter asks and answers this question in his article *Is Church Music Art?* [1] His reply follows: "If it be music which brings devotion to the devout (who may or may not be musically sensitive) and if at the same time it brings satisfaction and uplift to the musical person (who may or may not be devout) it is music which must be classed as art. If it fails in either function, it fails completely." It is interesting to note that Mr. Delamarter has spent his long career as a church musician in Congregational and Presbyterian churches where artistic music is a fairly recent development. It would be impossible to record three hundred and fifty churches in Philadelphia where music fulfills Delamarter's twofold requirement more completely than is done in the other half of the city's churches. Anyone attempting such a survey would surely find that a new organist had made sweeping changes in church number five while he was studying church number six hundred. A new minister or music committee may also cause radical improvements, or the reverse, in the musical course of a church's career. This chapter can merely point out some of the churches in Philadelphia that have consistently provided music far above the average over a long period of time.

Two views of music in any or every church will be helpful in attempting to summarize in a few pages the activities in over seven hundred churches. Some churches are musically important for their historic background, others for the elaborate program of music which they are including in their services at the present day.

---

[1] "Is Church Music Art?" appears in the *Proceedings of the Music Teachers National Association* for 1937 (p. 197).

A few are significant in both ways; they assumed a leading position in ecclesiastical music from fifty to a hundred and fifty years ago, and are still outstanding in that field. The historical chapters mentioned the earliest examples of music in the churches of Philadelphia. Briefly listed, the important churches were: Gloria Dei, 1700; Christ Church, 1730; St. Joseph's, 1750; St. Peter's, 1770; First Moravian, 1790; St. Mary's, 1810; St. Augustine's, 1830; St. Stephen's, 1850; St. Mark's and the Cathedral of SS. Peter and Paul, 1870; St. James' and Second Presbyterian, 1880; St. Clement's and Church of the New Jerusalem, 1890; St. Luke's in Germantown, 1900. The dates do not correspond with the beginning of music in the respective churches, but suggest a general period in which previous chapters mention them as rising to local prominence in their musical life.

During the years between 1890 and 1910 there were several city and suburban churches that followed in the paths blazed by such men as David Wood and Minton Pyne. The Hollond Presbyterian Church at Broad Street and Federal rose to a leading position in church music in the years when the music was directed by Charles M. Schmitz, Russell King Miller, 1893-1898, and David F. Crozier, 1898-1901. The music at Holy Trinity Church began a longer period of local leadership with the appointment of Ralph Kinder as organist in 1899. For nearly forty years Kinder's choral services and organ recitals were regular and well-attended features of church music in Philadelphia. In 1938 he was succeeded in that important position by Robert H. Elmore, an outstanding recitalist of the Philadelphia area. It is interesting to observe that Kinder's predecessor, Michael H. Cross,[1] stressed conducting in his church positions, while his organ playing leaned heavily on improvisation, according to James Huneker.[2] Mr. Elmore is Cross' exact opposite in his emphasis on organ technique and flawless accompaniment.

The Roman Catholic church may surprise some readers by its drastic changes in music since 1900. This ancient religious body is often considered to be free from sudden fads and sweeping changes in policy. The church music since 1900 illustrates quite

---

[1] Cross was organist at Holy Trinity Church from 1880 to 1897.
[2] *Steeplejack*, Vol. I, p. 142.

the reverse of the usual Catholic tradition of ecclesiastical consistency. In 1903 Pope Pius X issued the musically important document known as the "Motu Proprio," which called for a complete change in the music of most Catholic churches in Philadelphia. Compositions by such writers as Haydn, Beethoven, Schubert, von Weber, sometimes called the Vienna School of Sacred Music, were to be excluded from church services. Gounod and the older Rossini were obviously banned by the same decree. The types condemned were the secular and the theatrical. Music of a restrained and purer devotional nature was recommended, particularly the harmonizations as contained in 15th and 16th century masses and motets. The large church literature of Gregorian music, as brought to light by the researches of the Benedictine monks and the School of Church Music at Solesmes, was especially recommended for church use. Modern compositions in the religious styles of this older music were, of course, acceptable, and since 1903 much has been written that answers the purpose of the new music of the Catholic church, which is in reality a very old music after all. The 1903 edict suggests a modern tendency in the same direction as that fostered by an earlier Pius, the Fourth, whose activities toward purifying church music expressed at the Council of Trent, 1545-1563, brought the composer Palestrina into particular prominence. The Palestrina Choir of Philadelphia is directed by Nicola A. Montani, a musician who has done much to help the Catholic schools and churches follow the rules laid down in 1903. Montani spent the summer months of 1906 with the exiled monks from Solesmes who were studying Gregorian chant on the Isle of Wight. Dom Mocquereau and Dom Eudine superintended this summer school of mediaeval music. Mr. Montani is in many ways a present local analogue of the earlier Catholic musician, a Palestrina in other ways besides directing the Palestrina Choir. His compositions [1] and his many contacts as conductor and teacher have spread the doctrines of the Motu Proprio in Philadelphia and many other cities. The organization of a boys' and men's choir

---

[1] Nicola A. Montani is the composer of six secular and about thirty sacred works. As editor for Schirmer he has arranged and revised over three hundred liturgical compositions. His two volume book, *Essentials in Sight Singing*, is a publication of the C. C. Birchard Company of Boston.

at St. John's Church in Philadelphia, which Montani, and his wife Catherine Sherwood Montani, trained for seventeen years, is an important contribution toward carrying out the same papal edict; since one of the ideals expressed by Pius X was that mixed choirs should be replaced by boys and men as soon as possible.

Nicola Montani was born in Utica, N. Y., in 1880. His studies were begun in that city, and continued in Rome. Cappocci, Rella, and Perosi were among his teachers in the eternal city, as was Catherine Sherwood, his vocal instructor, who later became Mrs. Nicola Montani. Instead of dismissing Montani as a married singer, a step taken by the church in the case of the earlier Palestrina, St. John's Church in Philadelphia welcomed the two musicians as organist and vocal teacher for the founding of a male choir. Several public concerts were given by the choir of St. John's Church. A large repertoire of polyphonic works was developed for church services, including many of Montani's masses and motets in modern contrapuntal style. Many schools and religious institutions have engaged Nicola and Catherine Montani as musical directors and teachers. *The Caecilia*[1] lists no fewer than twenty-four academies and convents which have benefited by the Montanis' training. Present positions in Philadelphia include the directing of glee clubs at Hallahan High School, West Philadelphia Catholic Girls' High School, and St. Mary's Academy in Logan. Since 1907 Mr. Montani has been editor of liturgical music for G. Schirmer & Company of New York, and director of several musical groups near that city.

The Society of St. Gregory was founded by N. Montani, Leo Manzetti, and J. M. Petter in 1914. This organization of church musicians lists works as approved by, or antagonistic to the Motu Proprio, and holds regional meetings and national conventions for discussion and illustration of the most suitable music for Catholic services. Mr. Montani is a member of the special committee which lists both new and old music according to its liturgical merits.

Dr. James A. Boylan is a second member of the same committee of the Society of St. Gregory. Dr. Petter, one of the founders

---

[1] *The Caecilia*, a Catholic church and school magazine, for August, 1935, pp. 337-8.

of the Society, is the third man on this influential committee. James A. Boylan has been as influential in the advancement of American conformity to the Motu Proprio as has Nicola A. Montani, although his immediate contacts have all been in the Philadelphia area. The large seminary of St. Charles Borromeo at Overbrook has been musically guided by Dr. Boylan for over twenty years. As another leading advocate of purified music for the church, and of choirs of boys and men, Dr. Boylan's position at the seminary of St. Charles has enabled him to become one of the important figures in the new order of music in the Catholic Church.

James A. Boylan was born in Philadelphia in 1880, and is thus an exact contemporary of Nicola Montani. He studied piano and violin privately in Philadelphia, and prepared for the priesthood in that city and in Rome. His European musical training was received from Perosi, Rella, and Mocquereau—who also taught Mr. Montani. Before his appointment as musical director at St. Charles Borromeo, Dr. Boylan was an outstanding example of that powerful force in church music, a musical priest. Since 1917 he has concentrated on the field that was always his main interest, the choral service of the Catholic Church.

The music at the Cathedral of Saints Peter and Paul has been a noted feature of its impressive services since the construction of the present building in 1864. The series of leading local musicians who have directed the music at the cathedral is as follows: Michael H. Cross, 1862-1880; Samuel Herrman, 1880-1902; William S. Thunder, 1902-1924, and Reginald M. Silby. Since Dr. Silby's resignation in 1936, financial limitations have somewhat restricted the musical program, but the choir of boys and men continues to follow the course mapped out by the Motu Proprio. Mr. Gerard Stief is the present organist at the cathedral. Two large churches in less central sections of Philadelphia are noted for their fine choirs and the able use of the preferred type of liturgical music. St. Francis de Sales in West Philadelphia, Albert Dooner, organist, and the Church of the Holy Child in Logan, Philip Bansbach, organist, provide outstanding examples of the successful use of the approved musical system. The Catholic Church with its parish school possesses a perfect organization for a chorus of soprano and alto boys' voices available for daily rehearsals and occasional church services. It is stated elsewhere in this book[1] that the school music of parochial institutions is built around the old religious style, recommended comparatively recently by the Motu Proprio of 1903.

II

Among historic institutions the First Moravian Church presents a long and active record for over two hundred years of musical prominence. Ritter's book, which discussed their organization from 1780 to 1857, was mentioned in the chapter on music of the early nineteenth century.[2] The J. C. B. Standbridge organ installed at the close of this early period is still in use at the Moravian Church. It was rebuilt by the active firm of William Haskell and Company when the church moved to its present building at 17th and Fairmount Avenue, in 1892. The Moravians at Bethlehem, Pa., have made an impressive Easter Sunrise Service one of their main religious observances since 1754. The Philadelphia congregation has followed this custom from about 1895. Chorales by Bach, or from that period, are played by trombones at Bethlehem, and by a brass choir of ten instruments at the Philadelphia Moravian service. The Easter dawn services have been held at Ivy Hill Cemetery since 1928, a city-wide congregation being admitted to participate in them during the last ten years. One of the strongest religious-musical customs among Protestant denominations of Philadelphia has been the Easter Sunrise Services, especially those at the Temple Stadium and at Franklin Field. This development follows an ancient Moravian tradition which was introduced to Philadelphia by the First Moravian Church.

The United Churches, mentioned in so many connections in our earlier chapters, still preserve their traditions inherited from Philadelphia's first ecclesiastical musicians. Christ Church, founded 1695, and St. Peter's, 1761, were first called the United Churches in a charter granted by Thomas and Richard Penn in 1765. St. James' became a third united parish in 1809, but set up

---

[1] Cf., p. 282.
[2] Cf., *supra*, pp. 92-94.

an independent organization in 1829. The famous Bishop William White was rector of St. James' Church, at Seventh Street above Market, from 1809 to 1836. His views on church music have already been quoted in connection with early Episcopal churches in Philadelphia.[1]

St. James' Church had a quartet choir up to 1868, in which year this church organized one of the first boy choirs in Philadelphia. (St. Mark's boy choir was organized in 1867, St. Luke's, Germantown, shortly after 1870.) The organ was moved to the chancel end of St. James' Church in 1853. Expenses for music are recorded as $500 in 1842, $700 in 1844 and $1,200 in 1867. The present building at Twenty-second and Walnut Streets was opened in 1871. The organ was rebuilt and enlarged for the new church by Hall and Labugh of New York. This was the third rebuilding and enlarging of St. James' organ since 1809. The present organ was installed in 1903 by the Hutchins-Votey Company of Boston. at a cost of more than $8,000. This instrument was modernized and enlarged in about 1925, at which time a modern console was installed by the Austin Company. Recent organists and choirmasters who have served this historic parish are Edwin P. Chase, who introduced the boy choir in 1868; Charles M. Schmitz, choirmaster in the 1880's and up to 1895; Lacey Baker, 1895-1899; William Stansfield, 1899-1910; S. W. Sears, 1910-1929; Ernest White, 1929-1936, and Alexander McCurdy, choirmaster, and Richard Purvis, organist, from 1937 to the present time.

One of the recent developments in the organization of the choir at St. James' Church reflects the close connection that this parish has long held with the Episcopal Academy. These two institutions were originally close neighbors in central Philadelphia, and though both have moved from their original district, the connection has never ceased to exist. Ernest White, the organist at St. James', was also in charge of the music at Episcopal Academy. Alexander McCurdy, the present choirmaster, who is also director of music at the Episcopal Academy,[2] announced in October, 1937,

[1] Cf. *supra*, p. 12.
[2] Alexander McCurdy has been organist at the Second Presbyterian Church since 1927 and succeeded Lynnwood Farnam as head of the Organ Department of the Curtis Institute of Music. His recent appointment to St. James' Church and Episcopal Academy have made Dr. McCurdy a leading

that twenty boys would be given scholarships at Episcopal Academy in exchange for their services as members of St. James' choir. This arrangement has been of advantage to the boys, the church, and the academy.

For about twenty-five years after 1901, St. James' Church supported a choir school. The outstanding choir school of Philadelphia has been that of St. Peter's Church, organized in 1834 by Bishop White, probably as a parish school for that church. St. Peter's has maintained its Parish Day School since 1836, the year of White's death, reorganizing it as a choir day school in 1903. This choir school has an enrollment of forty boys and a faculty of eight teachers. The headmaster is Harold Wells Gilbert, Mus.Bac., who is also organist of the church, and director of the Mendelssohn Club of Philadelphia. The school resembles the public schools in curriculum and activities, with the special advantage of small classes and general selective policies of private school organization. Its graduates are prepared to enter high school, and usually have achieved more than average success in such higher institutions of learning.[1]

Among less historic churches it is difficult to select only a few from Philadelphia's hundreds of organizations that have had brief or even extended careers as important musical centers. The article by Charles N. Boyd, *Choir Development Since 1878*, has already been quoted as a source of information concerning Philadelphia churches and choir leaders whose fame transcended the limits of the vicinity of that city.[2] Mr. Boyd mentions the musical prominence of Samuel Herrman, Dr. J. McE. Ward, who has recently completed his fiftieth year as organist of St. Mark's Lutheran Church; the late Frederick Maxson, who for twenty-five years was organist at the First Baptist Church; Henry S. Fry, organist at

---

figure in Music in Philadelphia of the present day. The musical services at the Second Presbyterian Church in particular have been consistently artistic examples of choral work. He has continued and enlarged the tradition of fine choral singing begun by Hugh Clarke and carried forward by H. G. Thunder, H. A. Matthews, and N. L. Norden at that most musical Presbyterian church.

[1] Information from *Saint Peter's Choir School*, 1938-39, a booklet published by students at the school, and kindly provided by Mr. Gilbert.

[2] *Choir Development since* 1876, Boyd, from the proceedings of the Music Teachers National Association for 1928. Cf. also *supra*, pp. 145-146.

St. Clement's Church since 1911; Sears, Norden, Thunder, West, Matthews, Maitland and Addicks.

The beautiful Church of the Advocate and its music, particularly from 1901 to 1930, should be remembered in any account of Philadelphia music, as should also the ritualistic services at the Church of the Savior in West Philadelphia which continues to maintain an ambitious musical program. Afternoon services that were actually choral recitals at the Church of St. Luke and the Epiphany were notable achievements under the direction of Franklin W. Robinson (1904-1917) and H. Alexander Matthews (1917-1937). The organists of Calvary Presbyterian Church include a long series of names well known in Philadelphia music. From 1852 the directors of music at that church have been: J. C. B. Standbridge, who installed the first organ there; William H. Boner; Massah Warner in the 1880's; William H. Squires in the closing years of the century; Selden Miller from about 1900 to 1907; David E. Crozier, one of the earliest local enthusiasts for Bach's choral works, 1907-1925; and Robert A. Gerson, 1926 to 1928, in which year the Calvary and First Presbyterian Churches merged to form the present First Church in the building of Calvary Church. The writer counts it a high honor to be included in a list of such church musicians, and to play upon the organ which still contains many of the original Standbridge pipes. The organ at the First Presbyterian Church was rebuilt by Haskell in about 1900, and again by the Casavant Organ Company in 1926. The later rebuilding amounted to an almost complete renewal of this instrument. The new Casavant organ features a floating string and tuba section of great power, and a modern console of the usual four divisions.

III

When we consider the organs so intimately associated with all of the church music described above, many Philadelphia instruments should be discussed. The main organ from a historical viewpoint is that in St. Luke's Church, Germantown. This fine instrument is the fifth organ to be used at St. Luke's,[1] and was installed

---

[1] Previous instruments of very slight importance are recorded in *The History of St. Luke's Church*, R. K. Yerkes, as: an organ lent by Mr. Armat 1817, a new organ costing $425 in 1819, a third organ in 1841, and another in 1876

in 1894. Carlton C. Michell, who built the organ with specifications and other advice from George Alexander A. West, the organist of St. Luke's, introduced many features which have been copied by leading American organ builders.[1] The organ introduced heavy pressure reeds, harmonic reeds, new string timbres, and heavy swell shutters, all of which have since been included in most large organs of this country.

G. A. A. West, the organist who was largely responsible for this early fine instrument, has directed the music at St. Luke's Church since 1890. West was brought to the United States for this Philadelphia post at the recommendation of John Stainer, Frederick Bridge and Herbert Oakeley. For twelve years he was dean of the Pennsylvania Chapter of the American Guild of Organists, and for some time had charge of the music at Princeton University. Walter Henry Hall, his predecessor at the Germantown church, was imported from England in a somewhat similar fashion. B. Frank Walters, who introduced the boy choir in this historic parish, was organist there from 1868 to 1884. Walters was a thorough musician and one of the first Philadelphians to present a consistent program of church music of the Anglican type.[2]

St. Luke's still possesses the first great organ in Philadelphia. The Wanamaker organ is noted for quite different reasons. Since 1903 this instrument has been declared to be the world's largest organ.[3]

Some day there will be built a larger organ than that in the Wanamaker Store in Philadelphia. But it is hard to imagine any instrument retaining that title for thirty-six years. The St. Louis Fair organ of 1903 was declared to be the largest ever built. It was purchased by John Wanamaker for the Grand Court of his new store in 1909. The Wanamaker method of keeping the organ

---

[1] Yerkes, *Op. cit.*, pp. 113-114.

[2] Walters' daughter, Esther Palliser, was a favorite soprano in Philadelphia from 1885 to 1895, and later achieved international fame through a series of appearances in Europe.

[3] Information concerning the history of Philadelphia's most widely known organ—that of the Wanamaker Store—was kindly furnished by Mr. George W. Till, who rebuilt the organ for John Wanamaker in 1909, and headed the Wanamaker Organ Shop from 1905 to 1938. Full accounts of this instrument, and Mr. Till, are contained in *The Diapason* for October 1935 and March 1938, and the *Music World*, January 1931.

the world's largest has been very simple. Additions are made to it from time to time, and thus no other instrument disputes its mammoth supremacy. These enlargements have not been made with the purpose of outdistancing rival organs. When first installed in Wanamaker's this St. Louis organ was not found powerful enough to be effective in the court and its many large galleries. Revoicing and higher wind pressures were tried, and later the number of stops was increased from 141 to 232. The organ building department is a product of this and subsequent enlargements in the Philadelphia Wanamaker organ. This organ shop built the organ for the New York Wanamaker store in 1920. Further additions were then made to the Philadelphia instrument, bringing its total of pipes to 29,000.

The new console for this monster organ was the first six manual console ever used. More novel features of permanent importance were included in the console of this organ than in any other. When we realize that it was built between 1920 and 1925 it is remarkable that it possesses such features as adjustable tremolos, thumb operated expression pedal duplication, pedal divider,[1] and varied colors in the tilting stop tablets. The string division of twelve stops was designed by George A. Audsley. A newer string section has been added containing 107 ranks of pipes on fifteen and twenty-two inch wind pressure. The piano stop throws an actual piano mechanism into operation, a feature that has been copied elsewhere, but was put in at Wanamaker's in 1910.

Rodman Wanamaker was the patron saint of music at the stores founded by his father. He was no mean organist himself, having studied with Philadelphia's most celebrated organ teacher, David Wood. The noted performers who have given recitals on the Wanamaker organ include Dupré, Boulanger, Bossi, Vièrne, Lanquetuit, Hollins, Germani, and Courboin, among European celebrities, and a longer list of the great organists of America, particularly those of Philadelphia and New York. Many of these men played concerted numbers with the Philadelphia Orchestra at Wanamaker's.

---

[1] This arrangement makes it possible for one effect to be played on the top half of the pedal keyboard, while another is used with the left foot. Solo and accompaniment are thus possible on the pedal keyboard alone.

The music at the Wanamaker store was of such pioneering and historical significance that a brief account of the less stupendous predecessors of the present musical equipment is in order. An orchestrion only slightly less famous than that at the Centennial was in the Wanamaker store from about 1880 to 1906. The removal of this instrument was one of the first duties of George W. Till, who recently retired after superintending for more than thirty years the erection and repair of the organs in the Wanamaker stores.[1] Shortly before the removal of the orchestrion John Wanamaker had installed an organ built by Lew Harrison of Bloomfield, N. J., 1903. Frank Taft, who had been responsible for getting Wanamaker to buy the organ, played the first series of recitals on it. Taft was the American agent for the Casson Organ [2] and the first man to play organ recitals in a department store. In the years between 1903 and 1909 there were two Benig organs installed by Wanamaker in Philadelphia and New York, and a four manual Austin for Egyptian Hall in the former store. Alexander Russell became concert director in these years. Mary Vogt, who is still the organist at the Wanamaker store in Philadelphia, played her first concerts at that store in the same period. George Till came to Wanamaker's in 1905. These three, Russell, Vogt, and Till, are the musicians who have developed the ideas of John and Rodman Wanamaker, and have made the organ programs at the Philadelphia store both historically and artistically outstanding.

The present famous organ is played hourly during the business day by Miss Vogt and Alma Wilson. Other Wanamaker musical organizations include three bands, one for boys, one for girls, and a third for colored employees; and a bagpipe ensemble. The Rodman Wanamaker collection of string instruments, said to be the most complete in the world, was played in a series of concerts under the direction of Thaddeus Rich.

Before returning to the church organ, let us consider two other large organs in non-ecclesiastical buildings. The University of

---

[1] The orchestrion continues to perform its hearty strains from a pier at Longport, where Till supervised its installation.

[2] Called a "Hymnolia." This instrument had melody chest effects and bass sixteen foot duplication, all played from a single keyboard. In other words, the top tone could be mechanically emphasized, and the bottom one doubled in a lower octave.

Pennsylvania possesses the city's second largest organ in its Irvine Auditorium. The Sesqui-Centennial bought a large four manual organ from the Austin Company for its main auditorium. This instrument was later given to the University as a memorial to Cyrus H. K. Curtis. Mr. Curtis, a multi-millionaire publisher, was an ardent lover of music and a generous patron of all musical interests. The Curtis Institute of Music was named in his honor by Mrs. Bok, the former Mary Louise Curtis. The new organ at Christ Church is the large instrument from the Curtis residence, moved and rebuilt in 1935 for the use of that historic parish. The Curtis organ at the University is a third musical memorial to the late C. H. K. Curtis. Recitals have been given frequently on the organ in Irvine Auditorium. Some seasons have seen series of organ recitals given every Sunday afternoon on this large instrument. Faculty concerts often include numbers on the organ, or consist of organ recitals played as a rule by Dr. Morrison C. Boyd, the organist of the University. Since 1936 the auditorium has been used for many Federal Symphony concerts on Sunday afternoons, but the faculty concerts and organ recitals have also been given down to the present season. The Curtis organ at the University of Pennsylvania is noted for its size and power,[1] together with a modern console and a large number of beautifully voiced solo stops.

The organ at the Convention Hall is Philadelphia's largest example of an instrument with two complete consoles. One is constructed in the conventional church organ fashion, with stop knobs and a separation into the usual great, swell, choir, and solo divisions. The second contains a theatrical assortment of stop tablets, with an increased use of the unit system of duplication of stops. This theatre console contains several extra stops for sound effects usually found on such instruments, but hardly practical in this hall. Very little use has been made of the sleigh bell stop, or the baby cry either, up to this time. The unit system, when applied as completely as on the theatre console of the Convention Hall organ, has a tendency to make the four manuals sound very much alike. It becomes the problem of the organist to do all of the selecting of

---

[1] 180 speaking stops and 30 couplers, 23 general pistons, and many other mechanical accessories.

his sound effects, since the builder has not suggested by his attachment of a particular stop to a definite keyboard, that the conventional place to find it is the only one available. The organ at the Baptist Temple is one of Philadelphia's oldest large organs constructed on this unit principle, and presents a tremendous number of choices to the organist in a similar manner, but the modern application in the Convention Hall is far more successful. The expression pedals of the Convention Hall Organ make an unusually large dynamic range possible. Almost any stop can be loud or soft according to the finely shaded positions of very thick "swell shutters."

If we consider next the organ at Girard College we shall have returned half way to the church, for that instrument is Philadelphia's finest of the ecclesiastical variety, although its use is more as a school and recital organ. The new chapel at Girard College houses their famous Skinner organ, installed in 1935. Harry C. Banks has been mentioned as organist and teacher of piano at Girard College,[1] a position to which he devotes nearly his entire time. The two Austin organs and this recent Skinner instrument were all installed with the assistance of Dr. Banks' large fund of information concerning the needs of Girard College and modern organ specifications. The specification for the chapel organ is given, since at least one such list of stops belongs in any account of organ construction. Readers familiar with organ building will be struck by the small number of "borrowed stops," which are all acknowledged in the following list.

GREAT ORGAN

32′ Violone	8′ Erzahler Celeste	Harmonics 4 ranks
16′ Open Diapason	(enclosed)	16′ Trumpet
8′ First Diapason	8′ 'Cello (enclosed)	8′ Tromba
8′ Second Diapason	5 ⅓′ Quinte	4′ Clarion
8′ Third Diapason	4′ Octave	8′ Trumpet (enclosed)
(enclosed)	4′ Principal	Solo Reeds to Great
8′ Principal Flute	2⅔′ Twelfth	8′ Harp (choir)
8′ Stopped Diapason	2′ Fifteenth	4′ Celesta (choir)
(enclosed)	Chorus Mixture	Chimes (solo)
8′ Erzahler (enclosed)	5 ranks	

---

[1] Cf. *supra*, p. 285, in account of Girard College.

SWELL ORGAN

16' Bourdon	4' Octave	8' Cornopean
8' Open Diapason	4' Flute Triangulaire	8' French Trumpet
8' Geigen Diapason	2⅔' Nazard	8' Oboe d'amore
8' Gedeckt	2' Flautino	8' Vox Humana
8' Salicional	Chorus Mixture	4' Clarion
8' Voix Celeste	5 ranks	8' Harp (choir)
8' Viol d'orchestre	Cornet Mixture	4' Celesta (choir)
8' Viol Celeste	4 ranks	Chimes (solo)
8' Flauto Dolce	16' Posaune	Tremolo
8' Flute Celeste		

CHOIR ORGAN

16' Dulciana	4' Octave Dulciana	16' Bassoon
8' Geigen Diapason	4' Flute d'amore	8' Clarinet
8' Spitz Flute	2⅔' Twelfth Dulciana	8' Orchestral Oboe
8' Concert Flute	2' Fifteenth Dulciana	8' Harp ⎫
8' Viol d'orchestre	2' Piccolo	4' Celesta ⎬ 61 bars
8' Viol Celeste	Carillon Mixture	Chimes (solo)
8' Dulciana	3 ranks	Tremolo
8' Unda Maris		

SOLO ORGAN

8' Flauto Mirabilis	16' Contra Tuba	8' English Horn
8' Gamba	8' Harmonic Tuba	16' Corno di Bassetto
8' Gamba Celeste	4' Clarion	8' Corno di Bassetto
4' Flute	8' Tuba Mirabilis	Chimes (25 notes)
Grand Fourniture	8' French Horn	Tremolo
7 ranks		

ECHO ORGAN

8' Diapason	8' Dulcet	8' Vox Humana
8' Waldflute	4' Flute Triangulaire	Tremolo
8' Echo Gamba		

PEDAL ORGAN—Augmented

32' Resultant	16' Dulciana (choir)	Mixture 5 ranks
32' Open Diapason	16' Bourdon	32' Bombarde
32' Violone	16' Echo Lieblich	32' Fagotto
16' Diapason	(swell)	16' Bassoon (choir)
16' Contra Basse	8' Octave Diapason	16' Fagotto
(Violone)	8' Gedeckt	16' Trombone
16' Metal Diapason	8' Principal	8' Tromba
(great)	8' Still Gedeckt	Chimes (solo)
	(swell)	
	4' Flute	32 Couplers

The tuba mirabilis is on twenty-five inch wind pressure. A pedal divide, described as a new feature in the account of the Wanamaker organ, is also available on the organ at Girard College.

Other school organs that should be at least mentioned are possessed by Drexel Institute, the Franklin, Northeast, West Philadelphia, and Frankford High Schools, the Jay Cooke Junior High School, Mitten Hall of Temple University, and the Overbrook School for the Blind.[1] The three organs available for study purposes at the Central Young Men's Christian Association are noteworthy features of that institution's school of music.

An outstanding new organ is that installed at St. Mark's Church in 1937. This congregation seems to have been the first in Philadelphia to introduce a choir of boys and men, James W. Pearce organized this male choir in 1867 and directed its music until 1874. The activities of Kendrick and Minton Pyne have been recorded in the account of the late 19th century.[2] The organists since Pyne have been F. Averay Jones, 1905-1915; Lewis A. Wadlow, 1915-1929, and H. William Hawke, the present incumbent. The new organ embodies Mr. Hawke's ideals for an instrument that would be equally excellent for accompaniment and recital use. A few ranks of pipes from previous organs [3] were incorporated into the 1937 instrument of eighty-nine stops. The use of low wind pressures for most of the stops reflects a very new tendency in organ construction. Perhaps we should say that it resembles the newer music of the Catholic Church in being a recent restoration of a very old tendency. The Positif section of St. Mark's organ consists of ten stops on two and a half inch wind pressure. This positif organ is unenclosed, and is the most distinctive feature of the organ. The specification for this organ was made by G. Donald Harrison, its construction is the work of the Aeolian Skinner Company.[4]

---

[1] The Moller organ installed in April 1939 at the Overbrook Institution is Philadelphia's newest large organ.

[2] Cf. *supra* p. 145.

[3] A Roosevelt organ was installed in the 1880's, an Austin of 55 stops, voiced by Carlton Michell, in 1902, and a west end organ was installed by Midmer-Losh under the direction of Emerson Richards.

[4] The *American Organist* of October 1937 contains a full account of St. Mark's organ, with complete specification, pp. 335-339.

H. William Hawke was born in Ontario, Canada, and is a graduate of the Toronto Conservatory. In addition to the choir at St. Mark's, Mr. Hawke directs the Minton Pyne Singers, a male chorus made up of former choir boys of the church. He is an expert in matters pertaining to plainsong and the liturgical service of the Anglo-Catholic tradition.

The Swedenborgian Church of the New Jerusalem possessed the earliest Philadelphia organ with adjustable combination pistons, a Roosevelt instrument built in 1882, while their present Austin organ, installed in 1925, is this city's first church organ to possess double touch combination pistons. A light touch of the piston sets stops on the keyboard to which it applies, while a harder push produces these manual stops and a suitable selection of pedal stops.

In an earlier chapter, a program of an all-Bach recital played by David Wood at the Swedenborgian Church was quoted in full.[1] The present organist, Rollo Maitland, Mus.Doc., is carrying on the Bach tradition, begun in Philadelphia by his teacher D. Wood, as organist at the Swedenborgian Church. His annual series of Bach recitals have been given on the organ described above, every year since 1929.

> Rollo Maitland, Mus. Doc., F.A.G.O., was born near Williamsport, Pa., in 1884. He came to Philadelphia for schooling in 1897. His musical studies have been done under Wood, piano, theory, organ; Henry Hahn, violin; D. Hendrik Ezerman, piano; and Frederick W. Schlieder, composition. Dr. Maitland has given recitals in England and Switzerland, and on literally hundreds of organs in the United States. He has been an organist in Philadelphia since 1901, and since 1920 has held that position at the Swedenborgian Church of the New Jerusalem. The departments of organ, theory, and orchestration at the Philadelphia Musical Academy are headed by Maitland, who is the composer of many vocal and instrumental works. His daughter, S. Marguerite Maitland, is a gifted organist and composer, and holds the artist diploma from the Philadelphia Musical Academy.

The large Austin organ in the First Presbyterian Church in Germantown, a smaller but more effective Kimball instrument in

---

[1] Cf. *supra,* p. 108.

the Second Baptist Church of Germantown, and a powerful and very modern Welte organ at the Bryn Mawr Presbyterian Church are among the other notable organs in Philadelphia churches.

IV

Organ building in Philadelphia is closely related to both church music and to the organs themselves. Out of a vast number of local builders, let us pick a few who were more important than their fellows. John C. B. Standbridge seems to have been the earliest Philadelphia builder who achieved any particular fame in that field. He was the organist at Christ Church when the Erben instrument was installed in 1838. Standbridge submitted estimates, as one of the two local builders, on the organ to be installed in the First Presbyterian Church in 1847. The other Philadelphia builder to submit a bid was Henry Corrie. Standbridge was not successful in securing the contract of 1847, but was engaged to build the organ for Calvary Presbyterian Church in 1852 and became the first organist there as well. In 1856 he built an organ for the First Moravian Church. This instrument has been described in a previous chapter.[1] The organ recently removed from the chancel of the church of St. Luke and the Epiphany was originally built by Standbridge. It had been used at the Church of the Epiphany at Fifteenth and Chestnut, rebuilt in about 1885, moved to temporary quarters on Chestnut near Nineteenth Street, and finally set up in the chancel of the church on Thirteenth Street below Spruce when St. Luke and the Epiphany formed a combined parish at that location. The organ at Christ Reformed Church on Green Street was installed by Standbridge and rebuilt by Haskell. This same builder installed organs in St. John's and SS. Peter and Paul Churches. George W. Till, Philadelphia's leading authority on organ building, pronounces J. C. B. Standbridge to have been the outstanding builder of his time. His construction and voicing of wood pipes was considered particularly fine.

---

[1] Cf. *supra*, p. 94.

In the organ installed about 1865 at the Synagogue Rodeph Shalom both Standbridge and Knauff had a share. Henry Knauff and Sons were a second important concern in the middle nineteenth century. Knauff built the first organ for St. Mark's Lutheran Church in 1859. This instrument had three manuals and fifty-eight stops, a large number for that time. Knauff was organist at St. Mark's for forty years, and his successor, Dr. Ward, has been mentioned above as having been their organist for over fifty. These two long tenures cover the entire history of almost one hundred years in this church. J. McE. Ward, M.D., follows Standbridge and Knauff in his great interest in organ construction. John C. B. Standbridge was also a medical doctor whose hobby, music, became a main interest in his life. He was a graduate of the University of Pennsylvania school of medicine. Both Dr. Ward and Dr. Standbridge held the position of organist at Christ Church early in their musical careers. Standbridge went further than Dr. Ward with his organ building, eventually giving up his medical activities, and a thriving drug store, to concentrate on organ construction. The firm which he established at Twenty-second and Locust Streets in 1845 was continued by his sons George T. and Henry Key Standbridge until about 1890.

The firm of Wm. Haskell was more active, but less successful artistically, than either Knauff or Standbridge. As builder of several Philadelphia organs still in use and rebuilder of an even larger number, Haskell was an important figure in local organ construction. William Haskell was the foreman in the Philadelphia factory of the Roosevelt Organ Company for some years prior to 1896. In that year he founded the Haskell Organ Company and began the many installations and remodellings by which he is well remembered today. An early Haskell organ is that in the Church of St. Jude and the Nativity. The large organs at St. Francis de Sales and the Chambers-Wylie Presbyterian Church are two of his finest instruments. The First Baptist Church, Calvary Episcopal Church in Germantown, and the North Baptist Church in Camden installed some of this firm's larger organs. The chancel pipes of the organ at Holy Trinity Church are Haskell's work. This same firm rebuilt the older gallery organ in that church. Among his many rebuilding accomplishments were those in the First Presbyterian

Church in Germantown, Calvary Presbyterian Church, First Moravian Church, and the Christ Reformed Church. Since the last three organs were originally built by J. C. B. Standbridge, it is not surprising that William Haskell learned a great deal about the voicing and construction of wood pipes through his rebuilding activities. His wood oboe and saxophone stops, used for the first time in the organ at Holy Trinity Church, were possibly based on Standbridge models, with his own improvements.

George W. Till, the most recent Philadelphia organ builder to win widespread fame, is Haskell's exact opposite in method and activity. Till is an inventor who works long and hard at one idea, Haskell was an adapter and improver who spread his efforts over a wider area. The organ at Wanamaker's has been described in such detail that nothing further need be said except that Till built it. A string organ of great beauty was constructed by Till for St. Mark's Episcopal Church in 1922. This ten stop division is the only important unit retained in the 1937 organ at that church.

Mr. Till was born in Philadelphia in 1866. He was employed in the Wanamaker store as a young man, but left that institution to learn the organ building trade in 1886. From that year until 1905 Till was employed by the Odell Organ Company in New York. One year of that period found G. W. Till back in Philadelphia with the Haskell Company (1900-1901). From 1905 to 1938 Till had charge of organ building and repairs for the Wanamaker Company.

The Diapason of August, 1925, credits George W. Till with the following list of important inventions in organ construction:

1. Selective mixtures (*i.e.*, adjustable mutation stops),
2. Coupling expression pedals,
3. Divisional coloring of stops,
4. Humidified wind supply,
5. Introduction of piano mechanism within the organ case, with an automatic sostenuto for all pedal keys,
6. Master tremolo and adjustable tremolo,
7. Simplification and general improvement of electric action. (*The Diapason* article dwells on this last at some length.)

V

Most of Philadelphia's church organs have not been mentioned in this account. The large number of local theatre organs, more costly than valuable, have also had to be omitted. Perhaps a few theatre organs might be noted in concluding this subject. Small organs were a widely advertised feature of certain hotels and amusement gardens from as early as 1780. Christopher Witt's residence organ of about 1710 was the earliest non-ecclesiastical organ in America. The city tavern announced organ music in their concerts before 1800. Raynor Taylor played there, and from 1814 to 1819 on the organ at Vauxhall Gardens. J. C. Taws is credited with being the builder of the first barrel organ made in America. The organ from the old concert hall at 1217 Chestnut Street was rebuilt and installed in St. Clement's Church in about 1870. This theatre organ, remodelled by Roosevelt, was declared to be the most adequate organ in Philadelphia before the building of the instrument at St. Luke's, Germantown, in 1894.[1] The Austin Company rebuilt St. Clement's organ in 1915.

An organ formerly used at the Exhibition Hall in Chicago was installed in the Academy of Music in 1882. The pipes for this instrument were laid horizontally beneath the stage at that time. Twenty-five years later the organ was placed against the back wall of the Academy, while after twenty-seven more years this old instrument was removed (1929). For two more years the parts were stored in the cellar, then the demands of insurance companies led to its being removed altogether. This instrument was of great power, although it possessed only about fifteen stops.

A great increase in the number of theatre organs took place between 1910 and 1925. Over one hundred of these instruments were placed in motion picture theatres in those years. The old Stanley Theatre organ was an early example of this instrument as a featured attraction at a cinema. The Chamber of Commerce report for 1917 states that three-fourths of the city's motion picture theatres had organs, and one-third of these had both organs and

---

[1] Geo. Alexander A. West so describes the old organ at St. Clement's.

orchestras.   The organists' salaries ranged from thirty-five to sixty dollars a week in these theatres.[1]

This same report states that the average salary of a church organist in Philadelphia's seven hundred churches was six hundred dollars, and the range of these salaries extended from fifty to three thousand dollars.   Choirs cost about as much as the organists' salaries in the larger churches in 1917.[2]   The field of theatre organ music has practically disappeared since 1925, and the figures for 1917 would exceed those of 1940 in the realm of church music also.   The future of church music promises to include increased activity in chorus conducting and a possible lessening of emphasis on organ solos and remarkable organ installations.   If a current tendency in that direction continues to be characteristic of our church music, the people will be the gainers since they will participate in sacred works instead of merely hearing them performed.

---

[1] Philadelphia Chamber of Commerce report, 1917, *The Commercial Value of Music to Philadelphia*, p. 14.
[2] *Ibid.*, p. 13.

CHAPTER FIFTEEN

PHILADELPHIA MUSIC PUBLISHERS

I

Music publishing in Philadelphia goes back to the days before the widespread use of printed music in America. The German groups were noted composers and copyists of hymn collections. Johannes Kelpius' collection of nineteen hymns (with tunes) was composed about 1700 at Germantown. It is Pennsylvania's earliest musical composition. Schwenkfelder collections had often as many as one thousand pages. The hymns were not printed in this country, however. The Schwenkfelders, having brought one hymn book with them from Silesia, proceeded to copy and compose hymns in monumental volumes. The sect settled a few miles north of Philadelphia in 1734. Their voluminous hymn collections were not actually published, but such copying as they did took the place of the absent music printing industry for many years. German hymn books were published and printed in and near Philadelphia as early as 1730. Conrad Beissel is said to have composed fully one thousand pieces of music, and printed over four hundred hymns. He published treatises on voice and harmony, and a collection of "Choral Songs." The last named collection was printed at Ephrata, Pennsylvania, in 1754. Beissel founded the sect of Sabbatarians in Pennsylvania. An extensive Sabbatarian hymn book was published by the Franklin Press in 1730. Christopher Saur published four editions of a Mennonite hymn collection in Germantown, Pennsylvania. The earliest of these was printed in 1742. An edition of this same collection (Basel, 1838) is still used by the Amish in Pennsylvania. The Saur firm is still in existence, with headquarters on Eighteenth Street below Race.

II

Sacred music was published in large quantities in the late colonial years. The collections of the German mystics have been noted as quite voluminous.[1]   Lyon's *Urania* is typical of the English colonists' sacred music publications.   The Massachusetts composers and editors had assembled the most imposing array of religious musical editions in early colonial times.[2]   From Revolutionary times until about 1800 the Philadelphia musicians and music publishers came to be recognized as the most important in the new world.[3]   The post-revolutionary period being one of increasing secular interests, many of the musicians busied themselves with dramatic and concert works.   This swing away from the early Philadelphia attitude against music in general, and secular music in particular, is the chief characteristic of the period of Philadelphia's leadership in music and music publishing (1780-1800).   In a sense the growth of a varied assortment of musical fields marks the beginning of music publishing as we know it today.   The Hermits of the Wissahickon, or the minister musicians of early New England, printed their own sacred compositions or those of their neighbors, as an adjunct to their church services.   The first music store in America was that of Michael Hillegas of Second Street, Philadelphia.[4]   In 1759 there is record of his music store, while the *Pennsylvania Gazette* of January 5, 1764, advertises his extensive stock of instruments, music, and music paper.   Shortly after this date Hillegas gave up the music business to devote more time to the care of his fortune.   We cannot be sure, but it is quite possible that the "fortune" was the first to be made from music in Philadelphia.   Hillegas later became the first Treasurer of the United States.

Thomas Dobson was the first important figure in Philadelphia music publishing.   He printed and sold music at 41 North Second Street from 1788 or earlier, until 1809.   Two of Reinagle's collections of songs, and the celebrated "Seven Songs for the Harpsi-

---

[1] Pp. 5-6.
[2] Reverend John Tufts edited one of the first books of sacred music to be published in America with English words, *A Very Plain and Easy Introduction to the Art of Singing Psalm Tunes,* Boston, 1715.   Reverend (Thomas Walter of Roxbury followed Tufts' lead with a collection in 1721; Josiah Flagg's collection was printed in 1764.   William Billings' large collection of 1770 contained many original tunes.
[3] William A. Fisher, *One Hundred and Fifty Years of Music Publishing in the United States,* p. 23.
[4] William A. Fisher, *op. cit.,* p. 23.

chord or Forte-piano" by Francis Hopkinson were printed by Dobson.

Moller and Capron formed the first actual *music* publishing firm in Philadelphia, earlier firms such as Bradford, Dobson, and Franklin having been general printers and stationers. John C. Moller was a German organist, who came to Philadelphia in 1790. Henri Capron was a French 'cellist and composer who had been active in Philadelphia concert life since 1785. The *Federal Gazette* of March, 1793, advertised that Moller and Capron of 163 N. Third Street wished subscribers for a monthly music magazine to contain, in six pages, all "the newest vocal and instrumental music." Only a few issues seem to have been printed.

Benjamin Carr's manysidedness is again brought to mind when we realize the size and importance of his music publishing. The "Musical Repository of B. Carr and Co." was opened in July, 1793, at 136 High Street. Some of the publications omit the "and Company," suggesting that shortly after Carr's removal to 122 High Street in November, 1793, he carried on the business by himself. At about 1800 the firm is known as Carr and Schetky. Carr seems to have retired from the publication field in 1800. His father, Joseph Carr, founded, in 1794, the Baltimore music publishing firm, which under Benjamin's brother, Thomas, was the leading music establishment in Baltimore well into the nineteenth century.[1] Among the many notable publications by the Philadelphia firm (Benjamin Carr), the following possess particular historical interest: the original edition of *Hail Columbia,* songs by Benjamin Carr, Raynor Taylor, Didbin, Hook, Shield, Storace, Dr. Arnold, Canzonets by Haydn, and a song by the "new composer, Mozart."

Several less important publishing firms were active in the closing decade of the eighteenth century. John Aitken, Robert Shaw, Matthew Carey, J. Edgar, and Enoch Storey were among the music dealers and publishers in the same period.

George Willig became the chief and successful rival to the Carr firms in the Philadelphia music publishing field. Founded in

[1] The publications by the various Carrs are too numerous to include, even in list form. Several are named in the index of this book. Joseph Carr published Hopkinson's *Ode from Ossian's Poems,* and the first edition of *The Star-Spangled Banner* "adpd and arrd" by his son and successor, Thomas Carr. Cf. *supra*, p. 55, for the Philadelphia activities of Thomas Carr.

1794, Willig's Musical Magazine soon became the largest and eventually the longest lived music firm in Philadelphia. The location of the Magazine, 163 North Third Street, was the same as that of Moller and Capron—the first music publishing firm in Philadelphia. The continuity of interest between Moller and Willig is not known, but there is no doubt that from Willig's opening in 1794 there is a definite connection all the way to the Theodore Presser Company of today (1940). The name of Willig was retained until 1856, at which time the business was absorbed by the large concern of Lee and Walker. The Oliver Ditson Company of Boston bought out Lee and Walker in 1875, setting up a Philadelphia branch, known as the J. E. Ditson Company.[1] When the Theodore Presser Company of Philadelphia bought out the Oliver Ditson Company of Boston in 1931, Presser's became the remote, but quite direct, business descendant of G. Willig—if not of Moller and Capron, America's first firm of music publishers.

Before leaving the eighteenth century, some definite statement to summarize the enormous increase in the publication of secular music should make clear the course which has been suggested at the beginning of the above account. Of four hundred and forty-three secular compositions listed by Sonneck,[2] four hundred and forty were published after 1780. Thus over ninety-nine per cent of the secular music of the century was published in its last twenty years.

III

The nineteenth century, viewed from the particular temporal point known as the present (1940), seems to divide itself into two contrasted sections. The earlier years may be said to hark back to the glorious days of Philadelphia's position as the nation's largest city. This leadership terminated soon after the year 1800, at which time the music published seems to have been imitating older styles and of rather low calibre. There was an unquestionable

---

[1] A later firm also known as Lee and Walker revived the name and publishing interests of the concern purchased by Ditson. This second Lee and Walker Company published and sold music in the late nineteenth century.
[2] *Early Secular American Music* by Oscar G. Sonneck.

decline in the musical worth of Philadelphia publications between 1800 and 1820. Most music printed in these years was frankly aimed at the musical taste of the largest discoverable group of potential customers. The great increase in commercial music publishing was contemporaneous with an equally crescent wave of secular music—as has been noted in the conclusion of the preceding section. Not many years were to elapse before Philadelphia's loss of Capital society, coupled with a general lowering of cultural standards throughout the nation, were reflected in the music of the day. William Treat Upton calls the numerous songs of the early decades of the nineteenth century cheap and tawdry.[1] The fondness for the English ballad as popularized during the closing years of the eighteenth century, was continued throughout the nineteenth, with considerable falling off as regards musical originality and sincerity. The new trends of Italian opera and German instrumental music had not been firmly enough established in this country (prior to 1830) for a music publisher to hope for financial success through any but popular and ballad types of music. Paradoxically enough, the one Philadelphia firm which never abandoned worthwhile instrumental publications is the only one which has any link to later periods in music history. This was the Musical Magazine of George Willig, which led a continuous existence until 1856. Willig published many of the popular ballads, but continued to print considerable worthwhile instrumental music.

George E. Blake is second only to George Willig in importance as a Philadelphia publisher in the first half of the nineteenth century. His editions and publications were especially popular in the early years of the century, although the firm had a long career at various locations in the city [2] until 1871.

Another establishment in Philadelphia music publishing of the period was that of John G. Klemm and Brother. Both Blakes and Klemms were instrument makers as well as music publishers and dealers. Beginning in 1818 at 1 North Fourth Street, the Klemm firm was active at various addresses until 1880. Publishers

---

[1] *The Art Song in America* (p. 29) by William T. Upton.

[2] Fisher, in *One Hundred and Fifty Years of Music Publishing in the United States*, p. 87, gives Blake's headquarters as 1 South Third Street, 1804-1814; 13 South Third Street, 1814-1840; and 25 South Fifth Street, 1840-1871.

and publishers' addresses become increasingly complicated and numerous after the year 1825. Partnerships were formed, or dissolved, at the slightest provocation. The connection of Francis A. North,[1] G. Andrée,[1] Charles W. A. Trumpler,[1] Augustus Fiot,[1] Leopold Meignen, John E. Gould,[1] James M. Beck,[1] and Dennis Lawton,[1] is completely explained—necessarily at some length—by William Arms Fisher.[2] They were all mid-century publishers of the 1800's and share the destiny of having been bought out by the Oliver Ditson Company, which was in turn purchased by the Theodore Presser Company of Philadelphia in 1931.

IV

The name of Theodore Presser is Philadelphia's strongest claim to fame in the realm of the music publishing field. Very probably *Presser* is the most important Philadelphia name in music today. His influence as founder of the Music Teachers' National Association (1876) is important throughout the United States. The vast contribution he made as originator and editor of *The Etude Music Magazine* is world wide. The gigantic music publishing house, which is the outcome of Presser's business, is also internationally famous. What is less widely known is the indirect, almost accidental manner in which Theodore Presser, the obscure and far-from-mercenary music teacher, drifted into the commercial end of his chosen profession. Born in 1848 in Pittsburgh, his first study was in that city, in which he had a position in Mellor's music store. Later (1872) he went to the New England Conservatory and (1878) to the Leipsic Conservatory. His early music teaching was done at Ohio Wesleyan, Xenia College (Ohio), and Hollins Institute (Virginia). His leadership in the group that organized the Music Teachers National Association has caused him to be considered the founder of that large group. *The Etude Music Magazine* was started to further the ends of the M.T.N.A. The *Etude* was first issued in Lynchburg, Virginia, in October, 1883. Less than a year later, June, 1884, Presser moved to Phila-

---

[1] See Index.
[2] In *One Hundred and Fifty Years of Music Publishing in the United States,* pp. 88-89.

delphia where the *Etude* has been published up to the present day. The music for the magazine was to be teaching material, both new and old, and its goal of a circulation of five thousand copies was set so that the sales would cover the expense of the printing, and Theodore Presser could return to his teaching activities. Thus the Presser publications consisted originally of material for the *Etude*, and were intended merely to assist the music teaching profession— and to be a self-supporting journal of the Music Teachers National Association. It is not difficult to understand how the financial success of this helpful periodical suggested that separate publications of standard as well as new music would add to the resources of the publishing house. Although Presser's soon became a very large firm with the usual varied output of music and musical merchandise, the prime position of the *Etude* has never been challenged by any of the secondary interests which have grown so amazingly in the past fifty years. This is the more remarkable when we realize that the Presser Company is now the largest music firm in the world.

Mr. Presser has been reputed to have been a sharp business man and to have owed his tremendous success to his commercial acumen. His immediate associates declare that this report is vastly untrue. While the Presser Company has absorbed the music publishers in and near Philadelphia in a very comprehensive manner, the early ideal of true helpfulness to the relatively obscure is responsible for its large success. That the obscure are also the most numerous is not a difficult observation to make; nor could it have been hard to notice this fact in the late nineteenth century. The long credit and low prices of the Presser publications, particularly the *Etude*, were large factors in the success of this firm. Viewed from the angle of the town and village music teacher and pupil, these policies were truly helpful, since the music was actually made available to millions who could not have afforded to visit city stores, or to pay high prices to secure it. From the standpoint of many rival publishing houses, Presser's policies were ahead of their time as regards advertising, large scale production, low prices, and easy terms.

The following constitute the main facts in the Presser publishing and music dealing history. Theodore Presser came to Philadelphia in June, 1884, and opened an office at 1004 Walnut Street. The first years of the *Etude* and of the music publishing enterprise were an up-hill fight, but by 1886 it was possible to move to 1704 Chestnut Street and include a retail store in the business. Larger quarters were taken at 1708 Chestnut Street in 1893, and in 1904 the present address of 1712-1714 Chestnut Street was occupied. Theodore Presser died in 1925, but his business was so organized that it has continued and increased under the able management of his successors. The John Church Company of Cincinnati was purchased in 1930, and the Oliver Ditson Company of Boston was bought in 1931. It is as a combination of these three firms that the Presser Company has changed from one of this country's most successful music publishing houses to the world's largest music publishing firm.

The use to which the immense profits of Presser publications are put demands considerable mention. The distribution of large sums of money to musicians throughout the United States [1] from a foundation in this city, derived from the profits of a local enterprise, constitutes an important item in the field of Music in Philadelphia. The Presser Foundation was organized in 1916. Mr Presser sought to call this new project "A Foundation for the Advancement of Music," and it was only after much argument that he realized the proposed foundation would inevitably become known as the Presser Foundation.[2]

Theodore Presser's philanthropic ideas had begun to take definite form ever since the day his *Etude* became established and successful. A trip to Milan included a visit to the Casa di Riposo per Musicisti, the celebrated home for aged musicians, founded by Verdi. The endowment of a similar institution in America suggested itself to him before, or during, this visit to Milan. There is record of his advocating such a home at the meeting of the Music Teachers National Association in 1897. Ten years later Mr. Presser founded the Presser Home for Retired Music Teachers, in Philadelphia. This home soon moved to Germantown, a Philadelphia suburb, where it was housed in a fine new building, adjoin-

---

[1] And to a number of European musicians since the World War.
[2] *The Presser Foundation,* a pamphlet published by the Presser Company in 1931 at Philadelphia, p. 7.

ing the Presser residence. Five acres are devoted to the building
and its grounds. Nearly two hundred aged musicians have occupied this unusual institution. They have come from most of the
United States and from Canadian provinces.

The beginnings of the Presser Home in Philadelphia and Germantown will be seen to have antedated the organization of the
Presser Foundation by almost ten years. In fact, the later Foundation was in actuality a systematic reorganization of the Home
and Mr. Presser's many and varied other philanthropies into a
permanent and efficient foundation that would continue and
broaden the beneficent work which Theodore Presser had begun.
When we compare the date of the Presser Foundation's beginning
(1916), with its founder's early interest in the building of a Musicians' Home (1897 or earlier), the Foundation might seem quite
a new venture. It should be remembered in this connection, however, that the Presser Foundation is the oldest great musical foundation in America. The much older Musical Fund Society had a
similarly philanthropic purpose, but its relief of needy musicians
has had to be administered on a smaller scale, as will be seen from
the following summary of the activities of the Presser Foundation.

There are four main divisions of the Presser Foundation. The
oldest branch, which has been shown above to be older than the
Foundation itself, is the Presser Home for Retired Music Teachers.

A second branch is the Department of Scholarships. Each
scholarship amounts to two hundred and fifty dollars. The college selects its own student to receive assistance from the Presser
fund. Of course, only colleges and universities maintaining adequate music schools are considered in distributing these scholarships. There is also the wise stipulation that each scholarship student take a given proportion of academic work in addition to the
music studied. More than five thousand students in over two hundred colleges have been the recipients of scholarships from this
department of the Presser Foundation. The same department
has materially assisted worthy schools of music, among them the
American School of Music at Fontainebleau, the Edward Mac-
Dowell Association at Peterboro, New Hampshire, and summer
Band and Orchestra Camps.

The third branch of the Presser Foundation, in the order of organization, is the Department of Relief. Occasional and emergency spending in the interest of needy musicians is the main purpose of this division of Presser philanthropy. The Department of Relief has granted regular stipends to some musicians not found eligible for admission to the Presser Home.[1]

The fourth branch of the Presser Foundation is the ambitiously conceived Department of Music Buildings at Colleges. A substantial sum is donated by the foundation which is supplemented by the institution so favored. Eight large and beautifully planned Presser Halls have been erected in nearly as many states by this department of the Foundation. Over fifty additional applications for buildings so subsidized are awaiting consideration by the trustees of the College Building Department of the Presser Foundation.

Each of the departments of the Presser Foundation has a board of directors particularly qualified to administer the funds set aside for its special sphere. Space does not permit their being listed here,[2] but all are men eminent in Philadelphia affairs.

Mr. Presser, having completed the organization of the Foundation in 1916, retired from its presidency in 1918. He was succeded by James Francis Cooke, who for over twenty years has headed the Presser Foundation. Dr. Cooke came to the Presser Company as editor of the *Etude* in 1907, a position which he still holds.

The branches of the Presser Foundation, though springing from almost random beginnings so far as the order and relative importance of each is concerned, all bear a close relation to Theodore Presser's initial altruistic plans. Mr. Presser wished to see the *Etude* firmly established, and then return to his music teaching. When he found that the *Etude* was becoming amazingly successful, instead of merely a self-supporting music teachers' journal, he greatly extended the horizon of his aims. The fortune hoped for, and realized, through the magazine and the other publishing

---

[1] A musician between sixty-five and seventy-five years of age, who has taught music for at least twenty-five years and is in normal health, may be admitted to the Presser Home upon payment of four hundred dollars.

[2] The trustees of each branch are named in *The Presser Foundation*, pp. 9-24,

that grew around it was marked for benevolent purposes from its inception.   The present and future good which this endowment will accomplish is nearly impossible to estimate.   The spread of the *Etude* into all countries where music is taught in our staff notation is an achieved fact.   But the future of philanthropic aid to study, whether it be of music or any of the less ancient branches of learning, and the possibilities for good of such generous foundations as that under discussion, cannot be fully realized at this time.

There were many nineteenth century publishers in Philadelphia in addition to the twelve firms already discussed in this chapter.   Some additional names have been mentioned in the index.   So far as available material is concerned, the music publishers in the following list were not sufficiently important for more than a list of their names and addresses to be given.

> T. C. Andrews—Spring Garden St.
> A. Bacon and Co.—30 S. 4th St. (Bacon and Hart, Bacon and Weygant)
> Barclay and Culver—196 Chestnut St.
> James Couenhoven—162 Chestnut St.
> W. H. Coulston—147 N. 8th St.
> J. Edgar—68 S. 4th St.
> E. Ferrett—68 S. 4th St.
> R. H. Hobson—Chestnut St.
> Loud—174 Chestnut St.
> John Marsh—1102 Chestnut St.
> R. Meyer—722 Arch St.
> J. G. Osbourne—112 S. 3rd St., and 30 S. 4th St.
> F. Perring—198 Chestnut St.
> Wm. H. Shuster (also Winner and Shuster)—97 N. 8th St.
> J. C. Smith (also Smith and Rodden)—184 Chestnut St.
> W. R. Smith—135 N. 8th St.
> C. Taws—61 S. 3rd St.
> Septimus Winner (at seven addresses).
> R. Wittig—148 Arch St.[1]

---

[1] To complete the list of publishers in nineteenth century Philadelphia, many names would have to be added.   Among them are: Beckel, Bruce and Bisbee, Chalk, Duffy, Escher, Hupfeld, Kretschmar and Nunns, Mayer, L. Meyer, Munzinger, Schmitz, W. F. Shaw, Stayman, Swisher, Vogt, Warden, and J. Winner.

It is impossible to give a complete list of these firms, many of which must have led a precarious and transitory existence. The lengthy lists are given for the sake of showing how many publishing houses existed. The large companies (Blake, Willig, Andrée, Fiot, Lee and Walker, Klemm, and Presser), the firms of less importance (Boner, Gould, Beck and Lawton, North, Winner and Shuster), and the many small publishing houses existed in a complicated and ever changing web of commercial rivalry.

V

A contrast to this complex music publishing industry will be immediately observed as we review the publishers of today. The Theodore Presser Company has grown to such dimensions, both in Philadelphia and beyond, that a real unity of effort in the city's music publishing is suggested. There are, however, quite a few concerns that continue to lead an independent and successful existence. Among them the Cooperative Music Company at Sixteenth and Columbia Avenue is probably the most important. This firm is the successor to the Louis C. Gotthold Co. and the J. H. Faunce Co. In 1914 the Cooperative Music Company bought out the old firm of George Willig and Company of Baltimore.

Another present day publisher of music is C. Harold Lowden. Mr. Lowden had organized and directed the business of the Heidelberg Press since 1912, which firm was renamed C. Harold Lowden, Inc., in 1925. The Lowden Company has had headquarters at 514 Haddon Avenue, Camden, for the past few years.

An old firm still active is the Hall-Mack Company. Founded in 1895 by J. Lincoln Hall, the partnership of Hall and Irvin H. Mack was formed in the same year. In 1909 Hall-Mack absorbed the Adam Geibel publishing firm, while in 1936 this combined business united with the Rodeheaver Company of Chicago. Rodeheaver Hall-Mack has offices in Philadelphia and Chicago, and agencies in England, Australia, and New Zealand. Their concern is an important one in the publishing of Sunday School music. They have also a considerable catalogue of church and school music. Several Sunday School hymnals published by Hall-Mack have been printed and sold by the hundreds of thousands, one passing the half million mark. These figures are in order, since Hall-Mack has always emphasized practicality—and thus quantity,—the musicianship represented being always adequate while not strikingly original.

The opposite aim is stressed in publications of the Elkan-Vogel Company. This young but active firm was founded in 1926. In 1929 and 1930 Elkan-Vogel became exclusive American agents for Durand and Company, and seven other French publishers. The music thus handled includes much that is unusual both in its musical originality and in the novel instrumental combinations employed. It would be difficult for Elkan-Vogel's own publications to match the fine works imported by the firm; but they are rapidly building up a catalogue of new and original music.

The busy music publishing and printing work of the concern of J. W. Pepper and Son should not be omitted in an account of Philadelphia music publishers. Pepper's special field lies in music for instrumental groups.

Although so many publishers have been mentioned, this account has attempted to consider publishing houses only, and not to discuss agencies whose names might appear on printed editions. Thus, the J. E. Ditson Company has scarcely been mentioned, for it existed only as an agency of the Boston Ditson firm. These agencies are more numerous today than actual publishers in Philadelphia, so few firms being active as publishers owing to Presser's large share in the city's music publishing at this time.[1]

The condition of the music publishing industry in Philadelphia in the current period is a good one. While the Theodore Presser Company is outstanding in commercial music, it does not monopolize the field. On the other hand, the absence of a large number of constantly competing and frequently changing music publishers makes for a more permanent and successful organization of this phase of Music in Philadelphia.

---

[1] Philadelphia's musical agencies, past and present, have provided a large variety of music. At opposite artistic extremes lie the American agency in Germantown for Curwen of London, and the many popular song agencies for New York firms.

CHAPTER SIXTEEN

ADDITIONAL MUSICAL ORGANIZATIONS AND ACTIVITIES

I

MANUSCRIPT MUSIC SOCIETY

The final chapter consists of short accounts of several unrelated phases and societies in twentieth century Music in Philadelphia.

The Manuscript Music Society was founded by William W. Gilchrist in 1892. Its activities followed the obvious implication of its title. Concerts of new compositions by local composers were given in rooms and halls in Philadelphia. Between 1892 and 1915 there were usually two such concerts a year. After that year their programs were less frequent, until in 1936 this society ceased to be active, although it is still in existence. The 1915 date may be remembered as the year before Dr. Gilchrist's death, while Philip Goepp, the second moving spirit among the members, died in 1936. Nicholas Douty and Frederick Hahn are among present musicians who were active and interested in the Manuscript Music Society. David D. Wood and Camille Zeckwer were also prominent men in this club.

The usual places for their rehearsals and concerts were the Orpheus Club rooms, the Philadelphia Musical Academy, and the Church of the New Jerusalem, the last named being used for sacred programs. Most of the music played by the members consisted of vocal and instrumental works for soloists or small groups. A good idea of the type of music presented may be gained from the following program of May 16, 1894:

1. Quartet in D, for Piano, Violin, Viola and 'Cello........*H. A. Clarke*
   (Messrs. Jarvis, Stoll, [Richard] Schmidt, and Hennig)
2. Songs, "Wandering Spirits" }
   "Shade and Shine" } ....*Albert W. Borst*

3. Liebeslied, for Piano and 'Cello ....*M. Cross*
        (Messrs. Cross and Hennig)
    Romanza ed Arpeggio, for Viola and Piano ....*M. Cross*
        (Messrs. Schmidt and Cross)
4. Songs, "Crossing the Bar" ⎫ ....*Massah Warner*
        "May Song"   ⎭
        (Sung by Marie Kunkel-Zimmerman)
5. Theme and Variations for String Quartet (E major).....*M. VanGelder*
        (Messrs. VanGelder, Brill, Schmidt, and Trein)
6. Songs, "Nur um ein Wort"   ⎫
        "Und die Lerchen kommen wieder" ⎬.........*Maurits Leefson*
        "Lebensfrage"   ⎭
7. Nonet for Piano, Strings, Flute, Clarinet, and Horn....*W. W. Gilchrist*
8. Song for Baritone, from the Cantata "The Norsemen"....*Alonzo Stone*
9. Symphonic Variations on an Original Theme, for two Pianos
                                                        Henry A. Lang
        (Messrs. Jarvis and Lang)

This program is quoted from a long article in the magazine *Music* for July, 1894. The account continues with a glowing tribute for each of the nine numbers. Gilchrist's Nonet is often mentioned as an outstanding example of chamber music composed by a Philadelphian in the nineteenth century. Although all of the material played in the more than fifty concerts by this society could hardly achieve greatness, the influence of their activities on the musicianship in the vicinity of Philadelphia was very large.

II

THE MUSICAL ART CLUB OF PHILADELPHIA

This club existed during some of the years in which the Manuscript Music Society was active. It was founded in 1909, and Dr. Gilchrist was its first president.[1] The club's motto *Carpe diem*

---

[1] Other officers are named by Philip Goepp in an article, *The Musical Art Club of Philadelphia*, in *The Musician* for October 1913: A. C. Lambdin, vice-president, E. J. Keffer, secretary, and C. Gardner, treasurer.

suggests a less serious purpose than that of the contemporary Manuscript Music Society. The Musical Art Club was primarily a social group. Their original location at 17th and Chestnut Streets was directly above Thommen's restaurant. Luncheons, billiards, hospitality to visiting musicians were among the social activities of the club. Their weekly Scratch Night was an informal orchestra rehearsal in which members and their friends were invited to participate. This group, which took the name of the Scratch Club, continued to rehearse at the DeLancey Street residence of Philip Goepp's niece, Mrs. J. Claude Bedford, after the Musical Art Club ceased to exist. Active men in the affairs of this club included Maurice Weyl, Stauffer Oliver, W. H. Green, Philip Goepp, Constantin von Sternberg, and Nicholas Douty.[1]

In 1916 the Musical Art Club moved to larger quarters on Ranstead Street near Eighteenth. The Franklin Chess Club combined with the musical group in this new clubhouse. The Orpheus Club rehearsed there for some years prior to the building of their own headquarters at 254 S. Van Pelt Street. Receptions to Victor Herbert, Sousa, Samaroff and Stokowski, Gadski, Amato, Zimbalist, and Kreisler were important occasions in the social side of the club's activities. While their musical efforts were not of the most serious character, this club did hold several concerts in Witherspoon Hall. At a children's party given by the Musical Art Club the Scratch Orchestra was playing Haydn's *Toy Symphony* before a small but appreciative audience. Suddenly a large member of the club burst into the room carrying Thaddeus Rich disguised as a baby. The success of the stunt has never been forgotten by many of the children and adults present on that occasion. More serious musical programs were given at the club by members and by such distinguished guests as the Kneisel Quartet, Henri Scott, Leopold Godowsky, and Jan Kubelik.[2] Financial difficulties caused the Musical Art Club to give up its clubhouse and its many activities in about 1927.

---

[1] Mr. Douty, a former president of the Musical Art Club, provided many of the facts for the above account.

[2] These guest performers and other visitors are listed in *A Man and His Dream*, a pamphlet published by the Musical Art Club.

III

Music at the Sesqui-Centennial International Exposition

There exists a perfect reference work for the account of Sesqui-Centennial musical events. It was necessary to examine nine hundred and ninety-nine sources never intended for the gleaning of facts in preparing this book on Music in Philadelphia. Hence it was a welcome discovery when the writer found Herbert J. Tily's chapter in *The Sesqui-Centennial International Exposition* [1] while collecting material for this last chapter. Since Dr. Tily was chairman of the music committee for the Exposition, his account is authoritative. This committee of ninety-nine members included practically all of the important persons of musical Philadelphia in 1926. The ninety-nine notables make a long list,[2] but perhaps the fourteen chairmen of sub-committees might be mentioned by name:

> Clara Barnes Abbott, pageants
> James Francis Cooke, composition
> Dr. Charles S. Hirsch, orchestras
> Alexander Smallens, opera
> N. Lindsay Norden, chorus
> Henry S. Fry, organ
> Helen Pulaski Innes, soloists
> Albert N. Hoxie, bands
> George L. Lindsay, public schools
> Bruce A. Carey, private schools
> Rev. Hugh L. Lamb, parochial schools
> Gilbert Raynolds Combs, conservatories
> Nicholas Douty, teachers of music
> Nicola A. Montani, churches.

"The oustanding feature of the music program perhaps was the symphonic orchestral series given twice weekly and led by some of the world's most renowned conductors. The Philadelphia Orchestra was the official orchestra of the Exposition, playing from

---

[1] Chapter XII, "Music and Musical Organizations," in the official history *The Sesqui-Centennial International Exposition*. Current Publications, Inc., Philadelphia, 1929.

[2] The list is given in Tily's chapter, p. 211.

June 8 to September 25. Leopold Stokowski . . . was director of the Exposition orchestra program. The best of orchestral repertoire was given, including works produced for the first time anywhere and several numbers played for the first time in Philadelphia." [1] Each of the following conducted four concerts (and in the following order), Van Hoogstraten, Sokoloff, Hadley, Smallens, Rothwell, Rodzinski, Stock, and Stokowski. The final symphonic program was played by the New York Philharmonic Orchestra, under the direction of Willem Mengelberg. Howard Hanson conducted the first performance of his *Pan and the Priest* at this concert, October 13, 1926.

The Philadelphia Orchestra was an organization completely trained and ready to follow the various conductors listed above. When the Sesqui-Centennial Chorus was planned, the problem of finding a group equally prepared presented itself. While none large enough was available, several local singing societies cooperated in forming a chorus of 5,000 voices. Bruce A. Carey was in charge of sectional rehearsals for this chorus, and of the final rehearsals at the Metropolitan Opera House. The chorus sang under Mr. Carey's direction on the opening day of the Exposition, May 31, 1926, with accompaniment by the 108th Artillery Band.

The historical pageant of June 24 and 27 included many choral numbers. This elaborate affair was to have been given in the stadium on June 23, but rain caused its postponement. A description of the performance on the next night suggests the dismal possibility that the weather was still far from favorable. ". . . At five o'clock a steady drizzle made it questionable whether any participants or ticket holders would appear in the stadium. In spite of the rain, however, virtually all of the 15,000 participants as well as 60,000 spectators were in attendance. The festival was late in starting but the chorus procession marched across the damp field to the seats of honor above the tribune box. When they were halfway across the field the rain fell heavily, but at nine-thirty the performance was resumed and was concluded with a delay of only half an hour." [2] On the occasion of the Sunday performance, the

---

[1] Quoted from Tily, *op. cit.*, p. 212.
[2] Tily, *op. cit.*, p. 217.

weather being fine, the stadium was filled and thousands were unable to secure admission.

Twenty choral concerts were given in the Auditorium of the Sesqui-Centennial Exposition. The Saengerfest of German musical societies in Philadelphia was held there. The New York Liederkranz and the Philadelphia Junger Maennerchor gave interesting concerts during the summer. The first program of choral music was the Catholic Choirs' Festival, sung by 1,200 voices on the evening of June 9. The first performance of the *Missa Festiva* by Nicola Montani was directed by its composer as a part of this concert. One of the last choral concerts was sung by the Associated Glee Clubs of America. This male group of 2,600 gave a memorable concert under the direction of Daniel Protheroe on November 27. The many other choral programs, performed between these two outside dates, were sung by a variety of amalgamations of from two to ten choruses from the Philadelphia area. H. G. Thunder, James Hartzell, Alexander Smallens, Emil F. Ulrich, N. Lindsay Norden,[1] and Charles H. Martin, among Philadelphians, and Fred Wolle and Hollis Dann as visiting leaders, provided the conducting for these large choruses.[2]

An international musical prize contest was sponsored by the Sesqui-Centennial Association. Leading American musicians were on the board of judges for this competition. Prizes totaling $7,500 were awarded to composers in Europe and the United States for music submitted. Karl Seibeck, Vienna, won $3,000 for his opera *Toni;* Symphonic Fantasie by Gustav Strube of Baltimore, and *Passacaglia and Fugue* by Herman Erdlen of Freude, Germany, merited a divided award among symphonic works; Henry Hadley's *Mirtel in Arcady* and *Evening in Palestine,* by Jacob Weinberg of

---

[1] Press comments on Mr. Norden's conducting at the Sesqui-Centennial are quoted on p. 202.

[2] The choruses were: The Sesqui-Centennial Chorus of 5000, the West Philadelphia Musical Association, The Mendelssohn Club, Main Line Choral Society, Haydn Club Chorus, Pennsylvania Railroad Glee Club, Gimbel's Choral Society, Temple Chorus, Temple Glee Club, Temple University Glee Club, Tall Cedars of Lebanon Glee Club, Palestrina Choir, Penn Mutual Glee Club, Shrine Choir, Choral Society of the First Baptist Church, Lit Brothers Chorus, Snellenburg Chorus, Matinee Musical Club Chorus, Choral Society of Philadelphia, Chester unit, Bristol unit, Delaware County Chorus, Philadelphia Music Club Chorus, and the Y.W.C.A. Choral Society.

Jerusalem, divided the choral award. Each of these divided awards amounted to $1,000. A $500 prize was given to T. Frederick H. Candlyn for his a cappella work *Historical Suite*.

The large organ built by the Austin Company for the Auditorium at this exposition has been briefly described in a previous chapter on noted organs in Philadelphia.[1] Daily recitals were given on the organ throughout the Sesqui-Centennial, with the exception of its last month, when lack of heating facilities prevented further daily programs. The instrument was, of course, used frequently for preludes to meetings in the Auditorium, and in combination with instrumental and vocal groups during the entire exposition.

One of the later musical events of the Sesqui-Centennial was a contest for students sponsored by the National Federation of Music Clubs. Sixty-four contestants visited Philadelphia, and many local students took part in its different sections, on November 1-3, 1926. Eight classes of musical study were announced,[2] and a prize of $500 was awarded in each.

Judged on the basis of what was displayed and what was accomplished, the Sesqui-Centennial Exposition was a great deal more successful than its many detractors are ever likely to admit. Whatever its shortcomings as a large exposition, the music performed was one of the highest points, and surely the largest achievement in the long history of Music in Philadelphia.

IV

The Music League and the Philadelphia Music Bureau

The mammoth chorus and pageant of the Sesqui-Centennial will be better understood if we investigate the activities of a similar nature previously managed by the Philadelphia Music League. This group was founded mainly through the efforts of Clara Barnes Abbott, who was its only director from its founding in 1922 until its activities were taken over by the Music Bureau in 1929. Since Mrs. Abbott was also the only chief of the Music Bureau, 1929-1933, she was largely responsible for the accomplishments of both groups.

---

[1] Cf. *supra*, p. 320.
[2] Viz., piano, organ, violin, violoncello, soprano, alto, tenor, and baritone.

The special field of the Music League was the coordination of musical organizations in Philadelphia and the management of pageants and festivals in which a number of groups took part. Their first season included the first of a series of annual pageants, using mass choruses, dancing groups, and many soloists. The second pageant was far more ambitious than that of 1922. It was held at the Academy of Music as a part of Music Week, which was celebrated from May 13 to 19, 1923.

Music Week itself was an innovation which must be credited to the Philadelphia Music League. The celebrations of 1923, which took place slightly more than a year after the founding of the League, were elaborately staged in the Academy of Music and other theatres. On the Sunday which opened Music Week, May 13, 1923, free concerts were given in several leading theatres. The idea of combining many groups into one large organization, or into a festival program to which each contributed selections, was typical of Music Week activities, as it was of most undertakings sponsored by the Music League. National and racial groups were brought to the fore in certain concerts of the various Music Weeks from 1922 to 1932. The Welsh Eisteddfod, the United Singers of Philadelphia—a group of German singing societies—the Philadelphia branch of the Negro Musicians' National Association, and other ensembles similarly constituted took part in the 1923 Music Week. The Public Schools Day, May 14, was the forerunner of many festivals which have been given annually by the Philadelphia school music students since 1927.[1] Physical Education work was included with the musical numbers in this early Music Week event.

On May 17, the Thursday of Music Week, 1923, the Philadelphia Operatic Society performed *Aïda* as a final production before merging with other vocalists to form the Philadelphia Civic Opera Company. The Music League sponsored this performance to the extent of paying all rentals for the Academy of Music during the week. The Music League received $15,000 a year from the City of Philadelphia.

In November of 1923 the concerts at the Academy of Fine Arts were revived, and made free to the public, under the auspices of the

---

[1] Cf. *supra*, p. 279.

Music League.   These concerts were given every Sunday, and were performed by small vocal and instrumental groups.   Chamber music was the main attraction at the Academy of Fine Arts programs.   They continued until 1929, and very probably suggested the procedure followed by the Curtis Institute at the larger Art Museum on the Parkway.[1]

The pageants managed by the Philadelphia Music League were becoming constantly larger.   In 1924 the Academy of Music was again used, and a particularly well constructed historical pageant, *The Inspired City,* was presented.   This entire work was directed by John W. Harkrider, with able assistance from Thaddeus Rich, Herbert J. Tily, and H. Alexander Matthews.   Three thousand performers participated.   The festival of 1925 was given in Franklin Field on May 12, 13, and 14.   Five thousand took part as members of thirty-one adult choral groups, eight boy choirs, twenty bands, ten ballets.   John Philip Sousa and thirty-eight other conductors shared in directing all this music and dancing.   A scene from *Aïda* was given, and fireworks were also a feature of this first outdoor pageant given by the Music League.   Their activities in preparing and performing many of the musical programs at the Sesqui-Centennial have already been mentioned.

Annual Christmas carol singing sponsored by the Music League seemed to follow a course of steady growth similar to that of their constantly enlarging pageants.   The caroling was done at Independence Square.   By 1926 there was a large community Christmas tree, a throng of 10,000 carolers directed by Leopold Stokowski, and a combined band to provide the accompaniment.

The Philadelphia Music Bureau was active between the years 1929 and 1933.   Mrs. Abbott was the head of the bureau, and her assistant was Helen Pulaski Innes.   The average annual expense of the bureau, $60,000, was four times the amount that had been spent by the city to sustain the Music League.   The striking thing about the Music Bureau was not that it cost four times the amount appropriated for the League, but that it accomplished so

---

[1] Cf. *supra,* p. 229 for the chamber music at the Art Museum.

much more than four times the work done by the League through economical handling of all its projects. Its continuation of the free concerts at the Academy of Fine Arts, the Christmas caroling and other activities of the Music League, was to be expected since the same management was in charge of both organizations. The Atwater Kent contests were conducted by the Music League and continued by the Music Bureau.[1]

There were many new contributions to the city's musical life made by the Bureau of Music in its three seasons of existence. More than 1,500,000 song sheets were distributed by this bureau. Two Municipal Bands were managed and sustained by it. The Symphonic Band, led by George O. Frey, gave concerts each night for eight weeks during the summer of 1929. These band programs, given at Lemon Hill and Strawberry Mansion, evoked such enthusiasm that the Music Bureau included in its report for 1929 the recommendation that a new and larger home for outdoor concerts was the paramount need of Music in Philadelphia. The report declares: "A national survey of summer music given in the most representative cities of the country reveals the fact that the most acceptable offering a city like Philadelphia can present to its citizens is a series of high-class concerts at popular prices by our own Philadelphia Orchestra. To make these . . . concerts entirely successful there should be a bowl, a stadium, or amphitheatre erected in one of Fairmount Park's natural ravines." This recommendation received hearty approval and cooperation from public-spirited Philadelphians, several of whom had expressed the city's need for such concerts independently of the Bureau's official suggestion. Obviously the idea of outdoor summer concerts was not a new one to Philadelphia citizens. In addition to several concert gardens discussed in the early chapters of this book, Gray's Gardens (near Gray's ferry) and its summer programs of 1789 and 1790, and Harrowgate, 1789 to after 1800, might be mentioned as early locations for this type of entertainment. Outdoor concerts were given at the Maennerchor Garden by the Germania Orchestra, and by other orchestras and bands. The Willow Grove

---

[1] A. Atwater Kent offered large prizes to student winners in various classes of musical competition. These Atwater Kent auditions were held from 1927 to 1932.

summer concerts were celebrated examples of band and orchestra programs given in the open air.   A more immediate predecessor of the Robin Hood Dell project was the Fairmount Park Orchestra, which consisted of fifty men from the Philadelphia Orchestra and was directed by Richard Hageman.   The Fairmount Park Orchestra gave nightly concerts at Lemon Hill in the summers of 1924 and 1925.

The present concerts in the park are the most pretentiously organized that Philadelphia has yet known, as to the physical equipment, the orchestra personnel, and the music performed.   Arthur Judson, the manager of the Philadelphia Orchestra in 1929, responded with enthusiasm to the suggestion of the summer concerts as proposed by the Music Bureau, and gained the interest of the members of the orchestra.   The Musicians' Union surprised everyone by permitting the men to play on a cooperative basis, *i.e.*, salaries to be determined by the number of tickets sold.   The season of 1938 contained so many evenings of bad or uncertain weather that the sharing of receipts proved an inadequate method to pay the players.   Therefore in 1939 each member of the orchestra was guaranteed a set salary for his participation in the summer concerts at Robin Hood Dell.[1]

In addition to supplying the original impetus for the Robin Hood Dell programs, the Music Bureau provided publicity and conducted the membership drive for its first season of concerts.   Municipal authorities and prominent citizens assisted Mr. Judson and Mrs. Abbott in their selection of the site, erection of the orchestra shell, and management of the concerts.   Frances A. Wister and Herbert J. Tily were particularly responsible for the success of the opening season, which began on July 8, 1930.   Alexander Smallens was appointed general conductor.   Many guest conductors and assisting soloists and groups were engaged for small fees, or even on a volunteer basis, for the Robin Hood Dell concerts by the Philadelphia Orchestra.

These concerts have been truly a city project.   Newspapers, municipal authorities, schools, stores, railroads and street cars, and radio stations assist in advertising the annual series.   The work of

---

[1] For the nature and significance of these summer concerts, see the account of the Philadelphia Orchestra, p. 184.

motivating and coordinating such varied agencies in the interest of a musical project is the type of activity that was logically and efficiently accomplished by the Music Bureau.

Several less ambitious achievements by this bureau included the organization of rhythm orchestras for children, harmonica classes, folk song choruses, sight singing classes, the Municipal Amateur Symphony Orchestra, and the Contemporary Music Society. The Florence Nightingale Chorus of 500 nurses from 21 hospitals was begun and managed by the Music Bureau. This same bureau had charge of all music at public municipal celebrations. The preparation of the *Musical Survey and Directory* was an early accomplishment of the Music Bureau. Three thousand institutions, hospitals, community houses, settlements, and playgrounds were supplied with radios given by Atwater Kent and delivered and installed by the Music Bureau of Philadelphia. One of their most original activities was the equipping and management of a "music car." This automobile travelled throughout the city in the summers of 1930, 1931, and 1932, and provided popular music for dancing in streets roped off for the occasion. These many minor activities greatly enriched the musical life of every class of the city's population, and when added to the outstanding contribution of the Music Bureau—the establishment of Robin Hood Dell—make it the leading organization of Music in Philadelphia from 1929 to 1933.

V

THE MUSICAL FUND SOCIETY SINCE 1857

Since the so-called last concert of May 28, 1857, the Musical Fund Society has continued to further its second objective—"the relief of decayed musicians and their families." Little is to be noted concerning its activities from 1857 to 1900. The cessation of concerts made it possible to contribute more to needy musicians, since the concerts from about 1850 had been almost uniformly unsuccessful in a financial way. Eighteen fifty-seven provided a very wise stopping point because it was in that year that the Philadelphia Academy of Music was opened to the public. William L.

Mactier, a member of the society, states very definitely: "The opening of the Academy of Music virtually ended the public performances of the Musical Fund Society.   Operas proved more attractive than concerts." [1]   Mactier records further that over one hundred thousand dollars had been spent for relief of needy musicians prior to 1885.   Nor has this beneficent side of the society's activity stopped at any time down to the present (1940).   When Thomas J. Beckett retired from active service as superintendent of Musical Fund Hall he was permitted to occupy the society's house for the rest of his life, rent-free.   There has been a list of pensioners of the Musical Fund Society, for nearly one hundred and twenty years, and there will probably be such a group for many years to come.

The front of the Musical Fund Hall was completely rebuilt in 1891.   An orchestral concert was held to celebrate the completion of this new façade.   In the years 1895 to 1897 there were series of weekly concerts at the Hall, given by the Germania Orchestra.   At that time the Germania Orchestra was conducted by William Stoll, Jr.

"Mr. Thunder's Orchestra" [2] played its first season of ten concerts at Musical Fund Hall (1897-1898).   The season of 1900-1901 saw the newly organized Philadelphia Orchestra rehearsing four days a week at Eighth and Locust Streets (i.e., in Musical Fund Hall).   This long series of meetings was held in the building without any charge to the Philadelphia Orchestra Association.

The five hundred dollar gift to the Philadelphia Orchestra Guaranty Fund was a further donation by this society to the new orchestra under Fritz Scheel.   By these two large grants and by active support and attendance the Musical Fund Society may be said to have done more than any one group to sponsor this great orchestra.   The two purposes of the Musical Fund Society have been stated to be the advancement of musical culture and the relief of needy musicians.   Since a vicarious "elevation of musical taste" has undoubtedly been accomplished by the Philadelphia Orchestra,

---

[1] *Sketch of the Musical Fund Society*, p. 46, by Mactier; Philadelphia, 1885.

[2] Henry Gordon Thunder, Mus. Doc., leader of the Philadelphia Choral Society (p. 254), Fortnightly Club (p. 262), and the Bach Choir of Philadelphia.

the Musical Fund Society can rest content with its ably administered fund and its musical poor, who are ever with it.

A few items of especial interest remain to be mentioned in completing the story of this ancient and charitable institution. A charming anniversary concert was held at the Hall in 1920—one hundred years after the founding of the society. The event was entitled "Jenny Lind Concert," both the music and the musicians of Miss Lind's 1850 program being reproduced or imitated. Mabel Garrison was Jenny Lind, Hugh Clarke directed, as Signor Strakosch, and other performers were ably personified by Philadelphia's best musicians. Every desired antique restoration was achieved for this program—except that the unfortunate facade of 1891 could hardly be removed.

In 1925 the Musical Fund Society startled those of the musical world who mourned its "demise" in 1857 by offering ten thousand dollars in prizes for the best compositions for string quartet. This contest was closed in 1928, at which time the judges [1] awarded a divided first prize to Bela Bartok and Alfred Casella.

During this same prosperous period the Musical Fund Ensemble was organized (1927) to give concerts in Junior and Senior High Schools in Philadelphia. String combinations, often with piano, played the finest chamber music to the school children; and a lecturer supplied program notes appropriate to each selection.[2] Unfortunately the work of the ensemble was discontinued in 1934.

A prize of one thousand dollars from the Edward G. McCollin Memorial Fund was announced in 1929, for the best work for a rather vague combination: Orchestra and Quartet. In 1930 the Musical Fund Society appropriated one thousand dollars for the summer concerts of the Philadelphia Orchestra. These Robin Hood Dell concerts, begun that year and continued every succeeding summer, are, in the opinion of this humble scribe, and many not so humble also, the most important musical events in the city. They are important in that music is heard by thousands, and by different thousands on different nights. The setting is beautiful

---

[1] Among them were Willem Mengelberg, Fritz Reiner, Frederick Stock, and Thaddeus Rich.

[2] I have heard the Musical Fund Ensemble on several occasions. The audiences ranged from six hundred to two thousand in number, yet the chamber ensemble held them spellbound throughout the most abstract works.

and the price is low. The fence is also low for those without the price—not that they need to climb it, for the music may be heard far beyond the officially seated audience. No finer use could be made for the most recent special donations by the Musical Fund Society. They gave an additional five hundred dollars in 1931 and two hundred and fifty dollars in 1932, both for the summer outdoor concerts.

We can see how the society is still interested in its two objectives today. The elevation of musical taste and the relief of decayed musicians are still fostered to the utmost powers of a conscientious and able group of officers and members.

VI

COMMERCIAL PHASES OF MUSIC IN PHILADELPHIA

There are many musical manufactures in Philadelphia. It led the country in piano making from 1780 to 1840, and contained important organ factories from 1850 to 1900. In both of these fields Philadelphia has failed to live up to its promising start as a manufacturing center. Since 1900 the prominence of the Victor Company of Camden has placed the Philadelphia area in a leading position in the manufacturing of phonographs, and later of radio equipment. The Victor Talking Machine Company has long been more than a manufacturer of a new musical instrument: it has from its inception in 1898 been one of the pioneer agencies in the twentieth century's tremendous spread of the music of all instruments. Its vast artistic and commercial influence makes it imperative that a book on Music in Philadelphia should devote considerably more space to its history and its present activities than can be allotted to some of our less important though more narrowly Philadelphian musical industries.

The Victor factories, now called the Radio Corporation of America Manufacturing Company, are nearer the Philadelphia civic center than many of its theatres and most of its churches.[1] This geographical proximity may assist some readers to understand why

---

[1] "Commercial Value of Music to Philadelphia," p. 5; Philadelphia Chamber of Commerce report, 1917.

R.C.A.-Victor is included as a part of Music in Philadelphia—in fact, the most important part among its musical manufactures.

The invention of the Phonautograph, the predecessor of the modern phonograph, was the work of a Frenchman, Leon Scott, in 1855. The practical improvements made on this early instrument by Thomas Edison (1847-1931) are too well known to be listed here. Nor do they concern Philadelphia music history, except insofar as the gramophone as worked out by Emil Berliner and Eldridge Johnson in Camden from 1898 to 1901 is indebted to the Edison improvements and acoustical refinements. The instrument was called a Victor Phonograph in 1901, at which time Johnson had sufficiently improved Berliner's gramophone to consider it a marketable musical instrument. The manufacture was commercially unsuccessful until 1906, due to the apathy or hostility of musicians and the musical public. The signing of Caruso as a Victor artist in 1906 helped greatly to raise the public's estimation of the phonograph. The steady and very plentiful advertising programs helped to overcome apathy and indifference to the new *contraption,* as it was frequently styled. The Victor dog, first drawn by an English commercial artist, Francis Barrand, in 1902, has become one of the oldest and best known advertising symbols the world has ever known. "His Master's Voice" was first used by the London Victor affiliate, the British Gramophone Company.[1]

In 1903 the Victor Talking Machine Company opened its first recording studios, at Tenth and Lombard Streets, Philadelphia, where they were located for five years. In those studios Caruso and other great musicians of the day made their famous recordings. The Victor Company operated a matrix plant at the same address, where the master records were made and shipped to Camden for pressing. Their laboratory offices were also at that corner from the year 1903 to 1908.

The Victor Company, through its records by Caruso, Melba and other fine artists and groups, and through its well conceived advertising, was in the leading position in the entire field of musical manufacture by 1921, when radio became a formidable rival to

---

[1] Most of the R.C.A. Victor historical material is from "A Dog Has Nine Lives," an article by H. S. Maraniss, in *The Annals of the American Academy of Political and Social Science.* Philadelphia, September, 1937.

its commercial supremacy.   Radio was more fascinating and mysterious, and actually truer to the musical original than the talking machine had ever been.   After the phonograph industry had declined rapidly for five years, the Orthophonic Victrola was perfected by the Victor Company in 1926.   Though never rivalling the scientific mysteries of radio amplification, the orthophonic victrola does claim to be the tonal equal of most radio sets.   Its main advantages were, and are, the possibility of the listener's selecting his music, and his more secure confidence that "reception will be good" at all times.   While these are undoubted superiorities of a phonograph over a radio *as a musical instrument*, the timeliness, humor and many more non-musical features peculiar to radio have made it a more desired product for most home purposes.   The competitive stages of phonograph-radio rivalry did spur the Victor Company to make the great improvements embodied in the Orthophonic Victrola, and to introduce more refined processes into the making of records themselves.   Electric recording, with the use of a microphone, has vastly increased the realism of musical reproduction.   A happier ending to this commercial rivalry has been the merging of the Victor Company into the Radio Corporation of America.   This is seen in the combination Victrola-Radio sets, and in the device called a Record Player, which can be easily attached to the radio's amplification units and will thus run on the same electrical current as the radio set.   Mr. H. S. Maraniss[1] dwells on the advertising acumen of the R.C.A.-Victor Company, but finishes his article with a reflection on the present unification of victrola and radio:

> One of the mediums used today in advertising the story of Victor recording is not the newspaper, not the family magazine, but that one-time enemy of the phonograph itself—radio broadcasting. We use it every Sunday afternoon, for the plain fact is that the radio is a vital force in the conditioning of public appreciation, and a wonderful proponent of the music that is permanently recorded by Victor.

This concluding section shows a farsightedness unusual among men in the musical field.   Coming after the ruinous competition of the

---

[1] *Op. cit.*, page 6.

victrola against the radio, the amalgamation of the R.C.A.-Victor Company has insured the continued prosperity of this institution. Cooperation and united effort to serve the musical public should always be rewarded with the conspicuous success achieved by R.C.A.-Victor Company. Artistic aim, scientific method, modern awareness, and business insight constitute four sides of a firm foundation for this musico-commercial enterprise.

From twenty assembled "Interesting Facts about the Radio Headquarters . . . Camden, N. J.," the following few will give an idea of its gigantic size:

> More than 3,250,000 square feet of floor space are utilized by the RCA Manufacturing Company.
>
> At peak employment, more than 12,000 persons are employed in the factories, offices and laboratories of the Company.
>
> From three to five thousand complete radio receivers are turned out *daily* during the busiest seasons.
>
> The most complete radio organization in the world is that of the RCA Manufacturing Company, Inc., in Camden, N. J. It manufactures everything in radio from the microphone in the studio to the receiver in the home. Some of its products include Radio Receivers, Phonographs, Records, Broadcasting Stations, Photophone sound motion picture recording and reproducing equipment; aviation, police, and commercial sound apparatus.

Also from a press bulletin [1] come these significant statements concerning the scientific staff of the R.C.A.-Victor Company:

> . . . . Another group of buildings houses the largest and most complete radio research and engineering laboratories in the world. Here radio scientists create, develop and improve radios, the ultra high frequency police and aviation systems, the motion picture sound systems of today, as well as the television and other miracles of tomorrow. Locked doors and *No Admittance* signs are the only outward clues to the new wonders brought to life under the ceaseless searching and experimentation of a staff of radio scientists, who, because they already know so much, know how little of radio's vast potentialities have as yet been realized. For, as has been demonstrated many times, discovery in one direction often leads to new

---

[1] "R.C.A. Services Gird Globe" by Julius Haber, Camden, N. J., R.C.A. Press Division, pp. 3-4.

discovery in others, and wider vistas open up new worlds to be conquered. One door bears the legend, Dr. V. K. Zworykin, director of electronic research. Other doors bear other names, perhaps not so well known, but nevertheless important in some special field of research that may some day come to glorious life and everyday use.

Other large radio manufacturers in Philadelphia have been the A. Atwater Kent and Philco companies. The Atwater Kent plant discontinued its radio department in 1936, but the Philco Corporation is a very active concern at the present time. The Philadelphia Storage Battery Company and the Philco Radio and Television Corporation operate jointly as the world's largest makers and distributors of radio sets. The former company was founded in 1906 and began its manufacture of radios in 1928. There are eleven plants in northeastern sections of Philadelphia, others elsewhere in the United States, and four in foreign countries. The output of this company has been the largest among radio manufacturers since 1931. In 1936 alone nearly two million radio sets were made by Philco. There are 22,000 dealers who market this product in the United States, and 200 wholesale distributing centers in this country. Recent additions to the manufactures of the Philadelphia Storage Battery, and the products sold by the Philco Corporation, are refrigerating and air conditioning devices, which they placed on the market in 1939.

Let us close this section with some general figures on the music business in Philadelphia. Sales of pianos were recorded as in excess of $11,000,000 in 1917. The manufacture of phonographs during that year required the expenditure of over $75,000,000. These figures are quoted from a report of the Chamber of Commerce, "The Commercial Value of Music to Philadelphia." The following table is contained in their booklet:

BUSINESS RECEIPTS

Sales of music	$500,000
Receipts from music publishing	1,500,000
Piano and phonograph sales	11,150,240
Manufacture of phonographs	75,000,000
Manufacture of stringed instruments	225,000
Recitals and other receipts	100,000
Total	$88,475,240

INVESTMENT VALUES

Musical Fund Hall	$50,000
Orchestra Endowment Fund	800,000
Paid in past years for Philadelphia Orchestra..	1,000,000
Opera and other musical buildings	2,000,000
Settlement School	200,000
Musical Art Club	80,000
Presser Foundation	1,200,000
Talking machine plants	10,000,000
Piano and organ factories and stores	2,000,000
Value of organs in churches and theatres	700,000
Old musical instruments	200,000
Music publishing plants and music stores	2,000,000
Board of Education expenditures for musical work	86,488
Conservatories	200,000
Total	$20,516,488

These totals are considerably smaller than such a list would aggregate in 1940, in spite of recent drastic reductions in the money spent for certain types of music. A smaller and less inclusive commercial summary for 1882 is quoted from page 2245 of Scharf and Westcott's *History of Philadelphia*. It is given here because of its contrast with the larger list quoted above.

MUSICAL MANUFACTORY, 1882

	Number	Employees	Value of Product
Music printers and publishers	55	77	$154,000
Music typographers	2	24	43,200
Organ builders	4	18	35,000
Piano manufacturers	5	232	580,000
Other instrument makers	31	206	238,660
Total			$1,050,860

While the manufacture and sale of music and musical instruments constitute an important part of the commercial side of music in Philadelphia, there are many other facts and figures that apply in that field. According to the 1917 report the 15,000 musicians in Philadelphia earn an average annual sum of $7,000,000. Of these 2,000 are semi-professional, 2,000 belong to the American Federation of Musicians, and 800 are members of the Musicians' Union of Pennsylvania. Their salaries range from $800 to $2,000, and in rare instances reach $10,000. The 20,000 conservatory students pay a total of $800,000 annually to music schools. Four thousand music teachers earn approximately $4,000,000 a year.

Instrumental groups at social functions involve a large share of the money spent for the city's music. Fifteen thousand functions a year at which five or more orchestra members were employed are recorded in 1916.[1] It is not unusual for one hotel to have five different orchestras in as many rooms for one evening's social affairs. Music in the churches and schools has been sufficiently discussed elsewhere in this book for it to be evident that its prevalence in those institutions requires the annual expenditure of millions of dollars for salaries, instruments, music, and musical supplies.

Theatre music has always cost large sums of money, although in the past ten years this amount has dwindled considerably. Each opera sung in Philadelphia by the Metropolitan Opera Company of New York involves the expenditure of $12,500; receipts from the sale of tickets have been slightly in excess of that amount. These figures, gathered in the main from the most recent bulletin (1917) of the Chamber of Commerce, are often quite approximate, but they suggest several avenues through which large sums of money are exchanged as a result of the activities of Music in Philadelphia.

---

[1] Chamber of Commerce report, 1917, p. 13.

PART III

INDEX-DICTIONARY OF MUSIC IN PHILADELPHIA

This concluding and appendectal section must serve a double purpose. The main facts of Philadelphia's musical history were included in the preceding pages of the text, and as an index this section should locate such information as efficiently as possible. Many persons, or pieces of music, have not been mentioned, however, and the index cannot refer to them—as an index. These facts should be made available, since this volume appears to be the first attempt to collect them in book form. Hence the many items that might be valuable for reference purposes but could not be included in the relatively readable pages are added to the index in the manner of a dictionary. One difficulty was unavoidable. To discover some important fact the reader must use the index to refer to the text, while the less important information is the more easily found, since it appears in its alphabetical place.

the College Commencement of November, 1767, and at other concerts from 1767 to 1771.

Bansbach, Philip, 312.

Baptist Temple, 107, 321.

Barber of Seville, 69, 115, 233.

Barber, Samuel, b. 1910, West Chester, graduate of Curtis Institute of Music, winner of The American Prix de Rome, 1935, and the Pulitzer Prize for Music, 1935 and 1936. Composer of a symphony, some chamber music and vocal works.

Bare, Cynthia. Favorite soprano in the 1870's. Soloist at concert in St. George's Hall, April 27, 1878.

Bartholomay, Frederick, from 1900 to 1915 an organ tuner, and since 1915 a builder and tuner.

Barton, Andrew, 18-19.

Baseler, Dorothy Johnstone, harpist. Director of Matinee Musical Club Harp Ensemble and of the Baseler Harp Ensemble. Has played as soloist with orchestras and in prominent churches. Influential as performer and teacher in Philadelphia and the eastern states.

Battista, Joseph, b. Philadelphia 1918. Philadelphia pianist, studied at Settlement Music School, Philadelphia Conservatory, and Juilliard School. Frequent appearances in concert and recital work in Philadelphia and New York, including Youth Concert with Philadelphia Orchestra, January 18, 1939.

Battle of Hexham, or the Days of Old, historical play interspersed with songs, containing roundelay and chorus, etc. At New Theatre, July 17, 1801, and later.

Battle of Prague, 38.

Battle of the Kegs, 34.

Battle of Trenton, A Sonata, published by Hewitt of New York and Benjamin Carr of Philadelphia, 1797.

Bauer, Harold, 188.

Beals, John, 9.

Beatitudes, 254.

Beck, James M., succeeded J. E. Gould as music publisher, at 164 Chestnut St. in 1856. Partner of Dennis Lawton, 1856-63, and agent for the Ditson Co. of Boston.

Beck, Jean S., 305.

Beck's Brass Band, called "the first really good brass band" heard by Maurice F. Egan. (*Recollections of a Happy Life,* p. 46.)

Beckel, James Cox, b. Phila., 1811. From 1830 to 1880 held a series of organ positions in Phila. His father also had been an organist.

Bee Hive, The, or A Soldier's Love. Performed at New Theatre, January 4, 1815.

Bosio, Angiolina, 76, 77.
Bossi, M. Enrico, 318.
Boston Festival Orchestra, 160-1.
Boston Symphony Orchestra, 206.
Bottesini, 103.
Boudet, Victoria, 97.
Boulanger, Nadia, 318.
Boullay, Louis, announced on March 25, 1799, a "Grand con-
    cert, vocal and instrumental" for his own benefit.   Concert
    performer and orchestral violinist in Phila. and elsewhere,
    1793-9.
Bove, Domenico, 168.
Boyd, Morrison C., 293, 320.
Boylan, James A., 311-2.
Boyle, George Frederick, 303. B. Australia 1886.   Since 1910
    Boyle has taught at Peabody Conservatory of Baltimore, and
    Curtis Institute.   Now head of piano department at Phila.
    Musical Academy, and of the Boyle Piano Studies.   Also
    teacher at Juilliard School in N. Y. (since 1928).   Has pub-
    lished much piano music, and composed some orchestral and
    chamber works (still in MS.).
Bradford, Andrew, 9.   James Bradford was also a printer, of
    music as well as general works.
Braham, 77.
Brahms Chorus of Philadelphia, 202-3.
Braslau, Sophie, 225.
Braun, 71.
Braun, Charles A., 177.
Braun, John F. (d. 1939).   Played piano, violin, viola and 'cello.
    Majored in the study of voice in Phila. and Paris.   Several
    appearances as soloist with Phila. Orchestra, and as Wag-
    nerian tenor in lectures by Damrosch and Surette.   Parsifal,
    Siegmund, Samson sung in concert form with Stokowski.
    Soloist with many other local organizations, and with Cin-
    cinnati and St. Louis Orchestras.   Former president of the
    Art Alliance, and Pennsylvania chairman of community sing-
    ing during world war.   Former director of Phila. Orchestra,
    Presser Foundation, Musical Fund Society, and Pennsylvania
    Art Museum, and a president of the Music League of Phila.
Breaking Heart, The, 74.
Bremner, James, 11-12.
Brett, Miss, sang with Oldmixon and Broadhurst as a leading
    operatic actress in Phila. 1793-1800.
Bride of Messina, 120.
Brignoli, Pasqualino, 67, 78, 79, 121.

Carnival of Venice, 69.

Carncross and Dixey's, 11th St. below Market (1870-1895), a "minstrel opera house," centering around the stunts of the above two men. Other humorous acts in the style of a vaudeville program.

Carpenters' Hall, 57.

Carr, Benjamin, 26, 38, 56-64, 81, 95. For biography and works of the Carrs cf. 50-5. Influence of B. Carr on church music, 92-3. Carr publications, 332.

Carr, Thomas, 55, 89, 332.

Caruso, Enrico, 232, 358.

Casals, Pablo, 259.

Cassandra, 239.

Cassatt, Mrs. Alexander J. Active in the organization of the Philippine Concerts led by Scheel, 1899. Organized an opera class, which was directed by Scheel in 1899 and for a few following years. Mrs. Cassatt was the first president of the Euridice Chorus, founded 1886.

Castagna, Bruna, 185.

Castle of Andalusia, 39, 69, 72.

Castle Spectre, The, 40.

Caston, Saul, 185, 305. Associate conductor of the Phila. Orchestra since 1936. Trumpeter with that group since 1919, first trumpet for most of his twenty years with the orchestra. Has conducted regular concerts, and many programs on the tours and at Robin Hood Dell.

Catch Club, 88.

Catch Club, or The Feast of Anacreon, musical olio, given at the New Theatre, Mar. 21, 1801.

Catch Him Who Can, a two-act musical farce, followed Macklin's *Man of the World* at New Theatre, Feb. 28, 1810.

Cathedral of SS. Peter and Paul, 126, 143, 309, 325.

Cavalleria Rusticana, 128.

Cecelian Chorus, 142.

Cecillian Musical Society, 109.

Cella, Theodore, b. Phila. 1897, studied in Phila., New York, and Boston. Former Boston Symphony member. His relatively few works have been played many times by leading eastern orchestras.

Centennial Cantata, 135: Centennial Chorus, 136; Centennial Exhibition, 124, 135-141; Centennial Hymn, 135, 137; *Centennial Inauguration March,* 135; Centennial Organs, 136; Centennial Pianos, 136; *Centennial Triumphal March,* 137.

Centre House Tavern, had concerts by complete band and organ from 1799.

Cleopatra, 236.
Coal Black Rose, 86.
Coe, Robert, 9.
Cohn, Arthur, 210. B. Phila. 1910. Studied at Combs Conservatory, later at Juilliard School, New York. Mr. Cohn is particularly interested in chamber music, and has composed a considerable number of works for small ensembles of varied nature. He has been active in many recent Phila. music projects, especially the Phila. Music Center.
Cole, Lucius, 227, 299.
Collection of Chants (Carr) 91.
College of Phila., 12, 17. (Later the University of Pennsylvania, *q.v.*).
Colson, Mme., 79.
Columbian Garden, 461 Market Street, "after a long and tedious winter," announces "a concert by an excellent Band of Musicians Tuesday June 6, and every Tuesday and Friday thereafter from candlelight to ten o'clock." Prop. Laurence Astolfi and Co. Notices in the *Aurora* June 2, 1815, and June 13, 1815.
Columbian Light Infantry Band, 84.
Columbian Magazine, a monthly magazine published from about 1786, contained many articles on music, and music supplements. (Hopkinson's "Letter on the conduct of a Church Organ," September 1792; and his "Improved Method of Tongueing the Harpsichord or Spinnet," May 1787; music from Markoe's opera, *The Reconciliation*; odes, and songs.)
Columbia The Gem of the Ocean, 100. This song was entered by George Willig in the clerk's office of District Court of Eastern Pennsylvania, in 1843. Osbourne's edition of 1844 states that the song was adapted and arranged by T. à Becket from its original form as sung by Mr. Blankman and Mr. (David T.) Shaw in 1843.
Combs, Gilbert R., 220, 301, 346. Combs' Broad St. Conservatory, 220, 301-2.
Coming of Christ, The, 255.
Commercial phases of Phila. music, 357-363.
Composers' Forum Laboratory, 212.
Comus, first Phila. performance on Mar. 9, 1770, by Old American Co., conducted by Mr. Hallam.
Convention Hall Organ, 320.
Converse, John, 218.
Conway, Patrick, 196.
Cooke, Edgar M., 306.
Cooke, James Francis, 307, 339, 346. B. Michigan, 1875; studied

Auiol (active school at 5th and Walnut, many balls), Mr. Labbe's, Mr. Francis, Select Hall Dancing Academy, Masonic Hall Dancing School (Victor Guillou), regular balls, and Cotillon Parties at Masonic Hall; Harmony Ball Room, 119 Spruce Street.

Danks, Hart Pease (New Haven 1834-1903 Phila.). Active in Chicago, later in Phila., as singer and composer. Many hymns and popular songs by H. P. Danks. Composer of an operetta and several anthems.

Dann, Hollis, 277, 348.

Da Ponte, Lorenzo, 70, 71.

Darley, Francis T. Sully, 70, 89, 125, 175, 217, 273. John Darley, 70, 95, 217. J. C. Darley, 53, 95, 217. W. H. W. Darley, 87, 217, 298. William Darley, 217. Among published works by W. H. W. Darley the Congressional Library possesses: *They're a Noddin'*, with variations for pianoforte, and *On A Bright Sunny Morn* (Willig, 1822). W. H. W. Darley and J. C. B. Standbridge wrote or arranged jointly: *The Sacred Choirister* (Cowperthwaite, 1844), Eighth Edition of the L. Meignen System of Vocal Instruction (Lee and Walker *c.* 1880), *Four Voice Harmony and Piano or Organ Accompaniment, Chants of the Episcopal Church* (1840), and *Music of Christ Church and St. Stephen's* (Kay, 1839).

Dash, James Allan, 210, 257.

Daughter of the Regiment, 79.

Davenport, Josiah, 10. Early subscription concerts given at his house on 3rd Street, 1769.

Davis, Agnes, 188.

Davis, F. Edna. Special assistant since 1930 to director of music, supervisor of vocal music in Phila. High Schools.

Day in the Country, A., 74.

Dead Alive, The, "a musical farce by the author of *The Poor Soldier*" (O'Keefe), New Theatre, Feb. 4, 1801. Two Daileys, Durang, Mrs. Oldmixon, and Mrs. Francis in cast.

Deep River by W. Franke Harling, an opera with jazz that has operatic quality in spots—particularly its second act. Anticipates setting and character of *Porgy and Bess* by Gershwin. World première Lancaster, Pa. Sept. 18, 1926, then at Shubert Theatre, Phila., Sept. 21, 1926. Conducted by composer, sixteen consecutive performances in Phila., then two weeks in New York.

de Gogorza, Emilio, 304.

Del Puente, Giuseppe, Operatic soloist in New York, Phila., and elsewhere, 1870-1885. Lived and taught in Phila. 1890 to about 1910. (With Hinrich's Opera Co. at Broad above Co-

tion of Organists, officer in various musical organizations, authority and writer on church music. Composer of organ and vocal music.

Fry, William, 72-6, 79-80, 89, 101, 109; contrasted with Winner, 109.

Gabrilowitsch, Ossip, 172, 188, 235.

Gadski, Johanna, 132, 221, 232, 345.

Gaertner, Carl, 143.

Galton, Susan, 122.

Ganz, Rudolph, 266.

Garcia Opera Company, 70, 71.

Garden, Mary, 225, 233, 236, 238.

Garrison, Mabel, 225, 259, 356.

Gasparoni, 78.

Gauthier, Eva, 225.

Gazzaniga, Mme. Mariella, 78, 115, 121, 151.

Gehot, Jean. B. Belgium 1756, d. (?). Violinist in Wignell and Reinagle's Orchestra (1793 c.). Composer in New York and Phila.

Geibel, Adam, 283, 341. B. Germany 1855, d. Germantown 1933. Came to Phila. in 1862. Teacher, organist, publisher, and conductor.

Geiger, William, Mus. Doc. Associated with Henry Schradieck in the violin department of Combs Conservatory, 1898. Director of the violin department there since 1918.

Gentleman's Amusement. Selection of solos, duets, overtures, rondos, and romances from European composers (mostly). Also dances, marches, reels, sixty-four songs, flute method, musical terms dictionary. By R. Shaw and Benjamin Carr. In twelve parts, or one bound volume, $6.00. Issued at Carr's, 1794-1796. Supposed to be monthly editions, but only numbers 1-5, and 7 are extant.

George, Miss, cf. Mrs. Oldmixon.

Gerhard, Charles E., 168, 305.

German Grand Opera Company, 234.

Germani, Fernando, 318.

Germania Orchestra (Berlin), 85, 102, 167. (Phila.), 102, 142, 143; summer concerts, 150, 167-8, 258, 355.

Germantown Friends' School, 288-9.

Germantown Männerchor, 265.

Germantown Orchestra, 201.

German Washington Guards Band, 84.

Gershwin, George, 200.

Gerson, Robert A., 316.

Gerster, Etelka, 76, 130, 156.

Hatch Music Company in 1900 at Eighth and Locust Streets. Bought by Boston Music Company in 1915. He published *The Musician,* a monthly magazine in the intervening years, and was noted for *A Graded Course of Piano Studies* modelled after W. S. B. Mathews' revision of Theodore Presser's *Standard Graded Course of Studies.* Thomas à Becket was editor for Hatch Music Company for several years.

Horus, 240.
Hoshi-San, 242. Three act opera by W. Leps (and J. Luther Long.) Similar libretto to *Mme. Butterfly*—also by Long. Phila. Operatic Society sang *Hoshi-San* on May 21, 1909, under Leps' direction.
Hotz, Henry, 257. May Ebrey, 259.
Howard, James, 65.
Howe's Thespians gave *The Mock Doctor* many times in Phila., 1777-8.
How Sweet is the Morning, 53.
H. P., 190.
Hubbert, Mary S. One of the Enoch Pearson's original six assistant Music Supervisors, 1897.
Huguenots, 131.
Huneker, James G., 126, 134-5, 142, 158-9.
Hunter of the Alps, The. Two act musical drama sung at Wood's Benefit, Mar. 16, 1810, at the New Theatre.
Hupfeld, Charles F., and John, 49-50, 56, 57, 67, 81, 87, 96, 141, 219.
Hyperion School of Musical Art, 303.
Incledon, Mr., English vocalist, popular in 1818, *et seq.,* at the Chestnut Street Theatre.
Indian Princess, The, or La Belle Sauvage, by Nelson Barker, given first in Phila. 1808.
Independent Blues (Band), 84.
Ingham, John H., 175. Organized Sunday afternoon chamber music at Academy of Fine Arts shortly after 1900. Played piano in amateur chamber groups. Active in Musical Fund Society, Phila. Orchestra Association, and Manuscript Music Society.
Inkle and Yarico, 69.
Innes Band, 195.
Innes, Helen Pulaski, 168, 346, 351. Mrs. Innes managed radio station WIP for the first broadcasts of opera in Phila.
Invisible Girl, The. One act musical piece on program at New Theatre, Nov. 30, 1810.
Iolanthe, 122.
Iphigenia in Taurus (Clarke), 149.
Iron Chest, The, or Honor's Victim, 42. After lapse of twelve years, revived for Mr. Wood's Benefit, Mar. 16, 1810. Play interspersed with songs, at the New Theatre.
Italian Monk, The. Samuel Arnold's Opera composed in 1797, produced in America first time at New Theatre, Apr. 25, 1798. "Music and accompaniments by Alexander Reinagle."
Iturbi, José, 188.

O'Connell, Charles, 190. Came to Camden in 1924 as an executive in the "classical music division" of the Victor Company. His recordings of Schönberg's *Gurrelieder,* and of works by Mahler and Bruckner did much to restore the popularity of Victor records. Collaborated with the Phila. Orchestra in their recordings since 1932. Author of *The Victor Book of the Opera* (1935). Mr. O'Connell has conducted the Phila. Orchestra frequently, also on occasion the Chicago, Montreal, Toronto, Minneapolis, Rochester, and Boston "Pops" Orchestras.

Ode (Air, "Thou Softly Flowing Avon") for voice and piano, printed in the Universal Asylum, Phila. July, 1790. Written in memory of Benjamin Franklin, and given at the commencement of the College of Phila., July 17, 1790.

Ode on the birthday of George Washington, by a member of "The Adopted Sons," which met at Pennsylvania Coffee House, Phila. Words in *Pennsylvania Packet,* Feb. 24, 1786.

Ode to the New Year, 42.

Oedipus Rex, 190, 235.

Oellers' Hotel, 38, 42.

Of Age Tomorrow, musical entertainment in two acts, given Apr. 7, 1810.

Offenbach, Jules, 78, 123, 139.

Old American Opera Company, 10.

Oldmixon, Mrs. (née George), 68, 95.

Old Swedes' Church, 2, 3, 309.

Olney High School, 129.

Olympic Revels, 69.

Olympic Theatre. Cf. Walnut St. Theatre.

Onegin, Sigrid, 225, 253.

Onteora, 128.

Opera premières, 244-248.

Orchestrion (Centennial), 136-7. (Wanamakers), 319.

Orem, Preston Ware (Phila. 1862-1938), studied with Jarvis in Phila., and with Clarke at the University of Pennsylvania. Mr. Orem taught at the Philadelphia Conservatory and at the Combs Conservatory, and from 1900 to 1931 headed the editorial staff of the Presser Company. He composed a few works of importance, but is chiefly noted for his many transcriptions for organ, and for piano, as well as a series of popular books on harmony. Orem was organist at the Walnut Street Presbyterian Church, 1901-1910.

Organ: at Christ Church (1728), 2; at Old Swedes', 3; built by Witt, 6; and by Hermits of the Wissahickon, 7; opposed in colonial churches, 14; used in Moravian church, 17; and in the College of Phila., 17; built and bequeathed by M. Zimmerman, 21; Moravian organ of 1823, 94; of 1856, 94; at Christ Church (1836), 94; at Calvary Presbyterian Church, 94; at First Presbyterian Church, 94; at Centennial, 136; at Girard College, 321; leading organs in Phila., 316-325. Organ builders, 325-7. Theatre organs, 328.

Ormandy, Eugene, 177, 185, 187, 211, 266.

Ornstein, Leo, 299, 303.

Orpheus, Club, 133, 141, 144, 225, 258-262, 265, 266, 343.

Orpheus and Euridice, Grand Burletta. With the original music, accompaniments by Mr. Taylor, at New Theatre Apr. 10, 1801.

Orr, George P., 259.

Orthophonic Victrola, 359.

Ostralenka, 120.

Otello (Rossini), 71.

Padlock, The. A favorite comic opera, at the New Theatre, 1801.

Pagliacci, I., 128.

Paine, John K., 135.

Palestrina Choir, 210, 310. Founded in 1915 by N. Montani as the Catholic Choral Club. Membership of approximately eighty mixed voices. This choir sang at the reception to Cardinal Mercier (1918), at the opening of the Choral Concerts of the Sesqui-Centennial Exposition (1926), and participated in many choral festivals. It has made several Victor records of polyphonic music.

Palliser, Esther, 317.

Palma, John, 10.

Pan and the Priest (Hanson), 347.

Parepa-Rosa, Mme. Euphrosyne, 121, 130.

Parker, Horatio, 260, 267.

Parochial Schools, 281-2.

Parsifal, 190, 239.

Pasternack, Joseph, 200.

Pastorius, Franz D., 4.

Patrick in Prussia, or Love in a Camp, comic opera composed by John O'Keefe, Esq.

Patriot, The, or Liberty Obtained. Much of the music arranged or written by Benjamin Carr. (Hewitt version, N. Y. 1794; Bates-Carr version, Baltimore, Sept. 3, 1796.)

Patterson, Franklin Peale, 218.

Patterson, Robert M., 56, 75.

Patti, Adelina, 68, 76, 79, 115, 130, 156. Amalia, 90.

Patti, Carlotta, sister of Adelina and Amalia Patti. A brilliant coloratura voice, frequently heard in 1860's and 1870's in Phila., and New York.

tone of school children's voices, but the method of its operation was kept so secret that no one now knows much about it.
Too Many Cooks, musical farce in two acts, given at the New Theatre Dec. 28, 1810.
Torello, Anton, 305.
Tostée, Mlle., 78.
Tracy, Mrs. Henry M., 236, 237.
Trajetta (Traetta), Filippo, 298.
Traviata, La, 79, 115, 116.
Treash, Leonard, 214.
Treaty of William Penn with the Indians, Concerto Grosso (Heinrich), 104.
Treble Clef Club, 267.
Trilogy (Puccini), 241.
Trionfo della Musica, 71.
Trip to Fontainbleau, a three-act musical farce given at the New Theatre in 1801.
Tristan and Isolde, 132.
Trovatore, Il, 78, 115, 129.
Trumpler, Charles W. A.   Music publisher, 1865-72, at 632 and 926 Chestnut St. Bought out by F. A. North, 1872.
Tschaikowsky, P. I., 115, 161.
Tureck, Rosalyn, 301.
Turn Out, a comic opera at the New Theatre (or "Phila. Theatre"), Mar. 17 and 21, 1815.
Two Misers, The, a comic opera at New Theatre, c. 1794.
Ulrich, Emil F., 295, 348.
Uncle Tom's Cabin, 124-5.
Undine, words by Edwin Markham, music by Harriet Ware. First produced by Euridice Chorus of Phila.
United Churches, 313-314.
United Singers of Phila., 144, 350.
Universal Asylum, a magazine containing pages of music, published in late eighteenth century Phila
University Glee Club of Phila., 263-264.
University of Pennsylvania, 12, 17, 27, 28, 80, 95, 148-149, 185, 212, 216, 263, 290 294, 320.
Urania (J. Lyon), 15-16.
Uranian Academy, 26-7, 28.
Vampire, The, or The Bride of the Isles, given at the Walnut St. Theatre in Nov., 1820.
Van den Beemt, Hedda, 198, 220, 221, 291.
Van Gelder, Martinus, 344.
van Hoogstraten, Willem, 185, 347.
Van Rensselaer, Alexander, 175, 181, 183, 186, 261.

ACKNOWLEDGMENTS AND BIBLIOGRAPHY

Acknowledgments and bibliography are placed together since they constitute two sides of the topic *the source of information*. In preparing the early chapters of Music in Philadelphia, many books were made available at the larger libraries in that city. The New York Public Library, and more particularly the Library of Congress in Washington, supplemented the local storehouses of learning with their collections of early music. Acknowledgments should begin with the mention of many librarians who provided music, newspapers, and magazines of rarity and antiquity, as well as numerous books on Philadelphia music of all periods. Ann Harned, of the Philadelphia Library Company; Barney Chesney, at the Ridgway Branch of this company; and Daisy Fansler and other members of the staff of the music room at the Free Library of Philadelphia were particularly helpful in providing books, music, and periodicals quoted or discussed in this book.

As the years become more recent the printed material in book form appears to become scarcer. There seem to be five volumes dealing with the years 1750-1800 for every one on the 1801-1850 period. In the history of Philadelphia music from 1865 to the present, the acknowledgments are largely due to individuals connected with musical organizations who lent the writer their valuable records of former days, or shared their recollections on such relatively recent periods. The bibliography mentions several biographies of recent musicians, but the far larger part of the later chapters of Music in Philadelphia deals with men and women whose unpublished memoirs or musical recollections constitute the main source of our information. Thanks are due to Miers Busch for facts concerning the Musical Fund Society; to Clarence Scott Pedrick for an account of early music at the First Presbyterian Church; to Rosalie Hassler and Carl Buchman for the story of the musical Hassler family; to Abbie Keely for an account of her father, Henry J. Keely; and to Mrs. Minton Pyne for the data on Kendrick and

Minton Pyne. The late Howard E. Keiser made available several rare volumes of early programs at the Academy of Music. Further information was furnished by Harold T. Mason, his successor as manager of the Academy, and Abigail Eliza Evens, secretary to both of these managers. The memoirs in manuscript entrusted to the writer by Gustav Hinrichs contain much information concerning opera history since 1880. The autobiography of Willard Spenser, and other material kindly provided by Willard Spenser, Jr., contain a full history of the light operas composed by Mr. Spenser. Thanks are due to Mrs. J. Claude Bedford, Dr. R. Max Goepp, and Mrs. David D. Wood for material on Goepp and Wood and on Philadelphia music of the period 1870-1920; and to Henry Gordon Thunder for the history of the Thunder Orchestra, the Philadelphia Choral Society, and other musical organizations since 1880. Other men who have participated in the city's church music for many years gave generously of their time, and of their old programs and scrap-books, in the preparation of the later chapters of Music in Philadelphia. Among them should be mentioned David E. Crozier, George Alexander A. West, Henry S. Fry, and Dr. John McE. Ward.

In the section that deals with music in Philadelphia since 1900, only a few of the literally hundreds of musicians who assisted in providing material can be named here. Frances A. Wister, Dorothy Bauer, and Lóuis A. Mattson furnished most of the data concerning the Philadelphia Orchestra. The material on the other current instrumental groups was contributed largely by: Helen M. Guernsey, the Frankford Symphony Society; G. S. Dunn, the Roxborough Orchestra; N. Lindsay Norden, the Germantown Orchestra; David N. Phillips, the concerts at Williow Grove, and other instrumental activities of the Philadelphia Rapid Transit Company; Dr. Charles E. Hirsch, the Philadelphia Philharmonic Society and other recent musical groups; and Sidney Fox, the story of the Philadelphia Music Center. J. W. F. Leman and William E. Smith contributed much in time and material to the account of Federal Music Projects in Philadelphia, and of the other instrumental organizations with which they are associated. Information on chamber music of recent years was furnished by Thaddeus Rich, Mrs. Harold E. Yarnall, Samuel Laciar, and Dr. E. Brooks

Keffer. Many details concerning chamber music of the late nineteenth century were recounted by Dr. Oliver Hopkinson, who also provided some information relative to the musical descendants of Francis Hopkinson.

The history of opera performances since 1900 was prepared with considerable assistance from Henry T. Craven, and from special accounts of the Savoy Opera Company by Horace Mather Lippincott, and the Philadelphia Operatic Society by Dr. John B. Becker. The larger singing societies were described from material provided by:

Ian C. Somerville .... The Mendelssohn Club
Henry Gordon Thunder .... (Several choral groups)
H. Alexander Matthews .... The Choral Art Society, and the University Glee Club of Philadelphia
Henry S. Drinker .... Accademia dei Dilettanti
James P. Sims .... Orpheus Club
C. Bentley Collins .... Fortnightly Club
Mrs. Richard Sharpless Davis... Matinee Musical Society
Helen Ackroyd Clare .... Philadelphia Music Club

and supplemented with facts from programs and from other members of these choruses.

In the account of present day church music and noted organs in Philadelphia many authorities on that field gave generous assistance. In addition to the few organists whose help has been previously acknowledged, thanks are due to Rollo S. Maitland, James A. Boylan, Harold W. Gilbert, George W. Till, and Rev. A. W. Schattschneider. The facts for the history and present conditions of music in private schools and colleges were assembled from accounts kindly provided by teachers and officers in the respective institutions. Acknowledgment should also be made, although collectively, to the secretaries of conservatories in Philadelphia, who kindly mailed letters and catalogues with material on music schools in the city. Special thanks are due to Paul E. Duffield for his scholarly though unpublished research on music in the public schools, which work is the basis for the chapter on that subject. Many present day publishers assisted in preparing the later pages of the chapter on music publishing in Philadelphia. Dr. James Francis Cooke was especially helpful in the account of the

Presser organizations, and in the general discussion of the field of commercial music. Thanks are also due to Clara Barnes Abbott, Helen Pulaski Innes, Herbert J. Tily, and Harvey Watts for their help in the preparation of the chapters on recent musical developments in Philadelphia.

The writer gratefully acknowledges the particular assistance received from Dorothy Kulp Gerson, his wife, and Morrison Comegys Boyd, of the University of Pennsylvania. These two Philadelphia musicians have been a constant help all the way from assembling facts to criticizing the completed *Music in Philadelphia.*

BIBLIOGRAPHY

Abbott, Clara Barnes. *Musical Survey and Directory,* 1929. Published by the Philadelphia Bureau of Music.

Albrecht, Otto E. *Francis Hopkinson, Musician, Poet and Patriot,* article in the Library Chronicle of the University of Pennsylvania, March, 1938.

Armstrong, W. G. *Record of the Opera in Philadelphia.* Philadelphia, 1884.

Bispham, David Scull. *A Quaker Singer's Recollections.* Macmillan, 1921.

Boyd, Charles N. *Choir Development Since 1876,* article in the 1928 Proceedings of the Music Teachers National Association.

Brister, Emma Schubert. *Incidents.* Privately printed. Philadelphia, 1935.

Burritt, O. H., Cadwallader, Goepp, Grammer, and Bunting. *David Duffle Wood,* a series of accounts in a memorial pamphlet. Printed privately. Philadelphia, 1911.

Cheyney, Edward P. *A History of the University of Pennsylvania.* Boston, 1901.

Claghorn, Charles E. *The Mocking Bird, the Life and Diary of Its Author Sep. Winner.* Magee Press. Philadelphia, 1937.

Campbell, Jane. *Old Philadelphia Music,* pamphlet published by the Philadelphia History Society, 1926.

Chamber of Commerce, Report of 1917. Special booklet, *The Commercial Value of Music to Philadelphia.*

Clark, Kenneth S. *Municipal Aid to Music in America.* Published by the National Bureau for the Advancement of Music, 1925.

Cowell, Henry. *American Composers on American Music.* Stanford University Press, 1933.

DaPonte, Lorenzo. *Memoirs.* Lippincott, Philadelphia, 1929.

Dorr, Rev. Benjamin. *A Historical Account of Christ Church.* R. S. H. George, Philadelphia, 1841.

Drummond, Robert R. *Early German Music in Pennsylvania.* Appleton, New York, 1910.

Duffield, Paul E. *History of Public School Music in Philadelphia.* Manuscript (1935).

Durang, Charles. *History of the Philadelphia Stage.* Philadelphia, 1850.

Egan, Maurice Francis. *Recollections of a Happy Life.* Doran, New York, 1924.

Elson, Louis. *History of American Music.* Macmillan, New York, 1925.

Fisher, William Arms. *One Hundred and Fifty Years of Music Publishing in the United States.* Ditson, Boston, 1933.

Goepp, Philip H. *David D. Wood.* Manuscript (1915).

Good, Marian Bigler. *Some Musical Backgrounds of Pennsylvania.* Carrolltown News Press, 1932.

Herrick, Cheeseman Abiah. *History of Girard College.* Printed at Girard College, 1927.

Hinrichs, Gustav. *Memoirs.* Manuscript (1938).

Hipsher, Edward E. *American Opera and Its Composers.* Presser, Philadelphia, 1935.

Howard, John Tasker. *Our American Music.* Crowell Co., New York, 1936.

Hubbard, W. L. *History of American Music.* Toledo, Ohio, 1908.

Hughes, Rupert. *American Composers.* Boston, 1900, revised edition (Elson), 1914.

Huneker, James Gibbons. *Steeplejack.* Scribner, New York, 1922.

Krehbiel, H. E. *American Choral Societies and Conductors.* Supplement to *Harper's Weekly,* Feb. 1, 1890.

Lavignac, Albert. *Music and Musicians.* Holt, New York, 1903.

Lewis, Lester C. *History of St. James' Church.* Manuscript.

Mactier, William L. *A Sketch of the Musical Fund Society.* Philadelphia, 1885.

Madeira, Louis Cephas. *Annals of Music in Philadelphia and the Musical Fund Society.* Lippincott, Philadelphia, 1896.

Maitland, Rollo F. *David D. Wood's Life.* Article in *The Diapason,* March 1, 1935.

Mason, Daniel G. *Tune in America.* Knopf, New York, 1931.

Mathews, W. S. B. *One Hundred Years of Music in America.* Howe, Chicago, 1889.

McCabe, James D. *History of the Centennial Exhibition.* National Publishing Company, Philadelphia, 1876.

Melba, Nellie (Helen Porter Armstrong). *Melodies and Memories.* Doran, New York, 1926.

Musical Art Club. *A Man and His Dream* (descriptive pamphlet).

Parker, Mrs. Alvin Afflick. *Church Music and Musical Life in Pennsylvania in the Eighteenth Century.* Published by the Pennsylvania Society of Colonial Dames of America, Philadelphia, 1926. (Three volumes.)

Pennypacker, Samuel W. *Historical and Biographical Sketches.* Published in Philadelphia, 1883.

Philadelphia Rapid Transit Company. *Musical Offerings at Willow Grove Park.* Booklet published by the company in 1909.

Presser Company. *The Presser Foundation* (pamphlet). Presser, Philadelphia, 1931.

Reis, Claire. *Composers in America.* Macmillan, third edition, 1938.

Ritter, Abraham. *A History of the Moravian Church in Philadelphia.* Philadelphia, 1857.

Ritter, Frederick Louis. *Music in America.* 1883.

Robins and Church. *History of the Orpheus Club.* Private printing, Philadelphia, 1936.

Rogers, Joseph M. *A History of Grand Opera in Philadelphia.* Pamphlet published by Strawbridge and Clothier, Philadelphia, 1909.

Rosenfeld, Paul. *An Hour with American Music.* Lippincott, Philadelphia, 1929.

Russell, Charles Edward. *The American Orchestra and Theodore Thomas.* Doubleday, Page and Co., New York, 1927.

Sachse, Julius F. *The German Pietists of Provincial Pennsylvania, 1694-1708.* Philadelphia, 1895.

Samaroff, Olga. *Musical Life in America.* Norton, New York, 1939.

Scharf, J. T., and Westcott, T. *History of Philadelphia.* L. H. Everts Company, Philadelphia, 1884.

Seipt, Allen A. *Schwenkfelder Hymnology and the Sources of the First Schwenkfelder Hymnbook Printed in America.* Germania-Americana Press, Philadelphia, 1909.

Slonimsky, Nicolas. *Music Since 1900.* Published by Norton, New York, 1937.

Sonneck, Oscar G. *Bibliography of Early American Secular Music* (1905). *Early Concert Life in America* (1907). *Early Opera in America* (1915). *Francis Hopkinson and James Lyon* (McQueen, Washington, 1905). *Miscellaneous Studies in the History of Music* (Macmillan, New York, 1921).

Sousa, John Philip. *Marching Along, an Autobiography.* Hale Cushman and Flint, Boston, 1928.

Spenser, Willard. *The Wheel of Memory.* Unpublished memoirs.

Spillane, Daniel. *History of the American Pianoforte.* New York, 1890.

Sullivan, Mark. *Our Times.* Scribner, New York, 1927 *et seq.*

Thomas, Rose Fay. *Memoirs of Theodore Thomas.* Moffatt, Yard and Company, New York, 1911.

Thomas, Theodore. *A Musical Autobiography,* edited by Wm. T. Upton. A. C. McClurg, Chicago, 1905.

Tuthill, Burnett C. "Fifty Years of Chamber Music in the United States." Proceedings of the Music Teachers' National Association, 1928.

Upton, William Treat. *Art Song in America.* Ditson, 1930.

Watson, John Fanning. *Watson's Annals,* edited by Willis P. Hazard. E. S. Stuart, Philadelphia, 1877.

Wemyss, Francis Courtenay. *Theatrical Biography.* Glasgow, 1848.

Wister, Frances A. *Twenty-five Years of the Philadelphia Orchestra.* Stern, Philadelphia, 1925.

Yerkes, Royden Keith. *The History of St. Luke's Church* (Germantown). Private printing, Philadelphia, 1912.

MUSIC IN PHILADELPHIA

Among the many scrapbooks consulted, those at the Academy of Music and at the home of Henry T. Craven were particularly helpful, since they contain plentiful material (always dated) covering long periods of time. Mr. Craven is the author of a series of articles on the Academy of Music, published by the Philadelphia *Evening Bulletin,* between January and March, 1939. Newspapers in libraries, especially the Ridgway Branch of the Philadelphia Library Company, provided much first-hand information concerning our local musical happenings since Revolutionary days. Magazine articles and booklets, in addition to the few mentioned in the above bibliographical list, were also used for some of the later accounts of music in Philadelphia. Dictionaries and encyclopedias of music provide data for any historical account such as the foregoing. Grove's *Dictionary of Music and Musicians,* particularly its American Supplement, contained much that was used in Music in Philadelphia.